TRAJAN

TRAJAN

Rome's Last Conqueror

Nicholas Jackson

Greenhill Books

Trajan: Rome's Last Conqueror
First published in 2022 by
Greenhill Books,
c/o Pen & Sword Books Ltd,
47 Church Street, Barnsley,
S. Yorkshire, S70 2AS

www.greenhillbooks.com
contact@greenhillbooks.com

ISBN: 978-1-78438-707-5

All rights reserved.
© Nicholas Jackson, 2022

The right of Nicholas Jackson to be identified as author of this work has been asserted in accordance with Section 77 of the Copyrights, Designs and Patents Act 1988.

CIP data records for this title are available from the British Library

Designed and typeset by Donald Sommerville
Maps by Peter Wilkinson

Printed and bound by CPI Group (UK) Ltd, Croydon CR0 4YY

Typeset in 11.5/14.4 pt Arno Pro Regular and Arno Pro Display

To Carlotta, Linus & Alexine

CONTENTS

	LIST OF PLATES AND MAPS	ix
	PREFACE	xi
	TRAJAN'S FAMILY TREE	xvi
CHAPTER 1	IMPRESSIONABLE YEARS	1
CHAPTER 2	YOUNG ADULTHOOD IN A NEW ERA	18
CHAPTER 3	THE MAKING OF A MILITARY OFFICER	26
CHAPTER 4	THE MAKING OF A GENERAL	45
CHAPTER 5	ADOPTION AND ACCESSION	71
CHAPTER 6	THE DAWNING TRAJANIC AGE	103
CHAPTER 7	TRAJAN'S FIRST DACIAN WAR	119
CHAPTER 8	TRAJAN'S SECOND DACIAN WAR	148
CHAPTER 9	BIDING TIME BETWEEN GREAT WARS	170
CHAPTER 10	THE PARTHIAN WAR	196
CHAPTER 11	CONSPIRACY, DEATH AND DEIFICATION	234
	NOTES	251
	BIBLIOGRAPHY	284
	INDEX	292

PLATES AND MAPS

※

Plates

Marble bust of Trajan, from around 108 AD (*Venice National Archaeological Museum, Italy, Direzione Generale Musei, with the permission of the Ministry for Cultural Heritage and Activities and for Tourism*).

The amphitheatre in Italica, Trajan's birthplace (*Carole Raddato; CC BY-SA 2.0*); the three Flavian emperors, Vespasian (*Carole Raddato; CC BY-SA 2.0*), Titus and Domitian (*Ed Uthman, Ted Bobosh; CC BY-ND 2.0*); a tutor with his students (*GDKE-Rheinisches Landesmuseum Trier; Thomas Zühmer*).

Patrician children, Ara Pacis, Rome (*Dr Peter Ackermann*); Trajan's father, Marcus Ulpius Traianus (*National Museum of Belgrade, Serbia*).

Domitian's Palace, Rome (*Ken McCown*); Salonia Matidia, Mindia Matidia, Vibia Sabina (*all Carole Raddato; CC BY-SA 2.0*).

Trajan's private house in Rome (*Sovrintendenza Capitolina ai Beni Culturali, Rome*); the Warren Cup (*Frans Vandewalle; CC BY-NC 2.0*); Pompeia Plotina, Trajan's wife (*Carole Raddato; CC BY-SA 2.0*).

The benevolent Danube River god at the start of the First Dacian War (*Carole Raddato; CC BY-SA 2.0*); the opening actions of the Second Battle of Tapae (*Mike Bishop; CC by NC-SA 2.0*).

Dacia and the Dacian Wars (*map*); Jupiter intervenes in the Second Battle of Tapae (*Gary Todd; Public Domain Mark 1.0*).

Walls of Sarmizegetusa Regia (*Razvan Mateescu, National Museum of Transylvanian History, Cluj-Napoca, Romania*); Dacian assault on a Roman fort (*Mike Bishop; CC by NC-SA 2.0*).

Defeat of the Roxolanian cavalry (*Mike Bishop. CC by NC-SA 2.0*); a Dacian *pileatus* (*Paul Humphreys*); religious complex, Sarmizegetusa

Regia (*Razvan Mateescu, National Museum of Transylvanian History, Cluj-Napoca, Romania*).
Fall of Sarmizegetusa Regia (*Conrad Cichorius: 'Die Reliefs der Traianssäule'*); suicide of Decebalus (*Conrad Cichorius: 'Die Reliefs der Traianssäule'*).
Trajan's forum in Rome (*Jamie Heath; CC BY-SA-2.0*); the *alimenta* programme, Arch of Trajan, Benevento (*Carole Raddato; CC BY-SA 2.0*).
The Eastern Roman Empire and Trajan's Parthian campaigns (*map*).
Ruins of Dura-Europos (*Arian Zwegers; CC BY 2.0*); Persian cataphract in a relief at Taq-e Bostan (*Koorosh Nozad*).
The ancient port city of Spasinou Charax (*Hanming Huang; CC BY-SA 2.0*); the Great Iwans of Hatra (*Joe Welch*).
Reenactment of a Parthian shot (*Ardeshir Radpour*); bronze bust of Hadrian (*Edwin Robson; CC BY-ND 2.0*).
Photoreal portrait of Trajan (*Daniel Voshart*); the pedestal of Trajan's Column in Rome (*Dr Steven Zucker; CC BY-NC-SA 2.0*).

Illustrations in Text and Family Tree

All images of coins are reproduced courtesy of the Classical Numismatic Group, LLC.

Maps

The Roman Empire in 117 AD	opposite, page xii
Roman Spain	page 52
Rome in the Trajanic Period	page 110
Dacia	in plates
The Parthian War	in plates

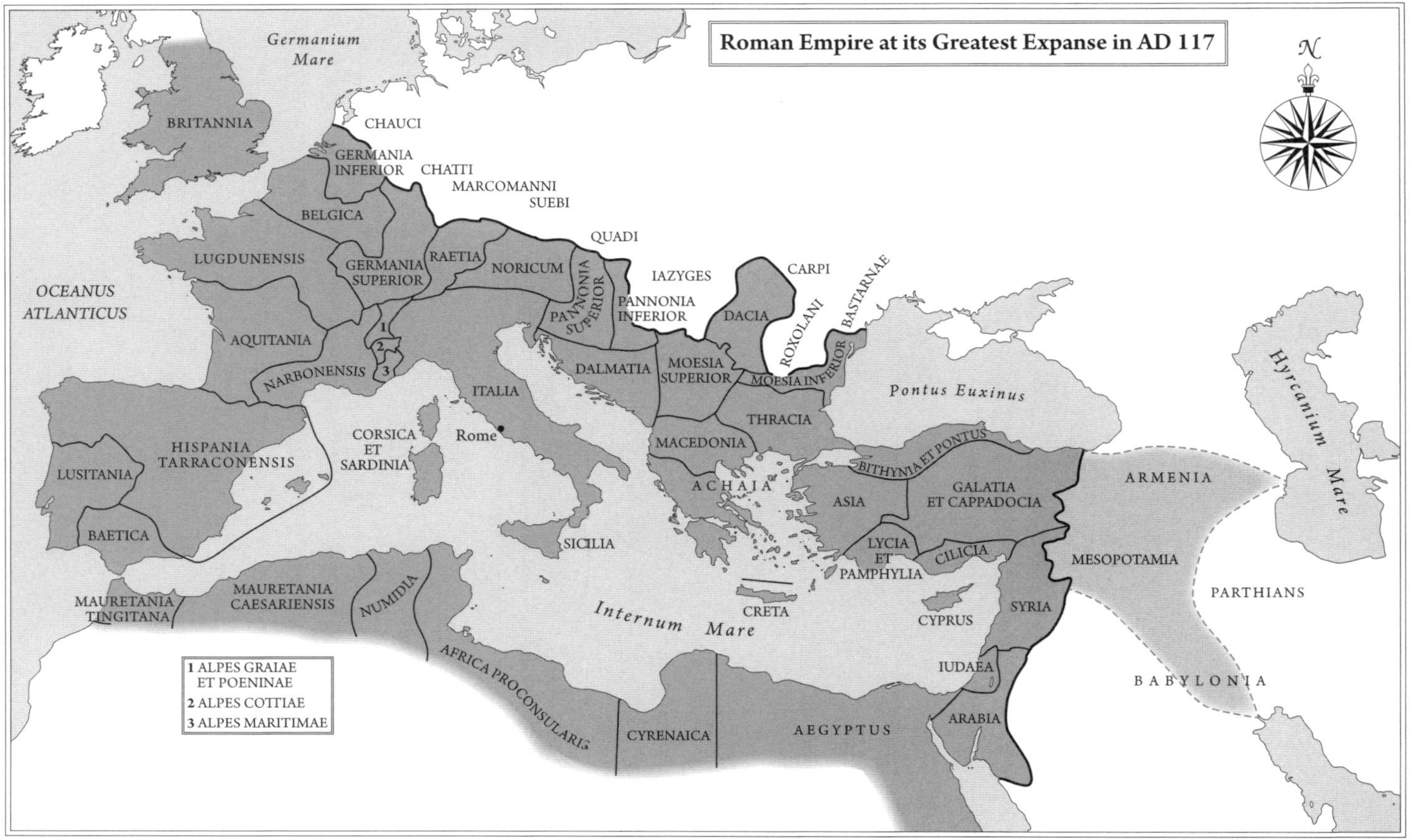
Roman Empire at its Greatest Expanse in AD 117
N
Germanium Mare
OCEANUS ATLANTICUS
BRITANNIA
CHAUCI
GERMANIA INFERIOR
CHATTI
MARCOMANNI
SUEBI
QUADI
IAZYGES
CARPI
ROXOLANI
BASTARNAE
BELGICA
LUGDUNENSIS
GERMANIA SUPERIOR
RAETIA
NORICUM
PANNONIA SUPERIOR
PANNONIA INFERIOR
DACIA
AQUITANIA
NARBONENSIS
1
2
3
ITALIA
DALMATIA
MOESIA SUPERIOR
MOESIA INFERIOR
Pontus Euxinus
Hyrcanium Mare
HISPANIA TARRACONENSIS
LUSITANIA
BAETICA
CORSICA ET SARDINIA
Rome
THRACIA
MACEDONIA
ACHAIA
BITHYNIA ET PONTUS
ASIA
GALATIA ET CAPPADOCIA
ARMENIA
LYCIA ET PAMPHYLIA
CILICIA
MESOPOTAMIA
PARTHIANS
SICILIA
CRETA
CYPRUS
SYRIA
Internum Mare
MAURETANIA TINGITANA
MAURETANIA CAESARIENSIS
NUMIDIA
AFRICA PROCONSULARIS
CYRENAICA
AEGYPTUS
IUDAEA
ARABIA
BABYLONIA
1 ALPES GRAIAE ET POENINAE
2 ALPES COTTIAE
3 ALPES MARITIMAE

PREFACE

Many books, have recounted the lives of illustrious and infamous Roman emperors such as Augustus, Caligula, Nero and Constantine. Yet very few have told the story of one of Rome's supreme conquerors, an emperor who extended the empire to its greatest expanse, a subjugator who crushed the Dacian kingdom, annexed parts of Arabia and for a short period conquered great swaths of the powerful Parthian domains. The first emperor to be born outside of Italy, he rose from junior officer to emperor in just over twenty years. He was a shrewd politician who maintained his absolute power and authority while promoting a relative sense of liberty in the Senate after years of unbridled autocracy from his predecessors. A prolific builder across the empire, he also constructed in Italy the largest forum ever seen. A visionary who wanted to extend the eastern boundaries of the empire and emulate the achievements of Alexander the Great, he likewise left an empire without a clearly identified heir. I write of the Emperor Trajan, whose reign defined a lasting age of prosperity and the last expansion of Roman imperial might.

With such deeds to his name, Trajan was feted both during and after his reign, earning from the Senate the unique honorific of *Optimus Princeps*, 'Best of Princes', which he adopted proudly into his titles. Though the lustre of his achievements lasted through the ages, this has not favoured historians with an abundance of detailed contemporary accounts of his incredible life. Indeed, any writer of ancient Roman history suffers from the frequent absence of hard facts, and as a consequence is forced frequently to use passive language like 'could', 'may', 'probably' or 'likely'. Writing about Trajan is no different and is more challenging than dealing with the many Roman emperors, certainly those of notoriety, who are covered more frequently in contemporary or near contemporary literature.

Effectively, there are only two contemporary authors who provide details on Trajan. The first was a senator during Trajan's reign called Caius Plinius Caecilius Secundus, better known as Pliny the Younger. A famous speech and a series of letters by Pliny have survived and they provide a narrow but direct observation into Trajan's life. The second is another senator, Lucius Flavius Arrianus, known as Arrian, who was consul before AD 130[1] and was possibly serving in Trajan's Parthian War while he wrote an account of that conflict. Unfortunately, only fragments of his history have survived. Otherwise, details come only much later after Trajan's death. Lucius Cassius Dio Cocceianus, more popularly known as Dio Cassius, wrote an account around a hundred years after Trajan's reign. A surviving digest of the volume that covered Trajan provides some useful details and insights.

That is effectively all that we have except for an array of epigraphic, archaeological and numismatic evidence and a handful of much later third century written summaries, presumably compiled from earlier Roman accounts. Trajan himself is thought to have written an account of his wars against Dacia, which is sadly lost today except for a single citation that is nothing more than a fragment of the original sentence. Therefore, to write about Trajan requires a detective-like approach to piece together the details of his life and reign.

Devoid of many details, I have adopted the following approach in reporting historical aspects: where fact is proven, fact is stated; where only marginal evidence exists, a position is taken based on the weight of evidence; where there is no constructive theory or evidence, reasonable conjecture is posed. As such, this account should not be considered an academic attempt to record what is incontrovertibly known about Trajan, but rather it is intended to provide an accessible portrayal of his life and afford a flavour of the daily workings and machinations of the Roman Empire at the end of the first and start of the second centuries. However, this account is by no means exhaustive and it is beyond the scope of this book to address the complex social, cultural and political details of the period.

In my research, I am principally indebted to three modern studies: the academic biography of Trajan written by Julian Bennett, *Trajan: Optimus Princeps,* which has provided an authoritative account of his life and skilfully fills many gaps in our knowledge; Frank Lepper's and Sheppard Frere's *Trajan's Column: A New Edition of the Cichorius Plates* which provided a groundbreaking account of Trajan's Dacian War; and Frank Lepper's *Trajan's Parthian War,* the seminal modern study reviewing the complex conflict.

Following convention, Roman costs are generally cited in this book in *sestertii*. Roman coinage was denominated as follows: 1 *aureus* (gold) = 25 *denarii* (silver) = 100 *sestertii* (brass) = 200 *dupondii* (brass) = 400 *asses* (bronze). To put the values of these into perspective: one loaf of bread was around two *asses*; one litre of average wine, five *asses*; a donkey, around 500 *sestertii*; an average slave 2,000 *sestertii* and a fine town house in Rome around two million *sestertii*. A Roman legionary soldier could earn 1,200 *sestertii* a year in our period. At state level, the largest annual cost was maintaining Rome's enormous professional army, which consumed nearly 80 per cent of the imperial budget (around 643 million *sestertii* a year).[2]

When possible, I tried to leave the confines of my desk to follow in Trajan's footsteps across Europe or see artefacts related to his life: Spain to understand Trajan's family roots and to get a sense of where he was born and where he spent a significant part of his life growing up; Germany to appreciate his presence in this region at a turning point in his career; Rome and Italy on several occasions to view, among other things, his building works; New York to examine the unique bust collection of Trajan's immediate family at the Metropolitan Museum; Romania to trace the events of the Dacian Wars, even camping in remote areas of the Carpathian Mountains to absorb the topography and terrain. Alas, the situation in Iraq and Syria at the time of writing precluded me from following Trajan's steps in the Parthian War.

*

This book has taken several years to research, develop and complete, and I would like to extend a particular thanks to the following people who have all kindly provided immeasurable help in that time: Professors Barbara Levick and Antony Birley for reviewing the complete manuscript and providing historical precision to the content; Drs. Julian Bennett, Richard Talbert, Claudia Winterstein and the late Peter Connolly, FSA, for their expert help on specific complex topics; David Swain for reviewing the manuscript several times and greatly improving the narrative; David Thomas for his invaluable critique and tireless review of the entire manuscript which resulted in major revisions; and Edward Handyside for his professional editorial review and wise adjustments to the manuscript. And lastly, thanks to Donald Sommerville for his expert editing and management of the book, and Michael Leventhal of Greenhill Books for his invaluable trust.

Nicholas Jackson

Trajan's Family Tree

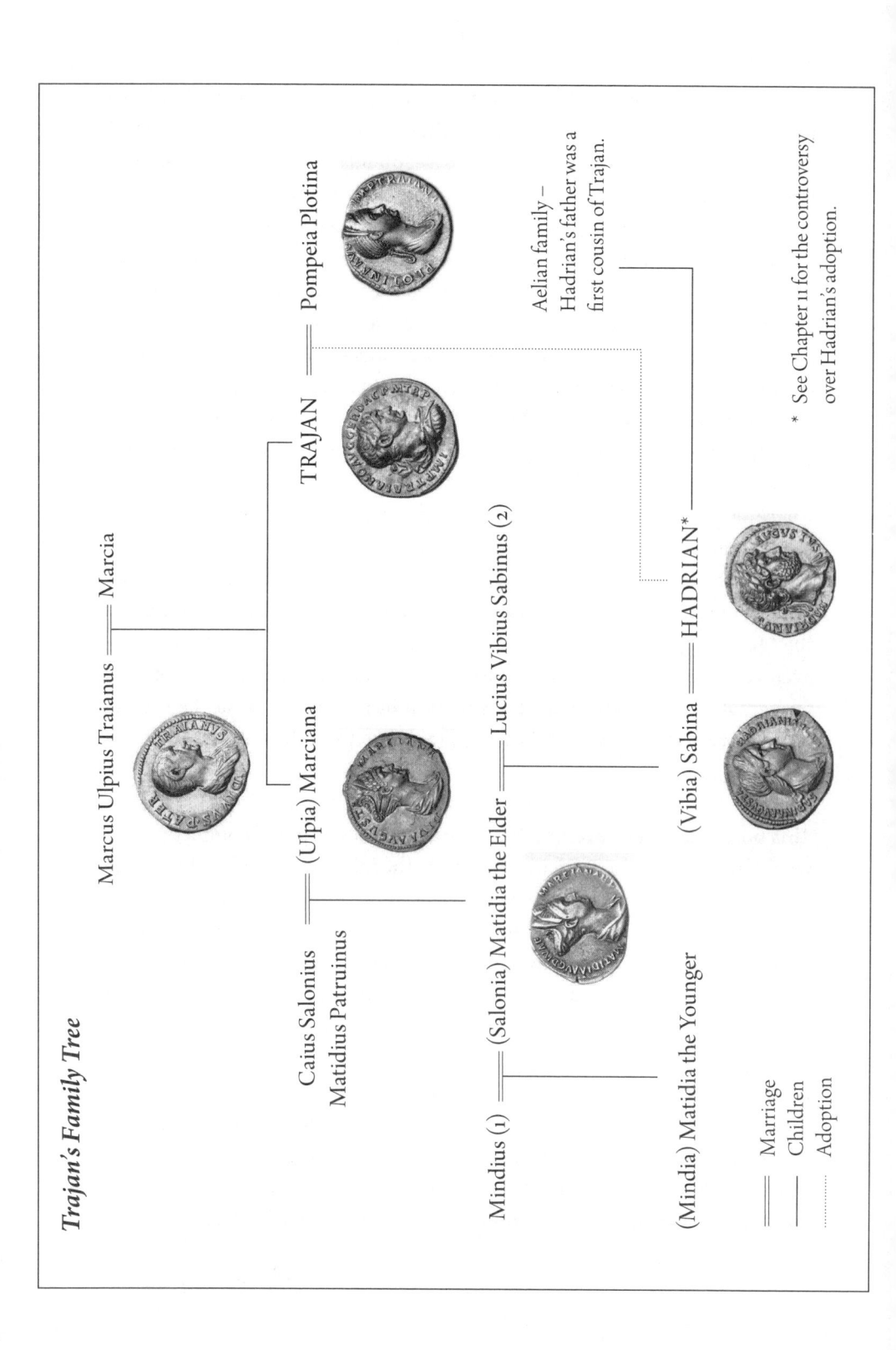

Marcus Ulpius Traianus ══ Marcia

    │

├── (Ulpia) Marciana ══ Caius Salonius Matidius Patruinus
│   │
│   └── (Salonia) Matidia the Elder ══ Mindius (1) / Lucius Vibius Sabinus (2)
│   ├── (Mindia) Matidia the Younger
│   └── (Vibia) Sabina ══ HADRIAN*
│
└── TRAJAN ══ Pompeia Plotina

Aelian family – Hadrian's father was a first cousin of Trajan.

* See Chapter 11 for the controversy over Hadrian's adoption.

Key:
══ Marriage
── Children
······ Adoption

CHAPTER 1

IMPRESSIONABLE YEARS

※

Born into the Roman World

The first-century Roman world can be a hard place to imagine in our current age, racing through a digital era, with few places escaping globalisation. It is equally difficult to envisage that, in the first century, the power of Rome, *imperium Romanum*, had created a city state which dominated an estimated sixty million people.[1] This was around a quarter of the world's population. At the time, Rome was one of the most civilised and advanced societies on earth, contemporaneous with the Han Dynasty in China, the Kushan empire in Central Asia, the Parthian empire in Persia and the Mayan civilisation in Central America.

Where did it all start for Trajan? It began in a wealthy Spanish region of the Roman Empire, surrounded by lush agricultural lands. This would make Trajan the first Roman emperor to be born outside Italy. Sadly we know very few reliable details about his early childhood, so the story of Trajan's youth and his early path in life will be brief, requiring some postulation based on the life of a typical contemporary Roman family with a comparable social background.

Yet, despite very few facts about his early years, we know that Trajan's path in life was one of power: power that launched his father's career; power within his family to leave Spain for Rome; power to become a senator and later a general; ultimately power to become emperor, a supremacy that would bring Trajan to the mountainous forests of Romania and to the rocky deserts of Iraq in conquest.

Back in Spain, even the year of Trajan's birth is uncertain. Deduction allows one to estimate he was born in AD 56, in the notorious reign of the Emperor

Nero and shortly after the 800th anniversary of Rome's celebrated founding.[2] We know his birthday was on 18 September.

He was born in the town of Italica, in the prospering Roman province of Baetica, which is now the Andalucia region of Spain. As a customary sign of recognition after birth, the midwife would probably have laid the new-born Trajan at his father's feet and his father in turn would have raised him above his head in acknowledgement of his kin and to establish his rights over the boy. On the ninth day after Trajan's birth, a purification festival, *dies lustricus*, would be held by the family for the official naming of the new-born.[3]

Trajan is the modern English spelling of his name. His full Latin name was Marcus Ulpius Traianus. A Roman citizen normally had three names. The first name (*praenomen*) was personal to the individual like a modern first name. The second name (*nomen*) referred to the *gens* or clan. The third name (*cognomen*) was the family name. Therefore, Trajan's father, also called Marcus Ulpius Traianus, belonged to the Traianus family branch of the Ulpian clan. Occasionally, a fourth name was added, an *agnomen*, to record an act of honour or define a branch of the family. Women were generally referred to only by the name of their clan, and sometimes the name of a wife or daughter was followed by that of the father or husband in the feminine form.

Later in life, Trajan was described as strong in body,[4] suggesting he started life in good health and development. This was an achievement for Trajan and his mother, because infant and maternal mortality rates were very high. Around 5 per cent of all Roman newborns did not survive beyond their first month and an estimated one in 4,000 women died giving birth.[5] Even after surviving birth and the precarious first month, around a third of infants died before their first birthday.[6]

Trajan's family belonged to the equestrian class and family life for the young Trajan would have reflected the comfortable and safe surroundings typical of this status. This equestrian class first formed within the Roman army – the men were rich enough to provide horses and serve in the cavalry – and evolved into a wealthy class of land and business owners. To qualify as an equestrian, a Roman citizen needed property to the value of over 400,000 *sestertii*, and could expect certain positions of authority in Roman society. Trajan's father, Marcus Ulpius Traianus (hereafter Traianus), could trace his roots to the ancestral home of the Ulpian clan in the town of Tuder (Todi), in Umbria, Italy.[7] Tuder was well positioned near the River Tiber and the Via Amerina road, both connecting the town to Rome.

Following the annexation of Spain into the Roman Empire, a family branch of the Ulpii probably left for the province of Baetica and settled in the town of Italica (north-west of Seville), lured by the promise of wealth from the prosperous agricultural region or for an administrative position in the province. Alternatively, a distant family member may have been one of the first Roman army veterans who set up home in the newly founded town of Italica. The Ulpii, like the Aelii and the Traii or Trahii were noble families in the region. Intermarriage between the Ulpii and the Traii resulted in a branch of Traianus' ancestors.

Traianus was born around AD 25 and probably married Trajan's mother, Marcia, at around twenty-five years of age.[8] Marcia's roots are even more obscure. Her ancestors may have come from the Marcii Bareae family that could have originated from wealthy landowners around Ameria (Amelia), also in Umbria near the Via Amerina. Some have pointed out that this possibly made Marcia's father, Trajan's grandfather, the prominent Quintus Marius Barea Soranus, who was consul in AD 52. If this was the case, the match with Marcia was a prestigious one for Traianus. Moreover, Marcia's half-sister, Marcia Furnilla, would later marry the emperor Titus and therefore tie Traianus to the imperial court, a linkage that would help exalt his family into the highest echelons of Roman society and power. After the marriage of Traianus and Marcia, Trajan's elder sister, Ulpia Marciana, was born. Trajan and his sister appear to have remained close throughout their lives.

The Romans did not have a definitive word for a new-born child.[9] Instead, during the period before he reached seven years of age, Trajan would have been referred to as an *infans*, literally meaning *not speaking* and from the time he learned to speak and walk he would have been a *puer*, a pre-pubescent boy. As a symbol of Trajan's vulnerability as an infant, he would have worn a traditional *bulla* around his neck, a gold charm to ward off evil spirits. This charm was given during the *dies lustricus*, the naming-day ceremony.

As a sign of free birth, a *puer* might sometimes wear a *toga praetexta*, a toga dyed to create a broad purple band around the rim. Children were viewed as requiring formation into human beings.[10] This formation was prone to 'corruption' through seduction and failure to resist the trappings of pleasure. Traianus and Marcia would have striven to protect the young Trajan from any abuse to ensure his correct formation into an adult. Thus, a paedagogue, or slave escort, was usually appointed to watch over a young boy like Trajan and to shadow his early years and shield him from dangers during the absence of his parents.

Traianus' Early Career

Before we can explore Trajan's education and his early years in Italica and Rome, we must first consider the early *cursus honorum*, or senatorial career, of his father, Traianus. Little is known of Traianus' initial career, but the different stages were prescribed by law and status. One can therefore piece together his path approximately, based on the elements of a typical career in the Senate.

Prerequisites for entry into the Senate included free birth Roman citizenship, no serious prior convictions, good health and a million *sestertii* or more in the census rating.[11] Essentially, one had to be wealthy and influential. A further precondition for any hopeful senatorial candidate was selection by the emperor into the vigintivirate: the twenty annual public posts in Rome held by men around twenty years old. Next was required a junior military position (*tribunus laticlavius*), typically for a year, and then a candidate could enter the Senate proper if selected for one of the twenty quaestorships, these being public financial posts. After a mandatory five-year gap, the next senatorial office was the praetorship. Eighteen praetorships, judicial in function, were hotly contended. Like the quaestorships, these positions effectively required endorsement by the emperor to ensure selection. There was also a 'fast track' route for favourites of the emperor who could be adlected directly into the Senate. Protocol allowed Rome's aristocrats to qualify for a consulship at thirty-two years of age and this was the pinnacle of a senatorial career, despite the heavy erosion of the position's power in the imperial era. Two consuls were appointed at any one time by the emperor, who could choose to hold one of the offices himself. As an ex-consul, a senator could expect the best military and governorship positions and perhaps the prestigious appointment of a second consulship or even the extremely rare honour of a third.

Working backwards from later dates that we do know, Traianus took a relatively risky step around the age of eighteen and broke away from his ancestors to seek a position on the first rung of the ladder towards a senatorial *cursus*, the vigintivirate. In this position, he may have acted as a junior magistrate dealing with civil cases. The post probably meant that Traianus had a helping hand from a senior senator or perhaps even direct selection by the Emperor Claudius himself, whose attention may have been drawn to his emerging talents.

Traianus would have next taken up the sword as a junior officer, a *tribunus laticlavius*, typically under a legion commander who was a family relative or close family friend. Following this military service, Traianus would be back in Rome for an annual post (*ca.* AD 51–52) as quaestor. Around the age of thirty-one, Traianus then held an annual praetor post in Rome (*ca.* AD 57–58). After Claudius, the reign of Nero saw steady promotions for *novi homines*, 'new men' from the provinces instead of the traditional aristocratic families in Rome. The *novi homines* like Traianus prospered in the new era and such patronage secured him a governorship of the senatorial province of Baetica, his homeland.[12] The date of this governorship is not known precisely. It has been argued that he was possibly the first provincial Roman citizen to govern his home province, and this was a change supported by Nero, who appreciated that a local man knew the best way to govern his own back yard. Despite this trend under Nero, this was rare because there were repeated rulings against governing one's own province of origin.[13]

In and Around Italica

Traianus' senatorial career involved a great deal of travelling across the Roman Empire and senators were expected to live in Rome when not away on state business, meaning that he would have spent limited periods in his Italica home.[14] As a result, bailiffs were likely appointed by Traianus to manage the family properties in Baetica in his absence. Nevertheless, around the middle of the first century, there was the opportunity for Traianus and his family to return to Italica, perhaps to attend to critical business and interests in Baetica. Consequently, the family was probably together in Italica for the period up to and around Trajan's birth in 56.

Before or after Trajan's birth, it is more than likely that Traianus returned to Rome and left his family in Italica, rather than drag them away on a long journey while his wife was pregnant or while Trajan was very young. Accordingly, Trajan likely spent his first months or years in Italica before moving to Rome and then, perhaps at around eight or nine years old, he almost certainly would have returned to Italica with his father during Traianus' governorship of Baetica (*ca.* 64–65).

The town of Italica was established in 206 BC by one of the greatest Roman generals of the age, Publius Cornelius Scipio. It was founded for his wounded troops and veterans following the victorious battle of Ilipa, where the Carthaginians were decisively beaten by an outnumbered Roman force. This battle marked the climax of the Second Punic War and effectively removed the Carthaginians from Spain, giving Rome a very large regional acquisition for its newly forming empire. The name Italica was chosen nostalgically in recognition of the troops' Italian homeland. It was the very first Roman settlement outside Italy and Scipio selected the area as a bastion of the Roman presence for two reasons: firstly, its geographical position lent itself well to transportation and communication within the region; secondly, it was an area blessed with substantial natural resources.[15]

The new town of Italica shared its plateau site with the native Turdetanians who already inhabited this fertile region. The Turdetanians were peaceful in nature and the Roman settlers integrated well, bringing Roman culture and technologies that would have been slowly accepted by the natives. To the north of Italica was access to the western Sierra Morena Mountains, rich in metal ores. To the east, plains stretched for miles, and to the west gentle rolling hills with rich soils. In the vicinity, the Huelva River flowed into the wide Guadalquivir River (then called the Baetis), which continued south to the sea. The riverbanks were cultivated and the river navigable from the coast to the town of Cordvba (Córdoba), which later became the capital of the province.

By the first century AD, Italica had flourished into a successful Roman town with municipal status while intensive Roman farming methods yielded a bounty of local produce. A complex irrigation network was developed, bringing the river waters further inland and allowing wine, oil and wheat production to rise substantially. Livestock was so abundant that meat was a regular part of the staple diet in the province. The Baetis River not only blessed the land with its life-giving waters, but it was also a highway for the export of produce down to the sea, and then on to Rome by ship along the coast. In particular, olive oil was liquid gold for the Italica residents and others in the region. In Roman times, olive oil was used for cooking, preserving foods, cleansing the skin after bathing, fuel for lanterns and even found other uses such as as a dubious contraceptive agent. The trade in olive oil therefore brought enormous wealth to those involved and aided the prosperity of Italica.

Still clearly visible today in the south-west of Rome, behind the ancient Tiber River wharves, there is an enormous mountain of ancient pottery rubbish over fifty metres high and a kilometre in circumference. The vast waste heap, called Monte Testaccio, is largely made up of broken large amphorae used to import olive oil from Baetica.[16] The amphorae could not be economically recycled and were spoiled by the absorption of oil into the clay structure. Instead they were carefully destroyed, stacked and treated with lime to stop the rancid smell of rotting olive oil; it is estimated that over fifty million amphorae were discarded, whose total capacity exceeded six billion litres of oil, a testament to the enormous olive-oil trade and export wealth of the Baetica region.

The Italica that Trajan would have known was not especially distinct from the other major settlements in Baetica, but it was able to boast a large and richly decorated theatre, constructed in honour of the Emperor Augustus in the early part of the first century. Parts of the theatre were financed privately by Lucius Blattius Traianus Pollio and Caius Traius Pollio, who were previously town magistrates and priests of the cult of the deified Augustus.[17] Traianus Pollio may have been Trajan's grandfather.[18] If that was the case, a man able to help privately fund the construction of a theatre was also able to ensure that Traianus had the substantial sum to qualify for entry to the Senate. A mosaic in Italica still exists today that identifies a Marcus Trahius in charge of constructing a temple of Apollo. This same Trahius could have been Trajan's great-grandfather.[19]

The nearby Via Augusta, the longest Roman road in the Iberian Peninsula, which linked the Pyrenees all the way to the southern coastal town of Gades (Cadiz) brought important communication and trade links to Italica, but it was not these links, nor its unique theatre, its auspicious historical founding, nor its strategic position in the province that made the town special to the Traianus family. Rather it was the very soil of the land and mineral reserves, blessed by the waters of the Baetis and the warm Mediterranean climate, that combined together to make Italica distinctive for the family and provided the ideal conditions for both agriculture and mining to generate vast wealth. This wealth was sufficient to fund an exit from provincial life, qualify for entry into the upper tiers of Roman society and gain access to the power corridors of empire. Traianus, and subsequently Trajan, indeed owed their positions largely to the fertile lands around Italica:

> ... large quantities of grain and wine, and also olive oil, not only in large quantities, but also of the best quality. And further, wax, honey and pitch are exported from there... and not unimportant, either, is the fish-salting industry that is carried on.
>
> Strabo[20]

Produce from agriculture was not the only blessing in Baetica. In addition, it had abundant mineral resources highly desirable to Rome:

> Up to the present moment, in fact, neither gold, nor silver, nor yet copper, nor iron, has been found anywhere in the world, in a natural state, either in such quantity or of such good quality.
>
> Strabo[21]

It was typical for wealthy families to own several properties. Thus, one can reasonably assume that Trajan's family kept a fine town house in Italica, as well as large country estates in the area. As a child for that short period in Baetica during his father's governorship, Trajan's social circle was probably restricted to the Italica household and estates or the governor's residence in Córdoba, meaning he generally had the company of his parents, his sister, nurses and slaves. On occasion, the circle would have expanded when certain family members, friends or clients visited. The living areas of an extensive home were open for Trajan to explore or play within except when social occasion or the conduct of family business dictated otherwise.[22]

Freeborn Roman children from families with disposable incomes could attend local schools to follow a formal education taught in both Latin and Greek. Wealthier families, such as Trajan's, would usually opt for private education from a tutor. Thus, typically from the age of seven, a private tutor would have attended the family home in Rome to teach Trajan. From seven to ten years of age, the elementary stages of education were taught. Reading, writing and arithmetic filled the teaching day. A social and historical context was applied to lessons, and Trajan would soon be versed in the many great legends and historical events of ancient times. In addition to formal education, Trajan would likely have been instructed by his father in Roman traditions and moral duties, as well as in sharing his general experiences. Marcia and Marciana would have also taught Trajan during those formative years, but ultimately it was Traianus' role as the father to instil his ideals in his son.

Besides the character moulding of the young Trajan through his education and fatherly instructions, what were the early factors of life in Italica that shaped the physique, nature and personality of Trajan? The mountainous regions to the north and the rolling hills and plains immediately around Italica were the perfect playground for a boy aged eight or nine to develop and hone his growing agility. The river afforded an opportunity to master swimming, sailing and rowing. A later liking for hunting and physical exertion were doubtless fostered by joining his father in pursuit of the abundant game around Italica. Being raised even briefly among provincial more humble Romans, away from the excesses and corrupting forces in Rome, may have reinforced a modest nature in Trajan. In turn this would enable him to connect better with people outside the upper classes. This type of lifestyle in and around Italica therefore provided an environment for Trajan, at an age of rapid development, to promote a strong constitution and a more amenable nature that would put him in good stead with his soldiers and the Senate later in life. The senator Pliny would later give a speech to Trajan in the Senate describing Trajan's inherently approachable nature:

> Anyone who approaches you [Trajan] can stay at your side, and conversation lasts until it is ended by his discretion, not by any loftiness of yours.[23]

Growing up in Rome and the Turmoil of Civil War

Although Italica and the region of Baetica must have played some role in influencing Trajan during his young impressionable years, further reinforced by the provincial background of his family, the majority of his childhood was likely spent in Rome. The epicentre of the empire therefore played a very important part in shaping his character. The family home in Rome, the Domus Traiana, was located on the Aventine Hill.[24] Recent excavations in the centre of the Aventine district, under a car park in Piazza del Tempio di Diana, may have identified the family's large suburban villa that likely became Trajan's private home before he became emperor. Ten metres below the piazza, six exquisitely decorated rooms with six-metre-high vaulted ceilings have been discovered.[25] Still well preserved, they were adorned with white marble mosaic floors, marble thresholds and fine frescoes covering the walls and ceilings. On white plastering delicate architectural elements are defined by red and other coloured lines, accompanied by finely painted birds, animals, insects, flowers, candelabra, theatrical masks and landscape scenes.[26]

Wealthy owners of large properties in Rome typically tried to replicate the space and features of their homeland estates.[27] The Aventine Hill had the space for such properties yet was only a fifteen- or twenty-minute walk north to the forum. The Aventine was traditionally the home of plebeians but suffered less overcrowding than other regions because it was slightly further from the forum than other hill districts.[28] With fine views to the north-west of the Tiber River snaking past and of the Capitoline and Palatine hills to the north, the area was fully inhabited by Republican times and, by the first century, it housed an increasingly wealthy set of residents.

The young Trajan was surely overwhelmed by Rome's sheer size, splendours and magnificence as he grew up. Already in this period, Rome had reached a population of around one million, making it the most populated city in the world. Incredibly, it held this record in the European region for over 1,800 years until the industrial revolution.[29] Multicultural, with many educated inhabitants bilingual in Latin and Greek, the organisation of urban life by the Romans is awe-inspiring even today. All Trajan's senses would have been excited by this metropolis at the heart of a vast empire: the sight of the gigantic Temple of Jupiter on the Capitoline Hill silhouetted against the sky and the gleaming white marble façades in the forum; the array of smells assaulting the nose in the crowded narrow streets on a sweltering summer's day; the intense roar of the crowd cheering their favourite charioteer at the Circus Maximus; the taste of exotic foods imported from all corners of the empire; the cool touch of a Lucullan marble column in such places as the Basilica Aemilia.[30] All would form memorable impressions on the young boy.

Absorbing and interpreting the spectacle that was Rome shaped Trajan's character, and he may have overheard adult conversations in the home about the sinister side of Rome's imperial court that festered in this period. In 65, the climax of hostility towards the Emperor Nero had materialised in a failed conspiracy, that ended in bloodshed for many patricians, including Nero's own tutor, the celebrated philosopher Seneca. Patricians were members of the group of citizen families who constituted the elite privileged class in Rome. Rumours and scheming were rife, fuelling Nero's increasing fear. Nero's vast Golden House, the Domus Aurea, was taking shape and sprawling across central Rome in the form of lavish villas and pavilions surrounded by impeccably landscaped gardens, fields, lakes, vineyards and woodlands.[31] Such extravagances alienated Nero further from the Senate. Yet Traianus was able to steer clear of the situation in Rome and was commissioned in the spring of 67 as a *legatus legionis*, commander of a legion, to campaign against the Jewish revolts in the province of Judaea (Palestine). Given the active campaigning involved, Trajan would have probably remained at home in Rome with his mother and sister.

The Jewish Revolt, which started in 66, was an insurgency on a scale not seen before within the Roman Empire. Years of poor governance, abuse of the region and internal bickering among the Jewish factions led to the annihilation of Roman forces garrisoned in Jerusalem by an army raised from the civilian population – shame indeed for Rome.[32] The immediate response was to send the governor of Syria, Cestius Gallus, with the Legion

XII *Fulminata* and supporting detachments straight into Judaea. However, the Roman force was routed at Jerusalem, sustaining major casualties, and the legion's eagle standard was lost.[33] Disgrace had descended on Roman efforts. No significant force was left in Judaea and the province was essentially outside Rome's control.

Nero responded vigorously. He replaced Gallus with Licinius Mucianus and appointed Titus Flavius Vespasianus (hereafter Vespasian) as general to reclaim Judaea. Vespasian had humble equestrian origins, but had demonstrated his abilities during the conquest of Britain and was one of the foremost generals available to Nero. Signifying the gravity of the crisis, three legions were mustered – equivalent to around 10 per cent of the entire Roman legionary force:[34] Legion XV *Apollinaris* was marched from Alexandria by Vespasian's son Titus; Legion V *Macedonica* came from an unknown location commanded by Sextus Vettulenus Civica Cerialis; and Legion X *Fretensis*, based in Syria, was commanded by Traianus.[35] The inclusion of Traianus as a *legatus* was a proud moment for his family and a defining stage in his career. Campaigning commenced and continued through the year with most of the province reconquered, except for Jerusalem and certain fortress strongholds.

Despite these promising advances towards bringing Judaea back under the yoke of Roman authority, rebellion was rising elsewhere in the empire, but this time in the form of Roman dissent. Nero's indulgences and excesses at the expense of Rome and its empire, as well as controversial executions of generals and senators, had gone too far. In 68 a chain of Roman rebellions started against Nero, including by the governor of Hispania Tarraconensis (Nearer Spain), Servius Galba. A loosely aligned group of governors, including Galba, precipitated the abandonment of Nero by his Praetorian Guard in Rome and the Senate found its opportunity to declare Nero an enemy of the state. After fourteen years of rule, Nero's principate (imperial rule with the pretence of partnership with the Senate) was now in ruins. Despite commanding significant support within the empire from the legions, Nero was unable to bear his desperate position and, with the help of his secretary Epaphroditus, committed suicide on 9 June 68. On hearing the confirmed news of Nero's death, the Senate hailed Galba as the new emperor. The great Julio-Claudian imperial dynasty, started almost a hundred years earlier by the deified Augustus, was at an end. When accounts of events in Rome reached the East, Vespasian called an immediate halt to all operations in Judaea and Traianus entrenched his legion until further notice.

Despite the instability of the period, Trajan's teachings would have continued. Starting at ten years of age he would have moved into the next phase of education with a *grammaticus* – grammarian teacher. His lessons would have focussed on the refined understanding of language and literature. Embedded within the content of learning was the need to study a multitude of disciplines: music, astronomy, philosophy and nature, and the need to appreciate fully the essence of literature.[36] There can be little doubt that he would also have continued to train with other boys in athletics, riding and other physical activities. In this period, Trajan's sister Marciana was married to Caius Salonius Matidius Patruinus, and left the care of her father to move into her new husband's home. In 66, Marciana had a daughter called Matidia, Trajan's niece.

As for the newly hailed emperor, Galba left Spain for Rome late in the summer of 68. He proceeded to instigate frugal financial policies, including a critical refusal to reward the Praetorian Guard financially for their allegiance. Furthermore, Galba had already committed another fatal error by not securing substantial support from some of the powerful military commanders dotted across the empire. As a result, no sooner had he arrived in Rome, than the legions stationed in Germania refused to renew their oath of allegiance and declared the governor of Germania Inferior, Aulus Vitellius, as their emperor on 2 January 69.[37] The mechanism of imperial accession now evidently resided in the might of the army.

Galba desperately attempted to shore up his position in Rome through the appointment of an adopted son as his heir. In doing so he unwisely overlooked his co-mutineer, Otho, who himself had high expectations of such an adoption. As a consequence, Otho moved rapidly to dispel any vestigial Praetorian Guard loyalty and, on 15 January, arranged the assassination of Galba and his new heir. With the support of the Guard, the Senate hailed Otho as the new emperor just 220 days after proclaiming Galba and despite the distant claims of Vitellius in Germania.

Civil war was now imminent and Otho foolishly assumed that his rival would back down. Instead, Vitellius moved to secure his claim and sent ahead two of his legion commanders, Valens and Caecina, with a substantial contingent of the Rhine forces. They crossed the Alps into Italy and joined forces at Cremona by the Po River. Otho was not completely without support, and forces along the Danube frontier and in the East proclaimed their allegiance to him, but, in practical terms, only the legions of the near Pannonia province were in a position to race to Italy in time to give real support.

Therefore, Otho's strategy was simple: send ahead his commanders Paulinus and Celsus with detachments of forces from Rome to unite with the detachments from Pannonia in early April; Otho would follow closely behind Paulinus and Celsus with the Praetorian Guard and then hold the Po River against the advancing Vitellian forces until the main relief army from Pannonia arrived.

Under this strategy, outnumbered Othonian troops engaged Vitellian units to the east of Cremona at the first Battle of Bedriacum (Calvatone) on 14 April 69. Otho was decisively beaten and his troops fled south in disarray and with great loss. The next day, despite the imminent arrival of his rapidly advancing Danubian relief forces, Otho decided that he was not prepared to perpetuate the loss of further Roman blood. Otho had no stomach for a protracted civil war, though he blamed it on Vitellius. He decided on the honourable Roman path of taking his own life in the hope that his act would be remembered for ending the civil war. Otho remained true to his decision, and the following morning, 16 April, he fell on his sword and his forces capitulated to Vitellius. He had been in power just ninety-four days.

Over the next few days, rapid dispatches to Rome brought news of Otho's defeat and suicide. On 19 April, the Senate hailed Vitellius as emperor. Trajan and his mother were doubtless increasingly confined to their home during this perilous period. The streets of Rome, dangerous even at the best of times, were particularly hostile in time of civil war. During the absence of Traianus, the family may have moved to the relative safety of a family villa outside Rome, eagerly awaiting Traianus' letters from the East to know he was safe and well.[38]

Vitellius' period of rule was soon to be challenged. A contender was rising in the East. Vespasian had not stood idly by as affairs in the West unfolded. Nor had he forgotten the manner in which Otho had been removed and the insult to his Eastern legions who had sworn allegiance to him. Vespasian sensed the strength of his position if the Eastern legions could be united securely with the legions along the Danube, against Vitellius' German legions and forces in Rome. Vespasian also had two sons, Titus with him in the East and Domitian in Rome, who were the necessary elements of a Flavian dynastic line. In addition, he was probably cognisant of his superior virtues and experiences compared to Vitellius and his close advisers would have counselled him on his encouraging position. However, Vespasian would not repeat the mistakes of Galba, Otho and Vitellius. This time, a greater level of support from provincial commanders and senators would be sought.

To this end, in urgent correspondence, Vespasian strove to secure all the Eastern forces through his loyal commanders. The governor prefect of Egypt, Tiberius Julius Alexander, was approached and his backing acquired. Traianus' support was also obtained and he was posted to oversee immediate operations in Judaea in place of Vespasian.[39] The assistance of Mucianus, governor of Syria, was also assured along with his three legions. Messengers were sent to commanders in the provinces of Pannonia and Moesia along the Danube, who had previously sided with Otho against Vitellius and were now ready to adhere to the Flavian cause.

In parallel, dispatches raced to Rome to rally influential senators dissatisfied with Vitellius. At that time, the Jewish revolt was under control and the Eastern frontiers were relatively secure. With all these elements in place, Vespasian was now ready. A meeting was held between Vespasian and his senior Eastern commanders in order to map out their clandestine plans, and Mucianus urged Vespasian to accept nomination. Vespasian accepted. The future of Traianus, who would almost certainly have been present at that critical meeting, was now inextricably linked to that of the Flavian cause. Back in Rome, the young Trajan would also be thrust unawares into the same cause by his father's actions.

The legions' declarations of allegiance to Vespasian were precisely coordinated. On 1 July 69, the governor prefect of Egypt and the legions III *Cyrenaica* and XXII *Deiotariana* in Alexandria (Iskandariya) hailed Vespasian as emperor. In succession, the Judaean, Syrian, Pannonian and Moesian legions made similar declarations.[40] With such dominant military support secured, Vespasian, Mucianus, Titus, Traianus and all the senior officers convened in Berytus (Beirut) in July to finalise the strategy to remove Vitellius. It was decided that Mucianus would depart for Rome in August on behalf of Vespasian with detachments from the East to unite with the Danubian forces. Mucianus would then present a formidable contingent that would force Vitellius to yield. But even before Mucianus could reach Thracia (approximating modern Bulgaria and the Istanbul peninsula), the legate of the Legion VII *Gemina*, Antonius Primus, made a dash for Italy in September to confront Vitellius with a significant contingent of Danubian forces. The act was a deviation from the careful plans laid out by Vespasian. As a result, Vitellian forces clashed with Primus, again near Cremona. The Second Battle of Bedriacum (24–25 October) was brutal. Vitellian troops had no general, since Vitellius was still in Rome, his general Valens gravely ill and his remaining general Caecina recently arrested for conspiracy. Vitellian forces were further demoralised having to bear the guilt of previous conflict with fellow Romans at the First Battle of Bedriacum, with Roman bloodstains probably still evident on the leather coverings of their shields. Bitter fighting continued into the night and eventually Primus overwhelmed the Vitellian forces, which fled in defeat and capitulated to Vespasian.

In Rome it was a fateful time for supporters loyal to Vespasian because, although Vespasian was victorious, Vitellius still controlled the city. The city prefect Sabinus, Vespasian's brother, having narrowly failed to convince Vitellius to abdicate after the defeat at Cremona, was forced to take refugee on the Capitoline Hill with a few Flavian supporters including Vespasian's own son, Domitian. Legionaries still loyal to Vitellius stormed the Capitoline and routed the group. Sabinus was caught and executed – a bitter moment for Vespasian to lose his brother.

During the fighting on the Capitoline Hill, the sacred Temple of Jupiter, the finest temple in Rome with its exquisite columns and reliefs, was set ablaze. The horror of civil war set the night sky alight for all of Rome to witness. Many Romans would have bowed their heads in shame. Primus was soon at the gates of Rome and Vitellius was captured and taken to the forum where he was tortured before execution. Vitellius' body was then dragged on a hook and flung into the Tiber.[41] By 20 December, Primus had Rome under control. The Senate reconvened and proclaimed Vespasian as emperor on 21 December, just 246 days after lauding Vitellius. The Flavian dynasty had risen and peace was restored to the empire.

Traianus had gambled everything by siding with Vespasian and his steady loyalty would now reap rewards and change forever the course of the Ulpii. Trajan had turned thirteen years old in the momentous year of 69 and the young boy learned a stark lesson from the events that saw four emperors in just one year: that the circumvention of civil war and establishment of stable government were only made possible with substantial broad support from powerful legionary commanders and influential senators.

All through the turmoil of these historic events, Trajan continued his education, which at thirteen years of age entered its final stage: the study of rhetoric. A rhetorician teacher would strive to instil the skill of public speaking into his pupil. Trajan was taught the best selection of words, as well as the correct structure of sentences. Among other aspects, the background to lessons included history, law, geometry and geography. Topics of speech and the composition of speeches formed the bases of exercises until the student was skilled in the art of oration and rhetorical discourse.[42] Yet Trajan is thought to have failed to fully master this art.[43] Perhaps his talents resided in other unexplored areas.[44] Though Latin was the official language in Rome and the western part of the empire, well-educated Romans were also expected to speak Greek which constituted a large proportion of classical literature and was the official language in the East.

On 1 January 70, while Trajan continued to study rhetoric, the new Emperor Vespasian in Egypt and his son Titus in Judaea, took up the positions of Rome's two consuls. The action was symbolic and Titus, taking the title of *Caesar*, signified his position as Vespasian's first heir. Titus was then appointed to lead the campaign against the remaining Jewish insurgents and bring closure to the rebellion. Traianus was relieved of his command and allowed to accompany Vespasian on his journey to Rome, as a *comes*, companion of the emperor. This was the first reward for Traianus' loyalty and it was a great honour for him to have access to the inner court around Vespasian.

Some five months later, Vespasian arrived in Rome with Traianus after being absent from the city for over three years. A much taller and more mature Trajan would have greeted the return of his father from the East. The new Emperor Vespasian was quick to reward men who were pivotal in securing his accession and Traianus was granted the post of *consul suffectus* for September–October 70.[45] Reaching the rank of consul, even the truncated *suffectus* version (who didn't open the new year as a consul), was a great distinction for Traianus and his family. Traianus' *cursus* was now open to ex-consular positions and he was soon appointed as the governor of Cappadocia (Eastern Turkey).[46] During Traianus' tenure, one legion was posted in this province, which bordered the important Armenia state between the Roman and Parthian empires. Under his new policies in the East, Vespasian had decided to garrison this province permanently due to increasing enemy incursions and the need to provide better security in the region.[47] Thus, Traianus was relocated to the governor's residence in the provincial capital, Caesarea Mazaca (Kayseri, Turkey). Given Trajan's stage in life he might have remained in Rome under the care of his mother because he was soon to reach the critical age of being able to claim manhood, but it is possible that the family joined Traianus in Caesarea Mazaca.

The End of Childhood

The end of Roman boyhood was officially assumed at the festival of Liber (the god of fertility) in the month of March following completion of the child's fourteenth year. Thus, Trajan likely assumed his manhood in 71. The event would be marked by the removal of his childhood *toga praetexta* in exchange for the *toga virilis* which was made of natural beige-coloured wool. The golden *bulla* charm, which had hung from Trajan's neck since he was nine days old, was also removed and dedicated to the *Lares*, guardian deities of the household. Celebration and feasting followed and family processions led into the forum to mark the occasion.[48]

Trajan's days at school were over. In the eyes of the state he was now a citizen and a *juvenis* – young man – able to take a position within Roman adult society. Although Trajan still fell under the authority of his father, he was expected to fend for himself and establish his position in public life. Assuming the family was in Rome, as the son of a senator he would now be allowed to attend certain Senate meetings to familiarise himself with proceedings.[49] Born in Spain, growing up in Rome, with a period spent back in his home province of Baetica and possibly some time in Cappadocia during his father's governorship, all had played a part in shaping Trajan's character. His father's successes had propelled the family into the upper echelons of Rome's society, including the favour of the Emperor Vespasian. Civil war had ravaged parts of the empire, including Rome itself, but the coming of the Flavian age offered the hope of stability. Foundations were in place for Trajan the *juvenis* to apply his learning and childhood experiences to the cause of regeneration and prosperity.

CHAPTER 2

YOUNG ADULTHOOD IN A NEW ERA

Transition into Manhood

In every society, ancient and modern, specific ages legalise certain activities that demarcate thresholds of adulthood. In Roman times, in this way, certain ages were also recognised as societal milestones. After Trajan proudly donned his *toga virilis* at just over fourteen years of age, he entered into a period called *adulescentia*, a phase of young manhood.[1] Though Trajan was presumably physically and sexually mature, marriage and participation in Senate politics were normally precluded until around twenty to thirty years of age.[2] In essence, *adulescentia* was a social release to explore adult life, including such potential trappings as sexual pleasure, aggression, gambling and drinking. Indeed, *adulescentia* was an emotive term for youthful adulthood.[3] It is easy to imagine this period of life having similarities with our modern world, where those in their teenage years can sometimes allow adult freedoms to turn into degeneration and excess. Certainly, Rome had much to tempt young adults into disproportionate exploration of these freedoms. The seedy ancient streets of the Subura district, for example, the fashionable Monti quarter of modern Rome, were home to countless brothels and drinking taverns, which many a young man frequented until the early hours.

As well as allowing the gratification of pleasure-seeking urges, Trajan's period of *adulescentia* was also an initiation into the world of adult responsibility in business and public affairs. If he had remained in Rome during his father's years as governor first of Cappadocia and afterwards Syria, Trajan could have aided his father's businesses during his absence. Traianus' military and political successes, as well as his close association with the Emperor Vespasian, would have earned him enormous wealth. Further family properties and estates were probably acquired, as well as substantial investments in businesses and major contributions to public works. Trajan would be expected to become more and more involved in the oversight of these interests, as well as the old family estates back in Baetica through bailiffs. Bookkeeping, the management of slaves, liaising with clients, monitoring repairs and numerous other duties would have helped to lighten the burden on his father, who had no other sons to rely upon.

The wealth of Trajan's family may have permitted him as a young adult to live in his own house, separate from the family home. However, only when he married and fathered children could he claim to be head of a household.[4] At this time, although formal schooling was at an end, Trajan likely acquired the guidance of one or two senior statesmen close to the family to steer the naïve youth through the ruthless and sometimes mortally dangerous world of Roman politics and business. Through these mentors and directly, Traianus would have additionally striven to keep Trajan from the uncontrolled debauchery to which Roman youths were so prone.[5] In any event, Trajan's later adult behaviour and reputation indicate that he emerged from the *adulescentia* period with his moral reputation intact. The humbler provincial origins of his family and his exposure to provincial life during at least his father's governorship of Baetica, combined perhaps with diligent guidance from family and mentors had kept him from going off the rails.

In Roman society, there were also points of transition through early adulthood that recognised physical changes. For instance, young men performed their first shave only after they had grown their first full beard. Once Trajan's downy growth reached a satisfactory beard-like appearance, a specific ceremony was held for the first shaving and the remnants of hair were dedicated in honour of a deity. Therefore, the growth of a beard delineated a point in the *adulescentia* period.[6] With puberty already past, Trajan's body was nonetheless still changing fast and he no doubt took regular exercise to tone his emerging strength and agility. There were numerous youth colleges and Trajan likely attended one or more of them. These were recreational clubs where young adult males could engage in exercises, athletic contests, hunts and games of physical power.[7] Trajan's later enjoyment of hunting suggests he may well have honed the necessary skills at a youth college.

Sex and Sexuality

Modern literature, films and television have often failed to address accurately the topic of Roman sexual habits. This is partly understandable given modern religious doctrine and social sensitivities. But one must cast away temperance for one moment to appreciate Roman sexuality and the period of *adulescentia*. This period can be viewed as a liberation into the adult world, where, in Trajan's case, a man could seek diverse and ready forms of sexual pleasure to feed his sexual appetite and abandon his sensibilities – in essence, a period of youthful sexual experimentation. With a highly charged libido, Trajan would have explored his developing sexuality during *adulescentia* to identify what satisfied his sexual desires and it appears that Trajan had a preference for male adolescents.[8]

But what were the socially accepted Roman sexual practices that would allow an understanding of the acceptability of Trajan's preferences? Firstly, it was acceptable for a Roman to purchase slaves for sexual pleasure, as they were of a lower social order. Moreover, since slaves were considered material property, it was legally acceptable for the owner to use and abuse them in any way to gratify his or her sexuality. Trajan may well have sought sex with the numerous slave boys working on the family properties or perhaps with girls if boys were not readily available. Secondly, male prostitution was legally acceptable in Roman times and particularly widespread in Rome itself. In fact, attractive young male prostitutes were exclusive and highly sought after; able to charge large sums of money for sexual acts; they could be considerably more expensive than their female counterparts. Trajan's access to substantial family funds would have allowed him to pay for the best and have them perform any act he so desired. Again, prostitutes were of a lower social rank, so it mattered little to demean their bodies, making the sexual encounter socially tolerable.

Roman society did not approve of sexual relations between a Roman male and another freeborn boy or man.[9] A homosexual act with a freeborn person of similar age or older was especially inappropriate, as it suggested the Roman male was becoming effeminate and not in a commanding position. A further debasement in any homosexual relationship was to act as the passive partner in an encounter. But, as with most prohibitions, the line was crossed frequently. Rumours circulated that Trajan himself breached this taboo of having sex with freeborn boys and men.

As a homosexual with a preference for adolescents, Trajan would be condemned both by the sexual mores of our own times and by those of the intervening centuries. However, in his own age this was entirely acceptable behaviour when the sexual act involved someone of a low social order. Yet Trajan was not reproached by his contemporaries for his sexual acts and the Roman historian Dio Cassius later wrote:

I know, of course, that he was devoted to boys ... in his relations with
boys he harmed no one.[10]

There can be little doubt that Trajan continued to indulge his desires beyond the period of *adulescentia* and despite his later marriage.

The Senatorial Career Ladder

In this period, a man fortunate enough to be born into the upper tiers of Roman society could expect a glorious career as a Roman senator, an honourable 'father of Rome', decorated and remembered through the ages. The various judicial, administrative and military posts strewn across the empire were not for the faint-hearted, but were laden with potentially rich rewards. Traianus' *cursus* had set a new high standard for any family member to follow, especially his son Trajan for whom expectations would be elevated. Since Traianus' risky but well-judged adherence to the Flavian cause, he had emerged from the civil wars of 69 as a proven senior military officer who had steadfastly supported the current Emperor Vespasian in his accession. Following the great honour of being *consul suffectus*, he is thought to have successfully completed a term as governor of Cappadocia (*ca.* 70–73).

Still greater things were to follow for Traianus that would directly impact Trajan's early advances. In 73, the Emperor Vespasian and his son Titus both assumed the highly respected censorship to maintain the population census, which was a register of Roman citizens and their property.[11] After the civil wars and the countless executions and banishments ordered by a succession of tyrannical emperors, it was apparent to the new censors that the Senate was in a depleted state that could only be addressed through fresh elevations to the patrician rank. Thus, for all his loyal service, Traianus and his family were raised to the patrician class.[12] Consequently, Trajan, at around sixteen years of age, was now a member of the Roman elite aristocratic class with all the privileges and prominence it bestowed.

Roman social structure was complex and had evolved over the centuries. In simplistic terms, at this period, based on his ancestry, a Roman citizen was either a patrician or a plebeian 'common' person. There were poor and wealthy in both classes, but wealth largely resided in the hands of patricians. Those few plebeians who had attained wealth were referred to as plebeian nobles. In addition to their ancestry, men could be appointed into the patrician class by the emperor because the censors' function had become annexed to the *princeps*. The census established two groups of higher-ranking citizens, senatorial and equestrian, based on wealth and property holdings. Men of the senatorial class generally pursued a political career; equestrians were engaged in enterprise and business. Equestrians, however, were not barred from holding military or administrative positions, as was seen with Traianus' career, and they could aspire to senatorial rank.

With the family's newly elevated status, Traianus was appointed to another governorship, this time in Syria.[13] He may have moved directly from Cappadocia to his new provincial capital at Antioch on the Orontes (Antakya) to begin his duties promptly in this highly important province. Syria was a crucial frontier zone adjacent to the looming Parthian Empire, but it was also blessed with vital ports and trade routes for the movement of lucrative produce from the East to Rome. Three legions were accordingly stationed in the province to be used for both security measures and engineering projects.

In the same year that Traianus moved to Syria (*ca.* 73), Trajan reached his seventeenth birthday and became eligible for the *latus clavus*, a distinctive symbol of the senatorial order; this was perfect timing for him to display his new patrician status. The actual *latus clavus* was a tunic worn under the toga with a woven broad purple band running perpendicularly from the neck to the bottom of the garment for patricians. Equestrian knights had two narrow bands of purple running down the tunic to distinguish them from patricians. Someone meeting Trajan in the forum at this time, would likely see a virile young man with a youthful muscular appearance, downy beard stubble and wearing a tunic with a crisp single purple band beneath the folds of his toga – perhaps with bags under his eyes from the previous night's excesses in the Subura.

As we have seen, the first prerequisite for a future senatorial career was entry into the office of the vigintivirate or, literally, 'the twenty men'. These were not positions in the Senate proper. Although these were only junior positions, specific postings within the vigintivirate dictated the course of subsequent entry and steps in a senatorial career.[14] There were four types of office: the *triumviri monetales*, to oversee the mint; the *quatuorviri viarum curandarum*, to look after the streets of Rome; the *decemviri stlitibus iudicandis*, assigned to the civil courts; and the *triumviri capitales*, assigned to the criminal courts.[15]

The most prestigious of the *vigintiviri* offices was one of the three *triumviri monetales* positions. Three elements would have secured this competitively sought place for Trajan: firstly, his father's ongoing and highly successful career; secondly, the elevation of the family into the patrician class; and thirdly, the indispensable bond between Traianus and the Emperor Vespasian.

As for so many other positions, a nod of approval from the emperor was a definite help with promotion. However, it should be noted that although the four colleges of *vigintiviri* had a ranking order, patrician status trumped any college affiliation for a future senatorial career.[16]

Therefore, around 74, it is thought that Trajan took up his *vigintivirate* office at the imperial mint in Rome. On a daily basis, he was probably responsible for helping to manage the production of coinage at the mint. Roman coinage was an effective means of publicity for the emperor, critical to his administration of the empire. The profile of the emperor's face, along with words and imagery, conveyed his achievements and values directly to Roman citizens right across the empire and even to traders beyond the borders using Roman coinage. It was therefore imperative that the mint liaised closely with the emperor's administrators and all major design themes would have been ultimately approved by the emperor himself. Different messages conveyed on the coinage were really intended to 'gratify the *princeps*' and display an image 'as he wished to see himself'.[17]

Trajan would have also been busy reviewing security at the mint, maintaining inventories and records of production, as well as ensuring production capacity was uninterrupted.[18] His role meant close association with the senatorial quaestors who supervised the mints, treasuries and financial affairs on behalf of the emperor and the Senate. By the end of his year in this post, Trajan would have gained a thorough understanding of the imperial mint and the importance of coinage both as a publicity tool and a means of imperial self-gratification.

The Dawning Flavian Age

Trajan would have observed considerable change in Rome between the period running up to his initiation into manhood and the completion of his first official public post at the imperial mint. In particular, Vespasian was primarily concerned with consolidating his position and the assertion of a new Flavian dynasty. This would not be palatable to all senators; why should the glorious Principate pass like a cheap inheritance from a father to his son? Might not Vespasian's heirs display the same tyrannical and narcissistic tendencies as the Julio-Claudian heirs of Augustus? Vespasian proceeded to counter this reaction in several ways. First, he quickly placed his principal supporters, like Traianus, in all the important provincial command posts and in key senatorial positions such as the consulships. The important censorships to restore the Senate were claimed by Vespasian and his eldest son Titus, his heir apparent. Their goal, obviously evident to most prominent people in Rome, was to ensure the elevation in rank of those they trusted and also to broaden membership of the Senate to include provincial men, rather than the previously narrow patrician contingent mostly from Rome and Italy. Vespasian himself was the first emperor from a plebeian family, so it strengthened his position to broaden the Senate in such a manner.

As part of his post-civil war consolidations, Vespasian strove to represent himself as a peacemaker. As we have seen, the machine of imperial coinage was hard at work churning out the message that Vespasian had restored peace to the Roman world. Vespasian added further gloss to his image by constructing a magnificent temple to Pax, the personified Roman goddess of peace. No expense was spared by the emperor and the temple was adorned with a lavish colonnaded precinct and spectacularly decorated rooms close to the forum.[19]

Besides restoring peace by ending the civil war, Vespasian could also claim triumph in the suppression of rebellion within the empire. Peace was restored in Judaea after several years of war against the Jewish insurgents. After a four-month siege of Jerusalem in 70, the city was taken under the command of Titus along with the shocking destruction of the great temple.[20] The rebellion was effectively over at this stage, although a defiant resistance at the mountain stronghold of Masada was not broken until 73. In fear of future uprisings, Vespasian approved the placement of a permanent garrison force in Jerusalem and the Legion X *Fretensis*, that had been commanded by Traianus in the Jewish wars, was selected to remain in this capacity under the authority of a newly appointed senatorial governor.[21] Vespasian was awarded a triumph in 70 for his feats in ending the Jewish revolt and he used part of the enormous wealth generated from spoils from the temple in Jerusalem to initiate the construction of the great Flavian Amphitheatre (Colosseum) in Rome. Nero's Golden House lake was selected as the site for the three-storey amphitheatre. It would take nine years to complete and would hold over 50,000 spectators, making it by far the largest amphitheatre in the world.[22]

In the west of the empire, Vespasian also claimed success for the crushing of a Germanic rebellion. A Batavian chieftain, Julius Civilis, who at some point had been made a Roman citizen and commander of a Roman auxiliary force comprising some of his tribesmen, had seized the opportunity to capitalise on Roman weaknesses caused by the civil wars. Civilis instigated a Germanic rebellion in a complex arrangement involving various tribal factions with different loyalties to the fallen emperors of 69. The revolt was initially successful in routing regional Roman forces, but Vespasian's relative Quintus Petillius Cerialis, with a substantial force was able to quash the uprising in 70.[23]

In the same period, announcements were made that Vespasian's eldest son, Titus, now a successful general of the Jewish wars, would be his heir and successor. The title of *Caesar* was bestowed on Titus in recognition, and coins hailing this title quickly followed; *Caesar* was now a title used to designate the emperor's heir. This was the final component for asserting the age of a new peaceful Flavian dynasty. In the summer of 71, Titus was also back in Rome and able gradually to take over more and more responsibility from Vespasian, now in his early sixties. In particular, Titus was made one of the two Praetorian Guard prefects, a position of power in which the emperor needed someone on whom he could utterly rely.[24] Vespasian's other son, Domitian, only in his early twenties at this point, was entering his *cursus* like Trajan. The absence of any sons of Titus, meant that Domitian was next in the imperial line, although he would remain in the shadow of his brother while Vespasian lived.

With Titus finally in place as his official heir and his position as emperor strengthened, Vespasian could risk being strict with his early fiscal policies, as the treasuries were seriously diminished after the costly civil wars. Much prudence in public spending and increased taxation would be required to return financial stability to the empire.[25] This slowed the initial reconstruction of the damage caused by the civil war; Vespasian needed to prioritise the initiation of much-needed works that had been postponed during the turmoil of recent years.

Consequently, the dawn of the Flavian age was a coordinated series of strategies and policies to restore the empire after civil war, to emphasise Vespasian's role in establishing peace and restoration, thereby consolidating the power of the new imperial dynasty. The cessation of uprisings and the discipline of certain Roman legions were pivotal factors to accentuate the new era of stability and the gradual construction of the immense Colosseum was to be one of the greatest symbols of prosperity for the Flavian age, a symbol so grand it would long outlast all the subsequent emperors of Rome and remains the unmatchable icon of Rome today. Trajan's growing awareness of the adult world was deeply embedded in this new dawning of the Flavian age, and it would have surely influenced his emerging political views as he embarked on his senatorial career.

CHAPTER 3

THE MAKING OF A MILITARY OFFICER

※

The Roman Army

The supremacy of the Roman army had made Rome the undisputed master of the classical world. The remarkable discipline, organisation and technical advances of the Roman legions, in combination with diverse and specialised troops from the provinces, made Rome the superpower of its day. The dominance of Rome even extended far beyond the edges of the empire through the influence of its military presence in frontier provinces. Rome's forces ensured the famous *pax Romana*, through coercion or force. They were normally used for reactive offensive action and their inherent flexibility allowed pitched field, guerrilla or siege warfare. In addition to military action, legionaries could also be employed in the creation of provincial infrastructure using their expert engineering skills.

All legionary recruits had to be Roman citizens. The legion was the largest separate military unit. Each legion was organised into ten tactical sub-units called cohorts, the first of which, thought to have been manned by elite legionaries, had 6 groups of 160 men, misleadingly called 'centuries'. The other nine cohorts had 6 centuries, each of 80 men. Together with around 120 horsemen for scouting and carrying dispatches plus all the officers, a legion at full strength was around 5,700 men.[1] However, detachments, sickness and injuries, deaths, desertions and other factors meant that legions were usually well below full strength. Each legion was given a unique name and number combination.[2]

The *legatus* was the commander of a legion. He was appointed by the emperor and was a senator. Next in command was the most senior tribune, the *tribunus laticlavius*, who was typically on his career path into the Senate. There were also five other tribunes who were equestrians acting as senior officers involved in administrative functions, the *tribuni angusticlavii*. Third-in-command was the *praefectus castrorum*, the camp prefect. The next lower tier of officers were the centurions, each in charge of a century of men. Usually veterans promoted through the ranks because of experience and acts of bravery, they were the cornerstones of tactical command. The most senior centurion was the *primus pilus*, usually a very experienced man who was appointed through merit and was assured later promotion into the equestrian class and could then aspire to the position of *praefectus castrorum*, military tribune or auxiliary prefect.[3] Other officers included an *optio*, a centurion's second-in-command, an *aquilifer* who carried the legion's sacred eagle standard and a *signifer* who carried the insignia of a cohort or century.[4]

In addition to the legions' efficient discipline and command structure, three key aspects distinguished them from other heavy infantry of the period: firstly, the continuous training of legionaries throughout their twenty-five years of service kept every man battle-ready and well disciplined; secondly, the effective role of logistical support over great distances, combined with self-sufficiency, meant that a legion could operate proficiently far from its regular garrison; and thirdly, state-of-the-art equipment – the segmented and articulated metal plate torso armour called *lorica segmentata*, plus a large composite rounded rectangular shield and a sturdy helmet with solid facial guards and an extended neck guard – provided steadfast defence in battle. Disciplined use of a short sword, for stabbing rather than slashing, was highly effective in close combat combined with this unique protection.

Complementing the legions' heavy infantry capabilities, *auxilia*, support troops, were an integral and essential component of the Roman army. *Auxilia* were non-citizens recruited from the provinces who, after twenty-five years of service were awarded citizenship along with their sons. In units of around 500 or 1,000 men, they provided specialised combat functions such as infantry, cavalry, archers and slingers. By the first century, the *auxilia* infantry were similar to legionaries in equipment and tactics and were generally tasked to man frontier defences in advanced positions, with legions stationed in deeper reserve.[5] The number of auxiliaries probably equalled the number of legionaries. Therefore, as *imperator*, or supreme commander, the emperor had an army of around 285,000 men at full strength in this period.[6] Though this figure would be diminished at any given time through attrition, it nonetheless gives a strong sense of Rome's professional military strength. The soldiers' loyalty was pivotal in the emperor's passage to and maintenance of autocratic power.

Trajan's First Taste of Life in a Legion

In around 75, the anticipated day had finally arrived for Trajan to take his *cursus* to the next level and join a Roman legion as a senior tribune, a *tribunus laticlavius*. This would be his first exposure to life in the Roman army, the world's first longstanding professional army, which demanded the utmost from its legionaries and officers. Trajan's father had already held several senior military posts and demonstrated able command during the Jewish uprisings, so it was now Trajan's turn to show he could follow in his father's footsteps.

It was customary for a *tribunus laticlavius* to join a legion that was under the command of a relative or close friend of the family. Consequently, Trajan was probably appointed to one of the three legions based in Syria, where Traianus was governor of the province at the time (*ca.* 73–77).[7] The role of a *tribunus laticlavius*, although technically second-in-command of an entire legion, was essentially a training post for a young officer on a career path to the Senate proper. The vastly more experienced senior centurions and camp prefect actually carried the burden of practical authority subordinate to the overall commander, the *legatus legionis*.

On arrival in Syria, Trajan transferred to the established fortress of his designated legion. These permanent fortresses followed a standard layout but varied in size and covered an area of around 200,000 square metres, roughly equivalent to the size of thirty football pitches.[8] The fort was likely surrounded by wood and earthen ramparts, with important buildings constructed from stone and the remainder being timber structures.[9] The precisely plotted area was shaped like a playing card with four guarded entrances and clearly designated roads: the *via Principalis* running laterally right across the camp and, perpendicular to that, the *via Praetoria* running down the middle to the headquarters building or *principia*.[10] For security, no building in the fort was within around thirty metres of the ramparts in order to create an empty perimeter that placed peripheral buildings beyond the range of most missile weapons should the enemy ever reach the ramparts.[11] On campaign, temporary camps using tents were constructed every night along a similar pattern to the permanent forts.

The *principia* was the administrative core of the legion's fort, containing the treasury, legionary standards, statues of the emperor, administrative offices and the important tribunal platform from which the *legatus legionis* could preside over formal proceedings within the headquarters. In the more established forts, the commander enjoyed the comfort of the *praetorium*, essentially a large Roman home complete with under-floor heating, private baths, open-air courtyards and luxuriously decorated private quarters. The far humbler barracks for legionaries were divided into simple blocks, each housing a century of men, petty officers, the centurion and storage space for equipment and military paraphernalia. Other buildings were allocated for the hospital, granaries, lavatories, stables, shared bath houses and various workshops.[12] Trajan, as the senior tribune, would have been given a small Roman-style home positioned along the *via Principalis* and been served by slaves and freedmen.[13] As a whole entity, the base was fundamentally an ordered, self-contained town. Over time, locals often established a settlement near the fort called a *vicus*, catering to the large military presence.

On a typical day in the fort, Trajan would have left his quarters early in the morning to join his fellow officers and aides in the *principia*. He would be provided with an escort, drawn from legionary soldiers on a roster, to guard him in the execution of his duties. He would have been given a dedicated office within the *principia* where he attended to his clerical and administrative tasks throughout the day before retiring in the afternoon or evening. His daily schedule would probably include time to exercise and bathe. One can assume that he would have eaten occasionally with the *legatus legionis* and his family, if present in the fort, in the *praetorium* and frequently with other tribunes and officers in their mess facilities or quarters.

Although Trajan's position was one of training, a proficient *tribunus laticlavius* could possibly be involved in an array of specific activities and actions, some of them distinctly not routine in nature: issuing orders on behalf of the *legatus legionis* when absent; condemning the accused and dispensing punishment; commanding manoeuvres and expeditionary patrols; negotiating with embassies and envoys; leading a division during battle; in extremely rare circumstances, directly commanding or joining the fighting line in hand-to-hand combat.[14]

Trajan's later reputation as an adept military officer, suggests he was recognised quickly as a promising and competent young man, showing aptitude in his duties and exceeding expectations. In contrast, other *tribuni laticlavii* often took the easy route of completing the posting with minimal effort and little professionalism.[15] This may have resulted in a division of competency among Rome's would-be commanders, with able young men such as Trajan earmarked for future distinction.[16]

All the official duties of a *tribunus laticlavius* did not completely deprive Trajan of the opportunity to seek pleasure and relaxation while posted in

Syria. Indeed, army life provided the surroundings for merriment beginning with the consumption of strong wines during manly gatherings of officers and legionaries. Within the vicinity of army camps wine merchants found ready customers, and soldiers received wine as part of their rations and for religious celebrations.[17] To meet demand, vineyards may have been established close to some permanent camps in order to supply the army directly alongside the expensive wine imports from Italy and Greece that were distributed throughout the empire.[18] For example, Trajan and his fellow officers could afford the more extravagant vintages, such as Falernian wine imported from Italy. Falernian wine was well aged and thought to have been derived from the Aglianico grape grown in the Falernus district of Campania, where the vineyards were cultivated between the River Volturnus and Mount Massicus to the north.[19] In the ruins of Pompeii, the following painted advertisement was found on the wall of an inn and one can easily imagine a similar range of choices in Syria when legionaries selected a wine:

> For one *as*, you can get a drink here.
> For two *asses*, you will get a better drink.
> For four *asses*, you will drink Falernian wine.[20]

All wines were much stronger in alcoholic content than wines today. They were often diluted with water and mixed with salts, honey, herbs and other spices.[21] Soldiers were known to drink their wine at full strength, undiluted.[22] Thus, heavy consumption started in the army may have seeded Trajan's habit and reputation for heavy drinking and the historian Dio Cassius records his 'devotion' to wine.[23]

On short leaves, Trajan could also have enjoyed entertainment in an amphitheatre, which sometimes accompanied a well-established legionary camp in a nearby town, hosting regular gladiatorial shows and other bloodsport bouts involving local and imported wild beasts. He could have also found relaxation in the fort bath house, not only a place for unwinding in a series of steam rooms and baths of varying temperatures, but also affording distractions in the form of massages, exercise, socialising and gambling.[24] The all-male environment of the camp would be in keeping with Trajan's sexual inclinations and desires. He may have enjoyed the discreet company of selected soldiers or even officers. Yet despite all these possible opportunities to seek pleasure and distraction, Trajan's time in Syria as a *tribunus laticlavius* was a productive period, inducting him successfully into military life in a legion.

First Military Action

Though not attested, Trajan's military baptism may have included combat action. Despite the warring and aggressive nature of Rome, a tribune like Trajan in the imperial era could easily complete his post without any experience of fighting, especially if posted to a legion in a congenial province with settled frontiers. Thus, Trajan's involvement in specific action so soon into his *cursus* would have been untypical but not improbable. In order to assess the likelihood of an early exposure to combat, we must first review the overall strategy of the Roman Empire and the evolution of frontier policies under the Emperor Vespasian. Much relates to the specific strategy for Syria around the time of Trajan's posting in 75–77, which may indeed have led to his first experience of warfare.

Contrary to what may be imagined, at the start of the Julio-Claudian period under the great Emperor Augustus, the frontiers of the empire had few or no specific boundaries or permanent fortresses for legions or auxiliary forces. Instead, the Roman army was organised along major access routes as 'mobile striking forces' able to react quickly and decisively against incursions or internal uprisings in an offensive or defensive manner. To support this flexible response, a series of client kingdoms and tribes were required beyond the periphery of some provinces to tackle low intensity incursions as well as mitigate the impact of major invasions. Under this system, if a large hostile force wanted to raid a settled Roman province, it would first need to contend with the forces and inhabitants of the client state as well as any natural geographical barriers, during which time an agile offensive Roman force could be deployed to the area of confrontation. Moreover, client kingdoms on occasion were able to provide substantial forces to assist Rome in times of need. The disadvantages of the Julio-Claudian system resided in the fact that certain client kingdoms and tribes could be unstable and at times incapable of coping with even minor incursions. Nevertheless, this geopolitical structure was well suited to the nature of Roman imperial expansionism in that era, allowing for an economy of force in the deployment of troops throughout the empire.[25]

However, the glory days of major expansion were shifting towards consolidation by the time of Vespasian's principate.[26] Consolidation rationalised the frontier and this meant the gradual demarcation of border zones that better defined the limits of Rome's direct influence. Certain client states were slowly absorbed where advantage could be gained in the establishment of superior frontiers in both political and geographical terms. A new strategic objective drove these changes: specifically, the need to provide enhanced frontier security against low-intensity incursions that the client states were unable to control completely. Provincial development could only flourish successfully through local stability, better daily management of security and further isolation from the unsettled hordes beyond. Consequently, forces were stationed more permanently along the frontiers, supported by a framework of fixed defences, 'intended to serve not as total barriers but rather as the one fixed element in a mobile strategy of imperial defence'.[27] As a result, an integrated system of trails and watch-posts called *limites* was gradually established to crudely demarcate a frontier and this was followed later by the development of trenches, palisades and roads in certain key zones.[28] The *limites* were by no means impenetrable, but they were able to deter minor incursions as well as provide surveillance against potential invasions.

Turning specifically to Syria, the region had prospered under Roman rule and established itself as one of the most important Roman provinces. Blessed with excellent agricultural conditions, it was especially suited to high-demand products such as grain and wine. It also reaped the benefit of its lucrative trade routes between the Far East and the Roman Empire, transporting high-profit products such as rare spices and silks. Even the Roman colour of authority, purple, came from an expensive dye extracted from various species of marine molluscs, notably *Murex trunculus*, found in the waters along the shores of Syria.[29] Around 130 snails were required for just 1 gram of purple dye worth more than its weight in gold, equivalent to approximately 200 *sestertii*.[30]

The Roman capital of Syria, Antioch on the Orontes (Antakya), was surpassed only by Rome and Alexandria and therefore of extreme importance.[31] It was an enormously wealthy city and its urban development was advanced and refined. Further south, Emesa (Homs), an independent and affluent city with territories stretching east, was embedded within the province of Syria.[32] Emesa had close ties with the city of Palmyra, 'City of Palms', situated at a large oasis in the Syrian desert. Palmyrene territory was part of the Syrian province and the city of Palmyra grew wealthy through its taxation of products passing along the trade routes. Hence, given the overall importance of Syria to Rome, it is no surprise that Rome appointed a consular *legatus* as the governor of the province, and Traianus was Vespasian's choice for a critical period when his new eastern policies required application. Traianus could be trusted as an experienced provincial administrator with some regional knowledge, as well as a loyal supporter of Vespasian; he was perfect for the job.

Before Vespasian, the Eastern Empire was an array of provinces and client kingdoms that followed the early imperial frontier strategy. Starting in the north, the provinces of Pontus and Cappadocia had no permanent legionary garrisons.[33] Four legions were stationed in Syria.[34] To the south there were no legions in Judaea. Therefore, the whole system of defence and security in the East relied on the ability of client kingdoms to diminish the impact of incursions and provide troops while Roman mobile forces were dispersed from Syria (with additional forces dispatched from the West in dire crises). Within this organisation, the Kingdom of Armenia was regarded as a neutral 'buffer' state between Rome and its traditional enemy, the Parthian Empire – the only polity capable of putting Rome in its place. But Armenia was not a true independent buffer state. During Augustus' reign, it had been agreed that client kings independent of Parthia would rule Armenia.[35] However, this situation unsettled both empires, each of which considered Armenia to be within its zone of authority. In 52 the Parthian king Vologaeses I placed his brother Tiridates on the Armenian throne and this inevitably led to conflict. Stability was eventually restored in 66 when Tiridates agreed to be crowned in Rome by Nero as King of Armenia: this expedient amended Augustus' policy such that Parthia would henceforth nominate a candidate for the Armenian throne and Rome would endorse the selection prior to any coronation. It would keep both Rome and Parthia comfortable for at least the foreseeable future and make Armenia a nominally controlled region.

The dependence on centralised offensive-defence legionary forces based in Syria and the precarious status of Armenia was clearly sub-optimal in Vespasian's view and not in accordance with his overall strategic vision. Offensive defence involved striking out against the foe at the outset to seize the initiative and force the enemy onto the back foot. Reacting to the Jewish uprising, Vespasian posted one legion permanently in the province of Judaea.[36] However, the whole region still remained vulnerable to future instability, particularly subject to the machinations of neighbouring Parthia. Moreover, the actual distance between the frontier regions of Syria and the critical core of the province was precariously short.[37]

Consequently, to reinforce security in the East, legions could still apply offensive-defence actions but Vespasian prepared an integrated plan to strengthen frontiers, clarify demarcation and absorb certain client states where beneficial. As we have seen, while Traianus was putatively governor of Cappadocia (*ca.* 70–73), one legion was permanently posted and appropriate infrastructure such as roads were established.[38] The legion was commanded by its own *legatus legionis*, while the province as a whole was commanded by Traianus as the proconsular *legatus*. The legion in question, XII *Fulminata*, was stationed in Melitene[39] (Malatya, Turkey) about ten kilometres southwest of the Euphrates in the vicinity of a critical crossing over the river at the foot of the Taurus mountains.[40] It was presumably supported by *auxilia* in the region. In effect, a military zone was now in place directly opposite Armenia in the vicinity of the Upper Euphrates. It was evident that the arrangement with Armenia was no longer trusted and that Cappadocia, as well as Pontus, needed this protection.[41]

In the early seventies, Caesennius Paetus, Traianus' predecessor as governor of Syria, advanced his forces into the kingdom of Commagene to face King Antiochiaus. The kingdom was taken and the Legion VI *Ferrata* was stationed at Samosata (Samsat) and the Legion IV *Scythica* at Zeugma,[42] both strategic positions on the western banks of the upper Euphrates. The outward justification for invasion was based loosely on accusations of clandestine relations between Commagene and Parthia.[43] The move was actually a veiled attempt to satisfy Vespasian's strategy of extending the Syrian frontier to the banks of the upper Euphrates, thereby creating more depth in the region to mitigate the effect of incursions, as well as establishing a frontier that was less dependent on client states. It also conveniently secured the fertile lands in the Commagene area. In the restructure, the city kingdom of Emesa was also absorbed into Syria.

The outcome of these initiatives was a line of three legions spanning a superior frontier position along the western banks of the Euphrates, from Zeugma in Syria to the upper Euphrates zone at Melitene in Cappadocia. In essence, a screen of legions ran in an axis roughly north to south, able to strike out and protect the fertile regions, trade routes, principal cities and road networks of the East against any insurgents or incursions. The Kingdom of Palmyra, although already part of Syria, was resolutely integrated into the province under Traianus' governorship through the construction of a road network. Syria also benefited from a substantial investment in infrastructure during Traianus' term using the engineering expertise of Roman legionaries. The Orontes River above and below Antioch was canalised to extend its navigability and extensive works improved the port at Seleucia Pieria that served Antioch.[44]

In the south of Syria, to bridge the gap between the legions along the Euphrates and the distant Legion X *Fretensis* at Jerusalem in Judaea, the Legion III *Gallica* was garrisoned at Raphanaea. The Legion XVI *Flavia Firma*, present in Syria during Traianus' term as governor and involved in the construction of the canal mentioned above, was moved around 75/76 and garrisoned in Satala (Sadak, Turkey).[45] In conclusion, from around the mid-seventies this meant two legions were stationed in Cappadocia and three in Syria. After just five or six years in power, Vespasian's new eastern security arrangements were in place and reasonably consolidated. Traianus and his family were right in the thick of all these changes, with Traianus as governor of Cappadocia and then Syria, and with Trajan possibly a military tribune attached to a Syrian legion.

All the visible modifications alarmed the Parthians. From their perspective, the new Emperor Vespasian was lining up his forces directly along their western borders after the aggressive acquisition of client states. Were the Romans planning incursions into Parthian territory? Did Vespasian have his eyes on the remaining major client states in the Upper Euphrates region, like the Kingdom of Osrhoëne or did Rome even have intentions to meddle with Armenia? To top it all, the great nomadic Alani, beyond the Caucasus Mountain region, were invading Armenia from the north. The King of Parthia, Vologaeses I, applied to Vespasian for help in 75. Vespasian declined Rome's assistance.[46] Consequently, Parthian tolerance of Rome was wearing thin, and as well as repelling the Alani, they may have flexed their muscles against Rome and tested the strength of the new Roman positions in Syria.[47]

So we return to the question of whether Trajan could conceivably have been involved in military action during his posting in the East. To have been part of these military confrontations between Parthia and Rome, Trajan would have needed to be the *tribunus laticlavius* of one of the two legions in the new frontier territory, either VI *Ferrata* at Samosata or IV *Scythica* at Zeugma.[48] Samosata was a fortified city that critically marked the end of the Taurus mountain course of the Euphrates.[49] A bridge at Samosata spanned the river over into the Kingdom of Osrhoëne and roads linked the city to the interior of the Syrian province.[50] Zeugma was a highly prosperous city on the western banks of the Euphrates. It also had roads to Antioch, which was about a week's march away.[51]

These two legions were critical to protect these cities with key positions next to the Euphrates, as well as extend the arm of Roman influence into the new frontier area. Hence, the two legions would almost certainly have been involved in any substantial engagements with the Parthians in the region. As an able *tribunus laticlavius* in one of the legions, Trajan may very well have been involved in skirmishes and battles with the Parthians, issuing orders from the *legatus legionis*, possibly overseeing a division of legionaries. Whatever Trajan's level of involvement, Vespasian's new system proved resilient and negotiations with Parthia concluded the fracas. Traianus, instrumental as the Syrian governor in the resolution of disruptions through his overall command of military engagements and diplomacy in Syria, was awarded the *ornamenta triumphalia*, a decoration that recognised successful commanders.[52] Once again, Traianus had served Vespasian skilfully, but this time his own son may have been involved. If so, Trajan had encountered the illustrious Parthians and been exposed to the complexities of engagement in dry and barren terrain. This knowledge would prove invaluable later in life when he would come up against the great neighbouring empire again.

Having possibly gained active experience against the Parthians but still keen to learn more about the operations and command of a Roman legion, a single posting in Syria was not enough for Trajan. It has been suggested that he seized upon the opportunity of extending his *tribunus laticlavius* term when his father's governorship ended in 77[53] until an appropriate post became vacant in Germania Inferior under the patronage of the governor, Rutilius Gallicus.[54] After a long journey across the empire, from the high arid wastes of the Syrian frontier to the wet lowland forests of the Rhine, Trajan may have joined one of the four legions stationed in the province (VI *Victrix*, X *Gemina*, XXI *Rapax* and XXII *Primigenia*).

In this period, Rutilius Gallicus and his forces were engaged against the Germanic Bructeri tribe inhabiting a heavily forested region north-east of Germania Inferior beyond the Rhine – the present-day Rhine Westphalia district in Germany.[55] The Romans had long grown to hate the Bructeri. Their resistance to Rome culminated in their union with others and the disaster of the Teutoburg forest in AD 9. Under General Varus, three entire legions and *auxilia* forces, totalling around 30,000 men, were utterly destroyed. Later, during the Gallo-German uprising of 69–70, the Bructeri had sided in a rebellion against Rome instigated by the Batavian Julius Civilis. After the uprising was quashed, punitive action against the Bructeri only seeded more hatred of Rome. That hatred later reared its head, fuelled by a mysterious prophetess called Veleda: hence the need for Rutilius Gallicus to campaign against the Bructeri around 75–78.[56] Trajan, presumably commended by his previous *legatus legionis* in Syria as an able *tribunus laticlavius*, plausibly had involvement in sorties against the Bructeri. If so, he would have witnessed the later stages of campaigning to subdue the tribe and the capture of the priestess Veleda.[57] It is not clear what happened to Veleda after her apprehension.

To sum up this stage in Trajan's *cursus*, Pliny later in his *Panegyricus* speech made the following remarks about Trajan at this time:

> A distant look at a camp, a stroll through a short term of service was not enough for you [Trajan]; your time as tribune must qualify you for immediate command, with nothing left to learn when the moment came for passing on your knowledge. Ten years of service* taught you customs of peoples, locality of countries, lie of the land, and accustomed you to enduring every kind of river and weather as if these were the springs and climate of your native land. Many were the times when you changed your mount and the arms worn out with service!
>
> Pliny[58]

After his eventful years as a tribune, the next stage in Trajan's *cursus* was beckoning back in Rome: the quaestorship. Trajan's induction into military life was complete and he was then entering the period in a Roman's life when the union of marriage was expected within patrician society. Therefore, his sword and armour had to be packed away and Trajan returned to Rome in 78 presumably to wed and stand in the quaestorship elections.

As Trajan travelled back to Rome through Gaul and then the Alps, he must have reflected on his encouraging initiation into military life. His years as a young junior officer had proved unusually active with the opportunity to include two postings in very different parts of the empire: Syria and Germania Inferior. He had excelled at his duties, despite the conventional training nature of the position. Again, Pliny provides an exaggerated description in his *Panegyricus* of Trajan's exemplary performance in this period. Surely an example of model behaviour for future tribune officers to follow:

> You were scarcely more than a boy when your successes in Parthia helped to win fame for your father, when you already deserved the name Germanicus, when the mere sound of your approach struck terror into the proud hearts of savage Parthians, when the Rhine and Euphrates were united in their admiration for you.
>
> Pliny[59]

---

* Refers to the customary ten-year period between the *toga virilis* and the quaestorship.

Marriage and Family Affairs (ca. 76–79)

The modern notion of marrying for love bears little or no resemblance to the driving forces behind a Roman marriage. Instead, social standing and the advancement of political or business influence through the new extended family, as well as producing children, were typically the principal imperatives.[60] Trajan's patrician status meant that his father, Traianus, and his bride's father were likely acquaintances who would have instigated and approved the betrothal in the traditional manner. Trajan's bride was Pompeia Plotina from Nemausus (Nîmes) in Gallia Narbonensis.[61] In this period, Nemausus was a prosperous colony blessed with a natural spring and surrounding fertile lands, well connected by roads within the region and with Italy. Plotina's family details are lost to us today, but the status of the Ulpii tells us she was probably from an equally affluent and influential family. Therefore, the union pulled together a network of family links whose roots were based in contemporary, wealthy and developed Roman provinces, Gallia Narbonensis and Baetica.

The legal age for female marriage was twelve or above, and many Roman girls were indeed married in their early teens.[62] Trajan, already twenty-one years of age in 78, would without doubt have had a younger bride. Legally, marriage was not constituted by a formal civic process; it was based simply on the consent of both parties to marry and the recognition that the couple were husband and wife. The day of a marriage was marked by adorning the family houses and giving offerings to the household deities. Plotina would have worn a bridal gown complemented by precious jewellery and slaves would have styled her hair according to the bridal fashion of *sex crines* (six tresses) crowned with a garland of flowers.[63] Brandishing torches, the bride's family would have guided Plotina to Trajan's house where he would welcome her into her new home. Lavish celebrations and feasting followed to complete the wedding ceremony.

And what of conjugal sex between the newly married couple? Trajan's sexual preferences may have made intimacy with Plotina scarce or, worse, non-existent. The newly-wed couple were nevertheless expected to reproduce. Thus, in the early period of their marriage, Trajan and Plotina would surely have tried to have children. Trajan could continue to indulge his sexual preferences elsewhere and as long as he was discreet and did not embarrass Plotina, their affiliation could flourish. Around the home, they would also strive to adapt to each other's company and domestic habits.

Plotina was known for her decency, dignity and simplicity, virtues that struck a chord with Trajan and likely governed their domestic lifestyle. In time, the couple probably established a stable relationship, each tolerant of the other's needs and, in essence, they appear to have experienced a contented Roman marriage.[64]

At this time, Trajan's family had its share of joys and tragedies. Perhaps two years earlier, in 76, Trajan's cousin from Italica, Publius Aelius Hadrianus Afer had a son called Publius Aelius Hadrianus (hereafter known as Hadrian).[65] Hadrian would play a pivotal and integral part in Trajan's life and we shall return to him later. Though Trajan gained a cousin, he lost his brother-in-law in 78. His widowed only sister, Marciana, would never remarry. Her only child, Salonina Matidia was eleven at the time of her father's death. Thus, Trajan's sister continued the upbringing of Matidia and she probably remained in the house of her deceased husband.[66]

In 79, Traianus reached the zenith of his senatorial *cursus* and was appointed proconsul of Asia. The proconsulates of Asia and Africa were normally allocated by lot to the senior ex-consuls without interference from the emperor, but it is possible that Vespasian's influence ensured that other candidates stood down, increasing Traianus' chances of selection for one of the two prestigious provinces.[67] Whatever the circumstances, the proconsulate of Asia was a very senior position, equal only to the proconsulate of Africa and awarded to Traianus in recognition of his highly successful career under Vespasian.

The province of Asia corresponded roughly with the western third of modern Turkey. This peaceful province with its prosperous cosmopolitan cities and string of bustling ports was an enormous asset to Rome, providing substantial taxation revenue as well as commanding the essential land routes from the East.[68] Together, the routes and ports made the province a crucial interface between the eastern and western components of the empire. Traianus and Marcia moved to the official residence in the provincial capital of Ephesus (Selçuk), a wealthy city on the western coast that was home to the celebrated Temple of Artemis, one of the seven wonders of the ancient world, and they remained there for the customary period of the governorship.[69]

Vespasian's Death and Titus' Accession.

Not long after Traianus was settled in Ephesus and while Trajan was in Rome attending to family business after his marriage to Plotina, the Emperor Vespasian became gravely ill. Vespasian developed a fever which later worsened into a 'stomach chill... and a sudden violent bout of diarrhoea'.[70] He weakened rapidly and died on 23 June 79, aged sixty-nine years.[71] The death of Vespasian marked the end of an era for Traianus. Long had he faithfully served his emperor and Trajan himself had entered his *cursus* under the principate of Vespasian. The era had seen the restoration of peace in the Roman world after the turmoil of civil war, and prudent economic policies had begun to repair the financial state of the empire. A new strategy of frontier demarcation and consolidation had also been implemented. Thus, the empire was passed in reasonable shape to Vespasian's successor, his eldest son and designated heir, Titus.

At his accession, Titus immediately assumed full imperial powers and received the endorsement of the Senate. The onset of Titus' principate was initially blemished because of his former role as Praetorian prefect. Understandably, given the responsibilities of this position, Titus had incurred hostility for oppressive actions in the interests of the Flavian dynasty. To recover popularity, the new emperor successfully presented a different image of authority through empathy and consideration. He dutifully recognised his father, who was deified with a cult established to honour his divinity. Titus also did not forget the loyalty of Traianus and appointed him as a *sodalis Flavialis*, a priest of the new Vespasian cult.[72] But without Vespasian as his champion and belonging to a different generation, Traianus, after completing his tenure as proconsul of Asia, returned to Rome and withdrew from public life, receiving no further senatorial positions under Titus. In short, he retired gracefully.

Present in Rome, Trajan was able to commiserate personally with Titus over the death of his father, as well as offer congratulations to Titus for his accession and affirm his allegiance to the new emperor. Ten years earlier, his father had made the same adherence to Vespasian's cause and such a gesture from Trajan to Titus was similarly critical to secure advantage and rewards under the new regime, as well as continue the family tradition of loyalty to the Flavian imperial family. Titus would also have need of such loyal men, not only as a bastion against treachery, but also to overcome three major catastrophic events on the Italian peninsula.

Firstly, just four months into Titus' reign, Mount Vesuvius in Campania erupted, wiping out the entire Pompeian plain and destroying the major towns of Pompeii, Herculaneum, Stabiae and Oplontis.[73] The pyroclastic eruption blasted out approximately three cubic kilometres of volcanic rock – around four times as much as the Mount St Helens eruption in 1980.[74] As many as 45,000 people were killed and countless numbers rendered homeless.[75] Titus acted decisively through the mechanism of a board of ex-consuls who were responsible for administering the relief campaign in the devastated region.[76] Moreover, Titus personally visited Campania to supervise relief efforts.[77] While he was in Campania, the second catastrophic affliction of Titus' reign struck. In 80, a great fire raged through Rome for several days.[78] Great swaths of Rome were burnt down, including the magnificent Temple of Jupiter on the Capitoline Hill.[79] Likely in Rome in this period, Trajan would have witnessed the shocking destruction of the great temple. Again, Titus acted dutifully and swiftly, using his own wealth to fund restorations in Rome, as well as appointing a board of equestrian knights to implement relief plans. Then, probably accentuated by appalling living conditions resulting from the devastations in Rome, the third disaster struck: a plague epidemic.[80]

Despite these terrible misfortunes during the reign of Titus, the Colosseum, started ten years earlier by Vespasian, was now completed and it offered a timely means for Titus to raise public morale. In 80, the inaugural ceremonies commenced and lasted for a hundred days. There were spectacular events and a myriad of gladiatorial combats, animal fights and the customary executions of criminals. The vast new stadium was also flooded to re-enact naval battles, complete with galleys and sailors. Trajan likely attended the initial days of the ceremonies, his patrician status ensuring him a place commanding the best views of the arena.[81]

The opening of the Colosseum marked an approaching change in Trajan's *cursus*, because in the following year he was eligible to stand for election as a *quaestor*.[82] His class and his family's loyalty to the Flavii secured his smooth election into the post through direct recommendation from Titus.[83] The quaestorship meant Trajan's first real entry into the Senate proper; the title literally meant 'to inquire' and the bureaucratic role entailed the administration of public finances.

Trajan's Gap Years and Domitian's Accession

Trajan was a *quaestor* in Rome for the statutory single year. As stipulated in the Roman *cursus*, once a young patrician senator like Trajan had finished his quaestorship, he was unable to take further senatorial office until completion of a mandatory five-year 'gap' period. It is not known how senators occupied their time during this imposed term without appointments. However, one can reasonably assume that an ambitious senator like Trajan threw himself into senatorial debates and proceedings. Without the formal duties of a specific magistracy, Trajan could dedicate his attention to the machinations of government, strengthening political connections and collaborations. One should not underestimate the importance of securing such allegiances, particularly given events that would unfold in the early eighties. Trajan would have also taken the opportunity to focus more on family businesses during this sabbatical from his *cursus*.

Just nine months into Trajan's post-quaestorship break, on 13 September 81, Rome was stunned by the unexpected early death of Titus at the age of forty-one, only two years after becoming emperor. Evidence suggests that natural causes were to blame.[84] His brother Domitian was hailed as emperor by the Praetorian Guard and his position ratified by the Senate the next day. Doubtless, just as Trajan had adhered to Titus, he would have manoeuvred rapidly to rally behind Domitian, who recognised the history of support from the Ulpii for the Flavii.

Domitian had always been overshadowed by Titus and had never attained the glorious military successes of his illustrious father and brother. Such success was pivotal to the foundation and security of an emperor's position and Domitian wasted no time in seeking immediate military conquest against the Chatti in 83. This Germanic tribe was located north of the Taunus Mountains in the river valley regions of the Moenus [Main] and the Visurgis [Weser] in a region corresponding approximately to the Hesse-Kassel district of modern Germany.[85] The historian Tacitus referred to the Chatti as a formidable force of foot warriors with more discipline than the average Germanic tribes:

> You may see other Germans proceed equipped to battle, but the Cattans [Chatti] so as to conduct a war.[86]

Domitian clearly had cause to launch a campaign against the Chatti, who had sided with the Batavian Julius Civilis against Roman authority in the Gallo-German uprising of 70, but punitive action was only part of the rationale: the ultimate driver was the desire to create a strategically superior frontier arrangement in the region. Hence, in 83, a large Roman force mustered in Germania Superior under the supreme command of Domitian and his general Velius Rufus.[87] In one campaign season, the Roman forces engaged the Chatti and military roads were constructed to penetrate deep into Chattan territory and strike at their strongholds. The Chatti could not sustain resistance and were compelled to capitulate. Once they were driven from the Taunus mountain area, new Roman *limites* effectively hindered their movement back into the Wetterau region and afforded surveillance for the detection of any subsequent incursions.

With the Chatti suppressed, Domitian claimed a victory triumph and the title *Germanicus* – 'conqueror of Germany'. It was a gross exaggeration on which to claim a triumph: the Chatti were defeated and displaced but not conquered. Nevertheless, Domitian had achieved his personal goal of securing a military victory. More importantly, Domitian's achievements were of strategic benefit to Rome. The expulsion of the Chatti meant the annexation of the fertile Wetterau region and the encircling Taunus Mountains. The subsequent *limites* along the upper ridges of the mountains provided a zone of security crucial to support control of the region to the south and east of the upper Rhine called *Agri Decumates*. The net result was an improved network of roads facilitating linkage between Germania Superior, Pannonia and Moesia, as well as a shorter frontier overall. In due course, Domitian was additionally able to concentrate more resources on the troubled areas along the Danube.

At the end of 84, while Trajan was probably in Rome during the penultimate year of his imposed sabbatical, a surprise attack on Moesia by the Dacians caught the Romans off guard. Dacia was a large kingdom north of the Danube, corresponding to modern Romania and Moldova. A civilized people with access to considerable natural resources, the Dacians were not an insignificant adversary. With the Danube frozen, the Dacians were able to cross over in strength and proceed to ransack Moesia, causing significant damage in the province as well as killing the Roman governor, Oppius Sabinus. In 85, Domitian hastened to Moesia with his Praetorian Prefect Cornelius Fuscus to deal with the crisis and was probably based at Naissus (Niš, Serbia). After considerable effort, the Roman forces were able to expel the Dacians. Cornelius Nigrinus and Funisulanus Vettonianus both won distinctions as senior commanders. With order restored in Moesia, Domitian returned to Rome in the following year, this time able to make a more reasonable claim to a decisive victory.

At the time of the Dacian invasion, a major senatorial milestone for Trajan was approaching that would ramp up his seniority: the praetorship. Therefore, at the end of 85, Trajan was busy in Rome preparing for the elections.

The last decade had provided Trajan with essential training in military life as a young officer, not only at the operational and logistical level, but also possibly in active combat with direct experience of the tactical deployment of Roman forces against formidable foes. Plausibly this military know-how was enriched through the diversity of opponents Trajan was able to observe: the Parthians and the Germanic Bructeri, each with unique tactics and fighting methods, each requiring the Roman forces to adapt accordingly. The variety of terrain had provided Trajan with a good understanding of topographical issues crucial for military deployment and engagement. He had also witnessed phases in the continued development of two major frontiers, the Rhine and the Euphrates Rivers. Despite having to tolerate the hardships of field operations, military life clearly appealed to Trajan as he drew satisfaction from the range of duties associated with his appointments.

In the same decade, Trajan had spent considerable time in Rome immersed in senatorial affairs, attending to family businesses and furthering his senatorial *cursus* in financial matters through the quaestorship. Married but still without children in the winter of 85, the hardened and more experienced young man was a promising future commander, well suited to military life and clearly qualified for the next major stage in his *cursus*.

CHAPTER 4

THE MAKING OF A GENERAL

※

Praetorship: Wielding Law before Senior Military Command

Before a Roman could command a legion or govern a minor province, normally he first had to be elected as a *praetor*. Since praetors were the judiciary of Rome, effectively one had to administer the law before obtaining senior authority in the army or provinces. Trajan's *cursus* had arrived at this watershed in power, and in 85 he was in Rome, eager to stand for election as a *praetor* starting in January 86.[1] Six years had passed since the fateful great fire had ravaged the city. Subsequently, the Emperor Domitian had ramped up his immense building campaign right across Rome, which was second only to the building efforts of Augustus.[2] At enormous cost the gilded roof tiles of the rebuilt temple of Jupiter now gleamed in the sun, proudly standing as a symbol of Domitian's magnificence.

As Rome outwardly prospered under Domitian's reign, Trajan's chances of success in the praetorship elections were certainly high. Such a capable young man, loyal to the Emperor Domitian and with a family history of service to the Flavian dynasty, could have every expectation of being elected as one of the eighteen annual praetors[3] and he was duly appointed in January 86. Under the Principate, praetors were essentially chief judges who presided over the series of Roman courts. The emperor and consuls had higher judicial authority, and often the emperor presided over the most important cases, but the praetors remained the principal embodiment of judicial authority in the city.

The sophistication and structure of Roman law is considered one of the greatest legacies of the Roman Empire. Fundamentally, a Roman citizen was protected by Roman law within the empire.[4] Although we do not know today precisely how Roman law was applied across the regions and in the provinces, certain local laws could be retained, but Rome's rulings were applied throughout.[5] Where no written law was applicable, local customs could have the force of law.[6] Such was the philosophy and scientific nature of Roman law. It has influenced the legal codes of western Europe and is the foundation of modern-day civil law in many countries.[7]

Three symbols were awarded to praetors to distinguish their rank and elevation within the hierarchy of the Senate. Firstly, they were entitled to wear a toga with a broad purple-dyed edge called the *toga praetexta*. Distinctive in their togas, when praetors presided over cases they were privileged to sit in a *sella curulis*, or ivory chair. Lastly, they qualified to be attended by two lictors, customary escorts for senior Roman officials who carried a tied bundle of wooden rods wrapped around an axe, called a *fascis*, to symbolise the authority of corporal and capital punishment.

Upon arrival in his office as praetor, Trajan may have been specifically appointed as the *praetor hastarius*[8] who presided over the *centumviri*, the court of a hundred men. Basically, the *centumviri* was an assembly of around a hundred representative citizens drawn from each of the voting divisions of Rome's various communities, who acted as panels of jurors. The title *praetor hastarius*, or spear praetor, referred to the tradition of using a spear to represent the court because a spear symbolised ownership, and related to the court that primarily addressed inheritance cases. The group was normally divided into four courts which could be held in session simultaneously[9] or convened as a whole for particularly prominent cases. The judge of the *centumviri* had final authority in all cases unless, unusually, the emperor or consuls intervened. If Trajan did take up such a role, he would have issued an edict setting out the practical law applications and procedures that the praetors intended to follow and the factors that would steer their judicial decisions. Since the edict was passed from one praetor to the next, it was a record of legislation that grew over time, amended and expanded by successors, evolving the very nature of Roman law. Trajan would have begun to work on his adaptations of the edict immediately after his election into the praetorship, and such a document likely required considerable effort to review, prepare and issue in a timely manner. Praetors like Trajan were thrown in at the deep end and any initial important cases would have been extremely challenging to judge while adapting to the office.

In addition to a praetor's duties as a chief judge, they were expected to finance certain annual *ludi* – public games. Trajan had to draw on his own private funds to contribute towards these events. No money was recovered by the praetors since all the *ludi* were free to the public. The line-up of events at the *ludi* could include gladiatorial games, theatrical performances, feasting and chariot races.[10]

The limelight of attention associated with funding the *ludi* was partially stolen from Trajan and the other contributing praetors in 86, because, in the early summer, Domitian re-launched the spectacular Capitoline Games, which had originally honoured Jupiter Optimus Maximus and marked the repulse of the invading Gauls from the Capitoline in 387 BC. The resurrected games were to be held every four years and multiple provinces within the empire competed against each other in a variety of activities ranging from oratory to field athletic events. Domitian's initiative was well received and the Capitoline games were a great success with the people of Rome.

Besides the obligations to fund public games and serve as a judge, Trajan's role as a praetor meant he could convene the Senate in the absence of the consuls. During any meetings of the Senate, Trajan's increased seniority as a praetor meant he frequently spoke and gave opinions on matters, according to the strict protocol of the Curia proceedings. In the Curia itself, Trajan now sat on a wooden bench allocated specifically for the praetors that was positioned close to the tribunal and was consequently more prominent in the seating arrangements. Prominence was always important in the Senate, especially during the period of Trajan's praetorship. Above and beyond the normal topics addressed, the subject of Danubian security and what to do about the menaces beyond the frontier occupied many sessions of the Senate. Trajan was thus immersed fully in the critical debates of the day.

Debate in the Senate would have become poignant, as events in Dacia took a turn for the worse in 86. Domitian's Praetorian Guard prefect, Cornelius Fuscus, left in command of operations since the expulsion of the Dacians from Moesia the previous year, had advanced into Dacia with an offensive Roman force. A general known to take risks, Fuscus was soundly defeated by the Dacians, lost his own life and the Legion V *Alaudae* was completely annihilated.[11] The news generated considerable concern in Rome, sufficient for Domitian to hasten to the Danube at the end of the summer. Entirely in character, Domitian was determined to control the enterprise.[12] The action he took was arguably decisive, far reaching and strategically astute. Moesia was divided into two provinces, Moesia Inferior and Moesia Superior, in order to regulate and manage the vulnerable frontier region better. Experienced governors were appointed and both of them executed prompt and successful retaliatory action against the Dacians. Domitian and his close advisers also sensed the need for additional forces to be stationed permanently in the

Danube area. Thus, he ordered the relocation of Legions IV *Flavia* (from Dalmatia), I *Adiutrix* (from Germania) and II *Adiutrix* (from Britannia) to strategically important sites along the Danube. Domitian then returned to Rome to plan a future campaign that would avenge Fuscus and crush the Dacians.[13]

Family Affairs (ca. 82–90)

Any future legion commander or general needed a unified and supportive family, able to represent his interests in Rome as well as extend political influence through powerful family connections. By the mid-eighties, Trajan's family was on track to secure for him these advantages. Traianus and Marcia, both presumably still alive and approximately in their sixties and fifties respectively, may have continued to live in the family home in Rome or retired to a country estate.[14] Despite withdrawing from public life, Traianus was still able to command respect for the Ulpii through virtue of his successful *cursus* and unquestionable loyalty to the former and now deified Emperor Vespasian, the current Emperor Domitian's father. However, there was no retirement for Traianus as we understand it today. There was no pension or state welfare for the elderly, nor any official age that marked the time when one gave up work. Instead, a man like Traianus withdrew from public service when he reached either a closure in his *cursus* or when physical and mental health dictated such. In fact, the definition of *old* appears to vary in Roman times from between mid-forties to sixty years of age.[15] Therefore, Traianus would be considered elderly at the time of Domitian's reign and released from public service, but was nevertheless still in control of his family as the patriarch. In everyday life, he was now a man of leisure and in Rome many patricians of similar age to Traianus took to the writing of philosophy or history.

Trajan's wife, Plotina, was by this time recognised as honourable and virtuous in character, commanding respect at the pinnacle of Roman society. In her early twenties, she attended to the family home and was supportive of Trajan's domestic and social associations.[16] Marciana, Trajan's sister and mother to his niece Matidia, was still under the guardianship of her father since her husband's death. Over time, Marciana and Plotina had developed a close relationship which continued to flourish.[17] Not to be underestimated, Plotina and Marciana in a cooperative mode, held considerable influence over Trajan.

Matidia, nearly twenty years old[18] in this period and supposedly beloved by Trajan like his own child,[19] was also involved in family development. Around the age of fourteen, Matidia had married Mindius and together they had a child called Mindia Matidia (hereafter called Matidia the Younger) around 82.[20] However, either due to death or divorce, Matidia soon remarried (*ca.* 84) to Lucius Vibius Sabinus. Matidia bore her second husband a daughter called Vibia Sabina around 86. Vibius Sabinus was a well-connected man with prominent and successful relatives. Trajan's only niece had thus provided him with two highly eligible great-nieces and had further expanded the family circle through marriage to include two new families. However, it was not long after the birth of Sabina before tragedy struck Matidia as it is thought that Sabinus died. As he was a supporter of Trajan, Sabinus' death was a loss to the family.

Finally in this period, Trajan's cousin died, leaving his nine-year-old son, Hadrian, to fend for himself.[21] However, since Hadrian had not yet reached manhood, Trajan and a fellow compatriot from Italica called Publius Acilius Attianus were appointed his guardians.[22] Trajan's role as a guardian was to protect Hadrian's future inheritances and interests. Hadrian, who had grown up in Rome, was by now coming to the end of his elementary education and about to start his secondary schooling. Trajan and Attianus likely approved a suitable private tutor for Hadrian and instilled in him the need to study diligently. Notably, Hadrian, Plotina and Matidia were of the younger generation, which surely facilitated the establishment of a fondness between them over the years.

By 85, Trajan and Plotina had been married for seven years. It was unquestionably a point of family gossip and despair for the couple that they remained childless. Roman marriage was expected to deliver progeny. Children were critical for family development and the extension of kin, as well as providing legitimate heirs. The ancient sources deny us any reasons for Trajan and Plotina's failure to have children, but one can imagine four possibilities. Firstly, the couple failed to conceive early in their marriage and then assumed a purely platonic relationship despite being biologically fertile. Secondly, one or both were biologically infertile. Thirdly, an unsuccessful pregnancy with complications left Plotina infertile. Fourthly, Plotina had one or more children but they died extremely young and their existence was never recorded. As a result, both Trajan and Plotina no doubt sought ways to fill the void through their immediate family – namely, Matidia the Younger and Vibia Sabina.

Trajan's ward Hadrian, after assuming his manhood at the age of fourteen or so and claiming his *toga virilis*, proceeded to leave Rome for Baetica where his ancestors had been established for many generations. Entering the local youth college like his guardian, he would have engaged in the competitive physical activities of the college. Passionate about hunting and with much game in and around Baetica, he pursued the sport to excessive levels and incurred a necessary reprimand from Trajan. Hadrian was probably recalled to Rome as a consequence in 90, where he was to remain until he embarked on his senatorial *cursus*.

First Legion Command

Following completion of his praetorship, Trajan had the necessary credentials for the next more senior stage of his *cursus*. A portion of patricians at this stage would wait for and strive to secure a consulship and many would fail to attain this prestigious position.[23] However, those like Trajan with ambition and drive sought additional praetorian positions in the run-up to a consulship. This was particularly difficult for someone whose father had already attained a senatorial career, as Domitian generally only promoted 'new men' who were the first in their families to serve in the Senate. Domitian's humble family origins, devoid of the illustrious backgrounds of the patricians, had seeded a determination in him to upset the old system of patrician dominance. Despite this, Trajan had clearly made an impression on Domitian and was favoured by him. In addition, Trajan's family had only held patrician status for little more than a decade. As a result, Trajan was appointed *legatus legionis* of the Legion VII *Gemina Felix* towards the end of 86. Leaving Plotina behind, Trajan headed out to Hispania Tarraconensis to take up the command of his first legion, stationed in a fortress called Legio (Léon), south of the stunning Cantabrian Mountains.

Having travelled from Rome, Trajan's arrival at the gates of the Legion VII *Gemina Felix* fort must have been a mixed moment of trepidation and pride. The whole legion would have been out on full parade to herald the arrival of their new commander with salutes and pageantry, the legion's standards proudly displayed and all the legionary soldiers' armour and weapons cleaned to look their best. The legion had a proportion of men who were Iberian-born Roman citizens and Trajan himself was their compatriot.

Galba had founded the VII legion in 68 to strengthen his position in order to claim the principate after Nero's suicide. He had then marched his new legion all the way to Rome and, once seemingly secure, sent it on to Pannonia. Towards the close of the civil war in 69, the legion rallied to Vespasian's cause against Vitellius. Casualties incurred during the war had significantly depleted the legion, which was supplemented by Vespasian with soldiers disbanded from another legion and it was given the name *Gemina*, meaning *the twin*. After a subsequent period serving in Pannonia again, VII *Gemina* performed notably enough to earn the aditional designation *Felix*, or 'lucky', before returning to its roots in Iberia where its new station marked the foundation of Legio.[24]

The location of the VII *Gemina Felix* fort at *Legio* provided a protective zone for the highly valuable Callaecia and Asturias regions.[25] These areas of the province (modern north Portugal and the Galicia district of Spain) comprised mountainous territory richly blessed with gold ore deposits. Dozens of mines were operational in the Roman period, such as Las Médulas and Las Omanas, providing Rome with Iberian bullion. VII *Gemina Felix* extended the arm of Roman authority to deter and tackle local tribal interference and raiding, thereby securing a steady supply of gold to Rome. The duty was not as sensational as fighting victorious battles in the name of Rome, but was nevertheless an essential military function that ensured the maintenance of one of Rome's major provincial assets. In addition, detachments of legionaries from VII *Gemina Felix* maintained security at other sites in the provinces such as important bridges. Large engineering projects may also have required the legion's expertise. Seconded legionary soldiers assisted too in guard or administrative functions in the governor's headquarters in the capital or other civil offices in major towns.

The provincial capital of Hispania Tarraconensis was Tarraco (Tarragona) with its important trading seaport on the Mediterranean coast. The governor at Tarraco was consular in rank due to the special historical significance of the province. One of Trajan's responsibilities as *legatus legionis* of VII *Gemina Felix* was to inform the governor regularly about the legion's major activities and status. Trajan, however, was a *legatus*, a representative of the emperor with delegated authority to execute orders according to his policies or direct instructions,[26] and not directly under the governor per se, although ultimately the governor was responsible for the security and military capacity of his province. As legate, Trajan was solely responsible for the legion's training and operations. His authority as commander covered a multitude of areas, including but not limited to, issuing of major orders to his officers, taking critical decisions on regional security measures and maintaining the legion's strength and state of military excellence. In executing his authority, Trajan relied significantly on his core of experienced officers. These men were primarily his long-service centurions, battle-hardened and respected.

Roman Spain

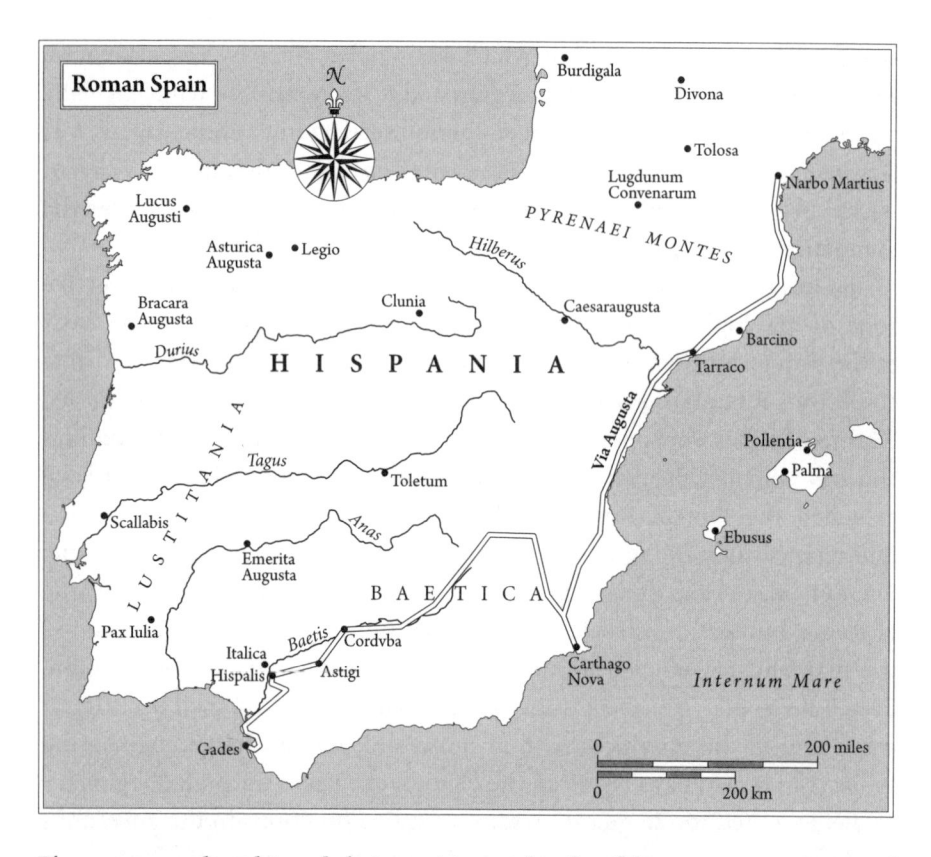

Map showing Roman Spain with locations including Burdigala, Divona, Tolosa, Lugdunum Convenarum, Narbo Martius, Lucus Augusti, Asturica Augusta, Legio, Hilberus, Bracara Augusta, Clunia, Caesaraugusta, Barcino, Tarraco, Durius, HISPANIA, Via Augusta, Pollentia, Palma, Tagus, Toletum, Scallabis, Anas, Ebusus, Emerita Augusta, BAETICA, Pax Iulia, Italica, Baetis, Cordvba, Carthago Nova, Hispalis, Astigi, Gades, Internum Mare, with LUSITANIA and PYRENAEI MONTES labeled.

They commonly achieved their position only after fifteen to twenty years of service in the ranks. The highest-ranking centurion in the legion, the *primus pilus*, would have provided close counsel for Trajan in matters of importance, and the camp prefect, or *praefectus castrorum*, who may have previously been *primus pilus*, was a pivotal source of support, with more decades of service in the legions.[27] A good legion commander like Trajan knew the value of such experienced men and the appropriate circumstances in which to seek their opinion.

Besides Trajan's responsibilities as commander of VII *Gemina Felix*, his posting in Hispania Tarraconensis surely allowed him the opportunity to return briefly to his hometown of Italica and the Baetica region, perhaps on official business. Many years had passed since he left as a child, and he would have enjoyed the chance to meet relatives, old friends and clients, as well as review the condition of family estates.

For the next two years, Trajan successfully led VII *Gemina Felix* without incident, maintaining internal provincial security and at the same time mastering the leadership skills necessary to command a Roman legion efficiently. Events in Rome and around the empire were shaping the future of Domitian's supremacy and it was imperative for Trajan to keep abreast of significant political events and subsequent repercussions, so he would have striven to stay in close contact with family and allies in Rome. Legio may have been a strategically important base for his legion in Hispania, but it was far removed from critical events, especially those involving the turbulent Danube region.

Domitian's Continuing Dacian War

After the reorganisation of Moesia into two provinces and the influx of three additional legions into the Danube region, Domitian anticipated 87 as a year to consolidate his Danubian forces and plan for a definitive campaign against the Dacians in the following year that would end the conflict that the Dacians had started in 84. This was to be a war that would restore Roman pride, re-establish firm authority in the region and take revenge for the loss of Roman blood in previous conflicts.

The high-level military plan for the war was relativity straightforward. Domitian appointed a new governor of Upper Moesia and general for the campaign, Tettius Julianus. He was to muster his force in time for the beginning of the campaign season, advance into Dacia through the western Carpathian Mountains via the Iron Gates Pass and across into the core of Dacian territory (modern Transylvania). Engaging any resistance, Julianus was then to advance on the fortified Dacian capital of Sarmizegetusa Regia to force capitulation. Accordingly, as the spring of 88 emerged, Julianus led his force from Viminacium across the Danube River and north-east towards the Iron Gates in a cautious advance. Beyond the Iron Gates, the Tapae valley plain opens up and here Julianus engaged the Dacians in open battle. The Romans were victorious and great numbers of Dacians were killed in the First Battle of Tapae.[28] To capitalise on the victory, Domitian issued an edict authorising tax relief for all retired soldiers and bestowing Roman citizenship on any who were not already citizens, including their spouses, children and parents. Such a gesture was intended to rally further support from the rank and file of the army for an emperor who rewarded success.[29]

The Dacian leader, King Decebalus, sensing the weakness of his position, withdrew back to Sarmizegetusa Regia and the network of strongholds that guarded the passes through the forested mountain region surrounding the capital. Ingeniously, the Dacians cut down trees and mounted armour over the trunks like mannequins, presumably in places short of warriors. At a distance, Roman forces were deceived as to the numbers of Dacian troops and consequently their advanced guards withdrew in places.[30] Though this bought some time for Decebalus, the main Roman column edged relentlessly closer. Julianus, confident that complete victory was imminent despite the closing season, corresponded closely with Domitian, who planned personally to accept the Dacian capitulation and outright defeat of Decebalus.

However, Julianus and Domitian were to be robbed of their total victory over Decebalus. The Dacians would have offered immense thanks to their gods for an unexpected reprieve at the eleventh hour for, several hundred miles to the west, the Governor of Germania Superior and the two Roman legions at Mogontiacum (Mainz) revolted against Domitian. History was repeating itself, with a Roman governor of Germania raising arms against the emperor. Horrified by events, Domitian was forced to cancel Julianus' remaining advances that season, and his preparations for actions planned for the following spring. Decebalus and the Dacians would live to fight another day.

Saturninus' Revolt

In 89, Lucius Antonius Saturninus, the governor of Germania Superior, initiated a revolt against Domitian.[31] The reason for Saturninus' bold action is unknown. It is speculated that Saturninus was in thrall to the attractions of a fellow officer. The inappropriate relationship that followed drew attention to his dubious moral character and the indiscretions were publicly noted.[32] This exposed Saturninus to a severe reprimand from Domitian, who was firmly opposed to what was conventionally regarded as moral depravity.[33] Whatever the reason, Saturninus must have felt his position was gravely threatened to have risen up against the emperor.[34]

Saturninus crucially misjudged the resources he needed to fulfil his goal of toppling Domitian. Such an objective required broad and coherent support both from well-placed senators in Rome and from influential commanders across the empire. Regardless, Saturninus moved to secure the loyalty of a critical mass of his officers from the two legions camped together at Mogontiacum and he assumed support would follow from the other two legions in his province. He also had erroneous expectations that one or more of the four legions in Germania Inferior would flock to his cause. Hence, on 1 January 89, Saturninus seized the substantial funds of the two legions in Mogontiacum to provide the immediate liquidity needed to kick-start the revolt.[35] The two legions at Mogontiacum, XIV *Gemina* and XXI

Rapax, hailed Saturninus as emperor and messages were sent accordingly to spread the news and recruit support. However, no other legion rallied to his side. Suddenly, Saturninus and his two legions were completely isolated. In desperation, he solicited the aid of the Germanic Chatti. As a result, Saturninus had at his disposal around 10,000 legionaries at the most, contingents of auxiliary troops and hordes of Chattan warriors. The armed rebellion facing Domitian was further accentuated by overstretched military resources elsewhere, due to his commitments in the Danube region.

News of the revolt reached Domitian in Rome around 13 January.[36] Acting swiftly and prudently, Domitian would have issued series of messages and orders. Firstly, a general call was likely sent to all the emperor's key military commanders and governors, reassuring them that the revolt would be dealt with and playing down the consequences. Specifically, Julianus was ordered to suspend military action in Dacia, releasing potential forces should the crisis worsen. In addition, Domitian still had one legion that in such circumstances could be spared from its present duties. It was also commanded by a *legatus legionis* who was trusted by Domitian and whose family had demonstrated the utmost loyalty to the Flavii. It was VII *Gemina Felix* in Hispania Tarraconensis commanded by Trajan. Pliny later recalled Trajan's support during a speech in the Senate:

> [Domitian] called you from Spain to be his surest support during those very German wars [Saturninus' revolt].[37]

Knowing that his 'surest support' would advance from the south, Domitian called to arms his Praetorian Guard and immediately left Rome for Mogontiacum.[38] The emperor and his advisers were by now aware that the other legions in Germania had not pledged allegiance to Saturninus, suggesting that the convergence of VII *Gemina Felix* and the Praetorian Guard with loyal legions would constitute an overwhelming opposition to Saturninus. Domitian was *en route* to Germania around mid-January with around forty days of marching time for his Guard ahead.[39]

The importance of the order from Domitian to Trajan warranted both land and sea modes of transmission using the imperial courier system with the highest priority clearance. In good conditions, the right winds would have allowed a boat to reach Tarraco from Ostia (Rome's port) in five days.[40] A relay of horse-messengers would have then conveyed the message to Trajan in Legio in another eight days.[41] As a result, perhaps as early as 27 January,

Trajan received his orders to proceed immediately and rapidly to Germania Superior with VII *Gemina Felix* to rendezvous with Domitian.

Meanwhile, the governor of Germania Inferior, Aulus Bucius Lappius and the procurator of Raetia, Norbanus, had advanced and defeated Saturninus in Germania Superior.[42] Incredibly, and perhaps aptly for the ill-fated Saturninus, on the very day that the Chattan contingent was due to cross over the frozen Rhine it is said to have thawed sufficiently to prevent them joining the mutinous legions.[43] Consequently, by 25 January the misconceived revolt was over.[44] Domitian's position held fast and his vigilant administration over the years had ensured that there was no widespread rebellion.

Nevertheless, Domitian and Trajan independently pressed on towards Mogontiacum. For this journey, Trajan demonstrated the marvellous mobility of a Roman legion. Within a few hours, the entire legion could be mobilised and on the march. Countless training exercises had perfected the art of mobilisation and the stamina to endure marches over vast distances, using the Roman roads famed for their quality of structure and sophisticated network. Following the main paved roads, unless shorter routes existed over reasonable terrain, Trajan first headed east. Probably only a skeleton detachment was left in the region to guard particularly vulnerable and important sites. Trajan then headed north over the Pyrenees before turning east to pick up the Via Domitia at Narbo Martius (Narbonne). Hurrying north up the Rhodanus (Rhône) Valley and past Lugdunum (Lyon), Trajan then turned north-east, skimming the foothills of the Alps, before arriving in the Rhine valley and heading due north towards Mogontiacum. Throughout the journey, Trajan drove the legion at a high marching pace and a reference from Pliny suggests Trajan was fit enough to lead by example:

> Throughout the entire journey, as you led, or rather, hurried along your legions* in your urgent haste, you never thought of horse or carriage. Your charger followed, unmounted, more for propriety's sake than to help you on your way.
>
> Pliny[45]

At a remarkable pace, Trajan and VII *Gemina Felix* arrived in the Mogontiacum area around the end of March 89, assuming a coverage of around thirty kilometres a day over the 1,900 kilometre journey[46] – an impressive feat, well noted by Domitian who had arrived in the region with

---

* Only VII *Gemina* is thought to have gone with Trajan to Mogontiacum.

his Praetorian Guard a few weeks earlier. By this time, Saturninus was already executed and trials were ongoing to determine which officers and ringleaders deserved similar fates. Methods of investigation were ruthless, as described by a Roman historian:

> [They] scorched the prisoners' genitals to make them divulge the whereabouts of other rebels still in hiding; and cut off the hands of many more.
>
> Suetonius[47]

Few rebel antagonists would have escaped prosecution. The treacherous legions, XIV *Gemina* and XXI *Rapax*, were eventually relocated to the Danube frontier in disgrace,[48] a harsh punishment that separated them from any of their loved ones settled around Mogontiacum.

As a reward for their loyalty, the four Germania Inferior legions were given the title *Pia Fidelis Domitiana*, 'faithful and loyal to Domitian'. Lappius and Norbanus were duly rewarded by Domitian with career advances. Trajan, because of his unquestionable loyalty to the emperor, was firmly integrated as one of Domitian's trusted *amici* or friends.[49] It has also been suggested that Domitian may have charged Trajan with responsibility to support Lappius who would lead a punitive war against the Chatti for siding with Saturninus.[50] Familiar with Chattan tactics from his youthful days as a military tribune, Trajan may have led VII *Gemina Felix* in the opening campaign of the war and it is not implausible that he excelled in his duties. Crossing over the Rhine into the Taunus mountain region and beyond, the Roman punitive action crushed the Chatti, who submitted to a peace treaty. This was an important event for Trajan if he was involved, to command a legion for the first time in a war involving other legions. It was a chance to observe the critical relationships and chain of command between *legatus legionis* commanders, their general and the emperor in the execution of a successful victory, although it is unlikely that Domitian took to the field in person.[51]

In the following year, Domitian manoeuvred to surround himself with yet more loyal supporters to secure his position against any possible ripple effects after Saturninus' revolt. During 90 he achieved this by appointing a large number of suffect consuls whom he trusted. Prudent administrative changes were also made in the Germanian provinces to prevent similar future rebellions. Firstly, legionary savings held locally were capped to prevent seizure of large sums to fund revolts. Secondly, forces at Mogontiacum were reduced to just one legion, rather than place the power of two legions together, which could be abused by a governor. Thirdly, the governors of Germania were now appointed as regular provincial governors, diminishing their military role. Lastly, the legions were redeployed so that each province only had three instead of four.[52] It was the end of an era for the Germanian legions, which had represented an enormous power-base for around eighty years and were now reduced in their potential to rebel against imperial authority. This was also made necessary because of the shift in risk from incursions to the Danube region.[53]

Domitian's First Pannonian War

Shortly after the quashing of Saturninus' revolt, dispatches reached Domitian in Mogontiacum reporting that the Suebic Quadi and Marcomanni were aggressively posturing against Rome. This situation was sufficient to trigger war, especially since Domitian still harboured resentment towards the Quadi and Marcomanni after their failure to support him in the recent war against the Dacians.[54]

The Suebi were Germanic peoples noted by the Roman historian Tacitus for twisting back their hair into a knot to create a forbidding image in battle.[55] The Marcomanni branch of the Suebi were widely settled at the time in Boihaemum (Bohemia, Czech Republic) around the upper Albis (Elbe) River region. The Marcomanni, meaning 'men of the borders',[56] were a tribe known for valour and strength.[57] The Quadi were settled further east, in and around the foothills of the Karpates (Carpathian) mountains, in the modern area of south-west Slovakia.[58] Warlike in nature and ruled by noble kings, the Suebic Quadi and Marcomanni clearly felt threatened by the Roman presence along the Danube but had tolerated treaties with Rome when necessary. Domitian and his advisers, now including the up and coming Trajan, crucially recognised that the threat from the Quadi and Marcomanni could lead to conflict on up to three fronts, two fronts potentially opening if the Quadi and Marcomanni launched independent offensives and a third from the Dacians. Even a fourth front was possible if the Iazyges, settled to the west of Dacia on the Pannonian plains, were drawn into a conflict. Of Sarmatian origin, this tribe is thought to have acted as a buffer state between Rome and Dacia in the early imperial period.

Repelling four simultaneous fronts in the Danubian region was unsustainable even for Rome and its mighty armies. Domitian had to act decisively to mitigate the risk of such an eventuality. However, on Domitian's arrival in Pannonia, the Quadi and Marcomanni were sufficiently intimidated to send peace envoys to try and appease the emperor and offer peace.[59] Sensing weakness in the Suebi and gambling that the Dacians were not an immediate threat due to their defeat at the Battle of Tapae the year before, Domitian decided to launch an offensive war, though it is thought that he did not take the field in person for the campaign.

The first Pannonian war was launched by Domitian in 89, using forces drawn from the Danubian legions. Advancing against the Marcomanni, Domitian's force was unsuccessful in suppressing the enemy. Domitian, perhaps overcautious about depleting too many resources along the critical areas of the Danube, may have failed to deploy sufficient strength. Abruptly, the risk of multiple fronts opening up seemed very real and Domitian was compelled to withdraw and secure a less than favourable agreement with King Decebalus, involving large payments and the provision of Roman engineers to keep the Dacians pacified. This negated the threat of having to deal with a Dacian offensive while the Quadi and Marcomanni were bolstered by their successful resistance. Domitian returned to Rome in October 89, leaving his commanders to consolidate the Danubian frontiers for a later second attempt at suppressing the Quadi and Marcomanni.[60]

Trajan may have still been in Germania Superior at this time, involved in the closure of engagements against the Chatti, which coincided with Trajan's last year as *legatus* of VII *Gemina*. Returning the legion to Legio in Hispania Tarraconensis in 90 if he had stayed on to fight the Chatti, Trajan would then have headed back to Rome in the same year. A proven reliable legion commander, Trajan may have been initiated into Domitian's *consilium*, the emperor's inner court of hand-picked advisers, where the promising commander likely provided fresh opinion and debate.[61]

Consulship

In Imperial Rome, the emperor was the supreme authority, whose absolute power (*imperium*) was legally appointed, but at odds with the constitution even at the end of the first century. The Senate, a body of around 600 of Rome's wealthiest landowners who had all either once been or were currently elected as magistrates, was responsible for central government. The body was led by two consuls, who were the formal heads of state, strictly speaking advised by the Senate. However, the power of the consuls had been eroded by a century of imperial authority. The Senate and consuls were largely symbolic in their political role and representative of a bygone Republican era; the Roman public assemblies that voted on magistracies had all but gone and the Senate had become the conduit for the execution of imperial autocracy. This role was further eroded with the gradual development of a professional imperial secretariat that directly served the emperor. Nevertheless, the Senate still formally bestowed powers on the emperor at his accession and conducted certain state business, and in the first century almost all the emperors' advisers, military commanders, governors and magistrates were still senators.[62]

Despite the downgraded office of Rome's two consuls, the positions still retained sufficient influence and prestige to represent a defining moment in any senator's career and a prerequisite for other subsequent offices. For these reasons, the appointment was a great distinction. It was customary by this time for many consuls to resign their office after a very short term to allow fellow senators to share in the position, the replacements being called suffect consuls. However, those select few who opened the consulship at the start of the year on 1 January, the *consules ordinarii*, had the esteem of linking their names to that year.

The Flavian dynasty was renowned for commandeering the ordinary consul positions, taking one of the two available offices on almost every occasion. Since 70, only three years had opened without one of the Flavian imperial family, Vespasian, Titus or Domitian, taking one of these posts. Consequently, it was an immense honour for Trajan to be singled out by Domitian for appointment as one of the *consules ordinarii* on 1 January 91.[63] Holding the other consular office was the equally privileged Marcus Acilius Glabrio.

How did Trajan achieve this appointment after completing his praetorship just five years previously? There are several plausible answers to this question. Firstly, Trajan had clearly demonstrated steadfast loyalty to the emperor by rapidly bringing his legion all the way from Iberia to Germania during Domitian's time of need. Subsequently, Trajan may have excelled as a legion commander in the punitive action against the Chatti, bringing military glory to Domitian as *imperator*. Such a reliable and competent military-minded senator was an asset to Domitian. Secondly, 'like father like son': Trajan's father had been a similar asset to Domitian's father, Vespasian. Domitian would have appreciated this loyal connection and seen that it further strengthened the relationship between them. Thirdly, Trajan may have been included in Domitian's *consilium* and impressed the emperor with his views and ideas. Finally, Domitian and Trajan were linked by marriage. Trajan's aunt had been married to Domitian's brother Titus. In summary, reliability, competency, connections, familiarity and trust were a potent mixture of attributes that propelled Trajan ahead of his peers into the prominent office of *consul ordinarius*.

After leaving his office as consul to make way for a *consul suffectus*, Trajan entered into the ex-consular stage of his career. In effect, an ex-consul was considered qualified to represent the emperor in the administration of an important province containing one or more legions. Accordingly, Trajan's expectation was to be directly appointed by the emperor to a three-year term as a *legatus Augusti pro praetore*, or governor of one of the imperial provinces. Until such a position became available in a province suitable for a junior consul, Trajan continued his attendance at the Senate house. On a typical day for a senator like Trajan, he rose at dawn, dressed and took light sustenance before receiving clients in his house. Shortly after, he travelled to the Senate house to attend meetings, debates, votes and other proceedings. Alternatively, a senator would attend important legal hearings. The middle of the afternoon marked the end of formal activities and Trajan may have visited the baths for exercise and cleansing. In the evening, Trajan ate the one substantial meal of the day, the *cena*, either at home with Plotina, family and other guests, or by visiting another prestigious house for the evening's feasting.[64] By now a seasoned drinker, Trajan drank wine sturdily during such meals before retiring at night to his bed, probably somewhat inebriated by his heavy consumption.

On occasion, the imperial palace might request Trajan's attendance if his opinion or role was considered applicable to any *consilium* gatherings, or perhaps even to dine with the emperor. In time, Trajan became 'one of Domitian's most influential courtiers', a position earned probably through consistent good advice and successful initiatives taken in his duties.[65] In this period, Domitian was instigating a diplomatic offensive to stabilise the situation beyond the Danubian frontier further following the unsuccessful First Pannonian War and the poor agreement established with the Dacians. His objective was to isolate the Quadi and Marcomanni by inciting hostility from neighbouring tribes,[66] and thereby reducing the possibility of having to deal with the Suebi at the same time as the Dacians – and potentially worse the Iazyges as well. These diplomatic activities and the consolidation of Roman forces in the region were critical topics addressed by the *consilium*, topics important to Trajan's continued learning and understanding of the increasingly complex and problematic Danubian frontier.

First Governorship

Two types of governor were appointed to the provinces. The first were *legati Augusti pro praetore*, or *legati*, appointed directly by the emperor who provided their mandate to govern. Depending on the priority of the province, the *legati* were either ex-praetors or ex-consuls and usually served a term of three years in an imperial province. The second were *proconsules*, also either ex-praetors or ex-consuls, appointed by the Senate and assigned by lot for a one-year posting in a public province. The exception to this format was the prefect of Egypt, also appointed by the emperor but specifically of the equestrian class, because the province was considered a personal possession of the emperor, and it was thought too important to risk the placement as governor of a senator who might have designs on seizing imperial power. Only imperial provinces were provided with legions with the exception of the public province of Africa and the equestrian province of Egypt. Both *legati* and *proconsules* governed their provinces independently, and both according to applicable laws and regulations issued either by the emperor or the Senate. Just because the appointment of the *legati* and *proconsules* was different did not mean that the *legati* only liaised with the emperor and the *proconsules* only with the Senate; rather it dictated the relative frequency of communications between them and the respective authority. The emperor could deal directly with both types of province and the Senate is known to have dealt with its provinces as well as communities within imperial provinces.[67]

It has been postulated that a suitable position as governor of a province became available in the year following Trajan's consulship. The position may have been in Germania Superior,[68] recently re-organised after Saturninus' rebellion. The three-year governorship of an imperial province with three legions was a moment to savour for the ambitious ex-consul. If Trajan was selected, the rationale for Domitian awarding him this appointment was the need to have a highly trusted man in place, especially as Saturninus' revolt was still fresh in the memory. The position would also groom Trajan in the art of provincial governance and open the path to even greater responsibilities in the future. Moreover, Trajan may well have been familiar with the region after his possible prior posting in the province as a young tribune, and feasibly involved in Domitian's wars against the Chatti.

Subsequently, at the start of 92, Trajan may have departed Rome for the capital of Germania Superior, Mogontiacum. The Roman legion fort at

Mogontiacum, from which the capital sprung, was founded in 13 BC by the Roman general Drusus to guard the strategically important region around the confluence of the Moenus (Main) River and the Rhenus (Rhine). By Trajan's time, the capital had developed substantially and sprawled out along the western and eastern banks of the Rhine, linked by a permanent bridge that was critically important to the area. Massive stone pillars supported the arched structure and the bridge deck was around twelve metres wide allowing two-way traffic. Flood plains beyond the riverbanks stretched out in all directions and, to the north, the Taunus Mountains framed the horizon. The legion fort was located just beyond the bridge on the eastern bank, surrounded by further settlement and close to a thermal spring. At this time, Legion XIV *Gemina*, recently disgraced by its support for Saturninus' revolt, was stationed in the fort, but soon after Trajan's putative arrival it was posted to Pannonia and replaced by Legion XXII *Primigenia*.

Mogontiacum was also close to the base of the Roman Rhine fleet, at Brühl, which consisted of patrol boats and transports for military provisions and personnel. A hive of activity around the harbour supported the fleet: new boat construction; maintenance and repair; and the constant loading and unloading of cargoes. Trajan's residence was probably located in the heart of Mogontiacum and well positioned in relation to the *basilica*, or town hall, which was the principal administrative building of the capital. The residence was a suitably luxurious arrangement of rooms following the typical plan of a large Roman town-house, probably complete with its own private baths and a large colonnaded private garden. As appropriate for a provincial capital, such residences, as well as important municipal buildings, roads and monuments, all created the necessary infrastructure for Roman administration and culture to flourish.[69]

Even though Domitian's re-organisations in Germania had reduced the potential for governors to revolt and diminished the military grandeur of the province, Germania Superior still had three legions present. Administration of this province containing multiple legions was therefore a major responsibility for Trajan if he was posted into this role. Besides XXII *Primigenia* newly seconded to Mogontiacum, VIII *Augusta* was located at Argentorate[70] (Strasbourg) to protect an essential crossing point on the Rhine.[71] VIII *Augusta* was only five days' march from Mogontiacum and able to strike out and protect the newly acquired Agri decumates region. Lastly, XI *Claudia* was based at Vindonissa[72] (Windisch, in northern Switzerland), poised to defend the upper Rhine and Danube regions and act as a deep reserve for

Germania Superior or the neighbouring province of Raetia. Although the legion commanders had their own mandates as appointees of the emperor, the governor was nevertheless responsible for all military forces (legions and auxiliaries) in the province with authority to use force where necessary in the maintenance of provincial security.

Of particular importance to frontier security and provincial prosperity in Germania Superior was the continued maintenance and improvement of the *limites*. By this time, the *limites* had developed further with progressive forest clearance along the trails and the construction of a series of wooden watchtowers. Invariably built on stone foundations, the wooden towers were primarily observation posts to deter minor incursions and monitor the potential for major ones. In the most strategically important frontier regions such as the Taunus Mountains, military roads supported the *limites* and a series of forward camps and forts provided immediate defence reserves. Entirely manned by auxiliary forces, the *limites* were continuously evolving and improving as the frontier matured and the legions remained as deeper reserves in the rear, not directly associated with the *limites*.[73]

Besides military and security aspects, a governor was the administrative head of the province. A high priority was ensuring financial efficiency and the continued flow of revenue to feed the coffers in Rome. In legal matters, the governor was the head of the judiciary and the presiding judge. For example, the governor of Judaea, Pontius Pilate, famously passed final judgement over Jesus Christ:

> He ordered Jesus flogged with a lead-tipped whip, then turned him over to the Roman soldiers to be crucified.[74]

Another critical component of the governor's diplomatic duties was hosting visits from dignitaries and emissaries to sustain dialogue with the leading native citizens of the region. To help in all these activities, a governor had at his disposal a retinue of staff, including but not limited to secretaries, scribes, law officers, guards, accountants, inspectors and various clerical officials.

If Trajan had been governor of Germania Superior, he would have returned to Rome in 94 at the end of the appointment. A successful governorship of Germania Superior would have raised his currency with Domitian even further and fully affirmed his new status as a senior ex-consul. His time in Germania Superior may not have involved major military exploits, but it would have provided the vital experience of governing a large and complicated imperial province. Security, diplomacy, provincial development and the upholding of Roman law were all part of the make-up of a successful Roman senator destined to be a general.

The Second Pannonian War

A feared eventuality now materialised in the Danube frontier region. No longer tolerant of Rome's diplomatic measures or activities, the Iazyges sided with the Germanic Suebi and were suspected of making preparations to cross the Danube and invade Roman territory.[75] In response, Domitian departed in May 92 for the Danube region to meet the threat of invasion.[76] He mustered a large army and, thanks to the treaty with the Dacians, the Roman force was allowed to cross their territory and outflank the Iazyges–Suebi alliance. Though fierce fighting resulted in the complete loss of the Legion XXI *Rapax*, the alliance was subdued. Domitian then returned to Rome early in 93 to claim an ovation for his efforts – a full triumph was untenable given the undefeated status of the two kingdoms and the terrible loss of a legion.[77]

Domitian had now entered the twelfth year of his reign. All factors considered, he could claim a number of solid achievements. Firstly, despite the difficult financial situation he likely inherited from his brother Titus' short reign, Domitian had successfully restored the finances of the empire and maintained a reasonably balanced budget that was only occasionally stretched.[78] This meant that he was able to sustain a massive restoration and construction campaign in Rome that was virtually unprecedented in Rome's history. He not only finished the uncompleted projects of Titus but began new and wondrous public works. In popularity, Domitian was favoured by his legionary soldiers because of their significant pay rise[79] and the additional rights he had secured them, as well as his recognisable presence as emperor in the provinces for many campaigns – although it is thought he did not actively take the field. His governor and general in Britain, Agricola, had campaigned in the far north of Scotland and his victory at the Battle of Mons Graupius was marked with the construction of a magnificent monumental arch at Richborough. Strategically, the frontier regions of Germania Superior had been improved with the beneficial annexation of the Wetterau and Agri decumates districts. Domitian had also stemmed trouble with the hostile Chatti, Suebi and Dacians through a series of military campaigns, settlements and diplomatic measures, all intentionally integrated. To all intents and purposes, Rome and its empire had prospered under his principate.[80]

Yet despite this positive state of affairs and Domitian's diligent imperial administration, there were signs that some of Rome's ruling class were becoming increasingly disgruntled and dissatisfied with him. Unlike some of his imperial predecessors, who had maintained a façade of power-sharing with the Senate, Domitian displayed and executed his power as emperor blatantly, as shown in his increasing alienation of patricians, his favouring of select senators and the transfer of some powers to his imperial administration.[81] Domitian may have had a low attendance record at the Senate, increasing the rift between the emperor and many senators.[82] Moreover, there were complaints about his 'inaccessibility and arrogance'. Domitian like to be saluted as *dominus et deus* – lord and god – an act that no doubt would have offended senators and alienated them further.[83]

Domitian had an autocratic style, striving to control all around him, and was consequently heavy-handed in his dealings with the Senate – a modern-day, hard-nosed 'micro-manager'. Domitian was also determined to improve morality in his subjects and he implemented related laws and policies.[84] His wine edict banned new vines being planted in Italy and ordered the destruction of certain vineyards in the provinces. On face value, this appeared to seek a reduction in wine imports and boost other produce during a grain shortage. However, it is thought that it was rather an attempt to curtail levels of consumption as it would have increased the cost of wine. Seemingly innocuous practices, such as pantomime, were banned and Domitian dismissed a senator from the Senate because of his pantomime acting.[85] In particular, sexual mortality was a concern of Domitian's. Laws against adultery and homosexual intercourse with a free-born male were enforced. He also upheld the strict punishment of priestesses of the goddess of the hearth, Vesta – so called Vestal Virgins – if their vows of chastity were broken. Initially, guilty Vestal Virgins could decide the manner of their deaths and their lovers were banished. Later, priestesses were buried alive in the traditional way and the lovers beaten to death with rods.[86]

Domitian was in essence a puritanical disciplinarian. His intellect would have fuelled additional fear and those who did not prosper under Domitian's open autocracy gradually edged towards dissent. As a result, Domitian had to contend with a growing number of challenges or conspiracies from senators,[87] which the emperor did not tolerate. Domitian exiled or executed a number of senators accused of treason who were unable to prove their innocence.[88] To increase the gravity of the punishment he also confiscated their estates as a warning to anyone else. Certain senators were horrified, while the less naïve recalled that most of the Julio-Claudian emperors had been more tyrannical in the frequency and manner of senatorial executions. But alarmed senators, mumbling in the back rows of the Senate house or scheming over clandestine dinners, were still a powerful and influential force to be reckoned with.

Trajan, likely privy to *consilium* meetings while in Rome in this period, would have been aware of the change in mood associated with Domitian's reign and the resultant signs of opposition. This was a highly important lesson for Trajan, who was able to observe the fundamental errors in Domitian's treatment of the Senate. Where there were irreconcilable policy differences that Domitian, like his predecessors, might seek to override, a degree of tact and a willingness to at least pay lip-service to senatorial sensibilities would certainly have helped. Instead of naked imperial control, a veneer of power-sharing could have been established and maintained, as exemplified in the reign of Augustus.

It is likely that Domitian still commanded Trajan's respect, especially on military matters, given the emperor's dedicated presence on the frontiers during major campaigns. In fact, contemporary Roman historians may have failed to value Domitian's efforts appropriately and, while he lacked the supposedly glorious achievements of Julius Caesar in Gaul or Vespasian in the Jewish wars, he actually coped relatively well with the highly challenging security threats along the Rhine and the Danube.

The Third Pannonian War

Assuming Trajan had governed Germania Superior, he was in a position to expect an even more senior consular governorship in one of the most significant imperial provinces. Trajan had acquired all the necessary skill and experience required to govern a heavily militarised zone and may have established a reputation for military proficiency during his early years as a tribune and later as a legion commander in Domitian's war against the Chatti. Crucially, Trajan had also demonstrated the utmost allegiance to Domitian during the Saturninus revolt, resulting in his prestigious appointment as a *consul ordinarius*. The subsequent trust that developed had spawned an acquaintance that drew Trajan into the inner circle of Domitian's *consilium*, establishing Trajan as one of his most important court advisers.

With these attributes in mind, it is reasonable to propose that Domitian may have appointed Trajan *legatus Augusti pro praetore* (governor) of Pannonia, although no evidence exists at present to support or reject this possibility.[89] In this period, Pannonia was probably the most important imperial province, not because of wealth or prosperity, but due to the proximity of the hostile and active Suebic Quadi and Marcomanni kingdoms and the equally problematic Iazyges who had so recently formed a formidable alliance with the Suebi. Consequently, the precarious status of Pannonia demanded a large deployment of legions and auxiliary forces strategically poised to provide protection for the Danube frontier and the provinces to the south. This outstanding appointment for Trajan thrust him to the top of his game. Not only would this mean a scale-up in his administrative duties as governor, but it was also a massive increase in his military responsibilities. Around 94, Pannonia was home to five legions;[90] a staggering total of 28,500 soldiers at full strength with an equivalent number of auxiliary troops. This was approaching 20 per cent of Rome's total military force. Such a concentration of power in one province was a force that Domitian would only assign to someone he held in the highest esteem and could trust completely. Additionally, Domitian shrewdly recognised that Trajan was appropriately experienced for the position: not too much so that he posed a clear threat of rallying a coup using the huge force available, nor with too little skill that he might fail in the complex duties that would be required. In short, the utmost trust had to exist and Trajan was perceived as posing little or no danger to the emperor.

At the start of 95, Trajan left Rome to travel overland through Italy and then across into Pannonia. On entry into his province, he assumed his *insignia*, the badge of office, and donned his military attire.[91] To the north and east the province was demarcated by the mighty Danube River; to the south lay the province of Dalmatia and in the west the province of Noricum and north-east Italy. Broadly speaking, Pannonia covered parts of modern-day eastern Austria and western Hungary and straddled several surrounding Balkan states. Essentially, it was a back door into Italy and a potential invasion axis, accentuated by few geographical obstacles once any hostile force crossed the Danube. To mitigate this weakness, a series of forts and *limites* lined the banks of the Danube at key locations in Pannonia.

Working from west to east along the Danube, XIII *Gemina* was based at the fortress town of Vindobona (Vienna) on the western bank. A short distance downstream, XV *Apollinaris* was based at Carnuntum (Bad Deutsch-Altenburg), the capital of the province, situated at an important strategic position near the Danube and the location of the governor's sumptuous palace. Next was XIV *Gemina* entrenched at Mursella (Petrijevci) and lastly I *Adiutrix* and II *Adiutrix* at Sirmium (Sremska Mitrovica) near the border with the province of Moesia. Interlaced and supporting the *limites*, large numbers of auxiliaries were also stationed throughout the province.

Trajan had a mandate as governor from Domitian. He was to ensure the overall security of the province against attack from another possible Iazyges–Suebi alliance and to prepare the province to support a Third Pannonian War in 95. Trajan would then very likely assume the role of a general of any expeditionary force derived from troops available in Pannonia. Any first strike against the Iazyges would plausibly have aimed at devastating their offensive potential and ability to provide meaningful support to an alliance with the Suebi. Next, one can suggest that the front would switch to engage the Suebic Quadi and Marcomanni, again to reduce their potential threat to Rome's interests.[92] Meanwhile, the two Moesian provinces would stay on alert just in case the Dacians abandoned the peace settlement and seized the opportunity to strike while Rome was preoccupied by the Iazyges and Suebi.

Consequently, in the early months of 95, Trajan needed to familiarise himself rapidly with the security of the province, which meant trips between legion bases and vigilant inspection of the *limites* to instruct improvements or additional construction. Once satisfied with his understanding of the province's offensive and defensive capabilities, he was able to muster an appropriately sized force in the south-eastern region of Pannonia, derived from various legion and auxiliary detachments. Applying all his experience, Trajan would have held councils of war with the legion commanders and senior officers to map out the first thrusts against the Iazyges.

Having gradually migrated from the southern Eurasian steppe, the Sarmatians were a diverse collation of nomadic peoples speaking forms of an Iranian language. Major branches included the Iazyges and the Roxolani who were Caucasian in ethnicity. By the end of the first century, the Iazyges had settled on the Banat (Hungarian plains) and the Roxolani north of the lower Danube River. The Iazyges, the initial target of the Third Pannonian War, were capable of fielding thousands of armed men composed of cavalry and foot soldiers provided by different tribal assemblies. Particularly formidable, the horse-mounted archers and lancers with intricate scale armour were deployed in discrete groups for forward or flanking manoeuvres.[93]

Crossing the Danube with his army to attack the Iazyges, Trajan almost certainly divided his force into closely associated columns under the individual control of the *legati*. Probably advancing close along the Pathissus (Tisza) River to protect one flank, the Roman force headed north, avoiding the marshy lands of the Banat where possible.[94] Trajan then successfully engaged the Iazyges during the campaign season of 95. Only under optimal conditions would he have issued the order for battle and he correctly judged the required tactics to overcome and rout the enemy. Critical to his success, Trajan's generalship needed to inspire courage, obedience and determination in his officers and soldiers and instil confidence that his tactics would prevail over the Iazyges.

With the Iazyges weakened by the end of the campaign season in 95, Trajan returned early in the following year to complete his victory. Domitian's faith in Trajan was confirmed. The general was no longer a novice. He had successfully commanded a large Roman field army against formidable opponents in hostile territory. At least in the short term, the Iazyges were sufficiently suppressed to pose little threat to Rome's authority in the region. As a result, late in 96, Trajan was able to change fronts as planned to start a new campaign against the Suebi, moving his army across to the new theatre of operations beyond the Danube north of Pannonia.[95]

At this juncture of the Third Pannonian War, how did the *legati* and officers view him prior to the campaign against the Suebi? Trajan was now approaching his forties but was physically fit and outwardly healthy in constitution. He was supposedly not unaccustomed to marching with his men or even eating the basic 'camp-fare' outdoors in their company.[96] A close association with the lower ranks combined with an acute military mind would have secured respect from his men and the admiration of his officers. Proud in his demeanour and of his achievements, he is thought to have nonetheless remained approachable and modest in his manner.[97] As well as in their accomplishments against the Chatti, his men had witnessed his capable leadership and military distinction against the Iazyges. In discussing news from Rome, no one would have dared criticise Domitian in front of his general, as they knew he maintained close links with the emperor and remained loyal. In short, they likely respected Trajan, who presented a figure of authority with intuitive military leadership and generalship skills. In just over twenty years, Trajan had progressed from a young tribune officer to a respected general of Rome. An impressive career indeed.

CHAPTER 5

ADOPTION AND ACCESSION

Fear and Conspiracy

Autocratic behaviour is not tolerated for long in a modern democracy, if at all. Conversely, in ancient Rome, the autocracy of an emperor was very much part of his imperial power. However, concealing any despotism and pretending to share authority with the Senate was an essential art in maintaining, at least minimally, the indifference of senators towards the Principate. Domitian failed in this art. Initially more endearing with his subjects and self-restrained,[1] by the mid-nineties the emperor was increasingly determined to enforce his puritanical views. These may not have been unusual for the time but his approach was too heavy-handed with the Senate.

In addition to Domitian's stance on sexual morality, he upheld religious virtue. As we have seen, he enforced the strict punishment of the Vestal Virgins if they broke their vows of chastity. Throughout his reign he had shown pious respect to Roman divinities and was devoted to Jupiter and the goddess Minerva. Prominence was not a defence. In 95, Marcus Acilius Glabrio, who was fellow consul with Trajan in 91, was charged with atheism and executed.[2] Doubtless more shocking to his peers in the Senate, the presiding consul, Titus Flavius Clemens, the emperor's cousin, was executed for the same crime in the same year. Clemens' wife, Flavia Domitilla, who was Domitian's niece, was banished. It is not clear what happened to their two sons, who had been Domitian's chosen heirs, but they were likely slain.[3] It is thought that these charges of atheism may have referred to their Christian faith.[4] Clemens and Glabrio had supposedly abandoned Rome's pantheon of gods, although other causes for their execution such as conspiracy against Domitian cannot be ruled out.

While there was no widespread assault from Domitian on other senators, the execution of these prominent men lost him further support from particular factions in the Senate. Moreover, it triggered anxiety and fear in those close to Domitian whose questionable behaviour might similarly jeopardise their lives or livelihoods. For this reason, even though Domitian retained a number of loyal supporters who respected his authority and successful reign, with others being at worst apathetic about his principate, he had made the fatal error of providing the right environment to nurture conspiracy among those who felt most threatened or discontented.

For conspirators determined to dispose of an emperor, the only option was assassination. Abdication had never happened and no legal method existed to remove an emperor. But the assassination of a Roman emperor was a task requiring the utmost courage, secrecy and ingenuity on the part of the perpetrators. It was a highly hazardous act only undertaken in extreme circumstances. An emperor was omnipotent and surrounded by rings of protection. The crack Praetorian Guard, drawn from the elite of Rome's legionary soldiers, provided round-the-clock armed protection in and outside the imperial palace and escorts for any excursions. A host of slaves operated constantly in the vicinity of the emperor to attend to his needs, as well as the aides who constituted the imperial administration. There were also family, friends and courtiers frequently close to the emperor. In addition, at any one time, Domitian could be in a number of locations: in his palace on the Palatine Hill or one of the many imperial villas in and outside Rome. Logistically, assassination had a very high chance of failure and of course failure would result in certain death for all conspirators if the plot was detected.

Yet, despite these perils, a small group of senators sharing a deep and common hatred of Domitian were drawn together in contemplation of assassination. After initial clandestine gatherings, the group was probably triggered into final action in 96 by a heightened sense of foreboding for their own positions or the disintegration of their values. The deaths of Glabrio and Clemens could have been the final straw. Having explored many options, they at last found a gap in Domitian's rings of protection. His senior chamberlain, a freedman called Parthenius,[5] had been driven to the edge of despair when Domitian executed one of the imperial secretaries, causing panic in Parthenius who feared similar retribution for a reprimandable act he had concealed. Probably by chance, Parthenius linked up with a member of the clandestine senatorial group and since this member was publicly known for his recalcitrant political views about the imperial administration, Parthenius divulged his discontent and a willingness to act. The senatorial conspirators now had a weapon able to strike within the tight security of the imperial palace. Time was of the essence, and Parthenius used his position to recruit similarly minded palace employees who feared Domitian enough to want him killed.[6]

The conspiring senators were also primed to act. An alleged plotter, Titus Catius Caesius Fronto, was set to become one of the consuls on 1 September 96 and thereby afforded the conspirators a degree of legitimacy and authority. They also perceived that the mood in the Senate was ripe for accepting change. But the assassination and coup required more than a disgruntled Senate house. Consequently, the conspirators may have very carefully approached a limited number of provincial governors and legion commanders who could be relied on either to support their deeds or at least remain indifferent.[7] With the same caution, they conversed with one of the two Praetorian Guard prefects, Titus Petronius Secundus, who agreed to control the Guard in the likely event that they reacted angrily to the loss of an emperor they favoured. Secundus would also ensure that the other prefect, Norbanus, was removed. Norbanus had loyally supported Domitian during the Saturninus revolt and his reaction to an assassination could fatally derail the subsequent transition of power.[8] Finally, considering how the legions and their commanders had reacted to events during the civil war that followed the death of Nero, the conspirators had one component to their advantage: the Third Pannonian War was still ongoing, tying up the enormous pool of legionaries in Pannonia and Moesia.[9] Therefore, despite Trajan's apparent loyalty to Domitian, the conspirators could risk his negative reaction to the assassination. It was presumably far too dangerous to lobby Trajan, so the conspirators probably had to assume that he was a level-headed patriot who knew that withdrawing legions from the war to avenge Domitian's death could destabilise the entire Danubian frontier. The transition of power to a new emperor could then proceed and hopefully Trajan would acclimatise to the change during his continuation of the war, whilst extensive lobbying could secure his acquiescence.

All that the conspirators needed now was a suitable replacement for Domitian, someone respectable, prominent and with a good family pedigree. In particular, they needed someone who could both fill the power vacuum left by Domitian and conciliate the senators in Rome and around the empire. Suitable candidates had to be approached with the utmost care and caution. Many would have rejected the offer, cognisant of the risks involved in the transition of imperial power and equally fearful that the proposition was in fact a test of loyalty concocted by Domitian.[10] Despite early setbacks, the group successfully persuaded Marcus Cocceius Nerva to accept, although it is unknown at what point he was approached. The later Roman historian Dio Cassius records exactly why Nerva was chosen:

> For [Nerva] was at once of the noblest birth and of a most amiable nature, and he had furthermore been in peril of his life as the result of being denounced by astrologers who declared that he should be sovereign. It was this last circumstance that made it easier for [the conspirators] to persuade him to accept the imperial power.[11]

Roman fear of astrological predictions should not be underestimated. As a result, this fear, mixed with a sense of opportunity, tipped the balance for Nerva to accept. After all, he was a political 'guru' who had survived the reigns of several emperors and he had every reason to believe that his intentions for the Principate would be palatable to the Senate. However, although Nerva was an experienced and astute senator, he had progressed through his *cursus* with extremely limited exposure to the armies or the provinces. The conspirators would have recognised this, but also appreciated that Nerva was in his sixties and in poor health. Thus, he was perfect in the sense that he was a temporary fix for the problem and, by the same token, controllable.[12]

Everything was then in place and the assassination plot was ready early in September 96. All the planned lobbying by the senatorial conspirators was completed. Fronto was in office as one of the two consuls and Parthenius was ready to strike. Thus, the conspirators gave the green light for the assassination to go ahead on 18 September.

Domitian's Assassination

On that fateful morning, Domitian completed his judicial duties in the spectacular *basilica* of his palace on the Palatine Hill. He then adjourned as usual to take his afternoon rest and bathe. Followed by a flurry of attendants he left the hall and likely passed into the vast public peristyle with its elegant sunken pool and fountain, surrounded by a refined colonnaded portico creating shade from the warm September noonday sun.[13] Paranoid about attacks while strolling around the peristyle, Domitian had commissioned the veneering of the walls with highly polished slabs of marble to reflect the image of any would-be attackers from the rear. But the assassination plans were far more subtle. Checking the immediate situation for last-minute risks, Parthenius judged that the moment was right to divert Domitian from his routine. Bidding the emperor's attention, Parthenius informed him that a freedman, Stephanus, was waiting in his private quarters with urgent details of a pending plot against him.[14]

Stephanus was an ex-slave of Flavius Clemens' banished widow, Flavia Domitilla, and he was also accused of misappropriation, both motives for his involvement in the plot. Domitian was apparently unconcerned with the former and the latter was unknown to him. Besides, Domitian was accustomed to Parthenius bringing such requests for audiences and Stephanus was known to him around the palace. The diversion was set and the first hurdle cleared with no suspicion raised. Eager to known the details of any plot, Domitian dismissed his attendants and hurried through the palace towards his private quarters.

With Parthenius accompanying Domitian en route to his quarters, they left the peristyle and entered the Domus Augustana, the private section of the palace, and they likely headed through the south colonnade of another large and lavish peristyle around a central pool. At the southern side of the peristyle they would have turned into the very heart of the palace where Domitian's private quarters were located. To bring Domitian here was an astute move by the assassins, as the private quarters were clearly separated from the public areas. Here the need for the emperor's privacy reduced security measures. It was the perfect place to lure Domitian.

Entering into his private quarters, Domitian was greeted by Stephanus. Also present was a palace page boy, attending to the shrine of the household gods. Parthenius held back outside to keep watch and direct any help required from the other assassins, who were strategically positioned in the vicinity should matters turn against Stephanus. These were two freedmen, a turncoat Praetorian Guard and an imperial gladiator. Stephanus had cunningly faked an arm injury for several days preceding this moment and the bandage on his arm did not trigger Domitian's suspicions. Another hurdle was passed, for beneath the bandage Stephanus concealed a dagger. Passing a document to Domitian with the supposed details of a plot, he distracted the emperor for a moment, during which time he got the dagger out and launched his assault. The aim was low and the dagger struck into Domitian's groin. Though chosen for his strength, Stephanus struggled with Domitian who was 'tall and well-made'.[15] Perhaps evenly matched, the two fought fiercely, Domitian tearing at his attacker's eyes and shredding his fingers in attempts to grab the blade.[16]

In the mortal struggle, Domitian had sufficient presence of mind to yell at the page boy to fetch his own dagger hidden under his pillow, but the assassins were one step ahead and had thought to arrange its removal that morning. They were equally thorough in ensuring that the other doors to the quarters had been locked to keep back the slaves and attendants now trying to reach the emperor on hearing the commotion. Realising that Stephanus required help, Parthenius decided to call in his back-up. The additional assailants dashed to the room and together they overwhelmed Domitian who was soon killed. While the dying emperor still bled profusely from several mortal wounds, the back-up attackers fled the scene. Parthenius coldly detained Stephanus and, after breaking through at last, Domitian's attendants set upon Stephanus who by now was exhausted and easily killed. In the confusion, Parthenius was able to claim his innocence by pretending to support the servants as they seized and slew Stephanus.

Fully assured that Domitian and Stephanus were dead, Parthenius withdrew from the private quarters, now in turmoil as guards and senior palace officials flooded the area. A prearranged rendezvous with one or more of the senatorial conspirators was then required to provide absolute confirmation that the plot had been successful. All conspirators were then promptly informed and Fronto used his authority as consul to issue a proclamation[17] for an urgent convening of the Senate the next morning, by which time he could ensure a substantial attendance from senators not immediately present in Rome. At this summons, all the conspirators would know their roles for the proposal of the nomination of Nerva to replace Domitian.

In the intervening time, Domitian's body was being viewed by officials, friends and relatives who wanted to see for themselves that the Emperor of Rome was dead. Domitian had died aged forty-four, coincidentally on Trajan's fortieth birthday, having ruled Rome and its empire for fifteen years.[18] Since he had no natural or adopted heir, the Flavian dynasty started by Vespasian in 69 and supported at its very conception by Trajan's father was now over.

Nerva's Accession

The next day at dawn, the atmosphere in the Curia or Senate house, was surely exceedingly charged.[19] Confusion reigned and few senators yet knew anything of the circumstances surrounding Domitian's death but were undoubtedly eager to understand the sequence of events and their implications; a mood of apprehension would have dominated the scene. It had been fifteen years since the Senate convened for the death of Titus and the accession of Domitian and twenty-seven since the assassination of an emperor, meaning that many senators had no experience of such circumstances.

With both consuls likely in place on the raised tribunal and other senators eventually settled in their seats, Fronto, who had issued the summons, took responsibility for opening and chairing proceedings. He officially announced that Domitian was dead and recounted the details of the assassination construed to the conspirators' advantage, putting heavy emphasis on the role of low-ranking palace insiders. No doubt a hefty measure of political 'spin' accompanied the depiction of the event. The senators were probably reminded of Domitian's despotic ways and how Rome and its empire were at least now relieved of the tyrant; all this was intended to draw immediate attention from the real force behind the assassination and distance the senatorial conspirators from any hint of involvement.[20] Of course, the more perceptive of the uninvolved would certainly have had their suspicions about a wider plot. There would have been a mixed reaction overall: those loyal to Domitian trying to conceal their anger or deep regret; those who harboured hatred of Domitian muting somewhat their sense of satisfaction and relief. The latter group may have overpowered or swayed those who were indifferent to the loss of Domitian.[21]

Fielding invitations to speak and trying to maintain order amidst the excitement, Fronto proposed a series of senatorial decrees. Firstly, an imperial successor was required. In the absence of any heir or designated replacement, Fronto proposed the nomination of Nerva as planned. A lengthy oratorical delivery described the virtues of Nerva and the nominee's respect for the Senate. The latter quality was critically important to emphasise given the recent disharmony between the Senate and Domitian. Senior senators responded to the proposal and Nerva probably pitched a coy initial refusal and feigned modesty. Yet the decree was passed and Nerva was acclaimed the new Emperor of Rome. Likely in the wings of the Senate house, the presence of the Praetorian Guard prefect, Secundus, offering no opposition to the nomination, supported Nerva's acceptance. Norbanus, the other prefect, was successfully removed from proceedings and was perhaps already dead at the bottom of the Tiber.[22]

The second series of decrees voted Nerva the titles and authorities normally bestowed on an emperor. They were the following:

> *Imperium:* Absolute power over the state, including the judiciary and the armies.
> *Tribunicia potestas:* All the powers of a tribune of the people, legally able to veto legislation as a representative of the people.

> *Pontifex Maximus:* Literally meaning 'Great bridge maker', the title
> appointed the emperor as chief priest and head of all Roman state
> religion.

Escalating calls from some senators for Domitian's vilification resulted in the passing of a final series of decrees to wipe Domitian from all records. Such damnation involved the removal of all his statues and his name from all inscriptions.[23] Little did the Senate know that this was a step too far, as it would later become apparent that not everyone across the empire was as enthused to take such action against one whose reign had provided reasonable prosperity in many quarters.[24]

The new emperor then stepped up to the tribunal to give his speech of thanks to the senators for their acclamations. Nerva also gave an oath that he would not authorise the death of any senator.[25] A close friend of Nerva, Cnaeus Arrius Antoninus, rose to embrace him and offer congratulations. In addition, because of his familiarity with the new emperor, Antoninus was able to speak out and warn him of the burden he was going to take up and of the hostility he was bound to incur from friend and foe whatever he did.[26] Such a warning would not have been lost on Nerva.

With the feverish session over, the bronze double doors of the Curia were flung open and the senators poured down the steps into a packed forum. A security cordon was doubtless arranged for the new emperor as he left the Curia and the immediate announcements spread out through Rome detailing the death of Domitian and the senatorial decrees for Nerva's accession. The people of Rome seem to have reacted with apathy to the news and Nerva was by and large accepted as they felt no loss or threat to their prosperity.[27] The Praetorian Guards, however, were angered and agitated as predicted. How dare some lowly palace employees murder their favoured emperor under their watch? But Secundus exerted his authority as their prefect and the promise of a large financial payment to each man from Nerva helped to pacify them – at least for the moment.

Leaving the excited atmosphere of the forum, Nerva's immediate task was almost certainly to issue urgent communications. With a group of makeshift advisers, including Fronto, Nerva would have devised and sent messages to all governors and senior military commanders across the empire.

Meanwhile, Domitian's old nurse, Phyllis, cremated his body in her own garden outside Rome on the Via Latina. She then bore the ashes secretly to the Temple of the Flavians, erected in honour of the deified Vespasian and

Titus, and mixed Domitian's ashes in with those of his niece Julia.[28] There was some dignity at least for one of Rome's great emperors who received an unjust damnation by the Senate.

By October, the news was starting to reach the provinces and armies dotted across the empire. The forces were 'deeply grieved' to learn of Domitian's assassination.[29] He had not been afraid to be present in the frontier regions as *imperator* during various wars, earning respect from his legions. Domitian had also significantly improved the salary and rights of legionaries. Soldiers even called for Domitian's deification.[30] Crucially, these grievances failed to materialise into action because Nerva's conspirators had lobbied sufficiently to prevent commanders from backing any dissent. At least to begin with, they accepted the transition of power to Nerva, temporarily quelling the army's dissatisfaction. Moreover, the general who commanded the largest assembled force, Trajan, held a key position if it came to any major instability. Many would choose to wait and observe his immediate actions.

Trajan's Reaction and Continuation of the Third Pannonian War

So it was in October that the imperial message arrived in Trajan's hands. At this time the campaign season for 96 had closed and his forces were withdrawing in good order from the Quadi–Marcomanni territories. With these Suebic tribes significantly weakened and access routes into enemy terrain cleared, Trajan was aware that a final campaign in the following year could well provide a substantial victory and conclusion to the Third Pannonian War. The message from Nerva would have tactfully and sensitively described events in Rome and explicitly reassured Trajan of his value to the new principate, as well as emphasising the importance of his continuation of the war in Rome's interests.

Despite these reassurances, Trajan was without doubt shocked by the news from Rome and humiliated by the disposal of an emperor he had loyally served and openly supported. Moreover, his father's and his own successes had been linked to the Flavian dynasty. His pride would have been bruised and he surely contemplated his options. He was presumably well aware that his ability to act was limited by the need to sustain regional stability. Despite the tens of thousands of legionary soldiers and auxiliaries all around him, and all at his command, the conspirators had correctly predicted that Trajan would not act rashly and jeopardise Rome's gains in the war for the sake of vengeful action. Trajan also knew that any retaliation would instigate civil war. From his childhood he recognised the destitution caused by the great civil wars of 69 that resulted in the loss of countless Roman lives and the shocking deaths of three emperors in a single year.

Thinking smartly, Trajan would have comprehended that a competent elder statesman had now been acclaimed emperor. And an elderly emperor needed an heir. Trajan was not unaware of his potential, and at the very least, he could influence the selection of Nerva's successor. He might even expect to be a viable candidate himself and by this time he likely had a sense of self-destiny.

Informing his chain of command of the events in Rome, Trajan had his forces declare their allegiance to Nerva. He expected his subordinates to keep their attention on the war at hand. It was imperative to ensure victory that would establish greater stability for the Danubian provinces and the glory of Rome. It would also ultimately exalt Trajan's own position of power.

It is testimony to Trajan's leadership that he was able to secure the compliance of his legions and the continuation of the Pannonian war. This meant mustering forces in the spring of 97 for another offensive against the Suebi, who would receive little support from the Iazyges defeated at the start of the war in 95. In addition, the XIV, I and II legions were respectively moved to Ad Flexum, Brigetio and Aquincum in Pannonia the better to support the river frontier of Pannonia and the forthcoming campaign. While Trajan worked diligently to ready his province and troops, letters and dispatches would have poured in from Rome. Of the utmost importance were letters from Nerva and his new imperial administration on the management of the war. Plotina and Marciana would have also written to him, likely describing the dawning of a new era in Rome under Nerva.

Nerva's Principate

The new emperor quickly installed himself in the Domus Tiberiana, an imperial palace on the Palatine Hill with spectacular views of Rome in all directions.[31] To exemplify his generosity, Nerva ordered that Domitian's decadent vacant palace, also on the Palatine Hill, be opened for public use. While the new emperor attended to the immediate affairs of state, news arrived that the western and eastern armies had sworn allegiance, thus providing immediate stability for his position.

Nevertheless, two factors meant to appease the Senate were instead causing unrest among its members. Firstly, Nerva wanted to promote an ethos of senatorial liberty and thereby distance himself from the disciplinarian rule of Domitian. Secondly, he pardoned those condemned for treason or exiled by the previous regime and 'no persons were permitted to accuse anybody' of treason based on a charge of defamation.[32] To strengthen this initiative, he swiftly executed certain prominent non-senatorial informers presumed to have been involved in such treason accusations.[33] However, Nerva's efforts to promote liberty and allow the return of punished senators instead created a wave of dissatisfaction. Many senators squabbled and accused each other of being party to Domitian's tyranny. Dio Cassius later claimed that, in at least one respect, this period of Nerva's reign was worse than Domitian's:

> It was bad to have an emperor under whom nobody was permitted to do anything, but worse to have one under whom everybody was permitted to do everything.[34]

The senatorial infighting escalated to the point where Fronto, still consul, openly questioned Nerva's ability to contain the uproar. This forced the emperor to issue a decree demanding a cessation of all the finger-pointing and unruly behaviour.

During this jittery start in Rome, Nerva amended the list of upcoming consuls to reward those loyal to his cause while retaining some of those already listed to minimise any affront. In addition, he lined up supporters to fill soon-to-be-available governorships and command posts across the empire. Closer to home, he also needed a new prefect for the Praetorian Guard. Even though he owed much to the incumbent, Secundus, he could not retain a prefect who had previously failed to protect his emperor. As a replacement, Casperius Aelianus was appointed as sole commander of the Guard. Aelianus was almost certainly not Nerva's ideal choice; as we shall see shortly, he would soon betray the new emperor he had sworn to protect. Gathering his new *consilium* around him, Nerva began to work on his imperial policies, recognising the need to continue many of Domitian's plans. His predecessor may have been vilified, but the majority of his policies were sound. For example, the Pannonian War that Trajan was commanding aimed to reassert Rome's authority beyond the Danube and thereby stabilise the whole region.

While Nerva continued to review all the policies with his advisers, there was one initial act that Nerva was obliged to execute without delay. Just like in our modern society, money talked in the Roman world and the new emperor needed to reward the people, the Praetorian Guard and the armies financially in acknowledgment of his accession. The reward was an essential gesture of imperial benevolence and Nerva was well aware that failure to issue the rewards could easily jeopardise the still fragile stability of his principate. The gift to the people was called a *congiarium* and that to the armies a *donativum*. The drain on the imperial coffers was huge, with every recognised citizen in Rome who was a recipient of the corn dole receiving around 300 *sestertii* and every legionary soldier probably receiving a higher sum. Nerva needed to be extra generous with the legionary soldiers to solicit their acceptance as he lacked military experience himself and the troops had been aggrieved by Domitian's assassination. This meant a much higher than normal payment to the troops. To put the *donativum* into context, a legionary soldier earned 1,200 *sestertii* per year, so it equated to a substantial bonus plausibly exceeding a quarter of a man's annual pay. Conceivably, Nerva also paid at least 1,000 *sestertii* to each Praetorian Guard, who typically received far more in wages than a legionary; the sum would help to appease their open dissatisfaction due to Domitian's assassination.[35] In short, Nerva's total bill for the *congiarium* and the *donativum* was over 105 million *sestertii*.[36]

Despite the eye-watering cost of these payments, the associated large scale distribution of coinage was a prefect publicity tool for Nerva. The imperial mints set to work issuing coins with all the appropriate messages to support his accession and to express how lucky the empire was to have such a worthy emperor – Roman advertising at its best. As the new coins were churned out, Nerva continued to spend heavily to ensure his smooth accession. Though the extravagance was not untypical for a new emperor,[37] the imperial coffers drained rapidly despite the inheritance of a reasonably healthy balance sheet from Domitian and in all probability normal reserves of bullion.[38]

An example of Nerva's additional spending was a new programme to issue land allotments to the poorest Romans, at a total cost equivalent to some sixty million *sestertii*.[39] This generous gesture to his lowly citizens equated to around 5 per cent of the annual imperial revenue. Nerva also approved a remarkable initiative in Italy to support disadvantaged families. The system was called the *alimenta,* and was essentially the first ever form of public child welfare. Its aim was to stimulate an increase in the Italian population, with the ulterior motive of helping local landowners in need of financial support. The *alimenta* worked by enrolling local landowners interested in participating. Once registered, some of their land would be mortgaged to the state. The landlord received the cash sum for the mortgaged land with favourable interest rates and the revenues generated from the interest were returned to the community by subsidising impoverished families with children – a Roman 'win–win' situation. In addition, various policies issued privileges to cities as well as alleviating charges and taxes in Rome and across the empire.[40]

The combined effect of Nerva's expenditure and a reduced flow of income into the treasury was the exhaustion of state revenue and a drain on reserve funds less than a year after his accession.[41]

The financial challenge was not yet a crisis. Nerva scrambled to implement initiatives that would remedy the situation.[42] As news leaked to the Senate about the economic deficiencies in the *aerarium* (the public treasury), Nerva had to accept the appointment of a senatorial economy commission, whose prime function was little more than to lend an appearance that the Senate was dealing with the situation on behalf of the emperor. It was also a political gesture to the Senate given that it aimed to improve funds in the *aerarium* and thereby give more power to the assembly.[43] Nevertheless, in time, Nerva's administration appears to have pulled in the purse strings and improved fiscal affairs overall. The healthy economic state of the empire at large meant revenues would soon create a healthy balance sheet.

Nerva generally avoided radically changing the way Domitian had actually run Rome and the empire. He recognised and maintained laws established by Domitian to sustain the status quo and this exemplifies how much of what Domitian had implemented during his reign was robust and effective. Witness an extract from a letter from Nerva to Tullius Justus:

> Any regulations laid down for matters begun or concluded in the last reign are to hold good; consequently letters of Domitian must also remain valid.
>
> *Pliny's Letters*[44]

In addition, Nerva issued an edict reassuring those who had received privileges from previous emperors that they would not be taken away:

> It is my wish that no one should think that I shall withdraw any public or private benefactions conferred by any of my predecessors, so as to claim credit for restoring them myself. Everything shall be assured and ratified: no one on whom the fortune of the empire has smiled, shall need to renew his petitions in order to confirm his happiness.
>
> *Edicts of the Emperor Nerva*[45]

Adoption of Trajan

Imagine trying to satisfy the views and concerns of around 600 easily disgruntled Roman senators of different generations, origins and political opinions. Many were immensely wealthy, aristocratic, demanding and highly ambitious, supposedly the honourable fathers of Rome. Since it was an impossible task to please everyone, a wise emperor had to try and secure the satisfaction of the majority. The conspirators who had masterminded Nerva's accession appear to have mistakenly assumed that their prior lobbying had sufficiently appeased the majority in the Senate. However, once the euphoria of senators pleased with Domitian's assassination had subsided, a large number of senators who had concealed their dissatisfaction at events were now poised to raise their concerns. A significant portion of this latter group were also serving in active senatorial offices with considerable influence and power to back up their discords with Nerva. Fundamentally, Nerva lacked military experience and connections with senior commanders, which meant he was unable to strengthen his position against the unsettled factions of senators with the might of the legions solidly behind him. It was this lack of military standing that constituted the Achilles heel of Nerva's principate. Furthermore, the rumour would have gradually circulated around Rome that Nerva had been involved in the murder of Domitian, which weakened his position still further.[46]

One senator emerged from the discontented factions with sufficient anger to plot against Nerva. His name was Calpurnius Crassus Frugi and he ineffectively courted the Praetorian Guard and a selection of his peers. Quickly discovered, he was exiled by Nerva who honoured his oath not to execute any senator.[47] Crassus' plot to overthrow Nerva so early after his accession, however unsuccessful the attempt, was a sure sign of wider discontent. The wolves were once again circling an emperor who was perceived as vulnerable. Moreover, Nerva was visibly frail and lacked a natural or appointed heir. This raised serious concerns in the Senate, including among those loyal to Nerva. If the emperor died suddenly, with no clear successor it would almost certainly result in civil war. And civil war was the greatest failing of the Roman state.

Nerva and his *consilium* were well aware of these issues and they probably started discussing suitable heirs soon after Nerva's accession. The position was not easy to fill. A successor needed the support of the armies and their commanders, as well as the senators and ideally the Praetorian Guard. Equally, the candidate needed to possess the necessary virtues and experiences to exert authority over his contemporaries. Age was also crucial; unlike Nerva, he should ideally be young enough to provide longevity to the next principate. In essence, this person needed to meet all the criteria that Nerva failed to fulfil despite his long senatorial *cursus* and reverence for the Senate. Regrettably for the new regime, it was soon becoming apparent that the appointment of such a successor was being unwisely left too long. No heir was appointed in the first half of 97.

In the meantime, the improved weather conditions of the season allowed the launch of another offensive against the Suebi. Capitalising on successes in the previous year and using the cleared access routes into enemy territory, Trajan's forces advanced swiftly and decisively against the Germanic tribes. The ruthless efficiency of the combined Roman legions and auxiliaries swept aside any resistance.[48] As the front advanced, Trajan would have dispatched regular bulletins to Rome detailing the progress of the war, and while encouraging news from the front would have bolstered Nerva's prestige, events in the summer of 97 were about to undermine his position completely.

Still displeased about the murder of Domitian, the Praetorian Guard was no longer able to contain its discontent. The large payment from Nerva at the start of his reign was now either forgotten or spent. Their commander, Casperius Aelianus, and other key officers may have been bribed into inciting the Guard by the governor of Syria, Cornelius Nigrinus, who was a highly decorated general under Domitian. Nigrinus was one of those senators whose prospects were dashed following Domitian's assassination and he is thought to have had ambitions for the principate, as well as a significant party of senators that supported him.[49] As a result, the Guard railed against Nerva to insist upon the execution of Domitian's assassins.[50] A desperate situation ensued: surrounding Nerva in his palace, Aelianus and select contingents of the Guard issued their mutinous demands for vengeance. Realising that his own life at that moment was not under immediate threat, Nerva offered his bare throat to the perpetrators in refusal and in a dramatic appeal to their common sense. Nerva's brave show was unable to defuse the situation and the Praetorians' two principal targets, who had taken refuge in the palace, were dragged out. Parthenius, the senior chamberlain who had managed the palace assassination from the inside, was supposedly killed with a single blow and Secundus, the ex-Praetorian Guard prefect who had allowed the assassination to proceed without intervention, had his genitals removed and stuffed into his mouth before he was executed. Completely humiliated, Nerva was then forced to thank the Praetorian Guard publicly for the execution of the assassins.[51]

Nerva's principate and authority were now in tatters. His support in the Senate and among the legions was waning, and he had been humiliated by his own Praetorian Guard and their prefect. Nerva and his *consilium* knew that they only had a matter of days or weeks to recover from this situation before the new regime was overthrown and Nerva probably killed in the collapse. It was starkly apparent that only a flawless, respected and well-positioned successor could quell the dissent against Nerva, and that person had to be identified without any further delay.

Trajan was the candidate selected as that successor by Nerva, probably after intensive lobbying by Trajan's supporters in the Senate. The kudos of the Ulpii was about to be raised further than ever. But why was Trajan chosen over his many peers? And what would have driven Trajan to accept? In essence, three main attributes made Trajan a good choice: his credentials, military influence and connections.

As for credentials, he was from a family with a newly acquired patrician status and his father's glittering *cursus* in service to the deified Emperor Vespasian underpinned the distinguished nature of the family.[52] This would satisfy those senators who expected an adopted successor to arise from a family with prestigious origins, even if those origins were established in recent decades. Trajan himself was born in the wealthy and highly Romanised province of Baetica. Therefore, senators could overlook the fact that he was not a true native born on Italian soil. Trajan had advanced well through his *cursus* with his reputation untarnished. He was also in his early forties. This particular attribute should not to be underestimated. It confirmed his appropriate level of experience and provided a foreseeable period of durable occupancy of the Principate, which would provide stability for other successors to be nurtured.

Trajan, like his father, was also known for his unquestionable loyalty to the Principate and particularly to Domitian. Despite Domitian's damnation by the Senate, this would actually help appease a significant number of influential senators who had benefited from Domitian's reign and may have been ostracised following his assassination. Finally, Trajan was amiable, humble in nature and, crucially, he understood the need to respect the Senate. Trajan had observed the detrimental effects of the alienation between Domitian and the Senate and it was clear he would likely be an emperor who would strive to avoid repeating this error. This would please those who expected a successor to be approachable and amenable to senatorial proposals and claims.

In terms of military influence, Trajan could boast a solid reputation in military affairs, quintessential in gaining respect from the legions and thereby helping avoid later rebellion. Basically, he was a younger version of Vespasian in the minds of many senators. Trajan could claim experience in several theatres of war, serving in Syria as a tribune, Germania as commander of a legion and now Pannonia, at that time the most critical theatre of war, as a general. To his credit, he was in tune with his men, sharing in their hardships on long marches and even eating their simple food with them outside.[53] He had a fundamental liking for military life and was favoured by soldiers and officers who recognised this discipline. His humbler nature, as opposed to lofty patrician superiority, explained his good relations with his men. This would mean that legionary soldiers and officers with whom he had served would warm to his appointment as Nerva's heir.

Trajan also had senior military positions under his belt. As a young commander, he had efficiently led the VII *Gemina* legion, now back in Spain. He had successfully held the governorship of Germania Superior and could probably still count on the three legions posted there to respect his elevation as designated successor to the Principate. Most importantly, he was currently the governor of Pannonia and general of a vast force actively engaged in the Third Pannonian War, deploying the resources of the five legions there and the supporting detachments from the Moesian provinces. Thus, Trajan was respected as a commander and general by a total of at least nine legions. In addition, in the summer of 97, Trajan was able to count on the governors of Germania Inferior and the two Moesian provinces and with them the seven legions stationed in their provinces.[54] If Trajan was forced to act, he had the potential to rally support from up to sixteen legions, over 90,000 men at full strength and approximately half of Rome's entire legionary force, not to mention an equivalent number of *auxilia*. No one in their right mind would contemplate challenging a successor with such military influence and the potential to draw on such power. In addition, Trajan was a commander and general with probable successes against the Chatti, Iazyges and imminently the Suebi. Glory was always the Roman general's greatest asset and an aspiration for any Roman. All these elements were indispensable for an imperial candidate who needed the power and strong arms of Rome's legions to secure his position.

Last in his line of attributes, Trajan was well connected in Roman high society through a series of networks arising from his near and extended family, friends, colleagues and Iberian compatriots. In particular, links to the wealthy and prosperous provinces of Baetica and Narbonensis, respectively through his own origins and marriage to Plotina, created an influential web in Rome and across the empire.[55] The following group of prominent figures were the most critical supporters of Trajan in the summer of 97:

Faction Leaders

NAME: Sextus Julius Frontinus.
LOCATION: Rome.
ASSOCIATION WITH TRAJAN: Critical ally in Rome.
POWER AND INFLUENCE: Military success against Civilis' revolt (70); former governor of Britain (73–77); served in Domitian's Chattan War;[56] former proconsul of Asia (85); military strategist; courtier and military adviser to Domitian; consul (73); member of Nerva's *consilium*.

NAME: Lucius Julius Ursus.
LOCATION: Rome.
ASSOCIATION WITH TRAJAN: Critical ally in Rome. Possible connections with the family of Trajan's wife.[57]
POWER AND INFLUENCE: Prefect of Egypt (date uncertain but possibly in the seventies or early eighties),[58] consul (84) and former Praetorian Guard prefect for Domitian; member of Nerva's *consilium*.

NAME: Lucius Licinius Sura.
LOCATION: Germania Inferior.
ASSOCIATION WITH TRAJAN: Closest friend and compatriot.
POWER AND INFLUENCE: Ex-consul (93); governor of Germania Inferior with three legions (since 95).[59] Considered 'most celebrated of learned men' by the poet Martial.[60]

Key Faction Players in Rome (or Unknown Location)

NAME: Cnaeus Arrius Antoninus.
LOCATION: Rome.
ASSOCIATION WITH TRAJAN: Former associate of Trajan's father.
POWER AND INFLUENCE: Former proconsul of Asia; recent consul (March 97) for the second time (first in 69); close friend of Nerva and a member of his *consilium*.

NAME: Lucius Neratius Priscus.
LOCATION: Rome.
ASSOCIATION WITH TRAJAN: Friend and Domitian loyalist like Trajan.
POWER AND INFLUENCE: Recent consul (May 97); highly respected jurist.[61]

NAME: Marcus Annius Verus.
LOCATION: Rome.
ASSOCIATION WITH TRAJAN: Possible ally.[62]
POWER AND INFLUENCE: Recent consul (March 97); on Nerva's *consilium*.

NAME: Cornelius Palma Frontonianus.
LOCATION: Unknown (probably Rome).
ASSOCIATION WITH TRAJAN: Close friend.
POWER AND INFLUENCE: Governor of a public province in Asia (details unknown); legion commander in unknown location (94–97).

NAME: Lucius Julius Ursus Servianus.[63]
LOCATION: Rome.
ASSOCIATION WITH TRAJAN: Loyalist; married to Hadrian's sister.
POWER AND INFLUENCE: Ex-consul (90).

NAME: Caius Antius Aulus Julius Quadratus.
LOCATION: Unknown.
ASSOCIATION WITH TRAJAN: Friend or someone tolerated and pacified by Trajan;[64] possibly a former colleague of Trajan's father; an elder statesman, once a loyalist to Nero and subsequently to the Flavians like Trajan.
POWER AND INFLUENCE: Eastern connections given his origins in Pergamum, ex-consul (94), possibly legate for Traianus while proconsul of Asia in 79;[65] governor of Bithynia-Pontus and Lycia-Pamphylia (probably under Titus and/or Domitian).[66]

Key Faction Players in the Provinces

NAME: Pompeius Longinus.
LOCATION: Moesia.[67]
ASSOCIATION WITH TRAJAN: Supporting Trajan in the Third Pannonian War and loyalist.
POWER AND INFLUENCE: Ex-consul (90); governor of Moesia Superior with two legions (since 94).

NAME: Octavius Fronto
LOCATION: Moesia Inferior.
ASSOCIATION WITH TRAJAN: Supporting Trajan in the Third Pannonian War and loyalist.

POWER AND INFLUENCE: Consul (86)[68] and probably posted as governor of Moesia Inferior by Domitian at the time he started his Second Pannonian War in 92.[69] It is thought that Fronto was still governor of Moesia Inferior (with two legions) until shortly before September 97.[70]

NAME: Quintus Sosius Senecio.
LOCATION: Germania Inferior.[71]
ASSOCIATION WITH TRAJAN: Loyalist.
POWER AND INFLUENCE: *Legatus* of I *Minervia* at Bonna (Bonn, 95–97). Influential connections in the eastern half of the empire. Would replace Agricola as governor of Belgica in second half of 97.[72] Son-in-law of Sextus Julius Frontinus.[73]

NAME: Quintus Glitius Atilius Agricola.
LOCATION: Belgica.
ASSOCIATION WITH TRAJAN: Colleague during Trajan's posting as legate of VII *Gemina Felix* in Hispaniae Tarraconensis.[74]
POWER AND INFLUENCE: Legate of VI *Ferrata* in Syria (*ca.* 91–93);[75] governor of Belgica (94–summer 97); upcoming consul in 97 (Sept–Oct) probably back in Rome in time to take up position.[76]

NAME: Sextus Attius Suburanus Aemilianus.
LOCATION: Belgica.
ASSOCIATION WITH TRAJAN: Ally or loyalist.
POWER AND INFLUENCE: Assistant to Julius Ursus when prefect of Egypt, financial procurator of Belgica (97) and therefore paymaster-general to the armies of the Rhine.[77]

These top supporters, plus Vibius Sabinus who was possibly still alive at that time,[78] and was married to Trajan's niece Matidia, were all individually powerful and influential men. They were all easily able to claim solid support from another ten or twenty senators each, and this created a faction of a hundred senators or more (factoring in some overlap between supporters).[79] This was equivalent to a sixth or more of the entire Senate. It has been postulated that the core of this faction was probably led by Julius Ursus and Julius Frontinus in Rome, who one can suspect were highly influential with Nerva and also had much to gain by foiling Cornelius Nigrinus' designs on the Principate. Nigrinus was almost certainly manoeuvring his own faction of senators at the time and he had probably been involved in the incitement of the Praetorian Guard against Nerva.

Presumably Nigrinus lacked the critical mass of support in the Senate and across the empire required to steer events and the leaders of the faction that supported Trajan managed to convince Nerva that their man was the best possible candidate. Ursus, Frontinus or Licinius Sura surely would have approached Trajan with the proposal for his adoption. Domitian's possible posting of Trajan as governor of Pannonia and the subsequent retention of Trajan in the position by Nerva, may have been partially thanks to the persuasive skills of Ursus and Frontinus.

Apparently hesitant at first to accept the adoption, Trajan was prudent to weigh up the immediate support he could depend upon before accepting.[80] He would not make the mistake of others who had underestimated the breadth and magnitude of support required to ensure a stable accession to the Principate. But Trajan could not contemplate his position for long, as the unrest in Rome against Nerva was filtering out to the armies, causing mutiny and rebellion in the ranks. The situation was dire and the empire was on the edge of a turmoil that could lead ultimately to civil war.[81]

Frantic communications certainly raced across the empire between Trajan and his closest supporters, including the astute Plotina and Marciana, who were probably aware of the mood among Rome's families. Likewise, correspondence between Trajan and his supporters would have intensified. Eventually, one of the top leaders of Trajan's supporting faction, Sura, urged Trajan to accept and worked hard on his behalf to champion his virtues to others.[82] Finally, the stark realisation came to Trajan: he had the quality and breadth of support needed to become Nerva's heir.

The die was cast.

Regardless of all the endorsements and assurances of support, one can reasonably suspect that Trajan's ultimate decision to accept the offer to become Nerva's adopted heir was driven by the imminent sense of immense power. All of his ideas for the glory of Rome could materialise if he was its emperor. It is even said that Trajan actually had a prophetic dream around this time as Dio Cassius records:

> [Trajan] thought that an old man in a purple-bordered toga and vesture and with a crown upon his head, as the Senate is represented in pictures, impressed a seal upon him with a finger ring, first on the left side of his neck and then on the right.[83]

Trajan evidently understood that the seal represented authority over Rome and stamping it into his flesh was a sign that he was marked to claim that authority. One can only guess whether such a dream influenced Trajan's resolve. Romans were far more superstitious than we are today and truly believed that dreams foretold the future.

Back in Rome, Nerva would have arranged the appointment of trusted men as consuls for the following year: Julius Frontinus, Julius Ursus and two other senators would receive their highly prestigious second consulships.[84] Despite the urgency imposed on Nerva by the humiliating activities of the Praetorian Guard a few months earlier, he had nevertheless managed to acquire a fitting successor as well as line up loyal supporters for the consulships in the year that would follow his public announcement on the matter of his adopted heir. In parallel, Cornelius Nigrinus was dismissed from his position as governor of Syria, thereby removing the three legions from his command and negating his potential to seize the Principate. All that was needed now was an appropriate event at which to ordain the successor, and the pending victory against the Suebi in the Third Pannonian War was perfectly apt. What could be a better accompaniment and prelude to ordination than the announcement of Trajan's victory, thereby further ensuring the respect of the armies?

Away in the depths of the Quadi–Marcomanni territories, Trajan's army had crushed resistance by the end of the campaign season and essentially bought the Third Pannonian War to a close. The war had successively suppressed the Iazyges and then the Quadi and Marcomanni tribes. Strategically, this was an important victory for Rome as it paved the way to revisit the unsatisfactory peace arrangements made with the Dacians. As pre-arranged between Nerva and Trajan, the victorious general issued the customary dispatch to his emperor in Rome: a laurelled letter – a letter accompanied by a wreath of *Laurus nobilis* leaves (commonly known as bay laurel), which traditionally symbolised victory and strength.[85]

By October 97, Nerva had received the laurelled letter from Trajan and he would have hastened to the Temple of Jupiter on the Capitoline Hill, followed by a select group of observers, advisers and his guards. Nerva offered incense to Rome's supreme deity, Jupiter Optimus Maximus (Jupiter the Best and Greatest), and laid the victory laurel wreath in the lap of the colossal statue of Jupiter made partially of gold and ivory.[86] The scene was stage-managed to signify the great extent of the victory, worthy enough to be dedicated to the almighty Jupiter and all thanks to Trajan in the name of his Emperor Nerva. Leaving the temple, Nerva then proceeded down from the Capitoline Hill into the forum where a crowd had been gathered. Stepping up onto the *Rostra* and gazing out over the old Republican forum, he announced loudly, 'May good success attend the Roman Senate and people and myself. I hereby adopt Marcus Ulpius Nerva Trajan.'[87]

A Syrian bronze coin, struck in 97, shows the laureate head of Nerva with his distinctive profile.

Nerva's Son and Heir

Following the dramatic public announcement, no surprise by now to many in the Senate, Nerva called the Curia into session and officially appointed Trajan as *Caesar*.[88] The title had now come to signify the emperor's designated heir. Both Nerva and Trajan were then hailed *Imperator* and awarded the title of *Germanicus* (victor over the Germanic tribes) in recognition of their success in the Third Pannonian War.[89] Nerva sent a message to Trajan conveying all the news in Rome and included a precious diamond ring to symbolise the adoption.[90] Soon afterwards, the Senate also formally vested in Trajan the powers of *Imperium* and *Tribunicia potestas,* which had been granted to Nerva the previous year at his accession. Quite simply, Trajan now lacked only the appointment as Pontifex Maximus and the title of Augustus, which were both exclusive to the emperor.[91] This made Trajan, to all intents and purposes, the subordinate partner in the Principate.[92] In the wake of the adoption, after the news spread across the empire, calm and stability were restored.

> Every disturbance died away at once; though this was the effect not so much of the adoption as the nature of the man adopted, sure indication that Nerva would have been foolish had he chosen otherwise.
>
> Pliny, on the year 100[93]

Clearly the combination of Trajan's attributes as an ideal candidate, rather than a hereditary successor, secured an acceptance that held firm during the transfer of powers to the adoptee. As discussed, one could never please the entire Senate, but at least a large majority were happy and for anyone harbouring any resentment, the force of the mighty Roman army provided a robust incentive to remain quiet and accept the turn of events. The indifferent portion of senators could at least console themselves that an influential heir was now undisputed and the fear of civil war was lifted.

With the Third Pannonian War concluded, Nerva and Trajan had agreed that Trajan would now take up the distinguished position as commander of all forces in the German provinces, both Inferior and Superior, with *Imperium* over the governors, legion commanders and the three legions stationed in each province. This was a prestigious position for Trajan, worthy of his new status as heir to the Principate. The Emperor Tiberius had given the same position to his popular adopted son Germanicus earlier in the first century. Transferring directly from Pannonia, Trajan travelled to Colonia Claudia Ara Agrippinensium [Cologne] in Germania Inferior, arriving towards the end of 97. A trusted supporter of Trajan, Pompeius Longinus, replaced him as governor of Pannonia and would be responsible for mopping up minor pockets of resistance and tying up any loose ends from the main war.[94] In Germania, other solid Trajan loyalists were ready to serve as governors of Germania Inferior and Superior: Sura and Julius Ursus Servianus respectively. Trajan was assured of total cooperation in his new provinces.

During this period, Hadrian was the military *tribunus laticlavius* of the Legion V *Macedonica* stationed in Moesia Inferior.[95] When the news of Trajan's adoption reached the province, the governor Octavius Fronto, who had supported Trajan's appointment, sent Hadrian to Trajan, then still in Pannonia, to convey his and the army's congratulations.[96] Hadrian was eager to visit his previous guardian who was in line to become the next emperor of Rome. His youthful thoughts may well have leapt ahead to a day when he, too, could be the next in line, being the only male in Trajan's immediate family. On Hadrian's arrival, he and Trajan would have had private meetings together during which time Trajan would have briefed the young man about his forthcoming proconsulship in Germania and of what he expected from Hadrian in terms of behaviour and performance, now that the Ulpii were connected directly to the Principate. From Pannonia, Trajan arranged for the transfer of Hadrian to Germania Superior to continue his tribunate with XXII *Primigeniae Piae Fidelis*. Hadrian would therefore fall under the direct authority of his brother-in-law, Servianus the governor, and ultimately under Trajan's umbrella in his new special role as proconsul of all Germania.

Once Trajan was settled in Colonia Claudia Ara Agrippinensium, he was undoubtedly in his element and extremely pleased with his circumstances as

Caesar, the presumptive successor to the Principate. A military man through and through, he augmented the proficiency of the Roman forces in earnest. The Rhine frontier required a thorough review to reassess the work started by Domitian to reinforce the borders. This was important because Rome had begun a gradual shift of its military powers away from the Rhine to the less stable Danube frontier. Therefore, one of Trajan's first areas to address was a review of the future arrangement of the six legions posted along the Rhine frontier, which was then arguably somewhat over-manned in places.[97]

While Trajan conducted his tour of inspection, most likely rearranging garrisons, directing the implementation of new *limites* or the reconstruction of established *limites*, he received news from Servianus that Hadrian's extravagances had led to notable debts with certain creditors.[98] Hadrian's indulgences were typical of many tribunes not serious about the nature of the position. He may also have been borrowing against his expectations, bolstered so dramatically by Trajan's exalted position as Nerva's heir. This would have displeased Trajan, especially having without doubt explained the virtuous behaviour he expected from Hadrian. Trajan chastised Hadrian, and the young man fell into disfavour. This was not to be the last time Hadrian had to be reprimanded.

Meanwhile, the rest of Trajan's immediate family adjusted to their new status as the imperial family. Plotina and Marciana continued to remain sturdy advisers to Trajan. Morally, they were a strong unit and no extravagances blemished their image and cast a shadow over Trajan, who was now highly visible and scrutinised by Rome's elite.

Nerva's Death and Trajan's Accession

Towards the end of 97, Nerva's feeble constitution was failing. Nonetheless, Nerva was delighted by Trajan's adoption and pressure on him would have eased.[99] In addition, some of Nerva's imperial duties could be shared with his heir even though he was absent in Germania.[100] But despite these alleviating elements, which reduced some of the strain on Nerva, a few of those close to him surely knew his days were numbered because of his frailty.

On 1 January 98, Nerva and Trajan, father and adopted son, claimed the prestigious honour of opening the year as *consules ordinarii*.[101] This was Nerva's fourth and Trajan's second consulship. Trajan held the appointment *in absentia* and Nerva, too frail to hold the office, passed his position on quickly to one of his old friends on 13 January. Nerva then withdrew to his peaceful imperial villa in the Horti Sallustiani, the Gardens of Sallust. Situated in the valley between the Pincian and Quirinal hills[102] (the Via Veneto quarter in modern Rome) the villa was surrounded by exquisite gardens and was an ideal place for Nerva to try and gather some strength. But a man unknown to us today, called Regulus, greatly angered Nerva over some matter that caused the emperor to raise his voice in anger. The stress and agitation were perhaps the final straw for Nerva who was subsequently 'seized by a sweat'.[103] A severe fever developed causing him to shiver profusely. Already very weak, Nerva was unable to resist the fever and died on 27 January aged sixty-five and having reigned for only a year and four months.[104] On that very day, there was an eclipse of the sun, an eerie coincidence that many in Rome would have taken as a sign from the gods that a great man had passed away.[105] Hundreds of miles distant in his winter residence in Colonia Claudia Ara Agrippinensium, Trajan was unaware he had just become the Emperor of Rome – the most powerful man in the ancient world.

Senior officials at the villa conveyed the news of Nerva's death to Trajan, the consul in Rome and the Senate. Trajan was proclaimed emperor and the order was given immediately to send a message to him in Germania. In transit, the dispatch first reached Moguntiacum in Germania Superior where the governor, Servianus, was informed of its contents. Hadrian, serving in the legion posted in Moguntiacum, was also told. Since Hadrian still needed to redeem himself with Trajan following the revelation of his extravagant habits, he seized on the idea of delivering the news of Nerva's death in person to Trajan. Servianus, however, was a disciplinarian and believed that an official messenger was more appropriate to deliver such crucial information.[106] Unable to order the unruly Hadrian to remain in Moguntiacum and perhaps a little afraid to vex him openly, Servianus instead told some of his men to cripple Hadrian's carriage. Undeterred, the defiant Hadrian was forced to head out on foot but soon found a suitable horse or new carriage to reach Colonia ahead of the official messenger.

One can imagine the highly charged scene when Hadrian was announced and permitted entry to Trajan's quarters, presumably crowded by his secretariat and other provincial staff close to him. Hadrian recounted the news from Rome written in the dispatch. Trajan would doubtless have remained composed. It was no shock to hear of Nerva's death given his fragile health and old age. Trajan also had little or no affection for Nerva: his adoption had been a political move and their subsequent relationship had been based on correspondence; it is very likely that they had never met during Trajan's absence in Pannonia and Germania.

Trajan would have immediately called for all his senior advisers, officials and commanders in the region, the first official court gathering under his principate. As the area began to throng with various people excited by the news, it may have taken some time for Trajan to appreciate fully that he was now the Emperor of Rome. The provincial boy who had grown up in Rome and spent a short part of his youth back in Baetica playing in the Spanish hills and fields, now had absolute power of life and death over millions of people in a vast empire. Stretching from the crags of northern England to the deserts of Egypt and from the rocky coasts of Morocco to the sandy beaches of the Black Sea, it covered a staggering four million square kilometres.[107] As head of the most advanced and powerful army of its time, the glory that was Rome was all his.

Receiving a flurry of condolences for Nerva's death and congratulations on his accession, Trajan presided over his makeshift court and almost certainly issued three immediate orders. Firstly, as a sign of respect, a message in his own hand was to be sent to the Senate assuming his position as emperor and stating an oath, like Nerva, that no senator would be executed under his principate.[108] Secondly, an order was issued for Nerva to receive appropriate funeral rites and deification and for his ashes to be placed in the one remaining space in the mausoleum of Augustus.[109] Having a deceased adopted father as a deity would solidify Trajan's position, but coins were not issued to commemorate Nerva's deification until 107,[110] suggesting that Trajan harboured a lingering dislike for his predecessor, perhaps because of his possible involvement in the assassination of Domitian. Thirdly, all governors and legion commanders were to receive messages detailing his accession with emphasis on the stable order of proceedings and orders to continue in their duties until otherwise informed.[111] In private, Trajan would then have likely dictated a series of personal messages to his closest and most significant allies as well as family and friends. To these people, he may have underscored caution during this initial period of his reign until the power structures of the empire were fully accustomed to the transition of the *Imperium*.

Once the funeral rites of Nerva were completed back in Rome, during which time the Senate received instructions from Trajan for Nerva's deification, the Senate convened to recognise Trajan formally as emperor and additionally elected him Pontifex Maximus. With this title Trajan was officially head of all Roman religion, which secured the last element of real authority that he had lacked as the subordinate partner in the principate with Nerva. In addition, formal acceptance from the Senate was the seal of approval required to legitimise his own principate. The title of *Augustus*, given exclusively to an emperor, could also now be claimed by Trajan. Originally the cognomen of the first emperor, the esteemed title did not bestow any official constitutional office on subsequent emperors, but rather recognised their revered position. Thus, Trajan's full names and titles in early 98 were quite a mouthful, including:

IMPERATOR	Commander of all Roman forces
CAESAR	Recognition of his dignified status, a designated heir
NERVA	His deceased adopted father's name
TRAJAN	His cognomen
AUGUSTUS	'Venerable' in recognition of his position as emperor
GERMANICUS	'Victor over the Germans' for the Pannonian War
PONTIFEX MAXIMUS	Head of all Roman state religion.
TRIBUNICIA POTESTAS	With the powers of a Tribune of the People
CONSUL II	Second consulship

The first emperor born outside of Italy was now fully vested in the powers he would need to control Rome and its empire.

The Senate had also offered Plotina and Marciana the titles of *Augusta*. The feminine equivalent of *Augustus*, this honourable title had first been posthumously bestowed on Livia, the wife of Augustus, after her years of service to the Principate and in recognition of her maternal dignity within the Julio-Claudian dynasty. Prudently, Trajan refused this title for his wife and sister, as it belittled the status of the title when granted so flippantly just because of his own accession. Neither Plotina nor Marciana would have been upset by this action. Both dignified and loyal to Trajan, they understood the need to remain above the trivialisations of honours to which others had fallen prey in the past.[112]

Trajan's first acts as emperor set the tone for his whole reign; he was in control. Almost immediately after coming to power, Trajan moved to deal with the Praetorian Guard, which had become too much of a liability to the Principate. History had shown its ability to influence the imperial succession and even participate in the downfall of emperors. Trajan would not tolerate this situation, especially after the Guard's humiliating and disgraceful behaviour towards Nerva when they had surrounded the emperor and demanded the execution of Domitian's assassins. Therefore, Trajan sent for the Prefect Aelianus and the principal Praetorians involved in this shameful riot. Thinking they were going to serve the new emperor, they travelled from Rome to Germania.[113] Aelianus may not have sensed a trap given that he had possibly been a friend of Trajan's father.[114] Even if he did suspect a threat he could do little else because refusal would expose him, and he had neither time nor means to rally a defensive coup. On arrival they were presumably seized by Trajan's guards and dispatched without a trial.[115] This was the end of the first prefect to have served three emperors.[116]

Next, Trajan severed his dependence on the Praetorian Guard for his personal security by acquiring the governor's horse guard and supplementing its numbers with recruits to create a new Imperial Horse Guard of 1,000 mounted men to oversee his protection.[117] The Imperial Horse Guard, called *equites singulares Augusti*, was composed of hand-picked elite cavalrymen, the majority from tribes in Germania Inferior – particularly the Batavians – who were renowned for their riding skills. Able also to provide protection on foot, the Horse Guard was famed for its loyalty as exemplified when employed by previous emperors such as Caligula and Nero. In addition, the new guard would eventually be stationed within the city walls of Rome, unlike the Praetorians who were garrisoned just outside. Given the added speed of the new mounted guard, the Praetorians could no longer surprise and surround the emperor if he was in Rome. This effectively side-lined the Praetorians, who were left to contemplate their once prestigious position guarding the emperor. Finally, Trajan appointed Attius Suburanus Aemilianus as the new prefect of the Praetorian Guard.[118] Besides the difficult task of maintaining the Praetorian Guard in its reduced role, Suburanus was wholly trusted by Trajan to keep them in good order and had proven his loyalty as paymaster-general of the Rhine armies during Trajan's adoption. While handing over command of the Praetorians to Suburanus, symbolised by a sword of office, Trajan remarked pertinently and controversially:

> Take this sword, in order that, if I rule well, you may use it for me, but if ill, against me.
>
> Dio Cassius[119]

Towards the end of 98, while arrangements concerning the Horse Guard and Praetorians were instigated, Trajan was en route to conduct an assessment of the Danube frontier. Rather than dash back to Rome to revel in his new imperial power and swan around the imperial residences, Trajan was an emperor unafraid of absence from the capital and aware that he was in a sufficiently secure position to circumvent the need to be in Rome to exert his authority. Trajan's extended assessment of the northern frontiers was a flavour of what was to come. The senators in Rome had no issues with Trajan's prolonged absence since his accession but, nevertheless, the people and the Senate called for his return, which for the moment Trajan continued to resist.[120]

Trajan's desire to ignore popular calls for his return to Rome and instead move over to the Danube to continue his frontier review was not without specific reason and foresight. With a component of his new *consilium* by his side, possibly including his close allies Servianus (who would stay on as governor of Pannonia from *ca.* 98/99), Pompeius Longinus and Sura, Trajan presumably worked his way along the Danube focusing on key strategic areas.[121] A diligent review of the entire frontier demanded an assessment of all significant *limites*, military camps, fortified towns and communication lines. At the same time, the forces along the Danube needed a morale boost, and a personal visit from a new emperor with a high military reputation was exactly what was required. Additionally, Trajan imposed discipline in areas where unruliness was evident.[122] The hard hand of obedience was unsettling but a proven practice to keep Rome's forces in a condition that ensured their military excellence above others. There can be little doubt that Trajan would have spoken personally with all the legion commanders, auxiliary commanders and provincial governors along the Danube. Although time-consuming, such dialogue instilled Trajan's vision for a Danubian strategy and military code of conduct. Diplomacy at the time resulted in formal terms of peace with the Suebi, whom he had defeated while governor of Pannonia in 96–97 – a critical achievement for Trajan who would later benefit from their acquiescence.[123] Furthermore, Trajan may have taken this opportunity to share with a select group of senior persons in the region his emerging ideas for military conquest beyond the Danube. By then, Nerva's chief secretary, the equestrian Cnaeus Octavius Titinius Capito, would have caught up with Trajan. Capito had served both Domitian and Nerva competently, making him a valuable asset to Trajan who needed a steady and experienced chief secretary to tackle his increased correspondence workload.[124]

As his tour of the Danube continued, Trajan became familiar with the geographical nature of the frontier and its defensive deployments and offensive capabilities.[125] This unique knowledge meant that Trajan was able to direct efficient preparations along the Danube that would support any future military campaigns. For example, the Djerdap Gorge of the Danube received such attention. Also known as the Iron Gate, the gorge, along with other ravines cut by the Danube, divides the southern Carpathian Mountains from the northern Balkan Mountains. Around 100 km long, the steep rock faces of the gorge reach hundreds of metres high in certain places, towering over the Danube River. Problematic for river transport, the Djerdap Gorge was a focus of Roman activities between the upper and lower Danube, as well as an access point north into Dacia and the Hungarian plains. To secure the gorge, Trajan commissioned the erection of watch towers in prominent positions along this strategically important region.[126] In addition, he ordered the reconstruction of the dilapidated Djerdap towpath, a unique cantilevered wooden platform that allowed the towing of river vessels through the gorge and thereby improved the thoroughfare for the Danubian military river fleet and commercial vessels.[127] Trajan also commissioned the enormous task of building a canal around the Gorge to avoid shipping having to face the very strong currents of the Gorge.

Overall, the result of Trajan's frontier tour undeniably meant a gradual improvement of military surveillance networks, defences and transport along the Danube. Trajan's military mind appreciated the value of such infrastructure to support the frontier, as well as his growing ambitions for offensive action beyond the river.

Despite Trajan's protracted absence from Rome, he did not neglect to recognise and reward those most loyal and supportive of his accession. For senators, the most coveted prize was to be appointed as one of the two consuls. For example, the esteemed 99 *consules ordinarii* offices were awarded to Cornelius Palma Frontonianus and Quintus Sosius Senecio for their roles in helping ensure Trajan's adoption by Nerva.[128] Julius Ursus and Julius Frontinus had already been awarded their second consulships for their part in supporting Trajan's adoption. Governorships, military commands, praetorships and various state positions were allocated to other loyal supporters. With all the immediate honours issued, Trajan decided to accept the title of *Pater Patriae*, father of the fatherland, from the Senate. Originally, the honorific title recognised outstanding service to the Roman republic and illustrious predecessors such as Julius Caesar and the great statesman Cicero had received it. In the imperial era, the title had somewhat lost its weight and came to represent a form of high admiration of the Senate for the emperor. Unusually, Nerva had accepted the title soon after his accession. Following convention, Trajan initially refused the title when similarly offered it soon after his own accession, but in 98 he finally accepted.[129] Perhaps he felt he had earned it after ensuring the stable transition of the Principate into his hands and his fatherly benefaction of those loyal to his accession.

After wintering in the Danube region, the year of 99 saw Trajan continue his absence from Rome and complete his extensive review of the frontier there. With his forty-third birthday approaching in September of the year, it is worthwhile considering how the emperor was perceived physically by the men and officers around him.

One can form a reasonable impression of Trajan in this period based on the profile depicted on coins and from statue busts. He was physically in good shape; active service and camp life had ensured Trajan remained toned and strong in stature.[130] A man not afraid to face the elements, his complexion was probably weathered and his face lined somewhat with age. A pensive expression was exaggerated by a compressed physical distance between his chin, mouth and nose tip, with the hint of a double chin giving away his increasing age. His hair was cut short and brushed forward over his forehead with a neatly cut fringe, typical of the military look he was fond of portraying.

At the end of the summer of 99, the new emperor could no longer postpone his return to Rome to greet the Senate that had endorsed his principate eighteen months earlier. He was probably satisfied by his assessment of the Danube frontier and knew enough to seal his ultimate plans. All that was needed was a short stint in Rome to please those who beckoned for his return and to attend to those matters of state that were more efficiently managed from Rome. The military-minded emperor had a scheme for restoring Rome's honour and conquering new lands. Trajan was ready to display true Roman expansionist behaviour, which was always a crowd-pleaser back in Rome, and he would soon reveal his intention to conquer Dacia.

CHAPTER 6

THE DAWNING TRAJANIC AGE

Modest Entry into Rome

With its origins steeped in legend, according to tradition the city of Rome was founded on the banks of the Tiber in 753 BC whence began its expansion to become the cultural, administrative and political capital of the Roman Empire. Originally the seat of kings, then republican government, by the imperial era Rome had developed into the most sophisticated city in the world. Nevertheless, for the first eighteen months after becoming Emperor of Rome, Trajan had delayed his expected return to the city in order to review the northern frontiers along the Rhine and particularly the Danube. Eventually, however, he could no longer resist calls for his return to the capital. Moreover, the new emperor seemingly had plans for the conquest of Dacia and he needed to launch these from Rome. Trajan also had to endure a lag period while necessary forces converged to where they could be deployed in a Dacian campaign and to allow frontier preparations to mature. Lastly, his return to Rome would allow him to catch up on his many civil duties, as well as set policies in place that would dictate the ethos of the new Trajanic age. It is this last element that is the focus of this chapter, before addressing Trajan's First Dacian War in the next.

Travelling back from the Danube, his centre of attention for the frontier review since the end of 98, Trajan would have arrived along the Via Flaminia at the northern outskirts of Rome in October 99. In keeping with plans for the emerging new age, Trajan had specific tactics for his entry into Rome. As he reached the Porta Flaminia, Trajan and his entourage saw vast crowds gathered around the arches of the gate and along the battlements of the old republican city wall.[1] Specifically choosing to approach on foot,[2] Trajan wanted to distance himself from lofty predecessors who entered Rome on decorative triumphal chariots pulled by four white stallions, or even borne on the shoulders of others. Instead, he wanted to show everyone that he was an emperor with Augustan principles – only the 'first among equals', moderate and approachable. Just like when a modern-day monarch leaves the comfort of a motorcade to proceed on an impromptu walk, the Roman people were delighted to see their new noble emperor on foot.

Beyond the Porta Flaminia itself, multitudes of excited people filled the streets, open areas and even the rooftops, eager to catch a glimpse of Trajan. Young, old, even the sick and frail had gathered to celebrate his return.[3] The *lictors*, customary escorts for Roman officials with their *fasces* symbolising the authority to punish, cleared a path ahead of Trajan through the swarms of cheering people.[4] Members of Trajan's own Imperial Horse Guard,[5] dismounted, were dressed in civilian clothes so they could blend somewhat into the crowds, although their tall stature and Nordic looks – fair-haired and blue-eyed – would have made them rather obvious to many.[6] Nevertheless, this gave the impression that Trajan needed no visible security deterrent, certainly not the imposing presence of an armed guard. Confident as he was of his position after a smooth accession, this was a further statement of Trajan's wish to impress on his people that he was an accessible emperor, a contrast to certain of his predecessors, such as Domitian and Caligula, who feared assassination deeply.

Massed in the Comitium, a sacred area of the forum right in front of the Senate house and shrouded in political importance, the senators awaited Trajan's arrival. As the crowd roared in recognition of Trajan's entrance into the Comitium, he proceeded to embrace senators with 'friendly greetings'.[7] Such an amiable emperor, arriving on foot, would have also impressed these fathers of Rome and secured respect for his 'modest demeanour'.[8] Taking time to circulate and personally greet as many of the senators as possible, Trajan eventually moved across to the western side of the forum to ascend the Capitoline Hill to make his expected dedications to the almighty Jupiter Optimus Maximus.

Beginning up the Capitoline Hill on a steep paved incline called the Clivus Capitolinus, a street still clearly visible today, Trajan passed between the closely opposed Temples of Saturn and of the Flavians. Trajan would have reflected to himself, perhaps even paused for a moment to acknowledge, that both he and his family owed much to the Flavian dynasty – in Trajan's case, to Domitian especially – who was not deified like his father and brother whose ashes officially resided in the temple. As he proceeded further up the steep Clivus Capitolinus, the vast Temple of Jupiter loomed above.

Built on an enormous foundation using blocks of grey native sedimentary tufa rock, which had supposedly not been altered since the Temple of Jupiter was first constructed in the sixth century BC, the vast marble-based podium of the temple covered an impressive area. It has been estimated that its façade was sixty metres wide, possibly as high as thirty-five metres from the ground to the apex of the roof and had three rows of six enormous Corinthian columns of Greek Pentelic white marble supporting the roof over the immense temple *pronaos* (courtyard). Six columns also ran along each side. In total, twenty-four columns, each twenty-one metres high, supported the whole roof structure. The sight was awe-inspiring. The proportions of the temple were of the same order of size as the modern-day pillar façade of Saint Peter's Basilica in Rome. Bright in the October sunshine, the roof tiles of the temple had been gilded by Domitian at enormous expense.

A myriad of gracious statues adorned the temple roof, the centrepiece a huge statue of Jupiter's *quadriga* (four-horse chariot) on the apex. Decorative marble ornaments completed the corners and edging of the roof, all complemented by finely sculptured cornices and metopes. The temple pediment contained a marble frieze that matched the beauty of the pediment of Athens' Parthenon. The frieze depicted the almighty Jupiter in the centre, seated on his throne facing left and holding his staff and lightning bolt. At his feet a great eagle, Jupiter's symbol and messenger, spread its wings. On each side, Jupiter was flanked by the goddesses Juno and Minerva: Juno was the goddess of the moon, protector of women and the wife of Jupiter; Minerva was the goddess of wisdom and the arts. Together, the three gods formed the 'Capitoline Triad'. On one side of the Triad, a two-horse chariot was driven by the personification of the Sun. On the other side, a similar chariot was driven by the personification of the Moon. On the far right of the pediment, the figure of Vulcan, the son of Jupiter and Juno, god of fire and volcanoes, was depicted collecting Jupiter's lightning bolts. The irony of Vulcan's presence was not lost on Trajan, because the great temple had been destroyed by fire twice in his lifetime (69 and 80) but now was restored to its former magnificence. In its entirety, the temple was doubtless a wonder for anyone who saw it from afar or close up. After all, Jupiter was god of light and the sky, as well as protector of Roman law and the state, the king of the Roman gods. It was a jaw-dropping immortalised abode for the Capitoline Triad, intended to inspire and humble any observer.[9]

Mounting the ornate steps up to the podium of the temple and leaving behind his entourage and the throng of senators who would have accompanied him to the Capitoline Hill, Trajan passed through the enormous hexastyle of pillars. Ahead of him lay three towering double doors, all of them gilded. The inside of the temple was divided into three large rooms, dedicated not only to Jupiter but also to Juno and Minerva. The central room belonged to Jupiter, and Trajan moved into this room to approach the colossal statue of the god within. The occasion would have been engraved on Trajan's memory forever. Almost two years before, Nerva had dedicated the laurels of Trajan's victory in the Third Pannonian War to Jupiter in this very temple. Just like Nerva then, Trajan would have burnt incense and bowed before the grand effigy of Jupiter. In the silence, Trajan realised his potential in this the most sacred of Rome's temples and he might have contemplated the enormous tasks and duties that lay ahead of him in the name of Rome and always under the gaze of the all-powerful Jupiter. Meanwhile, all around Rome, on altars at the foot of temples, sacrifices were given to Rome's pantheon of gods in thanks for Trajan's safe return and for future prosperity under his new rule.[10] As the blood of these animal sacrifices turned the altars of Rome red, Trajan left the Capitoline, marking an end to his entry into Rome.

Modest Living in Palatial Surroundings

Just like Nerva before him, Trajan had decided to take up his imperial residence on the Palatine Hill in the Domus Tiberiana, instead of the excessively opulent palace of Domitian which would have given the wrong message of overt decadence, and conflicted with his intention to launch an age of restraint and moderation.[11] However, Trajan was not forsaking comfort and luxury, since the Domus Tiberiana was still a palatial residence. Initially a series of wealthy republican houses, the Domus Tiberiana was created under Nero by amalgamating all the houses into one continuous palace, although it retained its attribution to Tiberius, hence its name. Stretched across the northwest corner of the Palatine and covering an area of over 18,000 square metres, the residence provided space and well-appointed accommodation for Trajan and his family. To the north, the Domus Tiberiana extended out beyond the slope of the Palatine Hill on vaulted brick and cement superstructures commissioned by the Emperor Caligula to create an arcaded façade with panoramic views over the forum below. A street, the Clivus Victoriae, ran below the façade and linked the palace to a covered ramp that led down to the forum. The western side of the Domus Tiberiana was delineated by the slopes of the Palatine Hill and to the south lay the old residential buildings that had belonged to the Emperor Augustus and his wife Livia, as well as the closely positioned Temples of Magna Mater and Victory. The eastern side of the Domus Tiberiana was bordered by another street, the Clivus Palatinus, which ran down from the Palatine into the eastern side of the forum complex. A central building within the Domus Tiberiana was surrounded by stunning gardens and on all sides by elegant pavilions offering respite from the intense Mediterranean heat of the summer months.[12]

A former residence for Tiberius, Claudius, Caligula, Nero and Nerva, the Domus Tiberiana was a perfect imperial retreat from the bustle of the forum below. The location was entirely suitable for an emperor of Rome: raised above the city and with spectacular views in all directions from the centre of a vast empire. Gazing out across Rome, surely it was impossible for Trajan not to feel a tremendous superiority, as if Rome was his own plaything? Only the strongest will could resist such a feeling from corrupting previously unassuming attitudes. And yet Trajan apparently had that will and strove to live modestly within the sumptuous palace. Equally, his family appears to have adhered to a similar ethos of unostenatious behaviour despite surroundings fit for the gods.

Both Plotina and Marciana had moved into the Domus Tiberiana ahead of Trajan to arrange the private areas according to his instructions while he was still in Pannonia. It was more than adequate for Trajan and his family and the imperial rooms were adjusted to match their own more modest tastes. On entry into the palace, Plotina, the very model of humble decorum, is recorded as having said:

> I enter here such a woman as I would fain be when I depart.
>
> Dio Cassius[13]

Family Affairs (ca. 99–101)

It is very likely that Trajan's father had died by the end of the century and that death would have been a particularly poignant moment for the family.[14] A great statesman, faithful to the Emperor Vespasian and instrumental in the Jewish wars and the civil wars of 69, it was he who had ensured Trajan's future. A prominent father was the key to many doors in the Roman social hierarchy and career progression. Traianus was undoubtedly honoured at his funeral and his death marked the end of an era given that presumably few from his generation remained. He would be later deified under Trajan and coins struck commemorating his divinity, *Divus Pater Traianus*.[15] With the death of his father, Trajan had become the head of the Ulpii family, and his immediate female relatives thus came under his direct patriarchal authority. Plotina his wife, Marciana his sister, Matidia his niece, as well as Sabina and Matidia the Younger, his great-nieces, could all call upon his protection. The family remained a strong unit and, once they were all settled into the imperial palace, harmony prevailed and was particularly noted between the two senior women, Plotina and Marciana, accentuating the upright nature of Trajan's family and the appropriate demeanour for the wife and sister of an emperor:

> Two women [Plotina and Marciana] in the same position can share a home without a sign of envy or rivalry. Their respect and consideration for each other is mutual, and as each loves you [Trajan] with all her heart, they think it makes no difference which of them stands first in your affection. United as they are in the purpose of their daily life, nothing can be shown to divide them; their one aim is to model themselves on your example, and consequently their habits are the same, being formed after yours.
>
> Pliny[16]

A gold *aureus*, struck in Rome *ca.* 112–13, commemorating the deification (*DIVI*) of Trajan's adopted father, Nerva (*left*) and natural father, Traianus (*right*)'.

But despite the apparent harmonious living, like every family, the Ulpii had their ups and downs. Again, Hadrian was the source of strife. At this time, Hadrian had returned to Rome[17] and was also installed in the Domus Tiberiana. Like Trajan, Hadrian had a partiality for young males and at one point he overstepped the mark by indulging his desires with Trajan's own personal selection of imperial page boys whom he kept around the palace and cherished.[18] Trajan likely reprimanded Hadrian. To smooth over the incident, Sura, now a very close adviser to Trajan, took steps to return Hadrian over time to good terms with his former guardian. Trajan eventually gave Hadrian permission to marry Sabina in 100, binding the family further. Moreover, the strong ties and affection that Plotina and Matidia both felt for Hadrian were highly instrumental in establishing this match.[19] Therefore, despite Hadrian's youthful excesses, which for the third time had required correction by Trajan,[20] the emperor's immediate family was irreproachable, an example of honourable and modest behaviour befitting an imperial family, all adhering to the doctrine of the new Trajanic age.

Trajan's First Acts in Rome

As we have seen, the manner of Trajan's entrance into Rome for the first time as emperor, the nature of his lifestyle and the generally harmonious existence of his family, were key components in his attempt to portray an image of a restrained, considerate and virtuous emperor. This was pertinent to the expansion and development he seems to have envisaged for Rome and its empire. However, the essential pieces required to solidify this emerging age were acts and policies that would enshrine Trajan's vision of an efficient and reliable imperial administration. His approach was based on the principles of Augustan respect and liberty for the Senate, seemingly in partnership with him; yet the reality was that he would remain firmly in control of all state business. As a result, certainly in consultation with his *consilium* and in consideration of the Senate's opinion, seven main areas appear to have drawn Trajan's attention in 99–100 during his first period in Rome as emperor: rewards, gifts and publicity; subsidies; crisis management; taxation and fiscal affairs; law and order; liberty; and public works.

Rewards, Gifts and Publicity

Benevolence was the mainstay of an emperor's supremacy. Only the emperor could give so generously and with sole discretion, securing an adoring attitude from the beneficiaries. Thus, Trajan acted swiftly to issue a *congiarium* and a *donativum*. He gave all adult Roman citizens resident in Rome and eligible to receive the corn dole – around 150,000 people – a *congiarium* sum of around 300 *sestertii* each. This amount per person was equivalent to a third of a legionary soldier's annual pay.[21] It meant that those impoverished citizens of Rome were given a life-saving or life-changing boost and the knock-on effect improved the overall economy in the city. Since Nerva had so recently paid the armies a very generous *donativum* upon his accession, Trajan was able to justify a reduced amount, giving probably around 150 *sestertii* per legionary soldier.[22] Officers typically received significantly more.[23] To help ensure the army did not perceive their amount as frugal, Trajan ordered that they

Rome – Trajanic Period

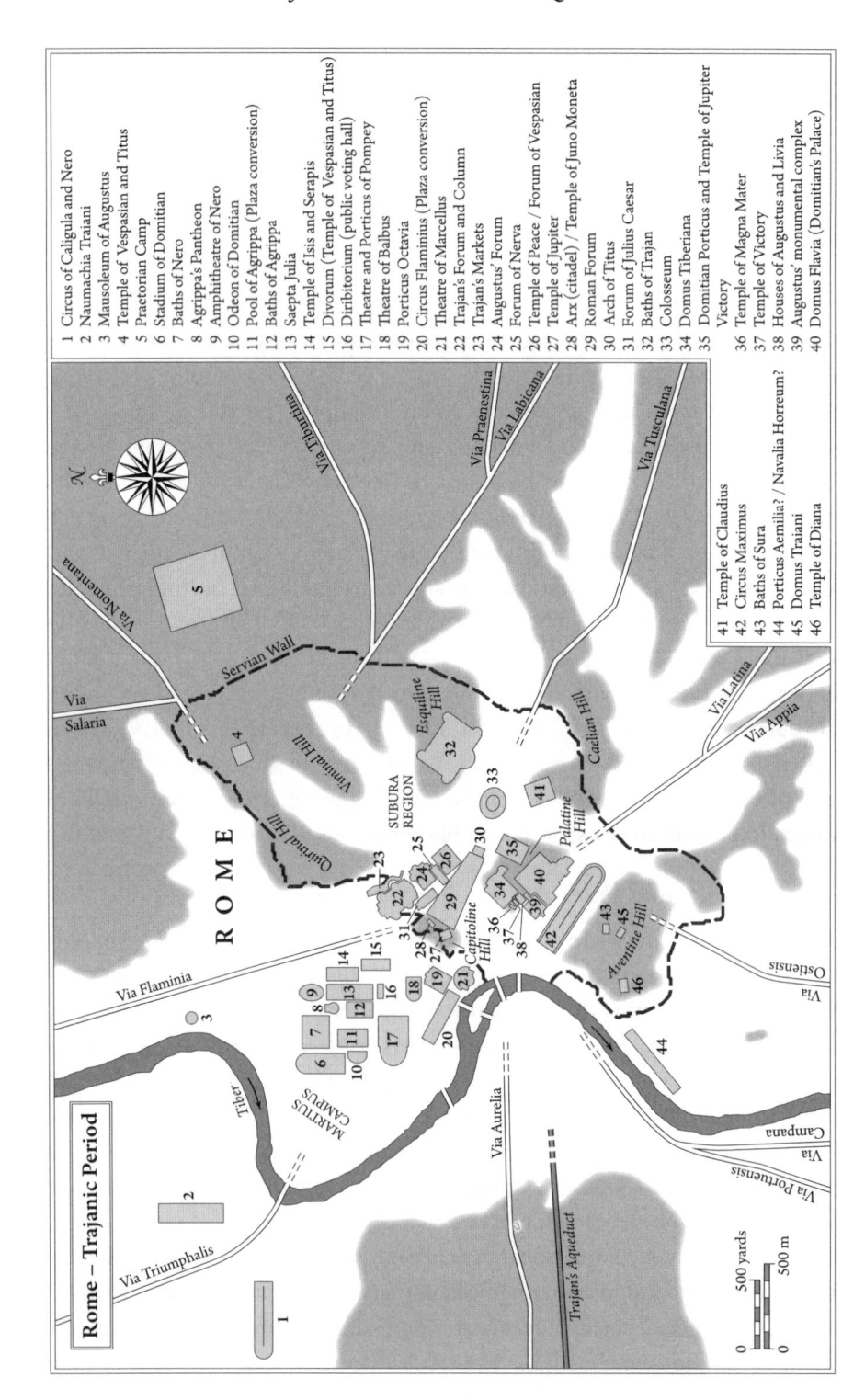

1 Circus of Caligula and Nero
2 Naumachia Traiani
3 Mausoleum of Augustus
4 Temple of Vespasian and Titus
5 Praetorian Camp
6 Stadium of Domitian
7 Baths of Nero
8 Agrippa's Pantheon
9 Amphitheatre of Nero
10 Odeon of Domitian
11 Pool of Agrippa (Plaza conversion)
12 Baths of Agrippa
13 Saepta Julia
14 Temple of Isis and Serapis
15 Divorum (Temple of Vespasian and Titus)
16 Diribitorium (public voting hall)
17 Theatre and Porticus of Pompey
18 Theatre of Balbus
19 Porticus Octavia
20 Circus Flaminius (Plaza conversion)
21 Theatre of Marcellus
22 Trajan's Forum and Column
23 Trajan's Markets
24 Augustus' Forum
25 Forum of Nerva
26 Temple of Peace / Forum of Vespasian
27 Temple of Jupiter
28 Arx (citadel) / Temple of Juno Moneta
29 Roman Forum
30 Arch of Titus
31 Forum of Julius Caesar
32 Baths of Trajan
33 Colosseum
34 Domus Tiberiana
35 Domitian Porticus and Temple of Jupiter Victory
36 Temple of Magna Mater
37 Temple of Victory
38 Houses of Augustus and Livia
39 Augustus' monumental complex
40 Domus Flavia (Domitian's Palace)
41 Temple of Claudius
42 Circus Maximus
43 Baths of Sura
44 Porticus Aemilia? / Navalia Horreum?
45 Domus Traiani
46 Temple of Diana

receive their money ahead of the people.[24] Trajan's total bill for these cash gifts reached approximately 71 million *sestertii*, nearly 10 per cent of the entire annual tax revenue of the empire.[25]

Although a massive drain on Rome's coffers, Trajan's *congiarium* and *donativum* were the ancient world's political billboard campaign, used by every emperor before him. The wide distribution of coinage would spread the image of Trajan across the empire, providing visible proof of Trajan's policies and virtues. Mint officials may have also intended different coinage types to boost Trajan's own ego, presenting to him a self-fulfilling image that they perceived he wanted to portray.[26] On such coins, personifications and representations carried a series of messages about Trajan's deeds, policies and virtues. For example, Concordia was the personification of unity and agreement, holding a *patera* (a bowl used in sacrifices to pour libations to the gods) and a *cornucopia* (a horn filled with agricultural produce to represent plenty). The message it conveyed was one of public unity behind Trajan and his policies – the emperor and his people were in harmony. Another example was Victoriae, the personification of victory, as a symbol of military success while also holding a *patera* and palm branch or shield.[27] This was a reminder that Trajan was already a victorious general against the Iazyges and Suebic Germans before becoming emperor – which his title *Germanicus* also reaffirmed.

As another gift to the people, Trajan paid for a spectacular series of public games to be held in the Colosseum soon after his arrival back in Rome. No expense was spared. Gladiatorial contests, which Trajan himself particularly enjoyed,[28] as well as animal fights against other animals or men, were staged over several days.[29]

Lastly, Trajan followed the classical approach of rewarding loyal senatorial supporters with consulships and other important positions of state. In particular, two *consules ordinarii*, the most sought-after positions for a senator as we have seen, were awarded in January 99 to Palma and Senecio for their dedicated loyalty in helping to ensure Trajan's adoption as Nerva's heir. Trajan had already awarded Julius Frontinus and Julius Ursus their second consulships in 98, but to acknowledge fully their instrumental roles leading the senatorial faction and the effort that probably convinced Nerva to adopt Trajan, the supreme honour of a third consulship was awarded to them in January 100, with Frontinus opening the year as *ordinarius* partnering Trajan's own third consulship. Trajan also had an additional motive: these men were highly regarded and influential senators who would now champion the emerging Trajanic age; their promotions would strengthen their influence still further and generate a solid power base for Trajan's administration and philosophy.[30]

Liberty

Nerva had already paved the way for Trajan in the restoration of senatorial liberty in order to distance his reign from that of the open autocracy of Domitian. But liberty has many forms and degrees, and Trajan presumably had his own clear plan to foster a type of liberty that would ultimately improve relations between the Senate and the emperor. Specifically, Trajan's idea of liberty may have been to give a sense of autonomy and freedom back to the senators. This would enhance the status of the Senate, whose role had been greatly diminished throughout the first century AD; this would benefit the administration of the state, while the imperial bureaucracy continued to hold the real and absolute authority. In effect, Trajan's support for liberty was a ploy. Give the senators a sense of liberty and the emperor's autocracy would seem less stifling.

To implement this policy in practice, Trajan encouraged senators to act more freely:

> You entered the Senate house and exhorted us, individually and collectively, to resume our freedom, to take up the responsibilities of the power we might be thought to share, to watch over the interests of the people, and to take action.
>
> Pliny[31]

In addition, the courage to act was also promoted under Trajan's era of liberty:

> You bid us be free, and we shall be free; you tell us to express ourselves openly, and we shall do so, for our previous hesitation was due to no cowardice or natural inertia, but to fear and apprehension, and the lamentable caution born of our perils which bade us turn eyes and ears and minds from our country, from that republic which was utterly destroyed.
>
> Pliny[32]

The Senate was freed to select its own consular candidates again (although ultimately Trajan had to approve any list) and the pinnacle of this new liberty, receiving high praise from the senator Pliny at the time, was the encouragement of the consuls to wield the original power of their office without intervention: Pliny was clearly exaggerating the situation, but perhaps some minor elements of power were returned to the consuls:

> You allow the consuls to act without interference, by which I mean that there are no fears nor perils as regards the Emperor to weaken and destroy their spirit; the consuls will not have to listen to anything against their will nor have decisions forced on them. Our office retains and will retain the respect due to it, and in exercising our authority we need lose none of our peace of mind ... So far as rests with our prince [Trajan], the consuls are free to fill their role as they did before the days of emperors.
>
> Pliny[33]

Public Works (ca. 98–105)

The renovation or construction of public works was a well-established process of pleasing the *populus* of Rome. It also promoted the elegance and status of Rome as the world's most refined city, a worthy capital of a great empire. Trajan did not intend to ignore this aspect and adopted policies to address public works accordingly. Funds were quickly released for one of his largest initial projects to restore the great Circus Maximus, the famous arena mainly dedicated for chariot racing and capable of holding around 150,000 spectators – especially impressive if one considers that Wembley, Britain largest sports stadium, only holds 90,000 people. Snugly positioned between the Palatine and the Aventine Hills, the huge lap of the arena track would take a Roman four-horse chariot two to three minutes to complete at race speed.[34] The Circus Maximus had been badly damaged by fire over thirty-five years earlier and had never been fully repaired. Trajan ensured a complete restoration of the massive façade of the Circus to its former glory and further enhanced its capacity, layout and architectural beauty.[35] The restored stadium was three levels high, the first level being completed in fine marble for the leading classes of Rome. In complete harmony with the image of a modest emperor not aloof from his peers, Trajan's seating arrangements allowed the audience to see him:

> Caesar as spectator shares the public seats as he does the spectacle.
>
> Pliny[36]

Soon after his accession Trajan ordered the extension of the *atrium* at the house of the Vestal Virgins in Rome, and the construction of a temple to the deified Nerva in Rome (which is lost today). He also commissioned the construction of a relief channel called the Fossa Traiana branching out west from the Tiber near its mouth, designed to help alleviate significant river flooding problems in the city. In this period, he also ordered the construction of a new aqueduct for Rome, the Aqua Traiani. Supporting trade and commerce, he started major constructions to modernise and expand Claudius' harbour at Ostia, including the creation of a vast hexagonal mooring area still visible today called the Portus Traiani. This was complemented by works to build a harbour to the north-west, Portus Centumcellae, near an exquisite villa that belonged to Trajan. Likely begun by Domitian just to the north-east of the Colosseum in Rome, Trajan completed a huge bath complex, the Thermae Traiani. It was the largest imperial bath, spread over eighty thousand square metres, and the new Aqua Traiani helped Rome cope with the enormous volumes of water required to run the facilities. The baths had a cistern able to hold eight million litres. Numerous other works were commissioned by Trajan including the improvement or completion of important roads such as the Via Appia, Via Aemilia, Via Sublacensis, Via Labicana and the Via Puteoli and enhancements to the aqueducts Anio Novus and Marcia.[37]

A bronze *sestertius*, struck in Rome *ca.* 103–11, shows the reconstructed Circus Maximus, including details of the outer colonnade and the central obelisk.

Crisis Management

At any given time, there would inevitably be a number of crises in the provinces or in Rome. Border incursions, revolts, disease epidemics, food shortages and natural disasters were the usual causes. An emperor needed to act quickly to tackle such crises and implement policies to mitigate the risk of them occurring. In this period, the first major provincial crisis occurred in Egypt where severe drought brought the province to its knees. The River Nile was extremely low and the normal process of seasonal flooding had failed. As a result, the agricultural areas in the flood plains had turned into desert. The abundant fields of Egypt, which 'could rival the most fertile lands',[38] were suddenly barren. Trajan ordered the return of a portion of stored corn previously sent from Egypt to Rome and surplus produce, probably from Africa, was diverted there too.[39] These actions avoided famine and demonstrated that Rome was not at the mercy of Egypt for food supplies, which was a perception at the time.[40] Clearly Trajan's action was intended to give the message that Rome could and would support its provinces in time of need and not just collect tribute.

Subsidies

As well as benevolent gifts, regular subsidies to the people were a significant output of a general imperial policy to consider the lowly citizens of the empire, those very people on whom Rome had often relied to fill the ranks of its armies or work the fields. One subsidy already existed, called the *frumentationes*, which was the distribution of grain to the impoverished people of Rome. To boost its impact, Trajan enrolled an additional 5,000 free-born children to receive the *frumentationes*.[41] This additionally perpetuated the impression that Trajan was considerate of his lowly subjects, and nurtured a future pool of possible army recruits, which would also ultimately reduce the number of dependents on the state:

> The army and citizen body will be completed by their [the 5,000 children] numbers, and they will have children one day whom they will support themselves without any need of allowances.
>
> Pliny[42]

Another policy for aid was affirmed by Trajan in order to promote and enhance Nerva's *alimenta* scheme. It is possible that the 5,000 children mentioned above were a means to extend the *alimenta* to other families.[43] It is highly likely that money acquired from Trajan's future conquests sustained financing of the *alimenta*.

Two marble reliefs (*plutei Traiani*) were unearthed in 1872 in the Roman forum, one of which commemorated Trajan's *alimenta* programme for children.[44] Sat on a platform in front of the arched colonnade of the Basilica Julia, the emperor is receiving a symbolic woman with an infant on her left arm and leading another older child with her right (missing from the relief).

Law and Order

During the imperial era, a breed of informer had evolved that often proved useful to emperors who needed any sort of accusation to justify a sentence of treason. This ruthless custom was loathed and feared by senators who were vulnerable to the unscrupulous informers. The situation at the end of Domitian's reign had encouraged informers who could benefit from their accusations. No lie or betrayal was too low for them. Many informers were even senators.[45] Trajan despised these informers and acted by rounding up some of those who had survived Nerva's first purge. During the series of public games held in the Colosseum after his return to Rome, Trajan put on a treat for the crowd by parading all these informers in order to disgrace them publicly. Their heads were even forced back for all to see and jeer at.[46] Trajan then devised an appropriate end for them. He did not break his vow and execute the senators who were among the disgraced, but instead packed them all onto disabled ships and abandoned them to the mercy of the seas. Interestingly, the Emperor Titus had conducted a similar purging of informers during his reign. He had marched culprits into the forum for a brutal public beating and he then paraded them in the amphitheatre before either selling them as slaves or banishing them.[47] In addition, Trajan effectively banned informers. He also established specific investigators to track down and root out any other informers in the future.[48]

In the administration of justice, Trajan was diligent from the start with a 'scrupulous attitude towards equity'.[49] His days as a conscientious praetor in Rome had laid a solid foundation and he gave great attention to detail when judging or presiding over cases. He was credited as being tireless in these efforts.[50] He also empowered the praetors by delegating important cases to their courts and even addressed them as his colleagues when in court.

Finance

As we have seen, all Trajan's initial acts and policies required large expenditure: the cash gifts to the people and the army; public construction works; famine aid for Egypt; increasing the number of children who qualified for the grain dole; expansion of the *alimenta* system; lavish public games. A precise figure for the total costs cannot be established, but an order of magnitude estimate suggests that a figure in the range of 506 million *sestertii* was required in the early period of his reign over and above normal spending.[51]

With such munificence, reminiscent of Nerva's situation in the early part of his principate, how did Trajan maintain a balanced budget? The short answer is that he could not. The annual revenues from provincial tribute and empire-wide taxation provided around 800 million *sestertii* a year.[52] Normal annual expenditure on the army and other regular state requirements was around this level of revenue, meaning that his additional costs threatened a large deficit. As a result, Trajan had to draw on the reserves normally held in the coffers of temples that maintained precious metal resources. At the end of 99, Trajan approved debasement of the *aureus*, the standard gold coin, by around 5 per cent. Effectively, this meant 5 per cent more coinage could be generated from the existing gold bullion reserves.[53] In any event, he would have counted on the general healthy financial state of the empire to gradually restore a fiscal balance. He also knew that conquest was a proven way to generate wealth.

As all these fiscal acts were known to certain senators, the heavy spending did not pass unnoticed. Pliny actually referred to the situation in his speech to the Senate in front of Trajan in 100 and questioned how the situation could be maintained:

> You will bear with my anxieties, Caesar, my concern as consul. Your refusal to accept gifts of money, your distribution of the military bonus and civilian largesse, dismissal of informers and reduction of taxes – the thought of all this makes me feel I should ask you whether you have given due thought to the Empire's revenues. Are there sufficient resources to support the Emperor's economy and enable it to bear unaided the cost of paying out such sums?
>
> Pliny[54]

Posing this question to Trajan in front of the whole Senate demonstrated the new liberty felt by the senators under Trajan's reign. Pliny went on to provide the explanation in his speech for Trajan's apparent overspending by comparing Trajan to some of his predecessors who were thrifty with the empire's revenues in favour of their own greed. It was a polite and diplomatic way of saying that Trajan was in fact being too generous to the detriment of the treasury.

In conclusion, if one was a recognised Roman citizen in Rome, the new Trajanic age was first felt through the pleasing distribution of a large cash hand-out. A select proportion even had their children enrolled to receive the sought-after grain dole. Lavish public games would have distracted temporarily from the grind of the normal working day. In addition, after a while, the population of Rome would start to benefit from the improved infrastructure in roads and ports to bring goods and produce into the city. Many may have also had their debts to the state cancelled, a significant relief given the ruthless nature of debt collection at the time. Others could have benefited from reforms in inheritance tax exemptions. Countless people would have sighed in relief thanks to the policies outlawing informers. A very privileged few, friends and trusted confidants of Trajan, reaped the reward of promotion within the Senate. But, whoever they may have been, Trajan had instilled a generally positive mood in this initial period of his reign and the spirit of liberty in the Senate, initiated by Nerva, looked robust enough to flourish in this emerging Trajanic age. Consequently, if everyone felt more secure, from the plebeian working on the streets to the wealthy patrician delivering his rhetoric to the Senate, this new age was precisely the right environment for Trajan to engage freely in what Rome had been built on: war and conquest.

A gold *aureus*, struck in Rome in 111, shows Trajan standing with his right hand extended towards two children, representing the *alimenta*.

CHAPTER 7

TRAJAN'S FIRST DACIAN WAR

Justification for War

With rare exceptions, the defining strategy of Roman warfare was to seize the initiative through outright, relentless aggression.[1] This aggression was usually calculated in its intentions. To respect the senators, justifications for war were best outlined to the Senate in Rome, despite Trajan's supreme military authority over all Roman forces. It would have been a political blunder to do otherwise and besides, Trajan's principate was not portrayed as a blatant autocracy that disregarded and superseded the Senate.

Trajan justified war against Dacia for five main reasons. Firstly, in recent years Dacia had acted aggressively against Rome. Significantly, the Dacians had invaded Moesia in 84 without warning and wreaked destruction. Two years later, a retaliatory Roman force in Domitian's First Dacian War had been defeated by the Dacian King Decebalus and the Roman general Fuscus was killed in action. Domitian's Second Dacian War also failed to suppress Decebalus. In 89 while in a weak position, Rome was forced to agree to an unsatisfactory peace settlement to keep the Dacians out of the picture so that Domitian could conduct his First Pannonian War unhindered. Therefore, Decebalus and the Dacians needed to be punished for their recent track record against Rome.[2] A successful punitive war against the Dacians would restore Rome's pride.

Secondly, the same peace settlement of 89 between Rome and Dacia involved the payment of substantial annual subsidies to appease the Dacians. Trajan took exception to these subsidies, particularly given the use of these payments to fund fortifications evidently constructed to resist Rome.[3] Instead of acting as a reliable client kingdom in the receipt of subsidies, Dacia was giving a clear message that it still saw Rome as an immediate threat to its sovereignty. Moreover, Decebalus was using Roman engineers, also provided under the terms of the treaty, to build these same fortifications.

Thirdly, Dacia was receiving a considerable number of deserters from the Roman forces positioned along the Danube, perhaps enticing them by the promise of rewards. This was a menace because these deserters could train Dacian forces in the art of Roman warfare. This would improve the fighting capabilities of Dacian forces and allow Dacian commanders to better predict Roman tactics.

Besides the strategic rationale, the kingdom of Dacia was wealthy and its riches were an attractive and motivating factor for war. Gold and silver bullion, extracted from the plentiful mines across the Carpathian Mountains or taken from the royal treasuries, could provide enormous booty for the emperor's private purse and indirectly a proportion would reach the Roman people. An agreeable bonus of war – the fourth reason.

Fifthly, Dacia was increasing in regional stature. The lull of the peace period had allowed Decebalus to strengthen and expand the forces he could field. In addition, Decebalus and his emissaries were hard at work trying to secure allies against Rome.[4] This raised the threat level and potential potency of any future Dacian attacks. This was particularly important at this time because frontier security along the Danube was uncertain. Despite years of effort by Domitian to improve security along the border, the empire remained distinctly prone to full-scale attack from multiple tribes waiting in their masses beyond the river. Trajan's own careful review of the Danubian frontier had allowed him to identify its vulnerabilities at first hand. Rome had always coped with individual incursions, but multiple simultaneous invasions on more than one front were now a distinct possibility and we can reasonably assume that Rome was cognisant of such a threat. Trajan and his advisers may have foreseen devastating damage in this eventuality and perhaps even a major risk to Rome's authority in the western half of its empire. This risk was accentuated by Dacia's active diplomatic efforts to form alliances against Rome. Dacia could spearhead the first attack into Moesia and two additional fronts could open up if the Germanic Quadi and Marcomanni tribes launched offensives into Pannonia. Even a fourth front could be initiated should the nomadic Roxolani of the Danube region also seize the opportunity for offensive action. Instead, if Rome struck hard at Dacia now, it would subdue a key antagonist and well-resourced enemy, and in turn lessen the potential for widespread invasions across the Danube.

Trajan's reasons for waging war boiled down to a desire to punish Dacia and to bring it to yield to the might of Rome. Just as Domitian had previously envisaged, a successful war against Dacia would re-establish firm authority in the region as well as avenge the loss of Roman blood in previous conflicts. The success of Trajan's war would be straightforward to measure and there would be one goal: to subdue Dacia. The kingdom would then become an obedient client state and there would be no more need to pay it any subsidies. As the war will have been long discussed and premeditated, Trajan and his close advisers no doubt consulted the Senate to ensure the founding fathers of Rome were not ignored and because experienced senators might even have had something worthwhile to say. No one is known to have challenged Trajan.[5] In January 101, the emperor then accepted appointment as one of the *consules ordinarii*, his fourth consulship, perfect timing for the year when he planned to invade Dacia.

Whatever the actual reasons for war, Trajan appreciated the age-old Roman formulas of power. A general plus victory equated to hero status and authority but an emperor plus victory equated to divine power. The divine power from victory would cement his principate and affirm his place in history as one of Rome's greatest emperors, a motivating factor for war indeed.

Dacia and the Dacian People

At the start of the second century AD, the kingdom of Dacia had vast lands stretching over an area approximately corresponding to modern-day Romania and Moldova, as well as the eastern part of Hungary. The western side of the kingdom was adjacent to the Banat (Hungarian plain) with its expanses of open grasslands and rolling hills. Here the border of Dacia merged into the realms of the nomadic tribes who had settled in the Banat region. The northern and eastern fringes of the kingdom followed the arch of the outer eastern Carpathian mountain range with its peaks approximately half the height of the Alps. Beyond were the Roxolani tribes in the east and the Carpi in the north-east. The southern lands stretched down over the Oltenia and Wallachia districts, fertile agricultural areas situated north of the Danube and south of the southern Carpathians, where the southern fringes of the Dacian kingdom's influence were demarcated by the wide Danube River and the opposite southern bank belonged to Rome as part of the Moesian provinces. The Oltenia region was blessed with lush vegetation and numerous river valleys running south into the Danube, creating an undulating landscape of soft ridges and forested hills. The area of the Danube itself was rich in game and wildlife: eagles, wolves, bears, deer, wildcats and numerous river birds. Two large tributaries of the Danube in Oltenia and Wallachia were the Rhabo (Jiu) and Alutus (Olt) respectively. These large rivers with their wide flood plains served as valuable transport routes down to the Danube from the southern Carpathian passes.[6]

As a massive ring of natural defence, the horseshoe shape of the Carpathian Mountains was the inner shell of the kingdom, encapsulating what we call today the high Transylvanian plateau. In the heart of this horseshoe are the lower Orăştie Mountains (or Sureanu Mountains), which were the epicentre of the Dacian kingdom. This core region contained a mountain sacred to the Dacians: Mount Kogaionon.[7] In close proximity they founded a fortress city that became their capital: Sarmizegetusa Regia.[8]

In ethnicity, the peoples of Dacia were descendants of the Thracians and spoke an Indo-European language with presumably numerous dialects. It is thought that the word '*dacia*' meant wolf and the military standard of the Dacian people was the head of a wolf – the notorious Dacian Dragon that led them into battle.[9] As a society, groups of families constituted tribes and all the tribes across Dacia were amalgamated into a dominion under the sovereignty of a king. The king, Decebalus at this time, ruled with counsel from the heads of powerful tribes and priests.[10] No Dacian texts or inscriptions have been discovered, although some names have survived the centuries. The Dacians may not have had a literary tradition but they had a rich culture exemplified by their well-developed towns and cities as well as a complex social hierarchy. Ordinary Dacian tribesmen were known to the Romans as *comati* and wore their hair long, while the *pileati* formed the ruling class, the leading men of the tribes. As a symbol of their position, the *pileati* sported Phrygian felt caps which were worn with the top of the cap collapsed forward over the head.[11]

The Dacians recognised many gods, but were dedicated to one: Zalmoxis.[12] Believed to have lived as a man and been resurrected after his death, Zalmoxis became a god and his followers expected a transition into a blissful afterlife, rather than the finality of death. As a consequence, the Dacians were unafraid of death and this created a potent warrior mentality in which Dacian fighters were often content to fight to the bitter end. The Greek historian Herodotus records the mysterious rituals by which worshippers communicated with Zalmoxis.[13] Picked by lot, a person was given messages for Zalmoxis about the people's needs and requests and then sacrificed in order to deliver the messages personally to their god. The sacrifice itself entailed the erection of three spears, each supported by a man. Others would then grab the messenger and swing him into the air so that he would be impaled on the spears and expire. A clean death on the spears was regarded as an effective delivery of the messages to Zalmoxis, while a failed attempt at the sacrifice was interpreted as the messenger being corrupt and another was found to replace him. A high priest led the rites of Zalmoxis and was clearly important to the king, not only as a spiritual adviser, but as a powerful motivator of his warriors in times of war.

With their rich natural resources, particularly in the Transylvanian basin, Oltenia and Wallachia, the Dacians were able and productive arable and livestock farmers, even skilled in the cultivation of vines and in the art of beekeeping.[14] Fruits and vines grew well in the hills and the plains provided excellent agricultural conditions, while the lower mountains supported lush grasses ideal for grazing animals. Dacia was equally blessed with plentiful mineral deposits, in particular of gold, silver and iron. The Apuseni Mountains were the site of dozens of *aurariae Dacicae*, Dacian gold mines, which were actively worked to extract significant quantities of gold from the primary deposits. Further south, mines provided iron ore and others still more gold and silver. The abundance of these ores had provided the Dacians with the means to create advanced tools and weapons as well as establish great wealth. These resources had allowed the Dacians to trade with their refined Greek and Macedonian neighbours.[15] As a result, the Dacians acquired new technologies and the various wares of Hellenistic society. All this was a far cry from the false image of a barbarian people scratching a living from the Dacian countryside and pillaging all those in their path.

Roman Senior Command

The Dacian way of life, their culture and resources were now threatened by the imminent conflict with Rome. Their war would be against an enemy with a structured chain of command based on an arrangement of generals and senior officers who all served under Trajan as follows:

Imperator

Trajan was the supreme commander of all the Roman forces against Dacia. Major strategic decisions, and where possible approval for significant engagements with the enemy, would all have required Trajan's personal authorisation.

Generals

Generals were commonly governors, *legati Augusti,* of those provinces in the vicinity that provided military support for the campaigns.[16] Trajan therefore hand-picked his generals, based on experience and trust, and appointed them governors of the key provinces that would be involved in the ensuing war:

> *Caius Cilnius Proculus*   governor of Moesia Superior.
> *Manius Laberius Maximus*   governor of Moesia Inferior.
> *Glitius Atilius Agricola*   governor of Pannonia
> [just before the start of the war in 101 he replaced Servianus, who had been in place since his tour of the Danube with Trajan to prepare the province for conflict. Servianus was then presumably a special adviser for the initial phase of the war][17]

These three would have commanded forces derived from their provinces and answered only to Trajan.

Legati legionis

Commanders of individual legions reported to their appointed general and had direct mandates from the emperor. Also important were:

> PRAETORIAN GUARD PREFECT   One of the Praetorian Guard prefects at the time, Marcus Claudius Livianus, commanded the Guard, which acted as a powerful heavy infantry reserve.
> HORSE GUARD PREFECT   Commander of the emperor's personal mounted horse guard. This guard had superseded the Praetorian Guard for the immediate security and protection of the emperor and could be used as a cavalry reserve in extreme circumstances.

Advisers

An emperor's prerogative was to consider advice from his *comites*, the hand-picked advisers who could accompany him.[18] *Comites* were a core component of Trajan's military staff and they almost certainly convened when possible to discuss campaign actions and to advise the emperor closely on military matters, diplomacy and strategy. This group would have been in addition to the senior commanders described above, and it is likely that there were discussions involving both the formal commanders and the emperor's additional advisers:

Senecio	*Legatus pro praetore* (special post); experienced general and friend to Trajan.
Servianus	*Legatus pro praetore* (special post); experienced ex-governor of Pannonia just prior to the war and friend to Trajan.
Julius Quadratus Bassus	*Legatus pro praetore* (special post); trusted friend to Trajan.[19]
Sura	Special adviser and ambassador,[20] loyal friend; ex-governor of Germania Inferior.
Pompeius Longinus	Special adviser, trusted confidant, ex-governor of Moesia Superior and Pannonia.
Hadrian	Special observer (now married to Trajan's great-niece); ex-quaestor.
Lusius Quietus	Commander of the Mauretanian light cavalry.
Caius Manlius Felix[21]	Campaign quartermaster (responsible for supplies of the whole force; worked closely with the quartermasters of individual legions and auxiliary units).
Unknowns	Perhaps included select senior centurions (highly experienced centurions were invaluable advisers, experienced in combat tactics and the bloody practicalities of war).

Roman Forces

The list below includes units, at their full theoretical strength, that were part of the expeditionary force or used to maintain security in the region.

PANNONIAN FORCES[22]
    Legions: I *Adiutrix*, II *Adiutrix*, XIII *Gemina*, XV *Apollinaris*
        22,800 legionaries

MOESIA SUPERIOR FORCES[23]
    Legions: IV *Flavia Felix*, VII *Claudia*, XIV *Gemina Martia Victrix*
        17,100 legionaries

MOESIA INFERIOR FORCES[24]
    Legions: V *Macedonica*, I *Italica*
        11,400 legionaries

LEGIONS DRAFTED IN FROM OTHER PROVINCES[25]
    I *Minervia* (from Germania Inferior); XI *Claudia* (from Germania Superior); parts of IV *Scythica*, XII *Fulminata*, and an unknown legion (all from Syria)
        14,400 legionaries

PRAETORIAN GUARD
    Half the Guard (five cohorts)
        2,500 Praetorians

IMPERIAL HORSE GUARD
    Full contingent
        1,000 mounted men

AUXILIARIES[26]
    Infantry cohorts (including Syrian archers)
    Heavy and light cavalry
        ca. 65,000 (more infantry than cavalry)

NAVY[27]
    Danubian River Fleet (transport boats and attack vessels)
    Detachments of sea fleets
        ca. 1,000 men[28]

SYMMACHIARII (mercenaries recruited from client states or tribes)[29]
    Aestii (infantry)[30]
    Palmyrenes (infantry)
    Getae (infantry)
    Turncoat Dacians (infantry)
    Britons (infantry)
    Cantabri (infantry)
    Mauretanian light cavalry[31]
    Balearic slingers[32]
        4,800 men

Legionaries:	65,700
Praetorians:	2,500
Imperial Horse Guard:	1,000
Auxiliaries:	65,000
Sailors:	1,000
Symmachiarii:	4,800
GRAND TOTAL:	140,000

It should be noted that all theese numbers assume that a legion or given unit was at full fighting strength. However, this was rarely the case because of deaths, injuries, sickness, desertions, lack of recruitment and other causes. Therefore, the actual force would have been lower by perhaps 20 per cent or more. We will never know the true number. However, this was a very large Roman force concentrated for war. From this number, Trajan had to leave a significant portion behind in the participating provinces of Pannonia, Moesia Inferior and Moesia Superior to defend against incursions, maintain internal security and to act as reserves. Therefore, Trajan strategically selected a combination of legions, or parts of legions, from various locations where depletion would not overtly jeopardise the security of any given area. His campaign invasion force was probably around 30,000 legionary soldiers and an equivalent number of auxiliaries plus the *symmachiarii* and the Guards; giving a total of approximately 77,000 men[33] – a staggering proportion of Rome's military might. Trajan meant business and clearly wanted to avoid a drawn-out war due to a lack of resources.

Dacian Senior Command

Although no details survive today that describe the Dacian senior command, it is known that they lacked a professional structure similar to the Roman army and they relied on royalty and tribal chieftains to lead their forces.

The King	Decebalus, King of Dacia, was the commander-in-chief of all Dacian forces.
The King's sons	Decebalus' older sons were generals by right of their royalty.[34]
High Priest	The high priest to Zalmoxis was a powerful spiritual leader and highly influential in the command of Dacian forces.

Possibly still alive at this time, Vezina was the high priest present at the Battle of Tapae against the Romans in 88 and he would have been even more valuable to Decebalus given his experiences against Domitian's Roman army.

Pileati	As the ruling aristocracy and chiefs of Dacian tribes, the *pileati* formed the mainstay of senior command. The *pileati* of a given tribe likely led their own *comati* warriors (see below). *Pileati* from the largest tribes held the most seniority and were probably generals alongside Decebalus' sons.

Council of war   Decebalus probably held councils of war in order to discuss strategy and military action as well as issue orders to his generals and senior chiefs. The high priest to Zalmoxis was also an integral part of this council. Roman deserters may have also contributed on aspects of Roman military tactics.

Dacian Forces & Allies
Comati

Each tribe contributed a force of infantrymen derived from the common male population, the *comati*. The size of the contribution depended on the size of the tribe. In peace time, the *comati* worked the lands, but when mustered for war they were fierce warriors. However, this ferocious nature in battle was let down by a distinct lack of helmets or body armour for the majority of *comati*, although each man may have had at least an oval shield. In contrast, the *pileati* chiefs were better protected with helmets and body armour.[35] The warriors' principal weapon was the falx, a two-handed battle scythe. This weapon was particularly effective at inflicting terrifying wounds on vulnerable limbs and its hooked pointed end could even pierce a Roman helmet. The Romans were later forced to strengthen their helmets against the falx with the addition of iron crossbar braces and some adopted additional armour to protect their forearms. A few *comati* were armed with advanced composite bows, technology acquired through lucrative trading between Dacia and the East. A small proportion were assigned to manage battle rams and ballistic catapults, either captured from the Romans in previous conflicts or built for the Dacians by Roman engineers provided under the terms of the peace treaty of 89 with Rome.

Total *comati* warriors: *ca.* 75,000[36]

Allies
Roxolani

A division of the Sarmatian people, the Roxolani were Iranian nomads who had settled north of the lower Danube River.[37] They had become an increasing nuisance and threat to Rome in the later years of the eighties, which had culminated in the destruction of a legion during a Roxolanian raid into Moesia. The Roxolani joined Decebalus against Rome in Trajan's First Dacian War and fielded heavy cavalry with both the horse and rider sturdily protected by intricate scale armour and each rider provided with a conical metal helmet, sword and a long lance.[38] These heavy cavalry were able to use shock tactics that could even break a disciplined line of Roman legionaries. In tandem, Roxolanian horse archers, each rider similarly protected by scale armour, provided a lethal accompaniment to the shock tactic – striking hard with their bows and then swiftly retreating to repeat the action again.

Total Roxolanian cavalry: around 9,000.[39]

Bastarnae

To the north of the Roxolani, the Bastarnae were of mixed Germanic–Celtic ethnicity. Hostile to the Romans, the Bastarnae sided with Dacia against Trajan and provided warriors with a good fighting reputation.

Total Bastarnae warriors: *ca.* 5,000.

Buri

The Buri were a Germanic tribe with similar language and culture to the Suebic Germanic tribes like the Quadi and Marcomanni. They lived along the north-eastern rim of the Carpathian Mountains in the Vistula river valley.[40]

Total Buri warriors: *ca.* 5,000.

Dacians:	75,000
Allies:	19,000
GRAND TOTAL:	94,000

Strengths & Weaknesses of the Roman and Dacian Forces
Roman Strengths

Discipline & training	Superior organisation and formation. Reliable fighting tactics.
Flexibility	Not only able to field forces for large scale pitched battles, but also smaller-scale guerrilla style actions.
Relentless nature	Roman forces rarely provided the enemy with opportunities for recuperation.
Legionary arms & armour	State-of-the-art body protection and highly protective surround shield. Javelin combined with short thrusting sword for attack.
Chain of command	Efficient issuing of pre-battle orders and enhanced discipline.

Use of reserves	Standard tactic of reserving forces for specific times of need.
Sieges	Expert siege warfare and engineering capabilities.

Roman Weaknesses

Vulnerable to ambush	Legionaries in close formation were particularly vulnerable in heavily forested areas.
Supply chain	Fielding large complex forces necessitated a sophisticated and reliable supply chain of provisions that was vulnerable to attack when over-extended.
Head protection	Initially susceptible to the hooked end of the Dacian falx able to punch through helmets.
Arm protection	The long reach of the falx inflicted serious injury to exposed limbs.

Dacian Strengths

Familiar terrain	An intricate knowledge of the topography and environment provided tactical and strategic advantages.
Defending existence	Highly motivated force defending their kingdom, tribal honour, homes and families.
Allies	Alliances with Roxolani and Bastarnae to the north-east and east.
Guerrilla tactics	Familiarity with the terrain supported guerrilla tactics.

Dacian Weaknesses

Poor protection	Majority of forces with little or no head or body armour.
Weak discipline	Poor tactical control and therefore less ability to cope with the disciplined efficiency of Roman pitched-battle warfare.
No western allies	Iazyges sided with Romans allowing access through Banat region to the Iron Gates Pass.

Roman Offensive Campaign I

Trajan's vast invasion force was mustered at Viminacium, the prosperous capital of Moesia Superior (now Kostolac in Serbia). Trajan had arrived in the theatre of operations in April 101, having left Rome in March. After reviewing the condition of his mustered force with his three generals, Proculus, Maximus and Atilius Agricola, he convened his senior officers and issued the first major order of the war: at the start of the campaign season in May, the force was to rendezvous, cross the Danube and advance on a single front from the west on the Dacian capital via the Iron Gates Pass in the Carpathian Mountains.[41]

Consequently, as the signs of spring emerged, Trajan led his force northeast along the Danube to the town of Lederata. Here, military engineers had prepared two vast pontoon bridges over the Danube. The two bridges were constructed by securing together two long lines of large river boats and building wooden pontoons across the decks between each boat.[42] At the head of the Roman host, Trajan led his mighty army across the makeshift bridges. For an entire day, the force crossed over and moved into marching camps beyond the northern bank.

At the start of a campaign, according to tradition, the *suovetaurilia*, or sacred sacrifice, was performed in the presence of Trajan, dressed in a toga with a fold of cloth pulled over his head to symbolise his role as Pontifex Maximus. The *suovetaurilia* involved the sacrifice of a bull, a ram and a boar in honour of Mars, the god of war. This purified the Roman army for the upcoming campaign and was intended to invoke the blessing of Mars.

After Trajan and his generals addressed sections of the army and other officers then conveyed the sentiments of these speeches to other divisions, the Roman column initially marched north up the Apus (Carasu) river valley. The army followed a specific marching order when campaigning. In the front, auxiliaries fanned out in scouting parties responsible for detecting ambushes and identifying enemy locations. Behind them the vanguard was composed of legionary soldiers with cavalry support. Next followed ten men selected from each century of a legion with the tools required to mark out and begin construction of the marching field camps, and behind them the Roman legionary engineers who could be called up to clear the way of obstacles or bridge rivers for the subsequent main marching column. Then followed Trajan, his generals and select senior officers or advisers like Livianus, Senecio, Bassus, Sura and Longinus with all their baggage, closely followed by the imperial Horse Guard and the Praetorian Guard. The combined legionary cavalry then followed ahead of the siege equipment, carried by a vast mule train. The legates, camp prefects and tribunes came next with all the remaining legions. Then followed the *symmachiarii* and auxiliaries and, finally, the rearguard, a composite force of infantry and cavalry.[43] A number of columns, each several kilometres long, made up the overall advancing host.

The march plan was the same each day. Breaking camp started before dawn and ended with the construction of a new temporary marching camp before dusk. Given the size of the force, the rearguard would commence its march when the vanguard had already arrived at the site agreed by the surveyors for the night's camps. As the force advanced, contingents of men were stationed along the route to assist in the maintenance and protection of the essential supply line. Although some provisions were carried by individual soldiers, supplemented by foraging en route, the supply line was absolutely critical to bringing a continuous flow of provisions up to the column from the supporting provinces that were themselves receiving extra supplies from across the empire to maintain the enormous invading army.[44] It was certainly one of Trajan's main roles to ensure such an uninterrupted and reliable supply chain to his extended forces.

Early during the march north, a strange form of message was delivered to Trajan. Mounted on a mule, a messenger from the Buri, allied to the Dacians, brought a very large mushroom cap or tree fungus to Trajan. On the top of the fungus, scratched into the smooth fleshy surface, a message had been written to the emperor. We will never know the details of this message, but one can assume that it warned Trajan to withdraw or pay the consequences.[45] Unperturbed, Trajan and his forces continued their advance.

The advance proceeded at a steady pace, probably covering around fifteen to twenty miles a day, up the Apus valley with the distant foothills of the Carpathian Mountains looming on the north-eastern horizon. The Romans faced little or no threat on their western flank because of their alliance with the Iazyges at this time. The column proceeded north before turning east into the upper valley of the Tibiskos (Timis) River. Here Trajan's army was strategically well situated at the interface between the Banat region and the rising Carpathian Mountains that protected the Dacians beyond. It was also a good position between the route they had just taken from Viminacium and another, some way to the east, which went due north from Dierna on the Danube along the Cerna River valley.[46] To the army's immediate east, within a day's striking distance, lay the Iron Gates Pass and from there access to the valley beyond and the inner core of Dacia. The region around the Iron Gates Pass was known to the Romans because it was the site of the First Battle of Tapae between Domitian's forces and the Dacians in 88.

Along the route just travelled from Viminacium, Trajan had ordered the construction of permanent forts at various key locations, and also at their present location which would later become the Roman town of Tibiscum (Jopta). This would not only solidify Roman presence in the Banat but also enhance communication and protect supplies along the route back to Viminacium. To reach the vicinity of Tibiscum, Trajan had covered around 145 km which, at their cautious pace was a five-day march from the crossing at Lederata. At this stage, it was likely Trajan decided to take stock of his advance and assess the security of the area through careful scouting and in particular to acquire as much information as possible about the Dacian defences around the Iron Gates Pass to the east. Trajan probably spent the middle part of May seeking optimal conditions and preparing for the imminent engagement with the Dacians in the first major battle of the war.

The Second Battle of Tapae

Domitian's general Julianus had narrowly defeated the Dacians at the First Battle of Tapae in 88. Thirteen years later, Trajan was about to face the Dacians in the same region for another major battle. Trajan and his senior commanders and advisers, well read in the military history of the region, would have been familiar with accounts of the first battle and these would have guided their tactics. Roman scouts returning from their reconnaissance missions informed Trajan that the Dacians were massed in defensive positions around the Iron Gates Pass and battle could commence once favourable ground was selected and appropriately cleared of obstacles by legionary engineers.

Topography

The exact location of Tapae remains unknown today, but it may refer to the region around the Iron Gates Pass including the valleys immediately east and west of the pass. The Iron Gates Pass itself was the last pass in the west before one entered the inner core of the Dacian kingdom. Between the Roman camps around Tibiscum and the Iron Gates Pass, lay the Bistra river valley, surrounded on both sides by the heavily forested high ridges of the Carpathian Mountains. Moving from west to east, the increasingly narrow Bistra valley rises up with narrow outcrops of rock dotted along the valley floor. Here Roman engineers would have cleared any obstructions, including areas of trees, to create open spaces suitable for a full-scale pitched battle if planned in that vicinity. Closer to the Iron Gates Pass, the valley narrows into a ravine rising up sharply to the pass itself, which is a tight gorge through the Carpathian Mountains offering access only to a narrow column.

Presumably, Dacian fortifications strengthened the wooded area of the pass as well as the valley plain immediately beyond. These areas closer to the pass were not suitable for the Romans to form up for open battle, so they would only have accepted a full-scale engagement in the cleared areas further back. Perhaps confident of his forces and his ability to learn from previous conflicts, Decebalus sensed that the conditions were also favourable from his perspective. He could move into these cleared areas and if necessary draw back into the pass, which he knew the Romans could not breach without passing through a narrow and vulnerable gap – in modern military terms, defiling. In addition, Decebalus could use the elevation to his advantage, moving his warriors down the slopes of the Bistra valley.

Engagement

On the morning of the battle, the Romans and Dacians formed up for what is now known as the Second Battle of Tapae, though it may have taken several such deployments on preceding days before each side was convinced it had the best conditions to engage. It was now probably towards the end of May 101. Having considered all the latest intelligence details, the tactical factors and the landscape of the battle arena, Trajan issued final orders to his commanders, almost certainly at a meeting of senior officers immediately prior to the battle.

We can never be certain of the exact Roman formations, but evidence from Trajan's Column in Rome, which depicts the war and remains standing to this day, suggests that the legionary cohorts formed up in the centre in a disciplined array across the cleared terrain of the valley with reserves held further back. Even deeper in reserve, the Praetorians were ready in their positions.[47] The forefront of the Roman position was held by the auxiliary infantry with support from the *symmachiarii* mercenaries.[48] The Roman cavalry was stationed on the wings. The whole arrangement was a classic Roman formation for open battle; the auxiliaries, more expendable than legionary soldiers, could open the fighting and when the enemy was sufficiently disrupted or the auxiliaries needed support the legions would move in, protected on the flanks by the swift-moving cavalry columns.

Reserves were held back at all times unless critical gaps emerged to be plugged with reinforcements. Trajan, accompanied by some of his generals and senior commanders, likely remained at a key vantage point within the Roman formation.

The Dacians formed up in front of the Romans probably with only a few hundred metres between the two opposing forces, and they likely kept their own reserves along the fringes of the open areas in order to rush out when needed. Decebalus remained at the rear in a wooded area but presumably with a good view of the battleground.[49]

Trumpet signals rang out and, in a disciplined and coordinated manner, the Roman auxiliaries and *symmachiarii* moved forward for the opening skirmishing with the Dacian *comati*, while the Roman cavalry moved to begin harassing the Dacian flanking positions. Meanwhile, the legions waited for the order to move forward. Gradually, the skirmishing shifted into a full-scale frontal engagement and the Roman auxiliaries successfully managed to drive a wedge into the Dacian formations with support from the *symmachiarii*.[50] According to the homeland customs of certain auxiliary units, the heads of slain Dacians were taken as trophies and even raised in honour for Trajan to witness. The trophy was prized to the extent that a slayer would reportedly bite the hair of the severed head in his mouth so that he could then fight on.[51] As the grim wedge of the auxiliaries and the *symmachiarii* tipped the advantage to the Romans, Trajan likely gave the order for the legions to move forward. Like a chainsaw cutting down anything in its path, the Roman legions tore into the Dacian force. First the legionary lines released a volley of javelins to shock and injure the Dacians as well as break the ferocity of any of their charges, then they engaged in a well-ordered attack using their short swords to make lethal stabbing thrusts out from behind their broad shields. Legionaries could be relied on to execute orders with discipline and their lines were less likely to waver than other units. The centurions, steadfast in their leadership and bravery, were the backbone on the battlefield, consistently directing their respective centuries as well as engaging in hand-to-hand combat along with the legionaries.

The Dacians fought fiercely and the long reach of their curved falx swords inflicted considerable causalities upon the Romans. The Dacians also used archery,[52] acquired through trade in the east. Volleys of arrows were fired into the Roman lines, perhaps somewhat unexpected by Trajan, who may have been unaware that the Dacians had acquired the same composite bow technology that his own forces possessed.[53]

During the battle, a storm drew in. This was not untypical for the region at that time of the year, as warm rising air and high levels of atmospheric moisture could create quickly moving storm fronts that unleashed heavy rain, lightning and thunder. This would be inspiring for the Romans: lightning was the tool of their mighty god, Jupiter, and the conditions may have increased their vigour despite the greater slipperiness underfoot and reduced visibility.[54] As the battle unfolded and the storm continued, it is quite possible that Trajan and senior commanders may have taken considerable personal risk by moving closer to the fighting lines at critical locations to observe conditions closely and direct reserves accordingly.[55]

Under the Roman onslaught, the Dacians were eventually unable to hold their positions and their lines began to break. Picking up their injured comrades where possible, the Dacians presumably fell back in good order and up to safer higher ground and the wooded areas around the Iron Gates Pass. Decebalus realised the battle was lost and issued a general order to retreat. The Second Battle of Tapae was a success for the Romans and cries of victory would have spread out across the Roman lines. Trajan received salutes and triumphal cheers as he moved through his force inspecting the scale of casualties and congratulating his men. Surely brimming with pride, Trajan had overseen his first major victory as *imperator*. He was forty-four years old.

Roman Consolidation and Dacian Counter-Offensives

It is probable that the Romans were able to force through the Iron Gates Pass in the wake of the Dacian defeat and establish control over the narrow gorge. However, the Dacians were by no means beaten and still able to offer considerable resistance and mount counter-offensives in the areas east of the pass. Trajan recognised their remaining strength and instead of dashing east across the Hațeg plain beyond the pass and into the Orăștie Mountains to strike at the heart of Dacia, he wisely opted to consolidate his position after his victory at Tapae. This prudent approach was the hallmark of a seasoned military mind. Instead, one can postulate that only reconnaissance activities were carried out on the Hațeg Plain beyond the pass during a period of consolidation for Trajan's main force in the Bistra River Valley to the west of the pass.

Consequently, as the Dacians pulled back into the surrounding mountains, along tracks and passes known only to them, the Romans torched abandoned buildings and Trajan took the opportunity to review Dacian defences in the area. One example that he inspected included a high stone wall on which skulls were displayed on stakes, perhaps Romans who had fallen in the First Battle of Tapae. The tails of Dacian dragon standards flowed in the wind among raised watchtowers behind the wall. In front of the wall, pits laced with sharpened stakes, known as *lilia*, or lilies, were intended to hinder assaults against the ramparts.[56] These defences were well noted by Trajan and his commanders as the type of barricade they would encounter in the remainder of the campaign, as they edged ever closer to the Dacian capital.

As part of this consolidation phase, Dacian forces were pursued by divisions of Roman units to the east of the Iron Gates Pass, possibly operating out of Roman camps in the Bistra river valley between the large Roman base at Tibiscum to the west and the pass to the east. Roman occupation of the pass after the battle would allow such movement. Roman cavalry swept across the countryside putting all in their path to fire and the sword.[57] Auxiliaries and legionaries spread out in relentless searches for Dacian positions.[58] In time, Roman bases for offensive operations would have been established to the east of the pass on the Hațeg plain. Few geographical obstacles were allowed to bar their way; for example, legionaries stripped naked to wade across rivers in their paths with their armour and weapons cradled in the curve of their shields carried above their heads.[59]

In addition, the constant diligent construction of roads and fortifications established the necessary infrastructure to stamp Roman authority firmly throughout the eastern Banat region. Meanwhile, Trajan addressed his troops and received Dacian *comati* as delegates of tribes possibly trying to broker peace terms.[60] Either as a result of the discussions with the delegates or on his own initiative to demonstrate his clemency, Trajan also gave orders that women and children should be spared in the sweeping consolidation sorties.[61] Given the savage nature of ancient warfare, this order from Trajan was probably a smokescreen for the reality of high civilian causalities during the war.

Around this time, General Maximus brought Trajan a coveted prize: a sister of Decebalus captured alive.[62] As expected for a captive of royal blood, Trajan approved her transfer back to Rome to remain under house arrest, probably until the end of her days. Her safety would therefore become a persuasive tool when negotiations opened with Decebalus. As the military consolidation continued through June and July, Trajan likely returned to Viminacium, escorted by his Imperial Horse Guard, delegating authority to his generals to continue to stabilise conquered Dacian territory prior to advancing deeper into Dacia later in the war. At Viminacium, Trajan was better connected with matters in Rome that might require his attention, and he could review the reserve forces retained in the region.

During this consolidation phase of the campaign at the height of summer in 101, the Dacian infantry and cavalry initially fled back across their own lands. In the panic, one Dacian cavalry column suffered heavy causalities trying to cross a treacherous river.[63] Yet despite such confusion and losses, Decebalus was able to rally and engage in counter-offensive actions that capitalised on the lull.[64] Various Roman forts were stormed, sometimes using battering rams, under protective covering fire from Dacian archers.[65]

With the news of Decebalus' counter-offensives, Trajan recognised the need to regain the initiative and return to the front line. He and his Guards may have travelled swiftly from Viminacium to Dierna using the naval fleet to sail downstream on the Danube and through the Djerdap Gorge with its rapidly flowing currents.[66] Messages were sent ahead for Roman forces to rendezvous with Trajan along his path due north from Dierna, with the objective of crushing any Dacian counter-offensives en route. This course from Dierna would have brought Trajan into the vicinity of Tibiscum and the Bistra River Valley from a more easterly direction, perhaps offering some element of strategic surprise given it was not the established route from Viminacium to Tibiscum.

Not afraid to immerse himself in the thick of action, Trajan led the swiftly moving column on horseback, his foot infantry marching at a pace of up to 40 km a day to stay within range. Firstly, from Dierna they moved north up the Cerna River valley. The terrain was rough, its dense deciduous woods rising up steeply on both sides before giving way to towering vertical faces of rock only broken by other narrow tributaries flowing into the Cerna. The route then left the Cerna valley to rise up and across into a wider open plain, lush with vegetation at the height of summer. On both sides of the plain, the high forested ridges of the Carpathian Mountains loomed in the distance with some of the highest peaks of the entire range, exceeding 2,000 metres, on their eastern side.[67] Gradually the plain narrowed as the mountains funnelled in towards the modern-day town of Teregova, which offered a route north through to Tibiscum beyond.

On this route from Dierna, Trajan's cavalry scouts informed him they had located a sizable force of Roxolanian heavy cavalry and mounted archers, allied to the Dacians.[68] This would have been far west relative to the Roxolanian region, but presumably they were fully exploiting the war to venture and raid westwards. With a clear advantage, Trajan ordered engagement and the Roman cavalry moved in to attack. Despite their heavy armour, the Roxolanians were overwhelmed by the Roman cavalry and defeated.[69] Next, the position of a Dacian infantry force was identified and subjected to a surprise attack. The camp was assaulted by the Romans under the cover of darkness. Surrounded and surprised, the defenders tried in vain to repel the Roman cavalry, auxiliaries and *symmachiarii*. All the Dacians were likely slaughtered and recaptured booty found in the camp was piled high in wagons.[70]

Trajan arrived back in the Bistra valley. His forces in the area had presumably dealt with the Dacian counter-offensives and now the emperor rallied his troops for another major engagement. Decebalus knew that he needed to make another stand against Trajan. The Tapae region was again selected because both sides recognised its symbolic, tactical and strategic advantages: for the Romans, it was within the Bistra River valley and included the zone of consolidation they had invested so much in securing; for the Dacians, it was part of their homeland to win back.[71]

It was probably around September by this time and the campaign season was closing rapidly as the days drew shorter and colder. Decebalus recognised that he needed to throw the bulk of his forces against Trajan and win a battle to stand any real chance of a good outcome to the war. To this end, he planned to break the Roman hold around Tibiscum and storm the new Roman positions in the eastern Banat region.

The Third Battle of Tapae

To win a major engagement in ancient warfare normally required a heavy commitment of troops to the battlefield. Experienced commanders like Trajan and Decebalus were cognisant of the devastating losses such a commitment could incur if events turned against them. Thus, as the two great armies readied themselves for battle, efforts at diplomacy still prevailed. Unusually for Trajan, prior to the battle, he gave audience to an embassy of Dacian *pileati*, inside the compound of a Roman camp. In the end, diplomacy failed and overtures from the Dacians were rejected. In all probability, Trajan sensed that his disciplined force would succeed and he knew that only an unambiguous victory would bring him true credit in Rome. Therefore, following a favourable review of the latest intelligence obtained from reconnaissance sorties and extracted from captured Dacian warriors, Trajan instructed his generals to prepare for battle.

Topography

In a similar manner to the Second Battle of Tapae, Trajan and Decebalus sought suitable locations in the vicinity that suited their battle plans. Only when both sides were satisfied, each thinking that they had the best possible positions under the right conditions, did the final orders go out to form up for battle. Even then, doubt on either side could frequently result in the assembled forces stepping down without any engagement.

Engagement

Aware of the high stakes, Trajan no doubt recognised that this would be the most important battle of the war so far, and crushing the Dacians at this point would essentially allow the Romans to advance on the inner core of the Dacian kingdom, the Orăştie Mountains, relatively unhindered. As a result, Trajan in all probability planned to take no unnecessary risks, forming up his force in the same classic arrangement as for the Second Battle of Tapae, banking on tactics, discipline and technical advantages in armour and weaponry to gain superiority in the field.

Again, the battle was begun by skirmishing between the Roman auxiliaries and Dacian infantry. Decebalus and his warriors were a resilient match for the Romans, and the fighting lines ebbed and flowed according to the strength, stamina and courage of the particular units engaged. At a critical moment, Trajan issued the order for his legions to move in, perceiving that their heavy infantry abilities were needed. The morale of units was also a pivotal factor for the outcome of the battle. As a professional army, the Roman legionaries were paid for their service and they fought for the honour of their unit and legion, for the emperor and the glory of Rome. No doubt many were scared as their line approached the Dacian hordes, while other more battle-hardened men were better able to close out fearful thoughts. Roman centurions were particularly known to play a key role in driving their men forward and leading by example in combat. The Dacians fought for their kingdom and the protection of their homes, for the honour of their tribe and king, and also for their families under threat from the invading Romans. With little fear of death in their culture, the Dacians fought fiercely as waves of well-organized legionary soldiers advanced relentlessly.

Casualties were heavy on both sides. The clean and swift stab of the Roman short sword was often a fatal injury and the Dacian falx inflicted particularly horrific wounds to the unprotected limbs of an opponent. Injured Roman troops and officers were not left to bleed to death on the battlefield, though. The Roman army had sophisticated combat medical aid for the period, unsurpassed until the nineteenth century. In dedicated field dressing stations, doctors (*medici*), and their assistants and orderlies tended to the wounded.[72] In this, the bloodiest of battles in the war so far, extra medical support was further provided by regular soldiers, presumably given minimal training in first aid.[73] The principal function of the medical staff during the battle was to remove any foreign bodies from the site of wounds, to stem the flow of blood or to amputate a limb. Next, the injury was cleaned and dressed in bandages. Many wounded would later succumb to fatal wound infections and sepsis. Given the scale of the battle and the high level of causalities, one or more of the field dressing stations exhausted its supply of bandages. Possibly near such a station, Trajan demonstrated great consideration for his injured men in an act that would have earned him much respect from his soldiers and was later recorded by a Roman historian,

> And when the bandages gave out, [Trajan] is said not to have spared even his own clothing, but to have cut it up into strips.
>
> Dio Cassius[74]

The *medici* may have even tried to alleviate pain for those suffering acutely. A wide range of analgesics and sedatives could have been prescribed, including opium poppy (morphine). Probably not without their own forms of compounds or remedies for pain relief, the Dacians were, however, far less fortunate than the Romans in their level of battlefield medical aid, and Dacian fatalities from injuries were likely significantly higher than for the Romans.

Continuously vigilant throughout the battle, Trajan personally interrogated Dacian prisoners, even as the battle still raged to try and determine the objectives and strengths of the enemy.[75] Where necessary, Trajan would have issued further orders to capitalise on any new information gained or to react to emerging dynamics of the mêlée. However, one must recognise that, once battle commenced, it was very hard to change orders in the confusion of combat.

As the battle drew on, exhausted combat lines retreated, creating lulls in the fighting so that fresher ranks could come forward and those seriously wounded be pulled back.[76] Gradually, the cycles of short fierce engagement and respites in fighting revealed the superior integrity of the Roman lines, presumably thanks to a combination of their discipline, skills, morale and better protection. Trajan edged towards victory. The legionaries and auxiliaries began to break the Dacian formations and the *comati* warriors became increasingly vulnerable and in places were probably outflanked.[77] All the time, Roman missile weapons harassed Dacian positions, inflicting injury and death.[78] In particular, *carroballistae,* mounted on carts, were drawn by mules into vantage points. These giant crossbows, powered by bundles of coiled cord, were capable of firing large bolts over considerable distances.[79]

As the Dacian momentum collapsed, their ground taken and formations broken up, with the slain and injured mounting all around them, the realisation that the battle was lost triggered sections of the Dacian force to retreat, and again Decebalus reluctantly issued a general order to withdraw. In greater disorder than in the retreat after the previous battle, the Dacians fled into the surrounding mountains and the Roman cavalry swept forward to mop up as many fleeing Dacians as possible.[80] Trajan had his decisive victory.

End of the First Campaign Season

In the immediate aftermath of the Third Battle of Tapae, Trajan addressed divisions of his men to congratulate them on their victory and to boost morale. Cavalry, auxiliaries and legionaries alike surrounded the emperor to hear his addresses, with unit standards proudly erected around the raised tribunal from which Trajan spoke. Later, Trajan sat on a similar tribunal and heard the evidence of deeds of bravery and honour undertaken by some of his men in the battle. Rewards were appropriately issued and the emperor's right hand was extended for the recipient of the reward to kiss. Fellow comrades observing the reward ceremony applauded. Other spectators kissed and embraced each other, perhaps recognising a close comrade who survived the battle, or to acknowledge a just reward at the ceremony.

Notably, the dependable Servianus, governor of Pannonia just prior to the war, and Trajan's most trusted friend Sura, who had both acted as special advisers in the first campaign, were rewarded by appointment as the next *consules ordinarii* and they probably left for Rome at the close of the campaign season in 101 to take up these posts in January of the following year. Trajan reshuffled his generals at this time and his friend Neratius Priscus replaced Atilius Agricola as governor of Pannonia while Senecio replaced Proculus as governor of Moesia Superior. Hadrian, who had accompanied Trajan closely during the campaign, gaining more intimacy with the emperor and perhaps even picking up Trajan's habit of heavy drinking,[81] also left for Rome to brief the Senate on the events of the first campaign season as part of his duties as a special observer of the war.[82]

Meanwhile, Dacian prisoners were rounded up from the battle, destined to become slaves or trophies of war for execution or combat in Rome's amphitheatres. In an equally unforgiving manner, Roman captives from the battle were likely taken away by the Dacians for torture, execution or long-term imprisonment. At this time, Decebalus doubtless sought advice from the leading *pileati* to decide the next steps after their defeat at Tapae, and routed *comati* warriors were regrouped at defensive positions within the core of Dacian territory. The situation for Decebalus was desperate, but the changing season would come to his aid. The closing campaign season around the end of September meant that Trajan was unable to press on towards the Dacian capital to the east. But this advance was only a postponement, as the emperor and his armies would return in earnest in the following year with plans to crush the remaining Dacian positions in the Hațeg region and in the Orăștie Mountains.

The Dacian defeat at the Third Battle of Tapae was a turning point in the war. They had failed to break Trajan's force and overrun the commanding Roman positions in the Banat. They had relinquished their hold over the Tapae area and the Iron Gates Pass. Effectively, Trajan had won the war. He had defeated the main force that Decebalus could field in open battle and the next campaign season would be about how long the Dacians could resist the Romans from their entrenched positions.

Roman Offensive Campaign II

Having wintered at various quarters along the Danube and with two victories over the Dacians at Tapae on their list of achievements, Trajan and his generals had reasonable justification to anticipate that the upcoming campaign season would bring closure to Trajan's Dacian war. A methodical and cautious approach would remain at the heart of their offensive strategy and the capital of Dacia, Sarmizegetusa Regia, and surrounding mountain-top forts were the principal targets in the second campaign.

With the coming of new spring growth in April 102, Trajan and his army again built temporary bridges to cross over the Danube into camps to the north,[83] and the sacrifices of the *suovetaurilia* ceremony were made once more to purify the army before advancing into enemy territory. Since the Romans had already taken control of Tapae from the Dacians and breached the Iron Gates Pass, the offensive column probably proceeded through the Roman-held regions in the Banat directly to the pass and beyond, using en route the network of Roman forts established in the first campaign.[84]

Beyond the pass, the Roman column advanced into the Haţeg plain and it must have been an impressive sight, as it is today, to see the stunning countryside of the plain open up rapidly. Along its southern border loomed the sharply rising Retezat Mountains and, on the opposite side, the Poiana Rusca Mountains which bulged out into the plain. Divisions of Trajan's light auxiliary cavalry and infantry branched off to assault villages and fortifications while the main column pressed forward, bringing the Romans within striking distance of the Dacian strongholds in the Orăştie Mountains that protected Sarmizegetusa Regia.[85]

Fully aware of the imposing Roman advances, Decebalus resorted to diplomacy in addition to continued resistance, and he sent out a group of envoys to speak with Trajan. Brought forward before Trajan, an envoy on his knees pleaded with the emperor to accept an audience with Decebalus or to send a Roman official to speak directly with him.[86] Sensing the value of the plea, Trajan sent Sura and Livianus his Praetorian Guard Perfect, to negotiate with the Dacian king. The mission was subsequently aborted because Decebalus failed to attend the negotiations in person, sending again his intermediary envoys.[87] Decebalus may have been bluffing about his desire for a peace settlement in order to buy valuable time.

Undeterred by the wasted negotiations, Trajan continued his strategy of widespread assaults on surrounding Dacian positions and pockets of resistance. At this juncture, a Dacian stronghold captured by the Romans led to a valuable discovery. Roman military equipment and a sacred legionary standard lost in the defeat of the Roman General Fuscus by Decebalus (in 84) were recovered. It was a great honour for Trajan and his troops to reclaim the prize and equally important to restore Roman pride since the defeat.

As spring turned to summer in 102, the Roman hold over the Haţeg plain strengthened and the first line of Dacian defences in the Orăştie Mountains was gradually overrun. Roman legionaries then constructed more permanent fortifications using wood and stone, and the growing network would have supported supply routes and critical lines of communication.[88] The multi-functional capabilities of the Roman force were proving highly effective in specific operations, gaining tactical advantages. For example, to execute a decisive flanking manoeuvre, Trajan ordered Lusius Quietus, commander of the Mauretanian light cavalry, to rapidly attack the Dacians in the Orăştie Mountains. The unit was perfect for such an operation. Lightly armed, highly skilled bare-back riders, they could negotiate some of the narrow ravines and steep climbs of the mountain range. It is likely that separate cavalry columns

Marble bust of Trajan, from around 108. This is one of the finest surviving busts and shows him with his hair brushed forward for a military appearance.

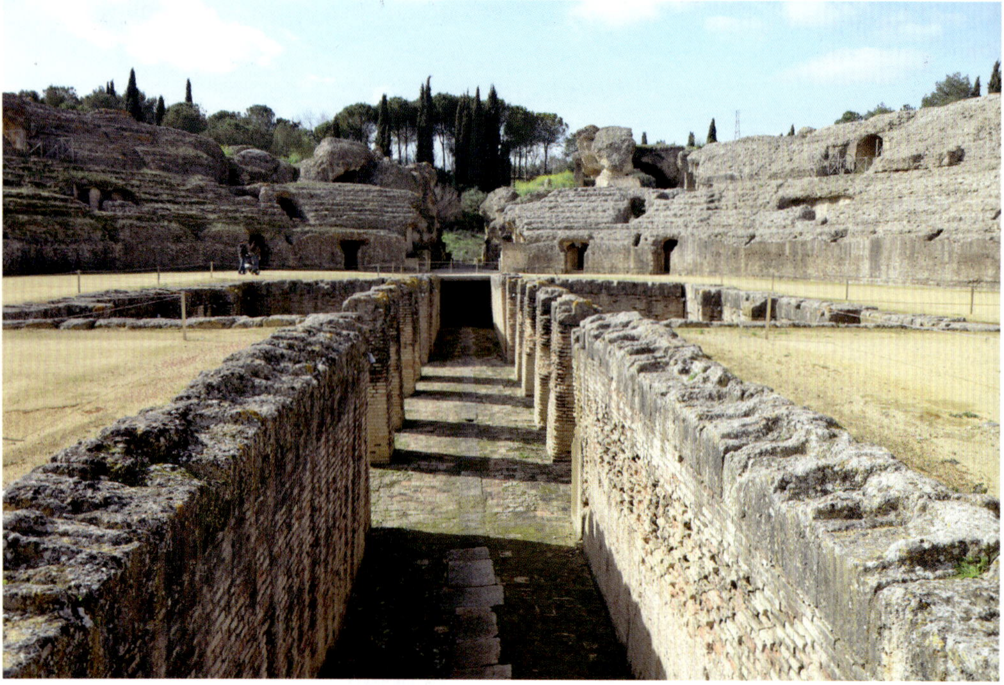

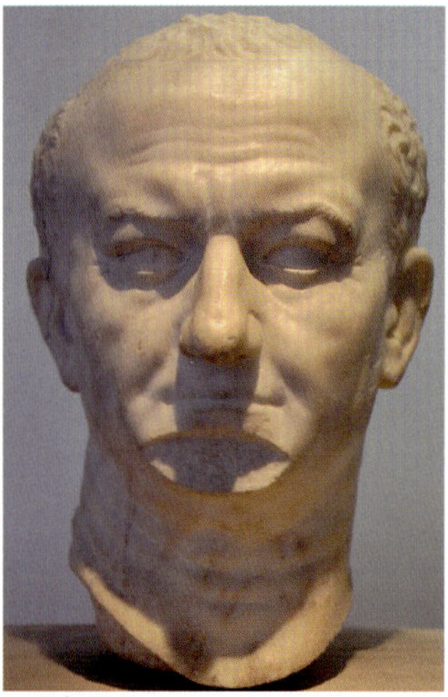

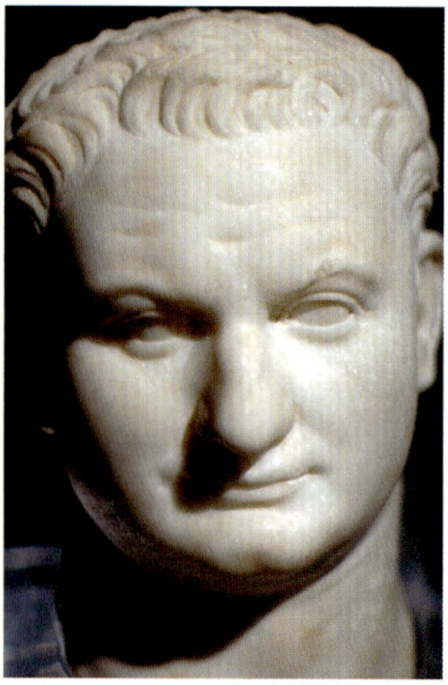

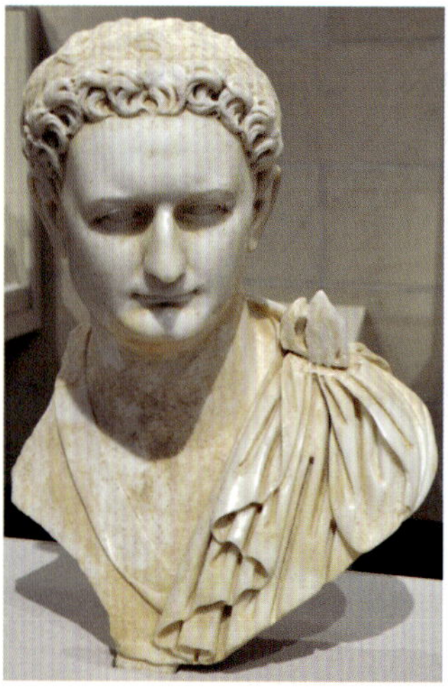

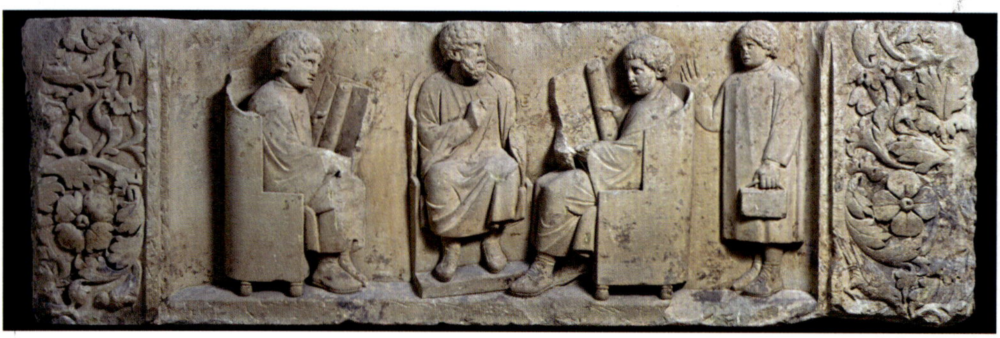

Left: Italica, Spain. Trajan's birthplace eventually had a 25,000-seater amphitheatre. Underground chambers, originally covered, were used to store animals and various gladiatorial paraphernalia. More recently, the location served as a set for the TV series *Game of Thrones*.

Right: Roman patrician children, as depicted on the Ara Pacis, Rome. As a distinction of free birth, children could wear a *toga praetexta*, as shown here. Boys wore the garment until puberty and girls until marriage.

Right: Trajan's father, Marcus Ulpius Traianus.

Left: The three Flavian emperors, all of whom Trajan served. Vespasian (*far left*) and brothers Titus (*centre*) and Domitian (*right*).

Left: Stone relief from a tomb showing a tutor with his three Roman students, *ca.* 180–5, found at Neumagen, near Trier in Germany. Trajan's early education most likely included scenes like this one.

Domitian's Palace, Palatine Hill, Rome. The emperor's lavish private living quarters, arranged on two levels, overlooked a courtyard with a magnificent Amazon fountain. Four elegant structures representing *pelta* – the round shields of the female warriors – formed the basis of the elaborate water works. The bedroom chambers where he was assassinated are thought to be amongst the rooms in the centre of the picture.

Salonia Matidia (*left*), Trajan's niece; Mindia Matidia (*middle*) and Vibia Sabina (*right*), Trajan's great-nieces.

Trajan's private house, on the Aventine Hill in Rome. This suburban villa boasted lavishly decorated rooms with six-metre-high vaulted ceilings and elegant frescoes fashionable for the period.

Trajan's sexual orientation is exemplified on the Warren Cup, a Roman silver drinking vessel from the mid-first century AD. Depicting a homoerotic scene of a type frequently displayed in Roman art, this piece shows two male lovers, a bearded active partner with a passive younger. A servant peeks from behind a door.

Pompeia Plotina, Trajan's wife, depicted in around 110–20. The bust depicts the austere demeanour of the empress, her hair elaborately styled with a high raised crown of locks.

Trajan's Column, casts 11–14: First Dacian War. The benevolent Danube River god (*lower left*), aids the Roman crossing that marks the start of the first campaign. Roman legionaries emerge through a fortress gate at Lederata onto a pontoon bridge, helmets slung over their shoulders, following their legate and numerous standard bearers. They carry their kit and provisions tied to wooden poles.

Trajan's Column, casts 56–8: First Dacian War. Likely a representation of the opening actions of the Second Battle of Tapae. Trajan, centre, his right arm and hand ready to signal another advance, is saluted by auxiliary troops bearing Dacian severed heads, as a division of Roman cavalry below sweeps into the melee.

Dacia and the Dacian Wars.

Second Battle of Tapae. Right of centre, Jupiter dashes down his lightning bolts on the Dacians. Roman auxiliary infantry and cavalry, supported by bare-chested *symmachiarii*, attack from the left. One keen auxiliary soldier fights with a Dacian's head held between his teeth.

Fortress walls near Sarmizegetusa Regia's eastern gate. The famously strong *murus Dacicus*, Dacian Walls, were constructed using composite materials, creating a formidable defence.

Trajan's Column, casts 78–9: First Dacian War. A Dacian assault on a Roman auxiliary fort. Importantly, the ram's head battering-ram exemplifies the sophisticated military equipment used by the Dacians.

Trajan's Column, casts 92–4: First Dacian War. Defeat of the Roxolanian heavy cavalry and mounted archers. Roman horsemen charge (*from left*) into the retreating cataphracts. The original miniature Roman metal spears are missing. A fallen Roxolanian cavalryman can be seen in the lower centre.

Dacian *pileatus*, 112–33 AD. Discovered in Trajan's forum, the bust shows the distinctive Dacian cap. It is thought that this bust may represent King Decebalus.

Religious complex, Sarmizegetusa Regia. A series of unique temples and sanctuaries dominated a large area to the east of the fortress. The large circular sanctuary seen in the centre and to its right the remains of an ancient sundial exemplify the sophisticated nature of Dacian culture.

Trajan's Column, casts 326–9: Second Dacian War. Fall of Sarmizegetusa Regia. One interpretation of this scene is that Decebalus (*standing right of centre*) is handing out cups of poison and is offering a choice to his remaining men: an honourable transition into the afterlife or an attempt to flee the besieged capital that he had ordered to be torched. Distraught Dacians crowd the scene and (*far right*) the dead are carried away.

Trajan's Column, casts 384–7: Suicide of Decebalus. Having escaped his capital, the king was eventually cornered in the Carpathians by Roman cavalry led by Tiberius Claudius Maximus. Despite Maximus' extended arm of clemency (*left of centre*), Decebalus, fallen against a tree, slits his own throat with a blade.

Trajan's forum was the largest ever built in Rome. Porticos on either side connected a triumphal arch entrance to a vast central basilica (*columns picture above*). A courtyard behind the basilica was dominated by Trajan's Column, flanked on either side by two libraries (now lost). His equestrian statue marked the centre of the forum square (not far from where the picture was taken).

Trajan's child welfare programme (*alimenta*) for destitute children in Italy, depicted on the Arch of Trajan in Benevento. The personification of Italy (*left*) holds a plough to represent the encouragement of agriculture. An infant and child (*centre*) embody the poor children of Italy, seemingly under the protection of Trajan's extended right arm (*now missing*). Two deities (*to the left of Trajan*) are probably Copia and Felicitas, goddesses of abundance and good luck respectively. The ominous presence of Mars, the god of War, may hint at a longer-term motive of nurturing children as prospective army recruits.

The Eastern Roman Empire and Trajan's Parthian campaigns.

Ruins of the city of Dura-Europos on the western bank of the Euphrates, Syria. This strategically located Hellenistic settlement in Mesopotamia was captured by Trajan in 114.

Persian cataphract, around 600 AD. This unique Sassanian stone relief at Taq-e Bostan (Iran), although depicting one of the Parthians' successors, shows the substantial protection and armament likely typical of a Parthian rider and his mount in Trajan's times.

The ancient port city of Spasinou Charax, near Basra, Iraq. This wealthy trading centre on the edge of the Persian Gulf, founded by Alexander the Great, was Trajan's most easterly acquisition during the Parthian War and the furthest reach Rome had ever established. Though it is prone today to annual flooding from nearby rivers, the earth and brick ramparts are still visible nonetheless.

Parthian shot, demonstrated during a reenactment of Sassanian archery. The highly skilled technique of shooting arrows whilst galloping seemingly in retreat was used to great success by the Parthians and later Persian armies. Prior to the invention of stirrups, the rider needed precision balance in the saddle.

Right: Bronze bust of Hadrian, dating from some point during his reign. Found in the River Thames near Tower Bridge, London

Left: The Great Iwans (Halls) of Hatra, Iraq. Approximately 180 km north-west of Baghdad, the ancient city was near the north-western limits of the Parthian Empire. It was initially seized by the Romans in 115, but could not be held. Trajan failed to re-capture the trading centre in the following year because of formidable defences and the surrounding hostile environment, even exposing himself to danger during an assault in which a mounted bodyguard near him was killed by archers.

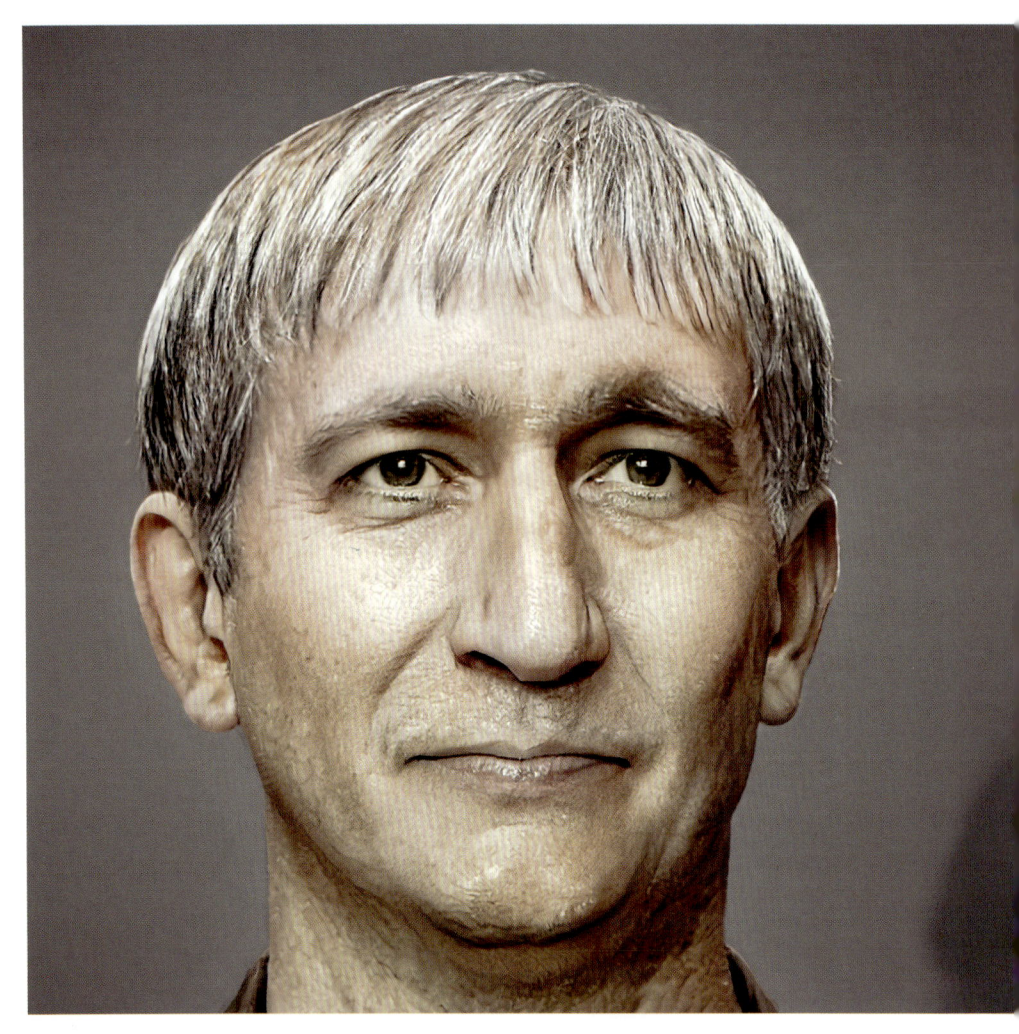

Above: Photoreal portrait of Trajan. Using state-of-the-art software and historical references such as his 'majestic-looking grey hair', marble busts of the emperor have been transformed into this real-life depiction.

Left: The resting place of Trajan's ashes. The emperor's cremated remains (later joined by those of Pompeia Plotina) were interred in the pedestal of his column in Rome. The remains of Rome's emperor and empress are now long lost, however.

advanced, able to slip swiftly through and unite against the Dacians on their flanks. They delivered a devastating strike. Chaos ensued in the Dacian positions and they were quickly defeated and forced to retreat deep into the deciduous forests of the mountains.

Lusius' success probably allowed Trajan to strike next at Costeşti Cetăţuie, a critical Dacian hilltop stronghold and religious centre.[89] It lay at the head of an access route to Sarmizegutusa Regia, which was just 15 km in a straight line to the south-east, and was part of a network of citadel forts around the capital. In a display of ultimate military power, demonstrating that no place could escape the might of Rome, Trajan ordered a direct assault on Costeshti Cetatuie, despite the long steep slopes up to the fortifications and the robust defensive ramparts.[90] Auxiliary infantry scaled the slopes and struck at the defences. Fire from Balearic slingers and Syrian archers compelled some of the Dacian defenders to seek cover on their own ramparts. *Carroballistae*, drawn into positions on constructed wooden platforms to give maximum vantage, provided effective long-range support. In addition, fire bolts that were wrapped in oiled swaddle added further destruction as their vulnerable targets went up in flames. With their ramparts collapsing, the Dacians had to resort to felling trees within the citadel to shore up the crumbling defences.[91] However, their efforts were in vain and the Roman auxiliaries were able to overwhelm the defenders and breach the ramparts.

In a similar manner, the nearby citadels of Blidaru and Piatra Roşie were subsequently taken by the Romans, probably during simultaneous attacks.[92] Each time, extensive forest clearance and basic road construction preceded the assaults to improve access for the Roman forces through the gruelling terrain of narrow gorges and valleys. The collapse of the network of fortresses around Sarmizegetusa Regia would have seriously undermined Decebalus' confidence. Holding urgent council with his generals and *pileati*, Decebalus had very few options left. Should he fight to the bitter end or broker a deal for peace while he still had some remnants of power? The news of the collapsed fortresses would have been greeted enthusiastically by Trajan; surely Decebalus would opt to capitulate? Typical of the unremitting nature of Roman warfare, immediate forest clearance commenced to open the way through to the capital. Nothing now lay between the Romans and Sarmizegetusa Regia except the difficult terrain and Decebalus finally decided to surrender unconditionally. Perhaps the Dacian king thought that it would be possible to emerge from defeat, while pieces of his army and military assets still remained intact, the better to live and fight another day.

Besides, the Dacians could retain some pride in having inflicted significant casualties upon the Roman army during the two years of the war. Thus, the Dacian nation surrendered before it was necessary for Trajan to throw a siege around Sarmizegetusa Regia and raze the capital and the following surrender terms were imposed upon Decebalus and the Dacians:[93]

Dacian Surrender Terms in 102

- King Decebalus to come and bow before Trajan as an admission of defeat and obedience to the emperor, casting aside his arms.
- The Dacians to hand over arms, military apparatus and engineers.
- Roman personnel (prisoners, deserters, slaves, etc.) to be returned and no further deserters to be received.
- Forts designed to oppose Rome to be dismantled.
- All lands captured by the Romans in the two campaigns to be ceded.
- Dacia to become a client state of the Roman Empire, obedient to Rome's policies.
- Dacia to allow the stationing of a legion on the Hațeg plain and other garrisons throughout the kingdom.
- Dacian envoys to go to Rome to ratify the peace treaty with the Roman Senate (another sign of Trajan's respect for the Senate and its duties).

In accordance with the terms of surrender, Decebalus left Sarmizegetusa Regia to capitulate in person to Trajan at his campaign headquarters at Aquae. The Romans had a special respect for natural springs and at Aquae hot water sprang from a natural fissure in the rock – an apt location for the Romans to maintain their headquarters.[94] In a scene that was surely charged with the highest emotions – utter disgrace for the Dacians and glory for the Romans – Decebalus came before Trajan. The emperor was seated on a stone tribunal, dressed in his finest full military panoply. Immediately behind him stood all his senior officers and advisers. Close by the tribunal, the Praetorian standard bearers and Imperial Horse Guard stood to attention in their ranks. Divisions of auxiliaries and legionaries stretched out in parade, all with cleaned and polished armour as expected on such an occasion. Decebalus then dropped to his knees at Trajan's feet, having first thrown down his personal arms. Behind Decebalus, *pileati* representatives from the various Dacian tribes bowed in surrender and, further back still, *comati* warriors threw down their arms and crouched with their hands raised in submission. It is likely that Trajan and

Decebalus would have spoken for the first time at this moment, but one can only guess at the discourse.

After the landmark surrender ceremony, Trajan addressed his troops as a true victorious *imperator*. He would have likely thanked his men and officers for their bravery and deeds, as well as offering sacrifice to the gods for their divine interventions. In addition, he probably expressed to his men the importance of the victory to the glory of Rome and that the Senate and the people of Rome would admire them for their achievements. The menace of Decebalus had been suppressed, or so Trajan thought, and the Dacians had finally been brought to heel since the first serious attempts to do so over eighteen years earlier. Trajan and his men might now hope for immortality, remembered in the glorious history of Rome.

However, after the sentiments of victory had waned, ensuring long term military success necessitated laborious and painstaking activities such as road construction, fort reinforcement and the development of agriculture.[95] Under the terms of the Dacian surrender, Roman garrisons stationed in Dacia would have begun these tasks in the expectation of taking many years to accomplish them.

CHAPTER 8

TRAJAN'S SECOND DACIAN WAR

Justification for War

Why did the Dacian King Decebalus, spared the humiliation of being totally defeated after Trajan's First Dacian War, provoke Trajan into a second war? Did the king believe that Trajan could not stomach another campaign or that his position in Rome was faltering? Did the Dacians defiantly believe they had the strength to resist the might of Rome's legions? Or were there allies waiting in the wings to join Dacia against Rome? With little doubt, Decebalus had capitulated in the first war to salvage what remained of his exhausted forces and to prevent the siege of his capital. He had also ratified peace terms with Rome that effectively left Dacia as a client state, supposedly obedient to the will of Rome. The proud Dacian king had likely agreed such terms with the simple intention of buying time to restore his military strength. As the Dacians had done in the past, he could then select a weak moment in Rome's fortunes to retaliate. Provoking Trajan into a Second Dacian War was therefore born out of defiance and the miscalculated judgement that the forces of Rome could be resisted yet again. As a result, specific peace terms were violated probably over a period from late in 104 through into the first half of 105.

Decebalus specifically ignored four parts of the peace treaty of 102. Firstly, he authorised the active acquisition of arms to replace those lost or handed over at the end of the first war. Secondly, the Dacians received Roman deserters into their realm. Thirdly, strategically important forts were restored to working order, likely housing some of the newly procured arms and deserters. Fourthly, efforts were launched to seek allies against Rome, and in parallel threaten or attack those who had opposed Decebalus in the first war. In particular, the Dacians captured lands in the Hungarian plains belonging to the Iazyges, who had sided with Rome during the first war. The net effect of these actions was perceived by Rome as open aggression against its authority, as well as potentially destabilising the Danubian region.[1]

The news of these actions filtered back to Rome from the garrisons in Dacia, as well as from spies and contacts across the region. Trajan and his advisers would have convened to debate the not entirely unexpected developments. It is possible Trajan decided to go to Dacia to see for himself the escalating situation. During his journey, violence broke out in Dacia, making war certain.[2] The Senate was called to session and Decebalus was again declared an enemy of Rome.[3] If Decebalus had calculated that Trajan would not rush to oppose him, then the Dacian king had foolishly misjudged the emperor.

Trajan and his *consilium* would have carefully considered the strategic viability of annexing Dacia if the second war was won. Removing Decebalus and converting Dacia into a province of the Roman Empire could help stabilise the precarious Danubian frontier. The new province would form a salient bulging out from the Danube and despite the considerable drain on resources to garrison the area, the Carpathian mountain range would delineate a new frontier that divided potentially hostile tribes to the west and the east of Dacia.

In addition, Trajan and his *consilium* would have recognised that the fortunes and resources of the Dacian kingdom could be fully exploited if it became a province. Although potentially not profitable as a province in the long run, the initial returns from the spoils of war and annexation would be enormous. Trajan could use the wealth to initiate wondrous new events, constructions and works in Rome and across the empire to solidify and glorify his principate further.

Finally, Trajan knew that complete annexation of Dacia to create a new province for Rome would allow him to claim expansion of the empire. This would link Trajan directly with the glorious heroes of bygone Republican days such as Scipio who removed the Carthaginians from Spain or Julius Caesar who had conquered Gaul. It would also link Trajan with the great rulers of the early empire like Augustus and Claudius who annexed Pannonia (Western Hungary) and Britannia (England and Wales) respectively. It would even allow Trajan to emulate Alexander the Great, whom we can suppose he admired greatly. This not only appealed to Trajan's desire for military glory and conquest, but would also strengthen his political status in Rome as a conquering emperor, traditionally associated with the favourable Roman virtues of vigour and military aptitude.

Roman Senior Command

The Roman chain of command for the war followed the same pattern as before. Trajan was *imperator* in the field with supreme authority, and the emperor surrounded himself with officers and commanders who were selected based on factors such as trust, experience and friendship. From the chain of command, Trajan hand-picked an inner group as his *comites* or military advisers. In particular, his most trusted and loyal friend Sura, who accompanied Trajan as a special adviser and ambassador in the first war, returned in the same role for the second war. Livianus, one of the Praetorian Guard prefects, present in the first war and with experience negotiating with the Dacians, was again selected to campaign with the emperor. Senecio, an experienced and trusted friend, who had acted skilfully in a special position as *legatus pro praetore* in the first war, presumably returned in a similar special post for the second war. Julius Quadratus Bassus, a skilled soldier and *legatus pro praetore* in the first war, returned for the second war in the same special role alongside Senecio. In the Banat region, an area now affiliated with Moesia Superior and a critical forward bastion close to Dacia, Pompeius Longinus was in place to command Roman forces. These five were evidently some of Trajan's closest advisers, his *crème de la crème*.[4]

Trajan's three generals, each a governor of his own province, were Lucius Fabius Justus, Lucius Herennius Saturninus, and Publius Metilius Nepos in Moesia Inferior, Moesia Superior and Pannonia, respectively. Hadrian was further advanced in his *cursus*, serving as legate of I *Minervia* in the second war. Serving on active duty was a major step up for Hadrian, and his experience as a special observer in the first war would help him command his legion more effectively.

Roman Forces

The majority of Roman forces used in the first war were also involved in the second war as they were stationed in the three critical provinces nearby (Pannonia, Moesia Superior and Inferior). Their experience gained during the first war would be invaluable to Trajan. The stationing of the legions and *auxilia* was not exactly the same as the first war because since then Trajan had shuffled some of the units around to reinforce the lower regions of the Danube and therefore better protect Moesia Inferior, which had proven vulnerable on too many occasions in the past. In addition, the area just north of the Danube, beyond the Moesian provinces, was also partially garrisoned with auxiliaries in a series of forts that effectively converted Oltenia and Wallachia into part of Moesia Inferior.[5] Moreover, the Banat region for all practical purposes became part of Moesia Superior and the military forts established in the first war were integrated with the placement of Legion XIII *Gemina* at Berzobis. The Hațeg plain, starting just beyond the Iron Gates Pass, was garrisoned, creating the most forward Roman positions after the first war.

To bolster the general pool of legions across the Danubian region, Trajan had recruited two new legions in or around 102, XXX *Ulpia Victrix* and II *Traiana*, and also transferred X *Gemina* from Noviomagus (Nijmegen). These additional 15,000 or more legionaries raised the overall total to a level sufficient to allow garrisoning of Dacia once it became a province. Given their experience in the first war, it is quite probable that the same vexillations of legions from Syria were brought back for the second war.

Therefore, the following legions were available for the Second Dacian War;[6] numbers provided are for units at full theoretical fighting strength but the actual number would have been lower:

GARRISONS IN DACIA
    Legions: I *Adiutrix*; IV *Flavia Felix*
    11,400 legionaries

PANNONIAN FORCES
    Legions: II *Adiutrix*; XV *Apollinaris*; XXX *Ulpia Victrix*; I *Minervia*;
        X *Gemina*
    28,500 legionaries

MOESIA SUPERIOR FORCES
    Legions: VII *Claudia*; XIV *Gemina Martia Victrix*; II *Traiana*;[7] XIII
        Gemina (in Banat region)
    22,800 legionaries

MOESIA INFERIOR FORCES
    Legions: V *Macedonica*; I *Italica*; XI *Claudia*
    17,100 legionaries

LEGIONS POSSIBLY DRAFTED IN FROM OTHER PROVINCE[8]
    Parts of IV *Scythica*, XII *Fulminata*, and of an unknown legion (all
        from Syria)
    3,000 legionaries

It is possible that, in addition to these 82,800 legionaries, a similar combination of additional crack forces was brought in for the second war as before: the Praetorian Guard (five cohorts; total: 2,500 men) and the Imperial Horse Guard (1,000 mounted men). As typical for the Roman army, the same number of auxiliaries as the total of legionaries was further available in the region (infantry and cavalry – around 80,000 auxiliaries at full strength), as well as naval forces (Danubian River fleet, around 1,000 men) and irregular *symmachiarii* (around 5,000 men, comparable to first war).

Legionaries:	82,800
Praetorians:	2,500
Imperial Horse Guard:	1,000
Auxiliaries:	80,000
Danubian sailors:	1,000
Symmachiarii:	5,000
GRAND TOTAL:	172,300

As described, all the numbers above assume that units were at full fighting strength. This was rarely the case and the units' actual fighting strength would have been smaller and there were casualties from the first war that might not yet have been replaced. Nevertheless, with the new legions, this was a considerably larger Roman force than before.

Trajan clearly wanted to guarantee enough resources to ensure that the second war would be over swiftly and cleanly. Once again, leaving a significant portion of the available force behind to maintain security in Pannonia, Moesia Inferior and Moesia Superior, Trajan would have had a campaign invasion force larger than in the first war at around 39,000 legionary soldiers[9] matched by an equivalent number of auxiliaries plus the *symmachiarii* and the guards, a total of around 86,000 men. The emperor had a far greater reserve that he could call on than in the first war. For practical purposes of governance, the huge influx of forces into Pannonia could have been the trigger for Trajan to divide up the province into an upper and lower region, as he did later, just as Domitian had done to Moesia two decades earlier.[10]

Dacian Senior Command

No specific details have come down to us about Decebalus' command structure in the second war. However, one can reasonably assume that Decebalus had a depleted group of commanders due to loses or defections during the first war. Nevertheless, Decebalus remained the commander-in-chief of all Dacian forces and no doubt his sons, close relatives and *pileati* noblemen again constituted the core of his senior commanders.

Dacian Forces & Allies

During the period between the first and the second war, Decebalus presumably plundered his resources to rejuvenate and strengthen his armed forces after the defeats suffered during the first war. Men younger or older than the ideal *comati* warrior age were likely drawn from loyal tribes and it is known that Decebalus actively rearmed his available warriors.[11] Despite these internal efforts, Decebalus appeared to lack support from allies that had come to aid the Dacians in the first war. For example, the heavy Roxolani cavalry were less active in the second war, either due to reluctance to support the waning Dacian kingdom or because of massive casualties incurred in the earlier conflict. Moreover, Trajan's own successful diplomacy and acceptance of Dacian defectors undermined Decebalus' ability to secure support from allies. In short, the Dacian force was well below previous standards. It would be unable to field a large army for open set-piece battles, and would have to be far more reliant on guerrilla warfare and the static defence of forts and citadels.[12] Decebalus may have had around 50,000 warriors at his disposal and probably very limited support from his remaining allies. Clearly the Dacians were heavily outnumbered and Trajan's force possibly constituted an over-kill assembled as much with planned garrisoning of the area after the war in mind as with actually winning it.

Start of Trajan's Second Dacian War
Escalations and the Partial Campaign of 105

In 105, Rome was again at war with Dacia, the fourth war in as little as twenty years.[13] Trajan, now with the title *'Dacicus'*, 'Conqueror of Dacia', awarded following his victory in the first war, was this time set on the complete annexation of Dacia and the removal of Decebalus from the throne.

The traditional campaign season was already well advanced by the time Trajan left for Dacia on 4 June, even crossing the Adriatic Sea at night, probably in order to capitalise on favourable sailing conditions. The emperor likely took the shortest route to the Danube, sailing from the seaport of Ancona to the province of Dalmatia and from there straight to Moesia Superior.[14]

The news of Trajan's approach unsettled many Dacians and led to large numbers of Dacians and their allies deserting Decebalus at this time.[15] These deserters sensed Decebalus' self-destruction. Even the Dacian king who had once defeated the Roman Emperor Domitian could surely not overcome the military aptitude and persistence of Trajan? Almost certainly filled with despair and anger at the desertions, as well as becoming increasingly aware of the weaknesses in his position, Decebalus tried to solicit peace from Trajan. The emperor, having presumably consulted those from his *comites* who accompanied him while travelling to the Danube region, insisted on unconditional surrender and for Decebalus to give himself up. But the stipulations were not acceptable to Decebalus, whose defiant nature would never consent to such terms. A second war was now unavoidable and Decebalus reacted by readying his forces openly for conflict. In sheer desperation, he then appealed to his neighbours to stand with Dacia before it was too late. Decebalus argued that failure to unite at this critical moment would only lead to their own demise in the future when the opportunity of uniting with Dacia would be lost.[16] In short, the age-old adage exemplifies Decebalus' plea, 'united we stand, divided we fall'. Alas, his neighbours, the likes of the Roxolani, the Buri and the Quadi never came to his aid and the once great kingdom of Dacia was left on its own against Rome.

Despite his pathetic situation, Decebalus wasted no time in seizing the initiative and launched guerrilla-style assaults on Roman fortifications in the Hațeg plain.[17] It is conceivable that such a strategy could have maintained resistance for a considerable period of time if successfully executed. Intimately knowing the landscape was another key advantage for an outnumbered and demoralised Dacian force.

Doubtless, the strategy was to topple the Roman positions in the plain and regain control of this vital area, with designs on recovering the Iron Gates Pass, which was a defensible barrier to entry from the west into the core of the Dacian kingdom. Even better, destroying or routing the isolated Roman forces garrisoned in the plain would seriously diminish Roman pride. By then in Moesia Superior and with the news of Decebalus' offensive manoeuvres, Trajan mustered his Imperial Horse Guard and cavalry forces in order to relieve his men in the Hațeg region swiftly. At full pace, it would have taken Trajan a few days to bring the mounted relief into the Hațeg plain following the shortest possible route. Trajan arrived in a timely manner, with his legionaries and auxiliaries desperately defending the walls of their fortifications in the plain, and he appears to have averted the loss of the Roman positions.[18]

Winter 105/106

Having dealt with the Dacian offensive at the start of the second war, Trajan returned to the Danube for the winter of 105/106. During this period, full preparations for the next campaign could be completed. For example, Roman forces and supplies continued to gather in the region and this required deployment and distribution respectively. New infrastructures supported these activities, such as a large permanent bridge over the Danube at Drobeta built by the architect Apollodorus of Damascus after the first war.[19] Strategically this was intended to provide a reliable means of transporting large numbers of troops and supplies over the Danube in this critical area and in particular to support the newly occupied Banat region.[20] The magnificent structure, parts of which are still visible today, had twenty stone piers connected by wooden arches that supported a vast deck fifteen metres wide across the entire river.[21] In total, the bridge was just over a kilometre in length.[22] It would have been a sight to marvel at both as a technical engineering feat and for its architectural beauty. To mark the inauguration of the bridge, Trajan gave sacrifice to the gods and made plans to use the bridge at the start of the campaign in 106.[23]

A bronze *sestertius*, struck in Rome ca. 107–9, depicts the magnificent architectural feat of the permanent bridge across the Danube, constructed in time for the Second Dacian War.

Like the completed engineering of Trajan's bridge, Roman diplomacy reached new heights during the winter of 105/106. With many states previously allied to Decebalus switching over to the Roman side and the increasing likelihood that he would defeat the Dacians, Trajan gave a combined audience to a host of foreign embassies. Dignitaries and ambassadors were invited to convene, probably at Viminacium, to state their support for Trajan in the war or at least their neutrality, and for Trajan to give assurances that they would be treated accordingly. Six different groups attended: the Bastarnae; Dacians independent of Decebalus' cause; the Roxolani; representatives from the Greek cities of the Pontic Coast; Scythians from the Pontic steppes; and an unknown Germanic tribe.[24]

With diplomacy tackled, Trajan could attend to his many duties preparing for the coming second campaign and addressing matters back in Rome and throughout the rest of the empire that required his urgent attention. It was during this time that Decebalus made a fraught attempt to have Trajan assassinated. This was a sign that the king was now resorting to desperate means as his power crumbled. Trajan would have had layers of security designed to safeguard his person. While on the Danube frontier in his winter quarters, the Imperial Horse Guard would likely have formed an outer cordon of security with check-points for those coming and going. Just like a legionary camp, the use of watchwords may have constituted one means of verifying the legitimacy of someone's presence within that outer cordon. An inner ring of security, manned by hand-picked guards, was probably the main barrier protecting Trajan's closer surroundings. Within that, the most trusted and able of all the guards were likely appointed to protect the emperor within his immediate vicinity, or at least a short cry away. Subject to this type of security, it is known that anyone of appropriate standing could request an audience with Trajan.[25]

The procedure for obtaining a meeting with Trajan would have been daunting given his heavy daily agenda. The process may have been based on a waiting list, with one's position on that list dictated by rank and seniority. Those intimately familiar with the emperor received priority. In such a system, senior officers of the guard, in consultation with persons highly trusted by Trajan in his administration, may have been responsible for vetting everyone requesting an audience. Trajan would likely have reviewed the list of appointments himself.

Knowing the basic details of Trajan's personal security, likely from information gathered from deserters from the Roman army, Decebalus hatched a devious plan. He first selected certain deserters, most probably military personnel who could appear credible when requesting an interview with Trajan through the normal channels. These deserters were then dispatched to Moesia to carry out the assassination plot. However, their plan was foiled as Trajan's diligent guards arrested the deserters on suspicion of malign intent. Under torture, the deserters revealed their treacherous scheme. Trajan's security had proved its worth.

Despite the failed assassination attempt, Decebalus actively continued hostile activities through other methods. This time he sent a message to Pompeius Longinus who commanded Roman forces with distinction in the vital Banat area. Decebalus apparently claimed that he was ready to accept any terms for peace in order to lure Longinus over into discussion. Longinus fell for the ploy and was detained by Decebalus' men. He was publicly interrogated regarding Trajan's plans for the upcoming campaign.[26] The loyal Longinus did not disclose any details to Decebalus who subsequently refused to let him leave.[27] Decebalus' action broke the basic code of conduct that respected an ambassador's freedom as an envoy.

Hoping to use Longinus as a bargaining chip, Decebalus sent a message to Trajan offering terms of peace in exchange for the safe return of Longinus. To put this offer in context, one has to recall that Longinus was a faithful supporter of Trajan with a highly prestigious background. He was an ex-consul who had supported Trajan's adoption and accession. In particular, he had supported Trajan in the Third Pannonian War and replaced him as governor of Pannonia during the critical period when Trajan needed the cooperation of the province to assure his smooth adoption by Nerva. Longinus had also accompanied Trajan immediately after his accession during his review of the Danubian frontier. Thus, Trajan would have greeted the news of Longinus' capture with a heavy heart. Trajan knew he could never agree to Decebalus' conditions. His only option was to protract negotiations and give the impression that he was indifferent to Longinus' fate, with the hope that Decebalus might see little point in detaining Longinus under such dishonourable circumstances. Trajan therefore sent an 'ambiguous' message back to Decebalus, leaving the Dacian king perplexed as to his next step.[28]

In the meantime, true to his honourable character, Longinus took steps to preserve Trajan from further embarrassment and perhaps he sensed the hopeless nature of his situation with little chance of ever being released. Longinus managed to acquire poison from a freedman of Decebalus[29] and he asked Decebalus to release this freedman in order to deliver a message to Trajan in which he would try to persuade him to concede peace terms. Decebalus accepted and when the freedman had left, Longinus 'drank the poison during the night and died'.[30] Longinus had proved his nobility and loyalty to Trajan beyond any doubt and to the very end.

Evidently furious at being tricked, Decebalus then wrote to Trajan stipulating the return of the freedman in exchange for the body of Longinus and ten prisoners of war thrown into the bargain. The message was delivered to Trajan by a centurion arrested with Longinus who was released to act as a liaison between the emperor and the king. However, Trajan was not to be bullied by Decebalus. Instead, he did not send back the centurion or the freedman, 'accounting the saving of his [the freedman's] life more important for the good name of the empire than the burial of Longinus' corpse'.[31] The whole Longinus affair was certainly viewed gravely by Trajan, his *comites* and other fellow officers who had known Longinus, as well as the Senate back in Rome. One can only assume that it was counter-productive for Decebalus, as it would have strengthened the resolve of the Romans to remove him as quickly as possible. He was now not only an enemy, but a dishonourable and disgraced king, a barbarian in the eyes of Rome.

Roman Offensive Campaign of 106

At the start of the 106 campaign season in April, Trajan issued his orders for the invasion army to muster and cross the bridge at Drobeta. On horseback, Trajan proudly led the vanguard of his infantry over the river, accompanied by his Imperial Horse Guard.[32] As before, the army assembled beyond the northern bank of the Danube in vast temporary field camps and the sacrifices of the *suovetaurilia* ceremony were made. One of Trajan's specific roles was to pour some of the blood from the sacrifices into the flames of an altar as libations to Mars.

Critical to the motivation and morale of his troops, Trajan then addressed his men,[33] perhaps instilling the need for diligence and bravery in the imminent conflicts, and explaining the importance of this war to the glory of Rome as well as the removal of the deceitful Decebalus. The recent Longinus affair may have provided a good example to include in his address to show the immoral nature of their opponent.

Trajan also called together his *comites* for what appears to be a council of war prior to the advance of his army.[34] The aim was without a doubt clearly agreed: capture the Dacian capital, Sarmizegetusa Regia, and dispose of Decebalus. No quarter would be given to the enemy. Tactically, a meticulous and methodical advance would be executed along two fronts: the first via the established route starting at Dierna and then the Iron Gates Pass into the Haţeg plain from the west; the second along a more easterly approach through the Vulcan Pass and into the Haţeg plain from the south-east. The two columns would then mass at a central strategic point close to the Orăştie Mountains and then advance directly on Sarmizegetusa Regia along parts of the mountainous terrain that had been overrun at the end of the First Dacian War. Arguably, the decision to advance along two fronts was to allow the much slower massive baggage train component of the advance to take the more secure route to the Iron Gates Pass, while a smaller and more agile fighting force took the Vulcan Pass to act as a flank guard in the east for the slower column. In addition, taking an enormous baggage train through a long defile like the Vulcan Pass would have been extremely problematic compared to the relativity short Iron Gates Pass. Furthermore, these tactics hinged on the fact that any major resistance or threat only existed in the south-eastern areas of the Carpathian Mountain range and in the Orăştie Mountains themselves.

With the strategy and tactics translated down the chain of command, the vast Roman army advanced on Sarmizegetusa Regia as planned. Without incident, the first column went due north and through the Keys of Teregova to the Roman fortifications at Tibiscum before heading east through the Iron Gates Pass, to the legionary fortress at the head of the Haţeg plain. This column, under less threat of attack, proceeded with helmets off and the legionaries marching ahead of the enormous baggage train in the rear.

The other column first headed north-east across the Oltenia region with its open flood plains and undulating hills. This column advanced according to the familiar set-up of a Roman army in hostile terrain, composed of legionaries, auxiliaries and the irregular *symmachiarii* troops. Where the Oltenia plains give way to the sharply rising Carpathian Mountains, the column had to form into a long line to proceed through the Vulcan Pass.[35] The pass itself is a deep river gorge, with sheer rock faces on either side rising up into the snow-capped peaks. In places, the line would have been as narrow as one or two men in order to negotiate the narrow spaces between the river and the cliff faces. Any heavy rain would have delayed the column's advance up the pass as the river would have quickly turned into a torrent. It would have taken the column two or three days to march through the pass, camping at night in makeshift conditions as there was no space for field camps except in two places where the pass opened up somewhat along its route. Once through the pass, the column emerged into the Petrosani Valley, with its steep glens and mountainous terrain, before heading west and dropping down slowly into the flat Haţeg Plain.

Thus the Roman army united without incident at their headquarters in the Haţeg Plain, the campfires of the enormous Roman force visible for many miles. Trajan and his generals would have been immediately occupied reviewing the latest intelligence gatherings. The Dacians had been noticeably unable to mount any resistance to the Romans as they advanced and the majority of Decebalus' available forces had pulled back to defend their capital in a last stand against Trajan.

The Fall of Sarmizegetusa Regia and the Dacian Kingdom

To reach Sarmizegetusa Regia, the Romans needed to pass through the densely forested, exceedingly steep and narrow ravines of the Orăştie Mountains. Access routes through the challenging terrain were guarded by hilltop fortresses in a cordon around the capital. Overall, five fortresses constituted the key elements of this network: Blidaru, Piatra Roşie, Costeşti, Căpâlna and Baniţa.[36] These fortresses created a defensive arrangement in the mountains covering around 500 square kilometres and could not simply be ignored because their inhabitants could easily sally out and attack the Romans from the rear if they tried to tackle Sarmizegetusa Regia. Although they had been destroyed or dismantled during the first war, the Dacians had rebuilt these forts before the second war.[37] Trajan and his generals issued orders for direct assaults on the forts, presumably repeating the successful tactics used in the first war.

With the ring of protective fortresses once in the hands of the Romans, Trajan and Decebalus both knew that nothing stood in the way of the overwhelming Roman force advancing on the last remaining stronghold, Sarmizegetusa Regia itself. The Dacian capital and its kingdom hung on a thread. Trajan would have reflected, with justifiable confidence, on the impending defeat of his foe and dispatched messages to Rome elaborating on all his achievements. The many hard days and nights spent campaigning in both Dacian wars were paying off. Probably with little hesitation, Trajan ordered his forces to encircle and lay siege to the capital. Decebalus would need all his leadership abilities to rally his remaining *pileati* and *comati* to defend their last refuge. Many probably deserted into the mountains. Nevertheless, with their backs against the wall, fighting for the very survival of everything they knew and loved, the Dacians who remained would be ferocious combatants.

Trajan's plans for taking Sarmizegetusa Regia were typical of Roman military tactics of the period and had been used with success by many of his predecessors. First, lay siege to the citadel and attempt to storm the defences and then, should that fail, starve the besieged from their stronghold and simultaneously prevent others coming to their aid from the outside. However, before describing the logistics of a typical Roman siege such as Trajan may have adopted, we must first consider the nature of Sarmizegetusa Regia's location and the surrounding topography, as well as the citadel's formidable defences.

Set in a stunning natural location in the heart of the Orăştie Mountains, Sarmizegetusa Regia sat on the top of a mountain ridge approximately 1,000 m above sea level, and flanked on the north and south sides by slopes running down into valley gorges. Spread along the whole ridge, areas over 1,500 m high posed formidable barriers with only precipitous barely accessible ravines providing routes through the gorges below. The single access route for any large force was effectively from the west along the Godeanu and Orăştie river valleys, and even these were logistical challenges for any army trying to negotiate the tight valleys that wound their way through the landscape. This route had been closely guarded by the network of Dacian fortresses and, with their destruction, the way through lay open to the Romans. The way up to Sarmizegetusa Regia itself was an effort even if one was a welcomed guest. Proceeding from any direction other than the west was a difficult scramble up steep and rocky forested inclines; it was a good 200 metres in some places from the gorge bottoms to the top. At best, a fully armoured legionary soldier would take a breathless fifteen minutes or more to scramble up to the top to reach the defences of Sarmizegetusa Regia if approaching from the south. Otherwise, from the west, the entrance trail was a longer incline with peaks and troughs, working its way up to the heavily defended western perimeter of the citadel's fortress.

Sarmizegetusa Regia was the religious and military centre of Dacia and the largest settlement in the kingdom. With enormous effort, the mountain top location had been extensively terraced by the Dacians to accommodate various public spaces and locations for buildings and defences in three zones: a central fortress, civilian areas to the west and east of the fortress and a sacred area to the east of the fortress.

It was approximately hexagonal in shape and the walls, surrounding an area of approximately 30,000 square metres, were constructed using the renowned *murus Dacicus*, or Dacian wall, technique.[38] It was essentially a composite wall with outer layers of stone using vast blocks, filled in with rubble and using timber to provide cross support. This created a sturdy structure, able to withstand powerful attacks given the shock-absorbing nature of the interior. The walls of the fortress typically reached four or five metres high and were three metres thick and would have had fighting ramparts at key locations. With remnants still visible even today, the vast outer wall followed the contours of the terraced areas with gates on the western and eastern sides. The north section of the fortress was more elevated than the south and provided vantage over the entire defences. With its natural defensive topography and remarkably strong walls, the fortress had no need for ditches.

The civilian buildings of Sarmizegetusa Regia spread out from around the fortress perimeter, particularly to the west of the mount. Dwellings of all shapes and sizes have been excavated to date, alongside workshops for the various industries of the capital. Advanced water-works supplied drinkable water to wealthy homes and water reservoirs served all the other inhabitants. Immediately to the east of the fortress, on their own distinct terraced platform, there were sacred religious constructions linked by a paved road to the fortress. One particular building, long thought to be a temple with rows of round stone bases, may have actually been a large warehouse.[39] Among these constructions was an astronomical instrument called the Andesite Sun, a large segmented stone disc whose markings allowed the reading of the stars. Sarmizegetusa Regia would have been regarded as a highly important hub within the Dacian kingdom, offering a thriving community centre, with fresh running water and food storage, all overseen reassuringly by the fortress and with fine views of the Orăştie mountains in every direction.[40]

In the summer of 106, these fine views included Roman siege constructions, a grim reality of war. The Romans were true masters of combat field fortifications and their highly skilled and experienced *cohors fabrorum*, military engineers, would have first surveyed the topography surrounding Sarmizegetusa Regia. With the surveying complete, recommendations for besieging Sarmizegetusa Regia were likely approved by Trajan. The citadel was almost certainly surrounded by Roman forces in order to prevent the Dacians from escaping en masse and to block all supplies of food and water reaching the besieged.[41] Forward position Roman forts were constructed close to the capital where troops could be concentrated in critical areas to support the siege or attack any relief forces coming to the aid of the besieged. Next, the engineers directed legionary soldiers to clear surrounding trees and vegetation. This removed any cover that the Dacians could use when trying to sally out from their fortress and provided materials for the fortifications that the Romans would erect. Protected by a screen of auxiliaries, the legionaries likely constructed various ramparts and fortifications around the capital. Each legionary was well trained and equipped for these engineering works and their field packs included a pickaxe, shovel, turf cutter, stakes for wooden palisades and a strong wicker basket for moving rubble and dirt. With their helmets off, but still wearing their body armour in case of a surprise attack, the legionaries relentlessly set about building the fortifications. At strategically important locations such as valleys, watch towers were erected and a series of communication routes would have supported the overall arrangement. Given the mountainous surroundings, there would be places where normal siege works would not have been possible, such as problematic inclines. Here, the engineers would have to be inventive to secure such areas. Observing these elaborate entrenchments from their fortress must have tested the limits of the Dacians' courage, but they could take some solace in the fact that all the women and children had been whisked away from the citadel before the Romans arrived.[42]

One can imagine Trajan's thoughts, alone in his field tent on the eve that marked the completion of all the siege works around the Dacian capital. Satisfied by construction reports, he would surely have reflected on all the events that had led up to this very moment, from his first surveying of the Danubian frontier in 98 to the conflicts of the First Dacian War and the hurried departure from Rome to commence the second war all fresh in his memory. He would have had no pity for his enemy. They had violated peace terms with Rome and defied his own victory in the first war. The Dacians were now merely an obstacle to be removed and their downfall would crown his imperial military successes. Any impatience to achieve complete victory over the Dacians had never swayed the emperor from the systematic and meticulous advance on Sarmizegetusa Regia.

With the wheat ripening in the heat of July for Roman foragers to crop and the Dacian capital besieged, Trajan would have made a series of addresses to his troops to instil courage for the impending assaults on the citadel.[43] Bolstered by the seemingly easy advance on Sarmizegetusa Regia, and with a vast force plus reserves at his disposal, Trajan was prepared to chance a direct assault to seize victory quickly. Flowing out from their entrenchments, combinations of auxiliaries and legionaries advanced towards the Dacian defences with scaling ladders to assail the walls.[44] Projectile weapons were critical to harass and hinder Dacians along the wall ramparts, such as auxiliary Balearic slingers able to release their lead shot with deadly accuracy. The Dacians responded vigorously, firing arrows and hurling spears and rocks down on the Romans below, as well as striking out at any ladders and scaling parties able to reach the walls. The Romans kept their large rectangular shields raised high to deflect the missiles cascading down upon them, their armour and helmets providing some protection where shields failed. Despite Dacian casualties, the Romans were unable to press any advantage and they were repelled by the defenders in their superior elevated position on the seemingly unassailable walls.[45] Viewing from a fortified vantage point, Trajan ordered his men to retreat.[46]

Perhaps sensing that the unsuccessful attempt by the Romans to scale the walls was a sign of weakness, Decebalus ordered a fierce counter-attack. Sallying out from their fortress, the Dacians swept down on the Romans, slashing with their lethal falx swords.[47] In response, a mix of Roman legionaries, auxiliaries and irregular troops, including Germans wielding clubs,[48] rushed forth from their entrenchments to engage the Dacians. From the rear, auxiliary Syrian archers provided covering fire in addition to the waves of Roman javelins thrown by the legionaries. With heavy casualties likely on both sides, the sally had run its course and the Dacians pulled back to the security of their fortress.

Not long after, Dacian traitors, eager to save themselves from their apparently impossible entrapment, brokered a deal with the Romans and opened a small concealed door in the fortress wall.[49] Roman legionaries were then able to enter a bastion of the stronghold and with pickaxes began to break down the ramparts. Simultaneously, Roman forces advanced on the breached point, but Dacian defenders quickly rallied and repulsed the assault before the collapse or loss of the bastion. With such an opportunity missed and a deadlock now evident between the Dacians and the Romans, Trajan decided that further direct assaults would be futile and the siege presumably switched into blockade mode to starve the Dacians into surrender.[50]

While direct Dacian accounts of the suffering and daily conditions inside Sarmizegetusa Regia during the siege do not exist, we can still piece together an idea of what the brave defenders endured. The key objective of a prolonged Roman siege was to force the besieged to capitulate by preventing any military relief, provisions or water from getting in. Equally, it aimed to contain all those besieged because letting the helpless out would alleviate the situation for those who remained.[51] Therefore, the Dacians trapped in Sarmizegetusa Regia were utterly isolated and left to contemplate their dismal future.

Focusing on daily routines may have provided some distraction for those within Sarmizegetusa Regia. This could have included tight management of rations, critical for survival, and the careful prediction of how many more days they could hold out for. In particular, water was always of the utmost concern. An unmet desire to quench one's thirst while on minimal rations could have a devastating effect on morale. And without rations, the heat of the closing Dacian summer combined with daily exertion meant that very few would survive more than a few days without ample water. Sarmizegetusa Regia did have sophisticated water-works, but like all the hilltop forts in the region, the city lacked springs and therefore relied on the volume of their water cisterns for the supply. Dispensing water from such storage and the security of the water reserves was likely managed by Decebalus' most trusted men.

Other routines surely included the continuous maintenance of weapons and armour, the sharpening of falx swords and reconditioning of damaged spears. The defences would have been kept under constant review, with appropriate repairs or improvements being undertaken to the perimeter. Rosters were probably required to share the risky business of patrolling defences. To counteract the undermining of the Dacian defensive walls, which could lead to their fatal collapse, it was also essential to listen and probe for any attempts by the Romans to tunnel under the walls.

Although we can easily imagine the variety of daily routines within Sarmizegetusa Regia, it is of course far harder to appreciate the true anguish that the Dacians experienced during that fateful summer trapped by the Roman siege works. Deep concerns for surviving loved ones must have challenged the strongest bravado. What could the besieged hope for, knowing that little or no resistance was left in their kingdom? Many must have considered that the end was near, but others probably remained in denial of the imminent Roman victory. A deep psychological war was waging and the Romans would have wanted to play on this vulnerability. Roman tactics to achieve this may have included taunting behaviour or the brutal catapulting of the dead bodies of fallen comrades – or diseased animals and people – into the city. A chilling first-hand description of such atrocities during the siege of Masada in Judaea illustrates the ghastly nature of Roman siege warfare:

> The noise of the instruments themselves [Roman siege catapults] was very terrible; the sound of the darts and stones that were thrown by them was so also: of the same sort that noise the dead bodies made, when they were dashed against the wall.
>
> Josephus[52]

It is not known how long the blockade of Sarmizegetusa Regia lasted, but one can estimate that after several weeks the Dacians had exhausted their supply of water and with no relief expected, the great Dacian king was forced to abandon the defence of his capital and, with it, the seat of his kingdom. In desperation and despair, Decebalus may have called his *pileati* together and, swallowing his pride, conceded that all was lost. Many long days and nights trapped in Sarmizegetusa Regia had allowed Decebalus to concoct a morbid exit plan. All his warriors would be offered a choice: drink a poison and die a noble death, transitioning honourably into a blissful afterlife to greet their god, Zalmoxis; alternatively, escape with their king deep into the mountains, slipping through the siege and living to fight another day in a guerrilla resistance against the Romans. Dacians were not afraid of death and many elected to follow the first option of mass suicide.[53] Bidding farewell to his comrades, Decebalus himself handed out cups of poison and the dead were carried away to a mass burial site in the grounds of the capital. Next, personal valuables and weapons were gathered and what remained of the capital was torched in order to leave nothing of use for the Romans. In the confusion of the fire and under the cover of darkness, the remaining Dacians miraculously slipped away with Decebalus somehow avoiding the surrounding Romans.[54] Probably woken from his sleep, Trajan would have been informed by his attendants that the capital was burning, and he may have immediately ordered extra vigilance along the siege entrenchments – too late to prevent the escape of Decebalus.

The magnificent Dacian capital, Sarmizegetusa Regia, had fallen. As the flames subsided, the Romans entered the empty city to seek out the besieged and to begin flattening all the charred remains in preparation for constructing a Roman fort on the site.[55] Trajan would have surely ordered messages to be sent to Rome stating that the kingdom of Dacia was now in Roman hands. But the victory was soon soured with the realisation that Decebalus had evaded capture. The vast Dacian treasures expected as booty were also missing.

Capture of Decebalus and the Annexation of Dacia

Late in the summer, with the days beginning to draw shorter, Trajan likely withdrew to his headquarters on the Haţeg Plain and instructed his cavalry units to scour the land in search of Decebalus. Defiant to the bitter end and able to operate on the run, Decebalus directed pockets of resistance against Roman outposts and camps. In the meantime, Trajan's fortunes were further improved following the capture of a well-informed Dacian *pileatus* called Bikilis, who divulged the whereabouts of the famous Dacian royal treasures. In an attempt to hide these, Decebalus had used Roman captives to divert the course of the Sargetias River which ran close to the citadel.[56] Non-perishable treasures such as gold and silver were then buried in the bed of the river, before it was allowed back along its course as if never disturbed. Perishable treasures were concealed deep in the mountains in well-hidden caves. All the captives employed for the work were then slain to limit knowledge of the treasure's whereabouts.

However, a companion of Decebalus betrayed the secret, and Trajan was able to retrieve the Dacian riches. It is said that a staggering 226,800 kg of gold and 453,600 kg of silver were found.[57] To put this fabulous wealth into perspective, it was equivalent to several thousand million *sestertii* – years of annual imperial revenues– and would later fund a vast array of public works and festivals to glorify Trajan's principate.[58] Under the protection of the most trusted guards and legionaries, the treasure was inventoried, loaded onto countless pack animals and sent back to Rome to fill the imperial coffers.

The loss of the treasures, doubtless unknown to Decebalus, had no impact on the defeated king's destiny. In the Carpathian Mountains, the pursuers had found their quarry. Perhaps by following along poorly concealed tracks or through betrayal of his whereabouts, a Roman *auxilia* cavalry unit from Pannonia finally had Decebalus in sight. Led by Tiberius Claudius Maximus, a soldier decorated by Domitian in the past, the mounted cavalrymen swept down on Decebalus and his immediate entourage. Lacking any significant guard or protective force, Decebalus knew his fate and, despite the cries and extended arm of clemency from Maximus approaching on horseback, Decebalus slumped down against a tree and slit his own throat with his falx to join his warriors in the afterlife with Zalmoxis and evade humiliating capture. So died the rebellious Dacian king, arguably his kingdom's greatest general and leader, who for nearly twenty years had manipulated, defeated and thwarted Rome.[59] It is thought that two sons of Decebalus were captured by Maximus and his men. Typically, their fate would have been distant custody far from Dacia, usually somewhere in Italy.[60]

Trajan would have taken little pleasure from the news of Decebalus' death, received while in Ranisstorium, an unknown Dacian settlement.[61] Nor would he have relished the grisly trophy of the king's severed head, collected and presented to him by Maximus, who thereby earned a second decoration. Far better to have captured Decebalus alive and paraded the Dacian king in chains through the streets of Rome to the indignation of Dacia and to the glorification of Trajan's imperial power. Instead, the head of Decebalus was sent back to Rome where, according to custom, it was supposedly hurled down the Scalae Gemoniae steps on the Capitoline Hill like that of other vanquished enemies in Rome's past.

A kingdom's way of life and culture are not destroyed simply when its king is killed or its capital ruined. Moreover, it was not normal practice for the Romans to try and eradicate a kingdom's identity and population when it was converted into a province of the Roman Empire. However, it is likely that the nation's people had suffered and continued to suffer from a decline in population. There were significant casualties of war, especially among the aristocracy. Refugees from the conflict, or civilians seeking to escape the new Roman province, may have emigrated. It is thought that around 50,000 captives[62] were rounded up and shipped off to Rome and across the empire to become slaves or to feature in Trajan's emerging plans for a series of massive public games to celebrate his victory. Among Dacian men who were lucky enough to avoid the fate of slavery, large numbers of able-bodied and skilled fighting men were further rounded up as conscripts to serve in auxiliary units dispersed across the empire.[63] Nevertheless, a large native Dacian population still existed and there is no evidence of genocide.[64] It was not the practice of Rome to wipe out the population in occupied territories.[65] Rome wanted productivity and growth from its new province to fill the imperial coffers.

Roman citizens throughout the empire were then invited to settle in the new province,[66] to farm the lands or play a part in the construction of urban life. With time, the typical infrastructure to govern a new province was put in place and, soon after the fall of Sarmizegetusa Regia, Decimus Terentius Scaurianus was appointed as the first governor.[67] A new city to accommodate veteran legionaries of the wars was founded on the Haţeg Plain, just east of the Iron Gates Pass on the site of the IV *Flavia Felix* camp.[68] Called Colonia Ulpia Traiana Augusta Dacica, the urban centre would serve as the capital of the province and soon became known as Sarmizegetusa Ulpia.[69] Across the province, military roads were constructed to facilitate transport and communication. Along the perimeter of the province, they served as *limites* to demarcate the boundary of the province under Roman control. At the same time, fortifications were erected to garrison the province's forces. IV *Flavia Felix* was based at Berzobis to defend the western reaches of the province and XIII *Gemina* was garrisoned at Apulum (Alba Iulia) to cover the eastern and northern frontiers. Supported by auxiliaries, the new governor had around 24,000 men at his disposal to police and protect the new province.[70]

With time, productivity returned to Dacia after the devastation of the wars, through the re-establishment of agriculture across the province. Newly formed imperial estates additionally generated substantial wealth, particularly those that exploited Dacia's precious metals. Fifty years old on 18 September 106, Trajan remained in the region into early 107 to oversee the beginning of the conversion of Dacia into a Roman province and coins were quickly minted to proclaim the capture of the new province, *Dacia Capta*. In stark contrast, the Emperor Claudius was in Britain (AD 43) for only a few weeks at the end of campaigning before returning immediately to Rome after the successful capture of Camulodunum (Colchester). The fall of the Dacian kingdom, with the death of countless innocent people and with the destruction and loss of many of its unique cultural features was a tragic event. But to well-informed Romans it was an accepted consequence in the process of expanding the empire and spreading the *Pax Romana* to those viewed as uncivilised. All Trajan's objectives had been skilfully achieved and he could claim complete victory over a difficult adversary, as well as the extension of the empire, recalling the golden age of republican and early imperial expansionism. At the expense of a once-great kingdom, Trajan's position in Rome had never been stronger.

A silver *denarius*, struck in Rome *ca.* 108–9, showing a defeated Dacian sat on a pile of captured arms, commemorating the successful end of the Second Dacian War.

CHAPTER 9

BIDING TIME BETWEEN GREAT WARS

❦

Triumphant Return to Rome

The conclusion of the Second Dacian War was unambiguous. Dacia's capital was destroyed and the kingdom ruthlessly converted into a province of the Roman Empire. Its king, Decebalus, had narrowly escaped the fall of the capital, only to be pursued as a fugitive through the Carpathian Mountains and when cornered had taken his own life rather than endure the humiliation of capture. Trajan had overseen a series of seemingly faultless campaigns in the war, taking to the field in person and probably on occasion at great personal risk. These endeavours were the very essence of Roman virtue to which every citizen could aspire: *firmitas*, persistence to achieve a goal; *pietas*, doing one's duty, and *virtus*, leadership with courage and boldness.[1]

An emperor in possession of such virtues was aligned with the Roman belief in their divine right to conquer and civilise the known world. A magnificent Roman triumph for the heroic *imperator* was therefore assured and Trajan arrived back in Rome to claim it in the summer of 107, having spent a total of two years engaged in the second war. Accompanied by his immediate entourage and probably his closest advisers during the war, Sura, Livianus and Senecio, he would have seen the final stretch of road down towards the gates of Rome lined with cheering crowds gathered to witness the return of their emperor who had conquered a formidable barbarian enemy and expanded Rome's territories.

The news of Trajan's triumphal return to Rome would have prompted many officials to begin preparing extravagant celebrations and ceremonies worthy of his victory over Dacia. These were not trivial affairs to organise and required considerable resources. The Senate had voted Trajan a triumph, which was an ancient religious and state ceremony to revere and honour a successful commander and to glorify the victorious power of Rome. This was Trajan's second triumph, likely held a few days or even weeks after Trajan's actual return into Rome because of logistical arrangements; the pageantry surpassed his first triumph in December 102, claimed after the First Dacian War.

Around mid-June, on the eve of the triumph, the soldiery marched out of their camps in the outskirts of Rome and it is thought that they mustered in and around the Campus Martius. These troops would have been selected from cohorts distinguished for bravery during the war and included individuals awarded military crowns to represent their units. Trajan may have actually slept in the Temple of Isis in the Campus Martius, where Vespasian and Titus spent their night in 71 before their triumphal celebration of the Jewish Wars.[2]

Very early the next morning while the procession assembled, Trajan's first preliminary act was to meet the Senate at the Porticus Octavia. It was important for Trajan, always respectful of the Senate, to attend to the official rituals of the triumph. After offering prayers and addressing the assembly, Trajan went back to a triumphal gate near the Campus Martius. The gate is lost today and, the precise location remains unknown. Here, Trajan ate breakfast dressed in his triumphal attire. He quite possibly wore a purple tunic, the colour of imperial power, under a suitably ostentatious gold embroidered toga, with a laurel wreath upon his head as a symbol of victory.[3] He then gathered his required paraphernalia: in his right hand a laurel bough and his left a sceptre topped by an eagle. Finally, his face was painted red, the colour of the God of War, Mars.[4] Trajan then mounted a spectacular ornate chariot, pulled by four immaculately groomed horses. He was ready to start the triumph heading off from the gate.

The following list outlines a generalised order for the assembled triumphal column possibly applicable for Trajan's victory over Dacia:

- 1st: Members of the Senate.
- 2nd: Trumpeters, heralding the advance.
- 3rd: A display of war spoils from Dacia, including treasures and a myriad of precious items captured during the campaigns.
- 4th: Flutists playing music.
- 5th: Sacrificial white bulls or oxen, adorned with decorations and led by priests.
- 6th: Native animals from Dacia, perhaps lynx cats and bears.
- 7th: A display of Dacian arms and the symbolic Dacian draco standard.

8th: Possibly the preserved head of Decebalus, followed by a selection of *pileati* and *comati* warriors presumably bound and gagged. Any surviving members of Decebalus' family, such as his sister captured during the first war and two of his sons during the second, may have been included here.

9th: Lictors of the emperor.

10th: Trajan in his chariot. Sura, his closest friend and a prominent figure in both wars, could have also been in the chariot. According to one ancient source, such a triumph may have involved a slave holding a golden Etruscan jewelled crown over Trajan's head, constantly whispering a warning into his ear, something to the effect, '*Respice post te. Hominem te memento*' ('Look behind you. Remember that you are a man.'), just in case Trajan lapsed into thinking all this display of power made him a god.[5]

11th: On horseback, a selection of senior officers representing the forces involved in the triumph.

12th: Last, the long column of soldiers, their javelins adorned with laurels, singing songs or jesting in verses at Trajan' expense in a unique moment when such freedom of speech was allowed.

The full procession first headed south, probably through the large open space of the Circus Flaminius located near the Tiber, a chance for many seated spectators to view the column. Following a south-easterly direction, the column next moved through the Forum Boarium, the oldest forum in Rome. All along the route, streets would have been cleaned, temples were opened and their altars bellowed out incense smoke, and numerous buildings and statues were adorned with garlands of flowers.[6] Every position was crammed with eager spectators.[7] From here, it is likely that the triumphal procession passed by the Velabrum, a commercial area in the valley between the Capitoline and Palatine Hills, and then proceeded through the Circus Maximus, from the north-west to the south-east end, allowing up to 150,000 spectators to witness the procession. Heading north, the parade circled left past the Colosseum and turned west onto the Via Sacra and up towards the main Forum Romanum. Here the crowds would have packed the streets in vast numbers as the column edged into the heart of the forum, past the Temple of Julius Caesar and then the Basilica Julia before arriving at the Temple of Saturn.[8]

At this stage, some of the Dacian captives were led away to be killed at the Tullianum (better known today as the Mamertine Prison), while presumably select components of the procession began the climb up the Capitoline Hill still along the Via Sacra. Dismounting from his chariot at the top, Trajan oversaw the sacrifice of the bulls or oxen and then the spoils of war were dedicated in the magnificent Temple of Jupiter. Entering the temple itself, Trajan laid his laurel victory wreath in the lap of the vast statue of Jupiter as a final dedication to the God of Gods. The procession was now officially over and dispersed. Around this time, it is possible that Trajan met a plethora of dignitaries and embassies from beyond the empire's boundaries, including locations as far away as India. They had gathered to pay their respects to the omnipotent emperor and it was a mark of Trajan's supremacy and far-reaching influence.[9] The evening's festivities typically proceeded with enormous public feasts and lavish banquets throughout the city, while Trajan and his close friends may have dined lavishly in the Temple of Jupiter.[10]

Today, it is hard to appreciate the scale of pomp and extravagance of Trajan's Roman triumph, suffice to say that it would dwarf many modern-day state ceremonies or global events in its grandeur and spectacle. Moreover, a victorious entry into Rome and an official triumph through the heart of the city was only the start of Trajan's victory celebrations for the Second Dacian War. Next came a series of games and spectacles that rivalled or exceeded anything witnessed before in Rome. Trajan laid on a spectacular array of unparalleled games financed with the booty and treasure taken from Dacia, as recorded by a later Roman historian:

> And [Trajan] gave spectacles on one hundred and twenty-three days, in the course of which some eleven thousand animals, both wild and tame, were slain, and ten thousand gladiators fought.
>
> Dio Cassius[11]

By providing such games, Trajan was following the typical tactic of Roman emperors to keep the masses in Rome happy through extravagant entertainment. During the celebrations, Trajan provided recognition for his close supporters during the war by setting up public images, presumably statues, in prominent locations.

> [Trajan] also set up images of Sosius, Palma and [Publilius] Celsus, so greatly did he esteem them above the rest.
>
> Dio Cassius[12]

In one very special case, a third consulship was awarded to Sura in 107. This was a high distinction and a prestigious award for the loyal adviser and friend.

Hadrian, who had commanded the I *Minervia* legion effectively during the second war and excelled during the campaigns through notable deeds, was also included in the recognitions for excellent service. But as he was not ready for a consulship, his reward from Trajan was in fact more personal: the same diamond Trajan had received from Nerva to commemorate his adoption in 97.[13] The gift would have raised Hadrian's expectations of succeeding Trajan, but was surely mixed with disappointment as Trajan did not actually adopt him as his son and heir, presumably yet to be convinced that Hadrian was the best candidate to succeed him. In addition, Trajan may have felt that appointing Hadrian as his heir too early increased the risk that Hadrian might not want to wait too long for his own succession.[14]

Not forgetting the Roman people, Trajan issued his third *congiarium*, his most generous so far, with every registered citizen in Rome who was a recipient of the corn dole receiving around 500 *sestertii*, at a total cost of around 75 million.[15] To appreciate the scale of this *congiarium*, a lucky recipient could have bought around 1,300 kg of wheat with the money.[16] With the masses of Rome content through cash gifts and lavish celebrations and important loyalists suitably rewarded, Trajan could turn his complete attention to matters of state, many aspects benefiting from his presence in Rome rather than distant correspondence from the remote lands of Dacia.

Managing Affairs of State
Administration and Corruption

In nearly ten years as emperor, Trajan had spent around 50 per cent of his time engaged in military-related activities or at war. Now his return to Rome in 107, with no immediate conflict in sight, marked a new era in his principate in which he could concentrate on acting as a 'civilian' emperor. After his triumphal entry to Rome it probably took several days for Trajan to adjust to urban life again, figuratively dusting off the campaigning grime and familiarising himself with the vast array of state affairs that required his immediate attention. To help him in his duties as the ruler of a vast empire of more than sixty million people, a staggering 20 per cent of the world's entire population by conservative estimates, Trajan finalised the work of his predecessors who had aimed to establish a professional imperial secretariat, and exclusively appointed Roman equestrians rather than freed slaves, thus taking to its ultimate conclusion a trend started by his Flavian predecessors from Vespasian onwards.[17] In so doing, he thus in effect created a *cursus* of respectable civilian service for equestrians in addition to the military career path that they could pursue.[18] A prominent example is that of Caius Suetonius Tranquillus, an administrator and prolific writer, who produced the famous set of biographies of *The Twelve Caesars from Julius to Domitian*. Under Trajan, Suetonius was appointed to the prestigious post of *studiis*, responsible for the emperor's personal library and *bibliothecis*, in charge of Rome's public libraries. Suetonius would have been an invaluable source of detail and references for Trajan.

Supported by this equestrian secretariat, Trajan could operate more effectively within the new boundaries he is thought to have established between the Principate and the Senate in the aftermath of the First Dacian War. Trajan had presumably rallied support from key opinion leaders in the Senate and, with input from his *consilium*, he better defined legal 'grey areas' that had existed between the emperor and the Senate since the time of Augustus. Although each emperor's scope of authority was defined in the legal enactment (the *lex imperii*) that constituted his formal appointment, vague legal statutes or practices still existed, such as the paradoxical role of the consuls as the most senior state magistrates. Since the onset of Trajan's principate, he had striven to emulate an Augustan style of authority that fostered a congenial relationship with the Senate whereby the emperor was only the *princeps*, 'first among equals', and thereby sustain a balance of liberty in the Senate that would distance his reign from the most recent open autocracy of Domitian. Trajan's mindset and strategy, consistent since his accession, was to appease the Senate and always remain respectful. However, rather than fully adopt the strategy of the Emperor Augustus, who camouflaged his power to pacify the Senate, it is thought that Trajan concluded an arrangement with the Senate that established a major constitutional milestone.[19] The arrangement reflected Trajan's skills as an administrator and his desire to acknowledge transparently the imperial power he held.[20]

The deal had two possible elements and was probably much easier to achieve because of the fear that lingered after Domitian's repressive reign. Firstly, in addition to all the powers already given to the emperor, it was openly recognised that all affairs of the state were delegated to the emperor, and, secondly, the emperor's dignity was ranked second only to Jupiter.[21] The Senate benefited from this arrangement by being recognised in turn as the 'source of all legitimate power'.[22] To herald the new agreement, Trajan was awarded the new title, 'Optimus Princeps', the 'best of Princes'. This was a significant recognition of his personal endeavours but his modesty prevented him from adopting the title until later in his reign (*see* Chapter 10).

Clarification of the boundaries between the Senate and the Principate did not mean any less work for Trajan and his secretariat in his managing of the empire with support from the Senate. On any typical day, Trajan needed to deal with a myriad of duties that required his explicit attention and authorisation, including but not limited to: corresponding with provincial governors;[23] approving major construction plans; attending Senate meetings; receiving foreign embassies; judging legal cases and reviewing financial affairs. Practically, this meant many hours a day involved in complex discussions, as well as reading and dictating. Indeed, Trajan was viewed by his contemporaries as diligent[24] in his imperial administration and a fourth-century Roman historian recorded that:

> [Trajan] was a man of extraordinary skill in managing affairs of state
>
> Eutropius[25]

In many matters of state, Trajan no doubt took the time to consult with his *consilium* and he probably followed their guidance unless he held a strong opinion on any given subject.[26] But all Trajan's efforts could never prevent the endemic corruption ingrained in the system of Roman governance and its propensity to surge during his periods of absence from Rome during the Dacian wars. An interesting example is found in 105 (between the two wars) with the court of the Centumviri, tasked among other things with the litigation of wills and inheritance. The court was marred by claims that lawyers were receiving inappropriate presents and gifts. As a result, a praetor called Nepos was forced to issue an edict warning plaintiffs and defendants that:

> All persons engaged in any lawsuit are hereby ordered to take an oath before their cases are heard, that they have neither given nor promised any sum to their advocates, nor have entered into any contract to pay them for their advocacy.
>
> Letter, Pliny to Rufus[27]

Nepos' edict should not be confused with the bribery of judges, but rather the remuneration of advocates which today we would view as normal. However, the Roman elite did not want to see them paid, because the advocates would then act for the elite who could reward them indirectly.[28]

There was also an issue with collusion between advocates so that lawsuits were withdrawn or collapsed, where it suited a third party of influence. As a result, Nigrinus, a tribune of the plebs, made a formal statement saying that the senators should:

> ... petition their excellent Emperor [Trajan] to find a remedy for such a scandal.
>
> Letter, Pliny to Valerianus[29]

Shortly after, Trajan issued his own edict, described by Pliny, as 'at once moderate and severe' to curtail the corruption.[30]

In this period, at the request of the consuls, Trajan was also asked to intervene in efforts to prevent the corruption of senatorial elections.[31] Candidates were resorting to long relied upon forms of bribery to secure election, such as treating the electorate, or giving out presents and money.[32] After several speeches at a meeting of the Senate, it was unanimously agreed that the bribery should be curtailed and Trajan's vigilant authority was required to correct matters. Trajan responded by passing a law against bribery during canvassing. To cement the commitment of candidates he demanded that the qualification needed to stand should be amended to make them invest in Italian land rather than have all their land in the provinces and live in Rome or Italy like transient lodgers. Candidates were henceforth required to invest a third of their estates in Italian land.[33] As a result, there was a profound impact on the price of land, as candidates strove to purchase their required quota and, in some cases, to sell their assets in the provinces to pay the inflated prices for Italian soil.

Clearly concerned with corruption issues in Rome, Trajan was equally active trying to ensure that dishonesty and graft were eradicated in the provinces. Bithynia-Pontus, a province corresponding approximately to the north-western region of modern Turkey along the Black Sea coast, provides an example of Trajan's diligence in attending to provincial corruption. The depopulation of old Bithynian cities due to migration into new Roman provincial cities had crippled the local economy, but the wealthy landowners suffering from the economic turndown had continued to spend beyond their means, resulting in a financial meltdown, accentuated by a series of corrupt Roman governors. A group of despairing Bithynian citizens therefore petitioned Trajan to fix the province's financial issues.

Trajan acted decisively and normal procedure was abandoned to create an unusual office that would remedy the widespread corruption in Bithynia-

Pontus. Trajan secured the appointment of one of his finest financial gurus, a friend and member of his *consilium*,[34] Caius Plinius Caecilius Secundus, famously known as Pliny the Younger, to be governor of the public province. However, Pliny was to act as an imperial governor on behalf of Trajan, even though Bithynia-Pontus was a public province that normally fell under the immediate responsibility of the Senate.

Pliny clearly possessed the right skills and qualifications for his appointment: a *consul suffectus* in 100, he had previously served first as the head of the military treasury and then the state treasury.[35] He had fiscal expertise. Moreover, Pliny is thought to have been relentless and highly diligent in his efforts compared to other governors.[36] Besides the normal duties expected of an imperial governor, such as maintaining frontier security and provincial administration, Pliny's highest priority was his special task to tour the province in order to examine and regulate public finances, which were in considerable disorder.[37] In addition, he was expected to focus on correcting any corruption and abuses he encountered during his investigations.[38] In this role, his scope of authority had limits. For example, Pliny required approval from Trajan for any major new constructions in the province, which consequently imposed restrictions on the local elite and authorities.[39]

Pliny arrived in Bithynia-Pontus on 17 September 109 and his correspondence with Trajan commenced accordingly.[40] Amazingly many of the letters have survived and provide a unique insight into the centralised management of the empire under Trajan and his attempts to suppress financial corruption. With so many duties, even the conscientious Trajan would have relied on clerks to help with his frequent and voluminous correspondence with governors. No doubt letters drafted by the secretariat were approved for dispatch by the emperor, but it is thought that some letters were dictated by him; one can detect the voice of the emperor in some responses.[41]

Therefore, it is worth dwelling on what the content of these letters can tell us about Trajan, his mindset and character. While recognising the challenges of trying to perceive subtle interpretations in his letters, we frequently find that he was keen to follow precedent set by his predecessors or according to law, but on occasion he was able to compromise.[42] Trajan's legal reasoning gives importance to what had been decided in the past. Consistency, candour and frankness all come across strongly in his rulings, giving the sense that Trajan was an emperor who stood by his convictions.[43]

Trajan held the same absolute power as had promoted vanity in many of his predecessors. In contrast, the letters to Pliny, give examples of Trajan's modesty. Pliny wrote to the emperor to request permission to erect his statute in a temple he planned to construct in Italy.[44] Trajan made it clear that normally he was reluctant to accept flattery in the form of public imagery, but he conceded only to avoid offending Pliny's 'loyal feelings'. We have many sound examples of vain emperors adorning Rome and the empire with their image on a grandiose scale. Trajan's aversion, despite his position of supreme authority, speaks to his principled humility and a different approach to the distribution of the imperial image.

Like other Romans, Trajan expressed in one letter a degree of condescension towards the Greeks.[45] To put this into context, the Romans thought highly of the Greeks as a cultured and refined people, admiring many of their great figures like Alexander the Great. Condescension from Trajan may reflect a slight snobbery towards the Greeks, long folded into the Roman Empire.

A number of letters from Trajan also show he was on occasion prone to frustration.[46] This is hardly surprising, given the need for endless correspondence with his governors on a wide range of topics and issues throughout the year, but it does reveal Trajan's human traits despite his imperial office. In one letter, Trajan's own words come through in annoyance with Pliny in his endeavours to fight corruption: 'But for goodness' sake apply yourself...'[47]

One pertinent letter reveals that Trajan could be very savvy when it came to local machinations far from Rome.[48] Pliny appears to have missed a case of collusion despite being on the ground locally. The letter pertains to a prefect in the region asking for additional soldiers for his guard. However, Trajan realised that the prefect was merely trying to extend his privileges and as a result drain soldiers from much-needed active service. It also highlights the keen military mind of Trajan when it comes to such topics.

Conversely, there is an example where the distance of Rome from the provinces and the imperial agenda to protect its control, result in a less sympathetic emperor.[49] A major fire in the province caused significant damage and Pliny put forward a proposal for a dedicated company of firefighters whom he would personally ensure were genuinely skilled and would adhere to their responsibilities. Trajan bluntly rejected the proposal, citing the risk of people assembling as a group for ulterior motives. He ruled that the local community in question should manage fire-fighting themselves with equipment provided to them. One can keenly sense the judgement of a remote authority, far removed from the local needs to have a first-line emergency service, because of fear that local factions would group against imperial rule. This was understandable for a wider policy of ensuring peace within the empire, but at a cost to local communities and their ability to provide an emergency service.

One of the longest surviving letters Pliny wrote to Trajan during his appointment addressed the persecution of Christians. In Trajan's age, despite Roman tolerance and even absorption of foreign religions, Christianity was officially illegal, given its strong antipathy to certain Roman principles and the perception that Christians were prone to degenerate and aggressive behaviour. Pliny had no difficulty prosecuting people for their Christian beliefs. If the accused confessed to their belief, they were punished. Those who denied ever being Christian he discharged, but he was less certain what to do with those who confessed to having been Christian but now repented. Pliny suggested clemency and sought guidance from Trajan, who agreed. While Trajan was merciful to ex-offenders for their beliefs, he remained ruthless towards those who continued to profess their faith. Here we have insight into Trajan's character in which he can be benevolent as well as tough when it came to the application of Roman rule against troublesome minorities.

Pliny's last datable letter to Trajan was sent on 28 January 111, meaning his term as governor had exceeded the customary twelve months for a public province. It is thought that Pliny died in office as there is no concluding letter describing his achievements or a request to return to Rome. We do not know how successful Pliny was in dealing with the issues in Bithynia-Pontus. The problems were deep-seated and it is likely that only the worst aspects were inhibited. Such was the nature of governing the vast empire Rome had established.

Despite all Trajan's diligence in managing affairs of state, particularly his efforts to deal with corruption, the 'best of Princes' could never please everyone all of the time, and during his extended period in Rome, a plot was uncovered against him. The ancient sources are silent on the details, perhaps not wanting to tarnish the impeccable reputation that Trajan had by then established. The conspiracy, the size of which remains unknown, involved at least two senators, Caius Calpurnius Crassus Frugi[50] and Manius Laberius Maximus.[51] Crassus had a probable motive for seeking Trajan's downfall if one looks back into the reign of Nerva when he formed a plot against the emperor that never materialised. It appears he was never punished, but the affair almost certainly ended his *cursus*. Thus, Crassus' hatred of Nerva had festered over many years and he bore a deep grudge against his heir and successor, Trajan. Laberius' motive is unknown. A distinguished general in Trajan's First Dacian War, he was awarded the great honour of a second consulship in 103 alongside Trajan himself. However, he evidently fell out of favour with the emperor, spurring a vengeful streak in the ex-general that was sufficient to have drawn him into the conspiracy. Whatever their real motives, their plans were uncovered and charges were brought before the Senate. Their punishment was banishment into exile. Trajan seems to have had no involvement in bringing forward the charges and their subsequent exile rather than execution adhered to his promise that senators would not be sought out and killed for treason. The whole affair would have been an acute embarrassment for Trajan, who would have felt keenly that he had real enemies in the shadows of the Senate who found enough excuse in what he did, or represented, to warrant treasonous acts.

Construction

In ancient Rome, constructing a wondrous building or completing a daring engineering feat that surpassed anything predecessors had achieved was a sign that the empire under generous stewardship, was flourishing and exceeding the efforts of previous distinguished emperors. Consequently, Trajan's objective after the Second Dacian War was very straightforward: to show the Roman people that he was the most benevolent emperor Rome had ever seen, raising the principate to a zenith of benefaction for the veneration of Rome. This required the initiation of many construction projects before the war and arguably a surge in activity once the war was over when booty was readily available.

This objective may have been partially inspired by Nero's massive construction campaign after the great fire of Rome in 64, after which 'Rome rose again from her ashes a truly imperial city in outward splendour, worthy of her position as the metropolis of the world'.[52] Trajan is even known to have remarked that no other emperor had yet matched Nero's efforts in improving the magnificence of the city in the last five years of his reign. To exceed Nero and all Trajan's other predecessors, but avoid self-aggrandisements such as Nero's Golden House, would mean Trajanic works superior in splendour and proportions to Julius Caesar's forum, greater in visual impact than Augustus' famous transformation of Rome from brick into marble, exceeding the practicality of Claudius' artificial harbour at Ostia and more striking than Domitian's dazzling gold leafing of the temple of Jupiter's roof – but equally not as self-gratifying as his sprawling imperial palace on the Palatine Hill. Thus, if the right balance could be achieved, the new Trajanic constructions would affirm Trajan's status as the 'best of princes' and win the many hearts and minds of the Roman people who adored wondrous new structures and public spaces. Execution of his building programme, far beyond his earlier accomplishments, required careful planning and Trajan probably hatched his plans in the run up to and during the Second Dacian War, following consultation with his principal architect, Apollodorus, so that on his return to Rome with a vast treasure to finance his ideas, he could patronise a construction surge that would see a string of dedications and inaugurations through 109–12.[53]

The quintessential example is the building of Trajan's new forum complex in Rome, which exemplifies above all others the remarkable construction campaign he sponsored. The Forum Traiani was started in 107 and dedicated on 1 January 112. Work in the area of this forum had actually started under Domitian, who undertook the task of chopping a section out of the Quirinal Hill to make space for an enormous complex. In 107 Trajan commissioned Apollodorus to design and build the last and greatest forum Rome would see.[54] It was probably destroyed by earthquakes in the ninth century but was in use for at least 500 years. To appreciate fully the sheer scale and grandeur of Trajan's forum, one should imagine being a visitor to Rome wandering through the complex. Approaching from the south-west, a mammoth triumphal arch with one gate allowed the visitor to enter the forum. On top of the arch entrance was a larger than life, probably gilt bronze, statue of the victorious Trajan riding a six-horse chariot. The entrance provided an immediate awe-inspiring effect and a reminder of Trajan's great Dacian victory. Passing through, the visitor entered directly into a immense open space, the Area Fori, or central plaza of the forum, approximately 120 m long and 90 m wide, paved in gleaming white Italian marble. One's eye would be drawn immediately to a colossal equestrian statue of Trajan in the middle of the space. Surely a breath-taking view in its entirety, to the left and the right two raised peristyles ran the length of the Area Fori, with three steps of fine Numidian yellow marble leading up to the Corinthian colonnade with 9-m high Phrygian white and purple marble columns. Above each column, large statues of Dacians appeared to support the ornate cornices topped by pedestals with military standards and, between each Dacian Atlas, the visitor may have recognised the framed portraits of historical figures carved in fine marble. If one walked closer to the peristyles, a large *exhedra* (semi-circular portico) on either side could be seen, divided from the colonnade by columns of yellow Numidian marble. The *exhedra* were two storeys high and exquisitely appointed with statues and fine marble veneers.[55]

At the far north-west end of the Area Fori, the visitor faced the Basilica Ulpia, the largest in Rome. Fronted by three porches, the Corinthian columns made of *giallo antico*, golden-coloured granite, contrasted aesthetically with the Phrygian purple and white marble columns behind that made up the Basilica aisles. Above the column façade, a highly decorative cornice supported more Dacian statues made from Phrygian marble with their heads made of white marble, and panels depicting piles of Dacian weapons. In the centre, a magnificent metal statue of Trajan riding a four-horse chariot, with his arm raised in salute, was flanked on either side by a two-horse chariot, each of them presumably ridden by one of Trajan's favoured generals in the Dacian wars. Behind these statues, the visitor could see another row of ionic columns made from a greenish Italian marble which supported the upper second tier of the *basilica* and the massive roof of the building.

Through one of the porches of the *basilica*, having ascended five steps of yellow Numidian marble, the visitor passed between the inner Phrygian columns and into the first vaulted aisle and finally past a screen of gray Egyptian granite columns before emerging into the stunning central nave, which was 88 m long and 25 m wide. With light beaming down through the columns of the second storey, the entire covered space must have been a marvel to behold. The floor of the nave was patterned by a refined geometrical arrangement of squares and circles made from fine coloured marbles. The visitor may have been informed that while Dacian booty paid for the forum itself, the *basilica* was paid for separately, from Trajan's own purse. Continuing forward, one would have observed two large *exhedra* at either end of the *basilica*, before passing through two aisles, identical to those used to enter the nave from the Area Fori, and into a colonnaded courtyard with two large libraries on either side, one for Greek and the other for Latin literature.

The same courtyard would also later house the freestanding Trajan's Column, 44 m high, with its spiral relief of the Dacian Wars, erected in 113 and still *in situ* today.

The geometric elegance and balance, the marble polychromic arrangements, the plethora of fine metal and marble statues, the enormous dimensions and the frequent images related to the Dacian war would have left the visitor in no doubt of Trajan's absolute power at the pinnacle of imperial omnipotence and Rome's mighty glory. When the Emperor Constantius II visited Rome for the first time in 359, his amazement at the splendour of Trajan's forum was recorded by a leading late Roman historian and succinctly describes the unparalleled beauty of the complex:

But when [Constantius II] came to the Forum of Trajan, a construction unique under the heavens, as we believe, and admirable even in the unanimous opinion of the gods, he stood fast in amazement, turning his attention to the gigantic complex about him, beggaring description and never again to be imitated by mortal men. Therefore abandoning all hope of attempting anything like it, he said that he would and could copy Trajan's steed alone, which stands in the centre of the vestibule, carrying the emperor himself.

Ammianus Marcellinus[56]

A silver denarius, struck in Rome *ca.* 112–15. Trajan's Column can be seen with the emperor's statue on top and two eagles at the base.

Fiscal Affairs

The last component to consider in Trajan's administration of the empire during his seven-year period in Rome was the periodic review of state budgets and financial resources, supported by the prefects of the treasuries. In the early period of his reign, Trajan had enough cash, inheriting a healthy fiscal position from his predecessors Domitian and Nerva.[57] After the Second Dacian War, Trajan returned to Rome with a vast wealth acquired from the Dacian royal treasures and newly acquired rich precious metal mines. However, at the same time, Trajan allowed a significant debasement of the silver *denarii* coinage by around 2 per cent in purity to a fineness of around 91.5 per cent.[58] Overall, this effectively meant a small but significant increase in the quantity of coinage that could be minted from the bullion reserves.

To understand why Trajan authorised this debasement, one must assess the balance sheet of the state in this period. While no definitive figures exist to support any robust assessment, totalling gross estimates for Trajan's expenses, based on reasonable conjecture, against the available income in the period, allows one to observe that Trajan may have enjoyed a healthy surplus despite his benevolent activities and substantial construction projects.[59] Therefore it has been suggested that the prudent fiscally minded Trajan debased the silver coinage to help preserve the fixed ratio of value between silver and gold coins in the wake of a massive influx of gold bullion following the conquest of Dacia. Because of this influx, the relative value of the precious metals changed, and debasement would have helped preserve the over-valuation of the silver *denarius* coin.[60] Whatever the reasons for the debasement of the *denarii* by Trajan, he did not draw complaints from the Senate and his reputation for skilful management of state affairs, which would have included fiscal success, remained thoroughly intact, as recorded by a third century Roman historian:

> He exercised the government in such a manner, that he is deservedly preferred to all the other emperors.
>
> Eutropius[61]

Arabia Provincia

In 106, during the closing phases of the Second Dacian War, Trajan was able to orchestrate remotely the annexation of the Nabataean kingdom with little resistance from the inhabitants.[62] Presumably after his return to Rome, he focussed on its adaptation into a province through his appointed governor. The Nabataean kingdom covered an area approximately equivalent to modern-day southern Syria, Jordan, the Egyptian Sinai Peninsula and Saudi Arabia's Gulf of Aqaba region. Given its geographical position bridging the Mediterranean and the Middle East, by the first century AD, the kingdom had monopolised highly lucrative trade routes passing through its realm that were reliant on its oasis settlements, which formed the backbone of the caravan trails. In particular, the Nabataeans controlled two major trade routes from the East to the Mediterranean, one between Egypt, Syria and Mesopotamia, and the return trade from the Mediterranean to the East. Goods included, among others, luxury species, prized perfumes and incenses, precious stones and high-value glassware.

In short, the Nabataean kingdom was a conduit for trade between five major areas of civilisation: the Roman Empire, Mesopotamia, the Middle East, India and China. Three cities had flourished into major centres of commerce along the routes because of their commanding positions at critical junctions: from north to south along an ancient thoroughfare called the King's highway they were Bostra (Busra ash-Sham, Syria), Petra (Jordan) and the port city of Aelana (Aqaba, Jordan) on the Gulf of Aqaba.

The Nabataeans had given no cause for Trajan to invade and take possession of the region for security reasons, but other motives for annexation can be deduced. Foremost, the kingdom's riches would have been well known and desired by Rome, and the prices of goods from the East were increasing for Roman consumers. The Roman writer Pliny the Elder, uncle of Pliny the Younger, protested in the first century about the cost of luxury items from the east:

> India, the Seres [Far East] and the Arabian Peninsula, withdraw from our empire one hundred million sesterces every year – so dearly do we pay for our luxury.
>
> Pliny the Elder[63]

With the kingdom controlled as a province, Rome could dominate pricing and improve revenue through direct taxation and levies, which would help to balance the mounting trade deficit between Rome and the East due to the importation of luxury eastern merchandise. From a military perspective, the province could be taken with little effort and easily maintained with just one legion, which at the time could be spared from Egypt without the need to raise a replacement. Therefore, when the last king of Nabatea, Rabbel II Soter, died after a reign of thirty-five years, Trajan was able to capitalise on the transition of power to the king's heir, Obobas.[64] Trajan called on his trusted friend Palma, who was governor of Syria at the time, and a Roman force with detachments from Egypt and Syria was able to seize the kingdom. Presumably, a successful short war was fought against Nabataean royal forces trying to defend the sovereignty of Obobas. The conflict would have been short-lived given the poor defences of the kingdom and the general lethargic nature of the Nabataeans, who were probably not inclined to fight a protracted war against Rome that they were bound to lose.[65] In addition, it is thought that the Nabataean kingdom's monopoly and power were somewhat eroded at this time due to the gradual loss of trade passing up the Red Sea directly to Egypt, and therefore coming under the Roman Empire would have had its advantages in terms of protection against growing external dangers.[66] Nevertheless, Palma was suitably rewarded for the successful invasion with triumphal insignia, a statue erected in Rome and the honour of a second consulship in 109.[67]

After the annexation, Legio III *Cyrenaica* was moved from Egypt to the new province of Arabia in 107 to be based at the important Nabatean city of Bostra, supported by auxiliary units throughout the province.[68] Strategically, the legion was well placed on the King's highway and between Aelana and the Euphrates town of Sergiopolis (Resafa), able to defend the south-eastern reaches of the empire's frontier with Parthia as well as the essential trade route cities of the new province down to the Gulf of Aqaba. The city of Bostra was soon renamed Nova Traiana Bostra and proclaimed the capital of the new province. It became the seat of the first praetorian governor, Caius Claudius Severus.[69] The city prospered under Roman rule and today a superbly preserved Roman theatre, able to seat 15,000 people, can still be visited, which illustrates the adornment of the provincial capital. To improve transport, Trajan's engineers in the province constructed a new road along the King's highway between Bostra and Aqaba, called the Via Traiana Nova.[70] In addition to improving transport, this road was essentially a form of defence along the desert steppe used by Roman forces to police the eastern rim of the province.[71] There were no victory celebrations for the new imperial province and Trajan never included reference to the subjugation of Arabia in his titles[72] in keeping with his policy of avoiding the extravagant claims of victory that some of his predecessors had often overplayed to their detriment. Modesty prevailed with recognition of the annexation described as *'Arabia adquisita'* – 'Arabia acquired' – on coins that were only issued around five years later during Trajan's fifteenth-year celebrations as emperor.

A gold *aureus*, struck in Rome *ca*. 108–10. The personification of Arabia and the camel were designed to commemorate the seemingly peaceful acquisition of the region.

Family Affairs (ca. 105–113), Friends and Trajan's Persona

Trajan's prolonged period in Rome during 107–13 was certainly a time for him to strengthen family bonds and closely supervise family affairs as the patriarchal head of the Ulpii. His wife and only sister, now in their early forties and late fifties respectively, had been faultless in their conduct during his absences from Rome for the Dacian wars and had never failed to support him or uphold the honour of the imperial family. Exceedingly grateful for their demeanour and to acknowledge them as the two most prominent women in Roman society, Trajan awarded them both the title of *Augusta* in

105. Augusta was the feminine form of Augustus, a title used by emperors as a cognomen to link them with the venerable first emperor. It was a high honour for Marciana and Plotina, in recognition of their model virtues, and the title had been awarded surprisingly rarely in the past. The first title was bestowed on Augustus' wife Livia after his death and then four more times, the last being the grand-daughter of Vespasian, Flavia Domitilla, some twenty-five years before Trajan's award.

In high Roman society, these two *Augustae* were clearly a force to be reckoned with, their de facto power arguably a match for even a distinguished Roman man. Not merely restricted to domestic life, the two *Augustae* would have played an active role in maintaining socio-political connections with the Roman elite. Furthermore, it is highly likely that they supported Trajan surreptitiously in matters of state and it is known that Plotina travelled with Trajan on occasion and would have acted as his close aide. They were not officially empowered to act on Trajan's behalf in such a capacity but their indirect influence through Trajan was probably very significant.[73] In any behind-the-scenes involvement, both *Augustae* appear to have remained above criticism, and in particular, Plotina's keen interest in Epicurean philosophy[74] was evident in her reasonable and modest nature, in contrast to the aggressive acts of intrigue that were the hallmark of some of the wives of previous emperors.

Trajan's niece Matidia, forty years old in 108, remained virtuous by all accounts and caring of her children, Matidia the Younger and Sabina, as well as a pillar of support within the immediate family.[75] Matidia, her daughters, plus Hadrian as Sabina's husband and Marciana, all resided with Trajan and Plotina in the Domus Tiberiana, where they were well established, having lived together for many years on the Palatine Hill. One can assume that the three older women all took great interest in the welfare of Matidia the Younger and Sabina who were in their twenties around 108. By this same time, Sabina had been married to Hadrian for seven years and they remained childless. Her sister, Matidia the Younger, despite being in the prime of her life, is thought never to have married nor had any children, which was highly unusual given the exceptionally advantageous connection to her great-uncle, Trajan. Everyone would have long ago given up hope that Trajan would father a child with Plotina and expectations were probably fading fast that Hadrian and Sabina would soon extend the family. It was also probably emerging that Hadrian and Sabina's marriage was not a happy one and their marital discord may have been very evident to the immediate family. Such was the friction between them that Sabina is said to have gone to the extent of deliberately trying to prevent herself from becoming pregnant.

> [Sabina] used to say openly that, because she had judged his [Hadrian's] character inhuman, she had taken pains lest, to the bane of the human race, she become pregnant by him.
> *Epitome De Caesaribus*[76]

It would therefore seem that the family's infertility curse, in the case of Hadrian and Sabina, was self-induced rather than having a biological cause. The whole situation was almost certainly compounded by Hadrian's homosexuality. In any event, the blood line of the imperial family was limited as a result of the family's lack of fecundity.

Around this same time, Hadrian was appointed governor of the newly divided 'Inferior' portion of Pannonia. It is possible he took up his position at the time Pannonia was divided, in June 106, relinquishing his command of I *Minervia* and thereby missing the climax of the concluding Dacian War.[77] Nevertheless, with the single legion posted in Pannonia Inferior, II *Adiutrix*, he successfully handled the Iazyges who were probably up in arms against Rome for two reasons: firstly, for not returning lands they had lost to Dacia; secondly, their traditional migration routes through Oltenia were hindered given that the region had become part of the Roman province of Moesia Superior. As an indication of his successes and for the next stage of his *cursus*, Hadrian was appointed *consul suffectus* in 108 at the age of thirty-two. However, he did not receive the more distinguished and coveted honour of opening the year as a *consul ordinarius*.

Loose tongues in the Senate would have noted this significant slight, given that Trajan personally approved the consulship lists each year. A number of factors would have raised Hadrian's expectations of receiving the more prominent position, such as his auspicious connection with the imperial family through his marriage to Trajan's great niece, his growing intimacy with Trajan during the Dacian wars and his notable deeds in the second war for which Trajan gave him the diamond he had once received from Nerva.[78]

Regardless of all these portents, Hadrian's unhappy marriage with Sabina was perhaps a source of discontent in the family and they may have persuaded Trajan to be less indulgent with his cousin once removed. Alternatively – or in addition – Hadrian's private social habits may have again diverged from the strict conduct that Trajan expected from his family and it was probably still not completely forgotten that several times in Hadrian's youth Trajan had chastised his inappropriate behaviour. As an extreme example, the Emperor Augustus had banished family members for unworthy conduct during his reign, so if Hadrian was behaving inappropriately he was potentially treading on thin ice with Trajan, who wanted to uphold an image of concord and decorum in the imperial family. But whatever the status of his evolving relationship with Trajan and the reasons for his appointment as *consul suffectus* instead of *consul ordinarius*, he retained the confidence of Plotina and Matidia throughout.

Regarding Trajan's friends, he suffered a grave loss when his closest companion Sura died in 108. Sura had consistently supported Trajan both in private and in public. A compatriot from Tarraco in Spain, no other person seems to have done more to champion Trajan's merits and lobby for his successful adoption by Nerva and ultimate accession to the Principate. At the critical time of Trajan's adoption, Sura had been serving as governor of Germania Inferior with three legions under his command. His loyalty to Trajan and his political clout were therefore instrumental in securing Trajan's smooth political elevation. He was also a man of great wealth who had constructed a public gymnasium at his own expense.[79] Once Trajan was emperor, Sura had acted as a close adviser in matters of state and had been a core member of his *consilium*. In this capacity he would have been highly influential in Trajan's policy and decisions. He also served Trajan as a special military adviser in both of the Dacian wars, where he probably accompanied Trajan closely on all his campaigns. In reward for his services and support, Trajan had granted him the extremely rare honour for a non-imperial family member of a third consulship in 107.[80] The imperial palace would have been a very sober place during the mourning for this distinguished senator.

During his life, a number of senators had been envious of Sura's privileged relationship with Trajan. They had vented their spite in a campaign to spoil Trajan's trust by insistently raising false suspicions of ill intent. An anecdote recorded by Dio Cassius describes how Trajan wanted to ridicule the accusations and show how much he trusted Sura. He decided to arrive unexpectedly one evening at Sura's house for dinner, presumably in Rome, without any guards. He then asked Sura's physician to anoint his eyes and his barber to shave him: both opportune moments for an assassination to occur. Afterwards, Trajan bathed and had dinner in the house. The next day Trajan remarked to those who had raised the false suspicions:

> If Sura had desired to kill me, he would have killed me yesterday.
>   Dio Cassius[81]

One can conclude from this anecdote that Trajan had lost a truly trusted companion; to honour his great friend he granted him a state funeral. On the day of the funeral, all public and private businesses were closed and Sura's body would have been taken from the place it rested in wake to the forum. Here, the *laudatio funebris*, funeral eulogy, may have been delivered by one of Sura's closest relatives and probably also by Trajan. Standing on the forum *Rostra*, they would have recounted Sura's many virtues and contributions of service to Rome. Surrounded by mourners, Sura's body was likely cremated on a pyre before his ashes were taken outside Rome to be interred alongside his ancestors.

In accordance with Roman tradition, a wax mask would have been made of Sura's face soon after his death to record his image, and the mask hung in the family house alongside other funeral masks as a reminder of the their illustrious past. The mask would also have served as a template to sculpt posthumous statues or busts of Sura. Trajan himself commissioned a statue in honour of Sura after his death and also constructed a prominent public bath, the Thermae Suranae, to immortalise his name. Dedicated in 109, and therefore built without delay soon after Sura's death, the baths were constructed on the site of his home on the Aventine Hill, which commanded fine views out across the Circus Maximus below and had been left in Sura's will to Trajan.[82]

Considering Trajan's general persona after a decade in power by 108, one can start by reviewing the images of Trajan and the imperial family, who were relatively well recognised, given that their statues and busts by then filled public areas, buildings and private homes throughout Rome and the empire. Public display emphasising one's status was an important aspect of Roman society, especially for the imperial family. Their images had to be visible to reaffirm constantly their eminent position, and the Ulpii portrayed a specific image of serenity and honour that is striking in the expressions of their portraits. The images were also somewhat idealised as part of imperial advertising to display the sort of youthful eternal persona that Augustus had used successfully during his principate a century earlier. Nevertheless, if one recognises the idealised elements created by the artists who prepared Trajan's statues and peel away the artistic licence, one can examine Trajan's likely physical form in this period to establish a reasonable impression of his appearance. Despite him being in his early fifties, statues continued to show Trajan with an athletic torso, suggesting he remained in excellent physical condition – not rippling with muscles, but strong and with little excess body fat.[83] This image is almost certainly exaggerated, but it is fair to assume that Trajan was in reasonable health given that we know he enjoyed physical pursuits and that during the Dacian wars he endured many hardships alongside his men. Earlier in his reign Pliny described how Trajan sought exertion as a source of relaxation from the rigours of his duties and it is possible he continued such recreations, perhaps to a lesser extent later in his life but enough to remain fit:

> Your only relaxation is to range the forests, drive the wild beasts from their lairs, scale vast mountain heights, and set foot on the rocky crags, with none to give help.
>
> Pliny[84]

In all his busts, Trajan's hair does not appear to be receding and the style had not changed since his accession, featuring the same military cut with a neat semi-circular fringe. It is more plausible that his hair line had receeded somewhat over the years, but we are not led to believe he was severely balding. In some portraits, signs of age can actually be found in his face, with a heavier expression and deeper lines forming just over his central brow and two either side of his mouth – overall, a more drawn appearance that somewhat belied the youthful image.

Still physically in good shape despite his increasing age, Trajan's temperament was considered milder as he grew older, and it is said that he never restorted to deception or harshness to achieve what he wanted.[85] He was open in his mannerisms to those that were worthy, as the Roman historian Dio Cassius indicates when he records that Trajan:

> loved, greeted and honoured the good, and the others he ignored.
>
> Dio Cassius[86]

Clearly respected for his abilities as Emperor, Trajan was able to mix pleasure with his work. For example, we have seen earlier that he called his *consilium* to a coastal retreat outside of Rome near Centum Cellae (Civitavecchia) where the emperor judged legal cases for three days. Pliny, as a member of the *consilium*, describes the pleasurable time away spent at Trajan's scenic imperial villa:

Thus you see how usefully and seriously we spent our time, which, however, was diversified with amusements of the most agreeable kind. We were every day invited to Caesar's table, which, for so great a prince, was spread with much plainness and simplicity. There we were either entertained with interludes or passed the night in the most pleasing conversation. When we took our leave of him on the last day, he made each of us presents; so studiously polite is Caesar! As for myself, I was not only charmed with the dignity and wisdom of the judge, the honour done to the assessors, the ease and unreserved freedom of our social intercourse, but with the exquisite situation of the place itself. This delightful villa is surrounded by the greenest meadows, and overlooks the shore, which bends inwards, forming a complete harbour [Centum Cellae].

Pliny to Cornelianus[87]

From this description, one can picture Trajan as hardworking, true to his humble character in terms of frugality, but able to charm and relax with his guests. A very rare remark by Trajan has been paraphrased that typifies this good nature. His friends queried why he was so courteous to everybody despite his exalted position and he responded to the effect that,

He was such an emperor to his subjects as he had wished, when a subject, that emperors should be to him.

Eutropius[88]

Modesty and adhering to the Augustan strategy that the emperor should pretend to be only the 'first among equals' underpinned the behaviour that Trajan practised.

It would therefore appear that age and his years in power had not altered Trajan's character or physical appearance detrimentally, but neither does it seem to have diminished his two major vices, the first being wine. It is supposed that many years of sustained heavy consumption of wine, while not interfering with his daily work, likely posed a threat to his health, especially as his tolerance for alcohol required ever-increasing quantities to achieve inebriation.[89] Aware of his weakness, Trajan had taken action to curb his drinking by asking the palace slaves to stop serving him when he was showing signs of intoxication.[90] His second desire was homosexual relations with attractive partners and his needs do not seem to have abated over time. For example, while back in Rome after the First Dacian War,

Trajan attended a pantomime performance and was attracted to one of the male performers called Pylades, likely named after Pylades of Cicilia who was credited with developing tragic pantomime. Pylades was presumably a slave selected to perform in the pantomime because of his beauty and condition. Overall, such relations as with Pylades or others did not dent Trajan's reputation and the respect he commanded.

A silver *denarius*, struck in Rome *ca.* 112–13. The personification of Via Traiana, reclining with a wheel supported in her right arm, is thought to refer to the Italian Via Traiana and the Via Traiana Nova in the East, both commissioned by Trajan.

The Path to War

As we have seen in this chapter, Trajan returned to Rome after the Second Dacian War and remained there for seven years, his longest period in Rome throughout his principate. He was by no means idle in this period. Initially, he provided extravagant and protracted celebrations for the victorious conquest of Dacia. In addition, he remained engrossed in the complex administration of state affairs, which he appeared to manage diligently and to the acclaim of his subjects and later Roman historians. Notably, he steered through a series of major building projects to achieve recognition as one of the foremost benefactors in Rome's imperial age. He was also attentive to the continued eradication of the endemic corruption in Rome and across the empire, with a centralised approach to government. In the east, Arabia was transformed into a province following its annexation. In private, there were probably issues stemming from Hadrian's unhappy marriage to Sabina but in public his immediate family continued to uphold an image of modest and virtuous behaviour, untouched by the trappings of their highly distinguished status. Emotionally, the sad loss in this period of Trajan's closest friend and ally Sura surely created a void in his life.

Yet despite all these events, distractions and activities, Trajan's attraction to military life and his evident desire for glory fostered a continued yearning for further military projects that would end his stint as a 'civilian' emperor in

Rome. An event in the east in 113 would trigger sufficient justification for the warrior emperor to seek other military triumphs, and the action would allow him to address a frontier he had conceivably contemplated since his first visit to the north-eastern edges of the empire as a young man. As events would unfold in the east, it would have not been unreasonable for some sceptics to assume that Trajan's protracted time in Rome had simply been a biding of his time between wars. His yearning for conquest had to be satisfied once again and at the peak of his power no one would stand in his way.

CHAPTER 10

THE PARTHIAN WAR

Justification for War

Since the fall of Carthage at the end of the Third Punic War in 146 BC, few nations or empires posed a threat to Rome's regional domination. The Parthian Empire was one of those few and the Euphrates River had essentially served as the boundary between the two great hegemonies. Sporadic, sometimes large-scale warfare between them had occurred over the two centuries before Trajan's time, provoked by the Romans or the Parthians, with responsibility for the conflicts evenly shared between the two.[1] At the core of the delicate stability between the two empires was Armenia. Much larger than the modern state of Armenia, the ancient kingdom covered an area stretching across modern-day eastern Turkey, Azerbaijan and northern Iran. Nominally controlled by both empires, Armenia cushioned the margins of political and military influence between Rome and Parthia. It is not clear what Rome and Parthia agreed for the nomination and endorsement of the Armenian king but it appears that the realities of the situation resulted in Parthia nominating a candidate for Rome to approve.[2] The Parthian candidate was selected from within Parthia's ruling Arsacid dynasty. Symbolically, this meant that the royal diadem, typically a decorated ribbon worn around the head representing an Armenian crown, was awarded by the absent Roman emperor to the Parthian candidate for his coronation.

In 113, the Parthian ruler Osroes I upset the balance of power between the two empires by meddling in Armenian affairs. He replaced one of his nephews with another, Parthamasiris, on the Armenian throne without Trajan's advance approval. Osroes' authority had been challenged since his succession by a claimant to the Parthian throne, the rival King Vologaeses

III, who ruled in the east of the Parthian Empire. Osroes' interference in Armenia was doubtless an attempt to gain more power against his foe in the east. Appointing Parthamasiris may have given Osroes more control over Armenian resources. The bold move may have also been a show of strength to his fellow Parthians. In any event, the Armenia status quo, as it had been for fifty years since the reign of Nero, was disrupted as a result and the treaty violation was enough for Trajan to justify war against Parthia.

A silver *drachm*, struck in Ekbatana *ca.* 109–29, features a rare depiction of King Osroes I, showing him with a traditional pointed beard and his hair in large bundles behind his ear and above his crown.

The arrival in Rome of news of Parthia's interference in Armenia was very likely a surprise, with little or no warning. However, the Armenian coronation crisis had opportunistic value for Trajan. He had probably long recognised the need to improve the northerly section of the eastern frontier and he could also seek further military glory, which he fervently desired. Around thirty-seven years earlier, as a young tribune on his first military posting, Trajan may possibly have witnessed part of Vespasian's reorganisation of the eastern frontier. This reinforced Cappadocian *limites* on the border with Armenia and garrisoned Syria in greater territorial depth the better to secure the western banks of the mid-Euphrates. Trajan's own father had been awarded the *ornamenta triumphalia* for his involvement in military action against the Parthians and it is likely that his opinions on the frontiers at that time influenced Trajan's later consideration of war against Parthia. Trajan had also witnessed Domitian's Rhine–Danube frontier developments and conducted his own detailed review of the Danubian defences after his accession as emperor. With an informed opinion and 'hands-on' experience in frontier development, Trajan may have realised for many years that, despite Vespasian's enhancements in the East, the frontier remained fundamentally flawed: the current northerly section may have enjoyed the geographical barrier of the mid- and upper Euphrates, but it lacked the ideal political and military zone of influence beyond the frontier that supported the perimeter defences, given the presence of two formidable adjacent entities, Armenia and the Parthian Empire.[3]

To improve the sub-optimal condition of the eastern frontier, Trajan had a grand vision of creating a uniform approach that integrated his efforts in Arabia with Vespasian's arrangements in the south-east of Syria and then with a new approach in the northern section to build a formidable frontier that would stretch over 2,000 kilometres from the Gulf of Aqaba to the foothills of the Caucasus Mountains. To achieve this vision, Armenia and northern Mesopotamia would need to be annexed. (It should be noted that Mesopotamia was not a kingdom but a geographical region roughly comprising the rich cultivated areas between the two great rivers, the Euphrates and the Tigris.) With Armenia as a garrisoned province and thereby removed from the equation, a new demarcation across Mesopotamia would provide an easily defensible frontier with the Armenian mountains to the rear and the forbidding mid-Mesopotamian deserts in front. From south to north, the eastern frontier *limites* would follow the existing Arabian infrastructure from Aqaba to Damascus before turning north-east to Palmyra and on across to the Euphrates. Such a frontier would be defensible given that the expanses of Arabian desert lying to the south-east had less than 200 millimetres of rainfall a year and that the few viable routes for invasion along desert trails could easily be cordoned off.

The new Mesopotamian frontier envisaged by Trajan could have run along a west to east axis that included Zeugma, Edessa, Nisibis and on to the Tigris at a similar latitude before rising up into the foothills of the Taurus Mountains, where the client states beyond could support the most easterly section of the new border. His grand design for the eastern fringes of the empire was intended as a defining moment in Roman history at the pinnacle of his principate – the far more assertive stance would eradicate the weaknesses of the Flavian frontier, incorporate Armenia and northern Mesopotamia and maintain in its entirety an arguably superior geographical position despite not taking in the mid- and lower Euphrates.

These plans were probably confided to a privileged few within Trajan's *consilium*. Had they been shared more widely with the Senate, they may otherwise have given rise to a sentiment that Trajan was on a war-mongering mission in the pursuit of personal glory. The Roman historian Dio Cassius, even so, not openly critical of Trajan before the Armenian coronation crisis, recorded his view on the real motive for war:

His real reason was a desire to win renown.

Dio Cassius[4]

Dio surely based his remark on contemporary criticism that had been handed down to him over the intervening eighty years or so.[5] Dio and the contemporary critics were likely right: it would seem that Trajan's evident love of military life could only be satisfied with yet another outstanding victory. Aspirant Romans like Trajan had long envied the exploits of Alexander the Great, the epitome of a brilliant military commander who, in his twenties, had conquered Achaemenid Persia, predecessor to the Parthian Empire. Moreover, formidable Roman generals like Marcus Licinius Crassus and Mark Antony had failed miserably to defeat the Parthians, resulting in enormous Roman casualties. The Armenia coronation crisis in 113 therefore provided Trajan with the excuse to implement a grand design for a new improved eastern frontier, and any success would emulate Alexander the Great and boost his own personal glory on an enterprise on which so many famous Romans had failed.

Heading for War

The execution of Trajan's vision for a new frontier in the east, with the annexation of Armenia and northern Mesopotamia, required a significant and gradual mobilisation of troops and resources to key centres of operation. Some premeditation was therefore required in advance of conflict. As such, Trajan ensured militarily adept and highly trusted men were in place in the East in or before 113. In particular, Quadratus Bassus, with a high reputation in military matters, was appointed governor of Syria. He transferred from governing Cappadocia and had held posts in both Dacian Wars. Marcus Junius Homullus, who was consul in 102, succeeded in Cappadocia and although little is known about this man, one can assume he was competent and held in high regard by Trajan. After Pliny's death, Cornutus Tertullus replaced him in charge of Bithynia and Pontus as consular legate. Claudius Severus, the long-standing governor of Arabia remained in place. Egypt, a more distant but still crucial eastern province, received a new prefect: Rutilius Lupus.[6]

Back in Rome, Trajan oversaw an empire-wide review of Rome's military strength in order to select legionary and *auxilia* units that could be spared at least temporarily from their current locations for transfer to the East. Rather like in a game of chess, Trajan needed to consider the empire strategically as a whole before moving his pieces accordingly. Probably in close correspondence with his trusted men in the East, the emperor was able to plan the direction of appropriate military resources to key strategic points. Rome's professional army had to be paid wherever they were moved and provisions had to be purchased. Around 112, Trajan approved the increased production of gold *aurei* coins and it has been claimed that there were large outputs from certain eastern provincial mints, in order to yield the enormous amounts of coinage required to pay for his invasion forces.[7]

When the news of Parthamasiris' coronation in Armenia reached Rome, probably in the second half of 113, Trajan's advanced logistical preparations for war were already well under way. With a clear justification for war now in hand, he was then able to switch focus to the specific campaigns ahead and to make the final selections of his most trusted and competent commanders to become his *comites*, or military advisers. The secret of the impending Parthian war was out, though it had been long evident to many able to recognise the signs of the preparations, started probably in 112, and doubtless it formed the source of much discussion and debate in Rome and throughout the empire.

The Parthian Empire

One of the great Persian hegemonies of the ancient world, the Parthian Empire had dominated the Iranian plateau for over 400 years. Originally nomadic Scythian people from the Central Asian steppe, a tribal branch called the Parni settled in Parthia (north-east Iran) and emerged as a kingdom in the third century BC, making Nisa, south-west of modern Ashgabat in Turkmenistan, their first capital.[8] Within a remarkably short period of time, the Parthians were able to defeat the successors of Alexander the Great's empire, the Hellenistic Seleucids, and rapidly expanded their empire until they dominated the Middle East and south-west Asia. At the height of its power, the Parthian Empire controlled modern-day Armenia, Iraq and Iran, as well as sections of Georgia, Turkey, Azerbaijan, Turkmenistan, Tajikistan and Afghanistan, and for limited periods after the Pompeian–Parthian campaign of 40 BC, parts of Syria, Lebanon, Israel and Palestine.[9]

To control their vast empire, the Parthians allowed a significant amount of autonomy to their subjects, with independent city states and a series of individual kingdoms, each of them ruled by a different king but with all the petty kings subordinate to an overall sovereign selected from the Parthian Arsacid dynasty. One of their greatest rulers, Mithridates II (*ca.* 123–88 BC), was the first to be fittingly named the 'king of kings'. Sovereign successors were elected from within the Arsacid dynasty by two groups: the Arsacid elite and a council of wise men. This system of government may have maintained control over a diverse range of peoples, but it was fundamentally flawed given that the 'king of kings' was entirely dependent on the backing of the various subordinate kings and vassals across the empire who provided troops and levies. He could easily be kicked out in preference for another favoured Arsacid family member. The result was a series of coups, which was exactly the case in 113 when Osroes' authority was challenged by Vologaeses III, and we will see that Trajan was able to capitalise on their diverted attention.[10]

Within the Parthian Empire, there were seven important regions relevant to understanding Trajan's Parthian War.

Northern Mesopotamia

In what has often been called one of the 'cradles of civilisation', elements of advanced culture emerged here in the period from 5,300 to 3,500 BC, with writing systems appearing as early as around 3,300 BC. In Greek the word 'Mesopotamia' meant between two rivers, which positions the region approximately between the converging mighty rivers Tigris and Euphrates. The region of northern Mesopotamia corresponds approximately to modern day northern Iraq, north-eastern Syria and south-eastern Turkey and north-western Iran. The ability to irrigate fertile soils allowed the development of productive agriculture in Mespotamia, although the region generally lacked good building stone and timbers. Around 139 BC, northern Mesopotamia was integrated into the Parthian Empire. Nisibis (Nusaybin, Turkey) was a major Mesopotamian city. In an area of the northern section of Mesopotamia (some distance from both the Euphrates and the Tigris) King Mannus of the Arabes Scenitae ruled over desert-dwelling people who were centred around the fortified town of Singara (Sinjar, Iraq).

Babylonia

One of the greatest cities in antiquity, Babylon (85 km south of modern Baghdad), with its roots in the third millennium BC, had controlled the fertile plains of Babylonia between the lower Tigris and Euphrates Rivers. Babylon was famed for its wondrous Hanging Gardens and the biblical Towel of Babel, but today is nothing more than ruined mud-brick buildings, archaeological remains and large mounds. Babylonia became a province in the heart of the Parthian Empire and the location of the winter Parthian capital, Ctesiphon, on the eastern banks of the Tigris about 35 km south of Baghdad. Ctesiphon was adorned by the Parthians with great buildings, including a palace where today the only remains of the city can be seen as a great arch called Taq-i Kisra, which is believed to have been the throne room of the 'king of kings' within a great palace complex. Directly opposite on the other side of the Tigris was the ancient great city of Seleucia, the first capital of the Seleucid Empire when Ctesiphon was merely a small suburb. Seleucia was easily one of the finest Hellenistic cities in the ancient world and, despite Parthian rule, it is said that the city retained its Hellenistic cultural identity almost entirely intact.

Assyria (and Hatra)

A powerful kingdom in still more ancient times, the core of Assyria equated approximately to the north-eastern part of modern Iraq, situated between the Tigris and Euphrates. Long past its glory days, the deserted capital of Assur was reoccupied during the Parthian period. In the third century BC, the fortress city of Hatra (al-Hadr, Iraq) was founded as an Assyrian city within the Seleucid Empire and it controlled the small semi-autonomous kingdom of Araba within the Parthian Empire. Hatra's location and resilient defences would prove to be a thorn in the side for Trajan.

Adiabene and Gordyene

A small but powerful kingdom within the Parthian Empire, Adiabene lay to the east of the Tigris. In this period, the king of Adiabene was Meharaspes whose capital was at Arbela (Erbil, Iraq). The important town of Nisibis in Mesopotamia was under his sovereignty, even though it fell outside his kingdom.[11] North of Adiabene, in the mountainous area to the south-east of Lake Van, King Manisarus ruled the kingdom of Gordyene. Like many other Parthian sub-kings, Manisarus was a member of the ruling Arsacid dynasty and therefore a contender for the Parthian throne.

Osrhoëne & Anthemusia

A kingdom born out of the dissolution of the Seleucid Empire, Osrhoëne covered a region to the east of the upper Euphrates, which is now the border region between Syria and Turkey. Osrhoëne was embedded within the region of Mesopotamia as a semi-autonomous vassal kingdom. Its prosperous capital city, the fortress town of Edessa (Şanlıurfa, Turkey), was the seat of the Abgar dynasty. In this period, King Abgarus ruled Osrhoëne. South of Edessa was the city of Batnae, an important centre for trade routes and capital of the semi-autonomous and fertile kingdom of Anthemusia, ruled in this period by King Sporaces.

In short, the Parthian Empire was a patchwork of semi-independent states and cities, many with their own unique language, ethnicity and culture – not entirely dissimilar to the different provinces within the Roman Empire – but all were dominated by high and low nobility under which were tiers of different ranking dependents.[12] The lowest class were not slaves. Passages about the Parthians written by Pompeius Trogus at the time of Augustus were later selected by another Roman historian, Justin, and they offer an insight into the Roman perception of Parthian characteristics, religion, habits and their accomplished horsemanship:

> Each man has several wives, for the sake of gratifying desire with different objects. They punish no crime more severely than adultery, and accordingly they not only exclude their women from entertainments, but forbid them the very sight of men. They eat no flesh but that which they take in hunting. They ride on horseback on all occasions; on horses they go to war, and to feasts; on horses they discharge public and private duties; on horses they go abroad, meet together, traffic, and converse. Indeed the difference between slaves and free men is, that slaves go on foot, but free men only on horseback. They dispose of bodies by leaving them to be torn apart by birds or dogs; the bare bones they at last bury in the ground.
>
> In their superstitions and worship of the gods, the principal veneration is paid to rivers. The disposition of the people is proud, quarrelsome, faithless, and insolent, for a certain roughness of behaviour they think becoming to men, and gentleness only to women. They are always restless, and ready for any commotion, at home or abroad; taciturn by nature, more ready to act than speak, and consequently shrouding both their successes and failures in silence. They obey their princes, not from humility, but from fear. They are libidinous, but frugal in diet. To their word or promise they have no regard, except as far as suits their interest.
>
> Marcus Junianius Justinus[13]

To Roman eyes Parthian men of the nobility had an effeminate appearance, with facial make-up and long elaborately plaited hair and beards.[14] Men wore kaftans and, depending on their wealth, either cotton or silk cloaks fixed down the front, beneath which they wore baggy trousers.[15] In terms of skills, across the Parthian Empire, consummate workers and craftsmen produced a variety of precious arts and materials, in particular, textiles.[16] Millennia of experience in the region opening up land to agriculture through irrigation technology allowed the Parthians to capitalise on the life-giving waters of the Tigris and Euphrates.[17] Other sources of wealth included the trade of special breeds of horse and from levies on lucrative trading routes. Resourced and skilled, the Parthians were a powerful amalgamation of civilised states and consequently a formidable match for Rome.

Travelling to the East and the Gathering of Roman Forces

In the final weeks prior to Trajan's departure, efforts were made to wrap up urgent matters of state and key senatorial officials and the imperial secretariat were instructed on how to deal with more routine business in the absence of the emperor. At this time Trajan received the tragic news that his sister Marciana had died. Aged around sixty-three, she passed away on 29 August 113. The loss of Trajan's only sibling, with whom he had maintained a close relationship throughout his life, and his only remaining link to the old days growing up in Rome and Italica, was a personal tragedy and it would have affected the emperor profoundly. Plotina, a close friend and companion to her sister-in-law Marciana, would have also felt the devastating loss keenly. Stricken by grief and yet under pressure due to his imminent departure for the East, Trajan had no hesitation in ordering Marciana's immediate deification and awarding her daughter Matidia the title of *Augusta* on the very same day.[18] Conferring a divine status on Marciana, *Diva Augusta*, allowed her to enter the Pantheon of Roman gods and goddesses and join her father, who had been deified by Trajan some time after his death. The act further strengthened the family power base of the Ulpii, given that Trajan was able to claim the divine status of his adopted father, biological father and now his sister. Just as he had for his most trusted confidant and supporter, Sura, Trajan arranged a state funeral for Marciana, befitting in splendour her divinity, and it was held five days later in Rome on 3 September.[19]

Trajan's departure for the East was probably delayed as a result of Marciana's death and the next opportune date was 27 October, the anniversary of his adoption by Nerva.[20] As he left Rome, the streets were lined with cheering crowds who had gathered to see their seemingly invincible emperor depart for the third war in his reign. No doubt accompanied by his usual entourage, which included Plotina, Matidia, his closest aides, *comites*, possibly his Greek physician since the Dacian wars, Titus Statilius Crito, and his young personal secretary, Marcus Ulpius Phaedimus, who had started out in service to Trajan as his chief butler, Trajan travelled at a modest pace, arriving in Athens around 7 December.[21]

While in Athens, Trajan united with Hadrian who is thought to have been based there since about 111.[22] Hadrian had enjoyed a cultural sabbatical during which time he had been awarded Athenian citizenship and then, possibly in 112, was elected *Archon Eponymos*, an honorary chief magistrate of Athens.[23] Presumably Trajan's own stay in Athens was short, but during it he received a Parthian embassy sent by King Osroes to negotiate peace. The embassy must have been sent on the knowledge of Trajan's planned departure well before he actually left Rome. Clearly cautious, knowingly ill-prepared or unable to wage war with Rome due to internal conflicts within his empire, Osroes attempted to resolve the crisis by firstly asking Trajan to confer the diadem on Parthamasiris to avert war and secondly by pointing out that the previous incumbent, Axidares, had been unsatisfactory to both Rome and Parthia.[24] As we have seen, Trajan's real motives for war could not be eradicated by Osroes' position and Dio Cassius records that:

> The Emperor neither accepted the gifts [brought by the embassy from Osroes] nor returned any answer, either oral or written, save the statement that friendship is determined by deeds and not by words, and that accordingly when he should reach Syria he would do all that was proper.
>
> Dio Cassius[25]

It was now clear to everyone that Trajan had no intention whatsoever of seeking peace with Parthia; he was evidently committed to war.

Using a combination of sea and land routes, now accompanied by Hadrian as part of his entourage, Trajan travelled across to Asia, destined for Seleucia Pieria (in modern Turkey) at the mouth of the River Orontes, the seaport for Antioch, arriving around 4 January 114.[26] It is thought that Trajan and Hadrian then proceeded to a limestone mountain known to the Romans as Mount Casius (Jebel al-'Aqra, on the Syrian–Turkish border), a 1,717-metre peak in a range around 7 km south of Seleucia Pieria that dominates the southern horizon of the port. With its stunning views out over the Mediterranean, the mount was the site for a temple dedicated to Zeus. The temple was a covered shrine supported by four columns and it housed a sacred stone of Zeus – possibly a meteorite – believed to have been cast down onto the earth by the great god. Physically fit enough to ascend to the shrine with the much younger Hadrian, Trajan dedicated captured treasure from the Dacian Wars to Zeus along with prayers for the successful execution of his pending war with Parthia.[27]

After visiting Mount Casius, Trajan proceeded to Antioch, arriving on 7 January to set up his imperial headquarters for the war, surrounded by his *comites* and gathering senior officers.[28] A significant force of three legions had been mustered on the outskirts of Antioch: X *Fretensis* from Jerusalem in Judaea; III *Cyrenaica* from Bostra in Arabia and III *Gallica* from Raphanaea in Syria. By now, Trajan almost certainly had specific plans laid out for the imminent war with Parthia, which started with the annexation of Armenia. However, he was unable to start the first campaign because of the bitterly cold snowy climate in the rugged Taurus mountains in winter that rendered many valleys impassable. Therefore, Trajan had to wait until April before he could march north and in the intervening period he would have attended to the critical supply chains required to sustain a massive invasion force, a vital matter for any Roman general. In addition, he dealt with state affairs and received embassies from the east.

One of the embassies granted an audience with the emperor was sent by King Abgarus of Osrhoëne. The king did not appear in person, wishing to maintain his neutrality because he was equally fearful of incurring the wrath of Trajan or the Parthians. Instead, he sent gifts and a message of his friendship to Trajan via his ambassadors.[29] Other overtures were sent from King Mannus of the Arabes Scenitae and King Sporaces of Anthemusia,[30] probably also keen to circumvent the looming war or at least buy additional time for their political manoeuvres. The Parthian 'king of kings', Osroes, also sent an embassy to Antioch to seek an answer to the proposals he had sent to Athens. To exonerate himself, Trajan pretended to desire peace but claimed he was unable to accept Osroes' terms, which proposed maintaining Parthamasiris on the Armenian throne with Trajan's approval. Trajan had already shown his hand when he decided not to address this proposal earlier in Athens and surely Osroes knew there was little or no hope that Trajan would accept. Instead, Trajan offered his own terms, which were doubtless deliberately unacceptable, and the ensuing war became unavoidable. One can only speculate on the content of Trajan's counter-terms, which possibly entailed the complete submission of Armenia for conversion into a Roman province. In any event, Osroes' embassy would have left Antioch with the dismal tidings of war to take back to their sovereign.

In April, with the melting of the snow in the Taurus Mountain passes and with diplomacy at an end, Trajan issued the order for his forces in Antioch to march north to gather additional legions *en route* and unite with others at Satala (Sadak, Turkey) in the Roman province of Cappadocia, a strategically well-placed launch-pad for operations into Armenia. Local guides and experienced Roman scouts familiar with the terrain would have sought out the most convenient route for the column via Zeugma, Samosata and Melitene to collect Legions IV *Scythica*, VI *Ferrata* and XII *Fulminata* respectively from these places. As a display of power, a division of the force struck east from Melitene across the Euphrates and captured the major Armenian city of Arsamosata (Aršamšat, Turkey). It appears to have been an easy victory, the city falling without a fight,[31] demonstrating that Armenia was poorly prepared and defended.

Returning to the Euphrates valley and continuing to bear north, Trajan's army passed through stunning mountain landscapes with thick oak forests and exposed rock formations, across deep crystal-clear streams and around snow-capped peaks, arriving at Satala towards the end of May. Satala was located north-west of the upper Euphrates in a wide valley region surrounded by thickly forested mountains. Here his force rendezvoused with the legion garrisoned at Satala, XVI *Flavia Firma*. In addition, two battle-hardened legions involved in the Dacian War had been called over to Satala, namely, I *Adiutrix* from Dacia and XV *Apollinaris* from Pannonia. A variety of legionary detachments from an array of several other legions were also gathered. In total, Trajan was able to muster the equivalent of twelve legions and a matching number of auxiliaries. Although more forces were probably available in theory for the Second Dacian War, many of those had had to be left in reserve in the provinces along the Danube. Even so, Trajan's army gathered in Satala that spring was probably one of the largest invasion forces Rome had ever mustered; the camps would have saturated the Satala mountain valley spaces and surrounding areas for many kilometres.

Roman command

As for the Dacian Wars, Trajan oversaw a chain of command as *imperator* in the field, with all major decisions normally requiring his authorisation through his generals and senior officers. The command structure *per se* was similar to that used in the Dacian Wars but with different people in the various positions, resulting in changes in those selected to act as his *comites*.

Comites for the Start of the Campaign of 114

Cornelius Palma	*Legatus pro praetore* (special post; twice consul)
Publilius Celsus	*Legatus pro praetore* (special post; twice consul)
Marcus Junius Homullus	*Legatus pro praetore* (special post; recent governor of Cappadocia *ca.* 111–14)[32]
Hadrian	*Legatus pro praetore* (special post)[33]
Lusius Quietus	General and commander of the Mauretanian light cavalry (trusted and skilled cavalry leader in Dacian wars)[34]
Marcius Turbo	Prefect of the Misenum Roman fleet

Roman Forces

Roman invasion force mustered at Satala in May 114 (numbers assume units at full fighting strength):

LEGIONS
- X *Fretensis* from Judaea
- III *Cyrenaica* from Arabia
- III *Gallica* from Syria
- IV *Scythica* from Syria
- VI *Ferrata* from Syria
- XII *Fulminata* from Cappadocia
- XVI *Flavia Firma* from Cappadocia
- I *Adiutrix* from Dacia
- XV *Apollinaris* from Pannonia
    - 51,300 legionaries

Detachments of around 2,000 men each from:
VII *Claudia*, XI *Claudia*, XIII *Gemina*, XII *Primigenia*, II *Traiana fortis*, XXX *Ulpia Victrix*, I *Italica* & V *Macedonica*
- **16,000 legionaries**

PRAETORIAN GUARD
Half the Guard (5 cohorts)
- 2,500 Praetorians

IMPERIAL HORSE GUARD
>   Full contingent
>   >   1,000 mounted men

AUXILIA
>   Infantry cohorts and cavalry equivalent in numbers to the combined legions. Almost certainly including units specifically able to counter Parthian light cavalry archers.
>   >   ca. 70,000 men

SYMMACHIARII
>   As in the Dacian wars, Trajan would have supplemented his force with *symmachiarii* particularly well adapted to cope with Parthian forces and the climatic conditions of the region.
>   >   ca. 5,000 men[35]

Legionaries:	67,300
Praetorians:	2,500
Imperial Horse Guard:	1,000
Auxiliaries:	70,000
Symmachiarii:	5,000
GRAND TOTAL:	145,800

These numbers assume that all the forces were at full strength. Accounting for typically undermanned legions and auxiliary units through injury, desertion and other factors, the total number would have been closer to 116,000. Nevertheless, this was an enormous Roman force. Trajan evidently envisaged a major war with Parthia, far beyond just establishing authority over Armenia. A proportion of this force would have remained in reserve at strategically important sites and to maintain security in the eastern provinces.

Parthian Command

The Parthian command structure was dictated by noble status. Loyalty within military units was therefore heavily dependent on kinship, reinforced by oaths. Unlike Rome, there was no professional standing army and instead warriors were raised specifically in the event of war from among the kingdoms, clans and tribes that constituted the Parthian Empire.[36] Osroes, the king of kings, was the ordained head of the Parthian Empire and the supreme commander of Parthian forces, although his authority was more reliable over his own clan and somewhat undermined by the rival claimant to his position at the time, King Vologaeses III. Sanatrukes, nephew of Osroes, would later emerge in the war as a designated commander, a *spadpat*, of a large Parthian force. The army was split into major divisions called *grunds*, within which were large detachments, *drafsh* and small companies, *washts*. The Parthian gentry, known as *azats*, commanded their levied kinfolk dependents who made up these groups. Except for his own muster of hereditary dependents, Osroes struggled to secure all the *azats'* contribution because of all the inter-clan bickering at that time.[37]

Parthian Forces & Allies

The superior horsemanship of the Parthians was the principal factor in the success and strength of their military forces. There were two types of horseman, the heavy cavalryman and the traditional light archer, usually used in a coordinated manner for the greatest impact. The heavy cavalry, or cataphracts, provided the shock tactics during combat. The breeds of horse commonly used have not been clearly identified but they were thick-set and so able to bear the weight of the heavy scale armour, made of steel or bronze, that protected the head, neck, chest, body and upper legs of the horse. The riders were also clad in heavy armour: generally a helmet with neck guard, scale or chainmail body armour, a corselet to provide extra protection for the upper body, and additional armour for the arms, legs, hands and feet. Both the rider and horse were thus effectively covered from head to toe and head to leg respectively in high quality armour. Each rider used a three and a half metre long lance as his main weapon to impale his enemies and they carried a secondary blade weapon.[38]

In stark contrast, the horse archers lacked any form of protective armour in order to maintain the speed and agility of their sturdy steppe horses or ponies. The 'Great Horse of the Persians' was the breed preferred by the Parthians for its speed, strength and beauty and it may have been the choice for many horse archers.[39] Each rider used a composite bow made from layers of animal horn, wood and sinew, and had a quiver of arrows 70–80 cm in length. A released arrow could be accurate and lethal at 40–50 m. Additional sidearms were carried for the eventuality of hand-to-hand combat. Neither the horse archers nor the cataphracts appear to have used stirrups. They depended instead on expert balance in a supportive saddle.

Infantry were also a component of Parthian forces but they did not play a significant part in battle and were perhaps useful only for specific activities such as assaults on fortifications. The Parthian army seems to have relied almost entirely on its cavalry for decisive action. During the battle of Carrhae in 53 BC, there were ten light archer cavalry units to one heavy, but it could vary and was presumably dependent on available resources and the prevailing battle circumstances.

Details of the total strength of Parthian forces are not known but it is likely that the Romans outnumbered the Parthians considerably. This is assumed given the unprecedentedly vast force Trajan had mustered and the fact that the Parthians were distracted by internal strife.

Roman Offensive Campaign 114

With his vast invasion force mustered at Satala and all his orders communicated through the ranks, Trajan was able to lead his army into Armenian territory in a historic act that put Rome on a collision course with Parthia for the first time in half a century.[40] It was a silent invasion, with no major physical barriers to scale under hostile fire and no waiting Armenian army to face in open combat. In fact, the historic event must have been something of an anti-climax as Trajan passed unimpeded east towards the Euphrates heading for Elegeia (Erzurum, Turkey). As the army swept through the terrain in separate columns, each under the command of a general, Armenian forward scouts would have surely informed Parthamasiris of the massive approaching Roman force.

Unable to mount an Armenian response that could cope even with Trajan's vanguard and without a Parthian army under King Osroes to come to his aid, Parthamasiris was alone and doomed. As a result, he agreed to meet Trajan at Elegeia, high up in the Eastern Anatolian Mountains, in the vain hope of negotiating peace. Arriving at Elegeia in early June,[41] Trajan probably ordered his force to disperse into the surrounding area and seek appropriate strategic points to set up camp and screen off any possibility of an Armenian or Parthian force penetrating the region. In his own camp, Trajan awaited the arrival of Parthamasiris, who was late for the agreed meeting. As Trajan was already clearly intolerant of Parthamasiris, this would have aggravated him further. When Parthamasiris finally arrived, accompanied by Parthian representatives and a group of elite Armenians, it was claimed that the party had been hindered en route from the Armenian capital, Artaxata (Artashat, Turkey), by attacks from supporters of the previously deposed King Axidares. Once cleared by Trajan's security, Parthamasiris was probably allowed to approach Trajan as he sat on a tribunal platform.

Parthamasiris came forward, saluted Trajan and laid down his diadem at the emperor's feet. Standing in silence, he expected Trajan to hand back the diadem,[42] thereby restoring Roman pride and averting conflict.

Evidently, Parthamasiris was totally dissociated from the reality of his position. Instead, the surrounding Roman soldiers cheered victory over the Armenians and the effect startled Parthamasiris who asked Trajan for a private audience. In response to this request, Parthamasiris was led away to a private tent with Trajan, who was presumably accompanied by his closest advisers and his immediate bodyguards. The uncrowned Armenian king reiterated his proposal to be recognised as a candidate for the throne whom Trajan could endorse and to whom he could then symbolically return the diadem crown. The atmosphere would have been highly charged and one can imagine that Trajan was calm and composed, supremely confident of his position and immovable in the face of Parthamasiris' arguments. Clearly used to getting his own way, Parthamasiris failed to hold his temper and stormed out of the tent in a fit of rage. Persuaded to return, Parthamasiris was led back to the tribunal that Trajan had remounted and the emperor asked the dejected Parthamasiris to recant his demands in front of all those assembled. From sheer desperation, Parthamasiris vented his anguish, claiming he was not a captive and had come in good faith voluntarily to seek his rightful appointment to the throne.[43] But the exchange was now over and Trajan is said to have stated that Armenia would not be surrendered to anyone and was now a Roman province amalgamated with Cappadocia, complete with a new governor, Lucius Catilius Severus.[44] Without a single battle, except the easy capture of Arsamosata, Armenia had fallen into Roman hands, although a struggle would lie ahead to root out Armenian resistance groups throughout the kingdom that were not prepared to give up without a fight.

Almost certainly still in despair, Parthamasiris was ordered by Trajan into exile to any location of his choice, but the accompanying Armenian nobles were to remain with Trajan as a token of submission as his subjects.[45] Parthamasiris was then told that he and his Parthian representatives would be accompanied by a Roman cavalry escort. With no regard for Parthamasiris' status and to prevent him from rallying any response, Trajan had secretly ordered the cavalry guard to lead Parthamasiris out of the camp and, once sufficiently out of sight, to execute Parthamasiris and all his entourage. A false report would then be issued that Parthamasiris had rashly tried to escape his escort and was killed as a consequence. To complete the charade, Trajan even wrote to Osroes about his nephew's death in an attempt to absolve himself of responsibility. The whole affair was in fact a well-managed display of Roman power, designed to send a stark message to Osroes and anyone else who might oppose Trajan that he would be intolerant towards even passive submission if Roman pride or authority was challenged. Trajan was evidently unashamed by this treacherous deed; it was another example of his darker side. He had acted in a similar manner with Casperius Aelianus soon after his accession.

Claiming Armenia as a Roman province with the murder of its candidate for the throne and actually converting the territory into a peaceful, flourishing, profitable region were two very different things. Directly familiar with the annexation of Dacia, Trajan knew success hinged on fanning out his forces to mop up any pockets of resistance and to start building roads, boundary walls and fortresses to make a reality of Roman rule, just as he had done after the fall of Dacia's capital. After dividing his available forces into five divisions, the first, under his direct command, was to consolidate and garrison the west of Armenia, including Elegeia and Arsamosata. In addition, this first division was ready to act against any Parthian intervention out of northern Mesopotamia. The remaining four divisions were ordered to eradicate or break up any Armenian resistance and, where applicable, extend the hand of Roman diplomacy to client states.

Campaigning in 114 to Secure the New Province of Armenia

The division under Lusius Quietus advanced to secure the region surrounding Lake Van. The lake, with its brackish waters, 1,640 m above sea-level, is dominated on its northern shores by the second highest volcano in Turkey, Mount Süphan, over 4,000 metres high. The lake was approximately in the centre of the Armenian kingdom. The tough, mountain-dwelling Mardi tribe posed a formidable resistance to its east and south in high mountainous terrain with peaks and ranges over 3,000 metres high.[46] Strategically, Quietus needed to secure the Bitlis Pass, a river valley through the high ground south of the lake that led through into Mesopotamia and the upper Tigris valley. This was a challenging mission, which required the dogged determination of a commander like Quietus, who had excelled in both Dacian wars and could be trusted with this vital mission. Also, as a Mauretanian, Quietus was probably familiar with the Atlas Mountains and therefore comfortable in the similar terrain around Lake Van.[47]

The second division, commanded by Bruttius Praesens, was tasked to flush out resistance in the high Armenian Taurus Mountains with Legio VI *Ferrata*.

Praesens' men ingeniously adopted the use of local snowshoes to cope with the deep snow conditions of the high terrain.[48]

The third division, whose commander is unknown, may have operated as far east as the Caucasiae Portae, or Caspian Gates,[49] an important strategic pass through the Caucasus Mountains into the vast Pontic–Caspian Steppe. The ancient sources confuse the location of the Gates but it is thought that they correspond to the Darial Gorge between modern-day Russia and Georgia. This represented a march in excess of 1,000 km from Elegeia over some of the toughest regions of eastern Armenia. The objective of this mission may have been diplomatic rather than strictly military, in order to extend Roman influence into this peripheral area. This division would have secured the Armenia capital, Artaxata, during its campaigning. The last division, the commander also unknown today, possibly pursued Armenian resistance forces or attempted a diplomatic mission, beyond Armenia as far as the Tzon Pass (Derbent, Russia). This was a narrow strip of costal land squeezed between the Caucasus Mountains and the Caspian Sea, linking the Eurasian Steppe in the north to Media (north-western Iran) in the south.

Each division was presumably successful in its missions, meaning that, by the end of the main campaign season of 114, Armenia was reasonably secure with essential garrisons in place at important strategic points and the beginnings of fortified boundary lines (*limites*) probably appearing along the forming frontiers of the new province.

To ensure the military efforts in Armenia provided long-lasting security to the province, vigorous diplomacy was required. Residing in Elegeia, Trajan applied his political skills and clout to the establishment of a ring of client states beyond the peripheries of Armenia that would help absorb external incursions into the new Roman province.[50] Military efforts and diplomacy were not mutually exclusive and some of the divisions that stretched out as far as the Tzon Pass and the Caspian Gates were surely engaged in displaying Rome's far-reaching power and securing the subservience of client states. As a result of all his efforts in Armenia, the Senate voyed Trajan the honorific *Optimus*, 'most excellent', which he proudly adopted into his titles around August 114.[51] They would have then read: IMPERATOR, CAESAR, MARCUS ULPIUS NERVA TRAJAN, AUGUSTUS, GERMANICUS, DACICUS, PONTIFEX MAXIMUS, TRIBUNICIA POTESTATE, CONSUL [six times], PATER PATRIAE, SPQR OPTIMUS PRINCEPS.[52]

Dio Cassius later captured the momentous event in these words:

> When [Trajan] had captured the whole country of the Armenians and had won over many of the kings also, some of whom, since they voluntarily submitted, he treated as friends, while others, though disobedient, he subdued without a battle, the Senate voted to him all the usual honours in great plenty and furthermore bestowed upon him the title of *Optimus*, or Most Excellent.
>
> Dio Cassius[53]

As the extremes of the Armenian continental climate brought in the harsh chills and snows of winter, Trajan remained at Elegeia in his new province and prepared for the upcoming campaign season of 115 which would drive his invasion forces into Mesopotamia to capture territories well inside the Parthian Empire and bring the war to Osroes.

Roman Offensive Campaign of 115

With the annexation of Armenia, all that remained to complete Trajan's grand vision for an improved eastern frontier was the occupation of northern Mesopotamia, a major region within the Parthian Empire. His campaign strategy appears to have been to split the region in half: he would tackle the west while, in parallel, the ever-reliable Quietus would first strike at the kingdom of Adiabene before sweeping into his allocated eastern half of the region. In short, the various vassal states of northern Mesopotamia would suffer the classic military approach of *divide et impera*, 'divide and conquer'.

Leaving a sufficient contingent of his invasion force behind in Armenia under the authority of Severus to maintain security and consolidate the new province, Trajan led his force down to the newly secured Bitlis Pass where the heavy winter snows were melting in the spring warmth. The pass was an easier way into upper Mesopotamia following ancient trade caravan routes. Despite his senior years, Trajan remained determined to share the toils of his men, marching on foot with them through the mountains, a trademark of his leadership which inspired great respect from the ranks:

> [Trajan] always marched on foot with the rank and file of his army, and he attended to the ordering and disposition of the troops throughout the entire campaign, leading them sometimes in one order and sometimes in another; and he forded all the rivers that they did.
>
> Dio Cassius[54]

Probably in May, Trajan reached the Tigris, which he crossed and thereby entered into Mesopotamia proper, continuing south through the Masius Mountains and dropping down into the desert plains of modern-day northeastern Syria.[55] Unopposed in the advance, Trajan understood the essential need to keep his men alert during the gruelling marches, so he issued false reports of enemy positions through his scouts that triggered the Roman columns to react accordingly and practise their critical manoeuvres.[56] Keeping his forces on their toes in this manner was a sign of Trajan's experience in the field.

His first goal in Mesopotamia was the capture of Nisibis. It was a critical city to dominate, as it straddled a major route east–west across Mesopotamia and therefore was a pivotal point from which to control movement in the region. Once it had been captured after a battle without further recorded incident, Trajan next advanced on the city of Batnae (Suruç), approximately 250 km due west across the open plains of northern Mesopotamia.[57] This was the capital of the kingdom of Anthemusia, ruled by King Sporaces. Again, the city was taken with relative ease so that Trajan secured an axis of Roman domination right across the northern section of Mesopotamia.

In the meantime, Quietus had led his division of infantry and cavalry, conceivably including two or three legions, probably along a similar route to that of Trajan through the Bitlis Pass. But instead of continuing south he had turned east towards the kingdom of Adiabene to attack King Meharaspes. The king had received support in the form of troops from another royal similarly under threat, King Mannus of the Scenitae Arabs. Nevertheless, the skills of Quietus as a commander and the superior strength of the Roman forces defeated Meharaspes.[58] Continuing on the heels of the retreating remnant of Meharaspes' routed army, Quietus was forced to stop at the mighty Tigris. The river is wide at this point and the semi-arid mountains were devoid of appropriate trees[59] for the Roman engineers to build a bridge to cross over. The river was also well defended by Adiabenian opposition on the opposite bank. As a result, Quietus went on to the second phase of his campaign and turned back to sweep across eastern Mesopotamia seeking out any forces that failed to submit to Roman authority.

Meanwhile, in the west of Mesopotamia, the emperor was setting up garrisons at vital defensive locations. It was absolutely crucial to secure supply lines because the barren lands demanded a continuous flow of provisions for the tens of thousands of men, horses and pack animals that constituted the invading force. Trajan then proceeded into the kingdom of Osrhoëne, heading for the capital of Edessa (Şanlıurfa, Turkey), and he may have led his force into the plains around modern-day Harran (Turkey), known to the Romans as Carrhae, around 85 km due east of the Euphrates. This was the site of Rome's worst military defeat. In 53 BC, the Parthians had wiped out a Roman force far greater than their own with only 1,000 cataphracts and 9,000 horse archers, resulting in the death of 20,000 Romans and 10,000 captured.[60] The harsh climate, with atrociously hot and arid summers, had played its part in this devastating defeat. The plains were dry and desolate, and not the reasonably well irrigated green fields visible locally today. The Carrhae battle site would not have been ignored by Trajan, who perhaps conducted a ceremony in recognition of the long-lost Romans who had perished in battle, while shrewdly reminding his current army that he would not allow history to repeat itself and that the Parthians were at present incapable of facing them in open battle even as the Romans swept through Mesopotamia.

As the army approached the outskirts of Edessa, King Abgarus of Osrhoëne finally came out to meet Trajan on the road.[61] Thus far, he had avoided direct contact to maintain neutrality, but he could no longer avert submission to the victorious Roman emperor on his doorstep.[62] But King Abgarus had a secret diplomatic weapon, an attractive young prince called Arbandes who had previously caught the attention of Trajan. While Trajan was staying in Antioch in 114, Abgarus had sent his son with an embassy, and Trajan's attraction to the beautiful young prince may have been the reason for him to pardon his father and grant Osrhoëne client status within the Roman Empire. To seal the agreement, a feast was held for Trajan and during the banquet Arbandes performed a dance.[63]

The tide was now turning against any vassal kings left in Mesopotamia who had not submitted to Trajan; in particular Manisarus of Gordyene and Mannus of the Scenitae Arabs, both of whom sent envoys to Trajan in this period in last-ditch attempts to obtain sympathy from the emperor.[64] However, they had evaded earlier opportunities to meet Trajan, behaviour which he viewed as contemptuous, and their embassies were presumably turned away without achieving their diplomatic goals. Instead, Trajan made his way east to punish Mannus initially and then to rendezvous with Quietus in eastern Mesopotamia.[65] Consequently, three important towns fell into Roman hands towards the close of the campaign. All three towns were 'advanced' positions, beyond the new eastern frontier that Trajan wanted to create, and each town commanded a vital route between Babylonia and Mesopotamia: namely, Hatra, Dura-Europos (Salhiyé, Syria) and Singara.[66] The capture of these towns would have certainly helped secure the new frontier by creating extended zones of military influence, like bastions stretching out into the deserts along limited access routes. All three towns were fortresses located in very inhospitable areas, but Trajan was able to seize them by capitalising on the continued internal feuding within the Parthian Empire and the consequent lack of any help from Osroes. Through well calculated, presumably swift surprise attacks, all three towns fell to the Romans without incident or lengthy sieges.[67]

In closing the campaign of 115 with a series of speeches to his assembled armies in Mesopotamia to commend them on their achievements, Trajan would almost certainly have emphasised how important it was for the garrisons he left behind to fulfil their duties in order to consolidate and secure the newly established province. To spread the news of all the achievements, a communication was sent to the Senate in Rome heralding the acquisition of Mesopotamia as a province, carved out of territory within the Parthian Empire. The letter is known to have arrived in Rome on 21 February 116, and the Senate rapidly awarded Trajan the honorific *Parthicus*, 'Conqueror of Parthia', which was adopted into his titles and versions stamped on coins to advertise the victory to the Roman world and beyond.[68]

Conceivably exhausted after the vigorous campaign, Trajan retired to Antioch for the 115/116 winter period. In that grand city, Trajan likely monitored the consolidation of Armenia and Mesopotamia into provinces and attended to pressing matters of state in other parts of the empire. Trajan's imperial stature had never been greater given the remarkable successes of the two campaigns and his *comites,* commanders and friends had much reason to congratulate him. Two major new provinces had been added to the empire, which bolstered Roman pride and echoed the glorious bygone days of the Republic and the early imperial era.

Despite the positive mood that winter, a very bad omen for Trajan was delivered in the form of a major earthquake in Antioch and the surrounding area. The clashing of the Arabian and Eurasian tectonic plates creates the East Anatolian fault line, which intersects with the Dead Sea fault line in the region of Antioch, making the area prone to violent seismic activity. From contemporary descriptions,[69] one can tentatively deduce that it may have measured 7 or more on the Richter scale,[70] causing widespread devastation to Antioch, surrounding cities and the countryside.[71] Many perished during the earthquake or from being trapped in the wreckage. The elected *consul ordinarius* in 115, Marcus Pedo Vergilianus, was among the casualties. Trajan had a miraculous escape from certain death as he was able to scramble out of a window in the room where he was staying and sustained only minor injuries. To avoid the risks posed by aftershocks, Trajan stayed in the open in the city's hippodrome, probably in a makeshift army tent. As earthquakes were perceived as fearful messages from the gods, it would not have escaped Trajan's attention that even Mount Casius, which he had visited two years earlier with Hadrian to deliver prayers to Zeus, had been altered by the power of the earthquake:

> Even Mount Casius itself was so shaken that its peaks seemed to lean over and break off and to be falling upon the very city. Other hills also settled, and much water not previously in existence came to light, while many streams disappeared.
>
> Dio Cassius[72]

Antioch was one of the finest cities in the Roman Empire and its desolation and the subsequent loss of life would have reminded Trajan acutely of the devastation caused by Vesuvius' eruption in 79. One can wonder if Trajan thought it prescient, since Vesuvius' eruption was not too long before Titus' death. Emperor Titus had overseen the relief efforts around Vesuvius, and it is very likely that Trajan similarly directed relief efforts in and around Antioch and used his available skilled legionary engineers and troops to support the immediate re-building of critical public buildings and infrastructure.

Roman Offensive Campaign of 116

As the slow process of reconstructing Antioch continued into the spring of 116 and beyond, many of Trajan's *comites* would have advised the emperor to advance his forces no further and just to focus on the consolidation of Mesopotamia and Armenia. Both regions had been captured with minimal casualties and the new complete Eastern frontier stretching from the Gulf of Aqaba to the Caucasus Mountains was in place. It offered a new era of Roman authority in the east of the empire. Trajan had succeeded where other famous Romans had failed. Now he wanted the ultimate: to strike at the heart of the Parthian Empire in Babylonia and hunt down the Parthian king of kings, just as Alexander the Great had chased the last king of the Achaemenid Empire of Persia, Darius III, through Assyria and defeated him at the Battle of Gaugamela.[73] The advance on the capital, Ctesiphon, would be a crucial part of the war. The king of kings had dodged a direct encounter with Trajan and an attack on the capital had enormous prestige value.

It appears the first major objective of the new campaign was to deal rapidly with the kingdoms of Adiabene and Gordyene and to start off where Quietus had reached the obstacle of the Tigris River in the previous year. Testament to the skills of the legionary engineers, bridge pontoons in collapsible and transportable segments had been constructed at Nisibis, where timber was readily available from the forested foothills of Mount Masius (Tur Abdin), and were then carried over 100 km to the selected river-crossing point.[74] The Romans were expert at crossing wide rivers on quickly constructed wooden pontoon bridges and despite the hostile fire from the enemy on the opposite bank, they were finally able to cross by creating a series of fake bridges to confuse the enemy and with moored sections in front for infantry and archers to return fire.[75]

Once they were over the formidable Tigris, little prevented the Romans from laying waste to Adiabene. Trajan handed over command presumably to Quietus or one of his generals who led a division to secure the regions around the city of Nineveh (near Mosul), corresponding roughly to the modern-day province of Erbil in the Kurdistan region of Iraq. Nineveh and Gaugamela fell into Roman hands, as well as Arbela, symbolically the very city where Darius III fled after being defeated by Alexander the Great in the Battle of Gaugamela.[76] Adenystrae, the stronghold of King Mebarsapes in Adiabene, was also besieged and, by a stroke of luck, a Roman centurion called Sentius, who was being held captive in the town after a diplomatic mission there, was able to pull off a heroic act that committed his memory to history. He managed to persuade his fellow prisoners to help him escape his confinement, kill the commander of the stronghold and open the gates for his compatriots,[77] thus ending what would otherwise have been a lengthy siege. The rapid loss of Adenystrae was a final fatal blow to Meharaspes, who effectively lost his kingdom as a consequence. Presumably the kingdom of Gordyene was also taken in this period and Manisarus deposed at the same time. Trajan was then plausibly able to claim a third new province, called Assyria, and again without any attempt by Osroes to prevent Trajan's seemingly unstoppable advance.[78]

While this single division swept through Adiabene, possibly another Roman column advanced with amazing ease and totally unopposed down the Tigris all the way to the famed ruined city of Babylon:

> After this [the Romans] advanced as far as Babylon itself, being quite free from molestation, since the Parthian power had been destroyed by civil conflicts and was still at this time a subject of strife.
>
> Dio Cassius[79]

After the tricky crossing of the Tigris, Trajan had taken a different route, heading for the fortress of Dura-Europos on the western bank of the Euphrates, which had been captured by the Romans in the previous year. It was a formidable march of around 300 km south-west across forbidding terrain along Trajan's new frontier route passing near Singara and down the Chaboras River tributary to the Euphrates.[80] The rationale for this manoeuvre was to link up with a river fleet that had assembled somewhere in Syria on the banks of the Euphrates and then sailed down the river to Dura-Europos to collect Trajan and bring a mass of provisions down to Sippar (Tell Abu Habbah, Iraq). At Sippar the Euphrates runs very close to the Tigris, the two being within 30 km of each other, thereby putting Trajan within striking distance of the Parthian winter capital, Ctesiphon, on the eastern bank of the Tigris.

Lucius Flavius Arrianus (better known as Arrian), a Greek historian who probably witnessed Trajan's Parthian War first-hand, wrote an account of the campaigns, and fragments of his work survive, one of which describes the fleet that Trajan led down the Euphrates towards the heart of the Parthian Empire. Trajan is described erroneously as a 'king' by Arrian:

> Trajan the king had fifty ships. Four carried the royal insignia and they pulled the commander's ship with long ropes. The ship had a length corresponding to that of a trireme, but the depth and width of a cargo vessel, like the very large Egyptian [ship] *Nikomedis* [a famously large vessel]. In it the living quarters were suitable for a king. [The ship] displayed golden railings and at the top of the main mast the king's [Trajan's] name and those of whomever the king honored were incised. The fleet was divided into three parts so that they would not become confused by an unbroken sailing [line].
>
> Arrian[81]

With his legionary and *auxilia* divisions marching along the bank of the Euphrates and not burdened by the mass of provisions being carried by the fleet, Trajan was able to travel with lightning speed down to Sippar. A journey of around 400 km, taking around two to three weeks at a forced march pace, meant that Trajan arrived within sight of Ctesiphon in May or June.[82] With typical Roman audacity, Trajan then ordered his entire fleet to be hauled 30 km overland to the Tigris River, probably using massive rollers and sledges.[83] The whole advance was executed so efficiently that the Parthians had no time to formulate a defensive plan for the cities of Seleucia and Ctesiphon. Trajan was able to capture Seleucia, the prominent former capital of the Seleucid Empire, and with his navy afloat on the Tigris he ferried his army across and entered Ctesiphon without having to draw a single sword.[84]

It was a historic moment for the emperor. Trajan was the first Roman to capture the Parthian winter capital of Ctesiphon. It was the jewel among the cities he had captured during his war. Sprawling along the banks of Tigris, Ctesiphon was adorned by luxurious royal palaces, refined temples, gracious public buildings, and had huge prestige value as a prized city of the king of kings; the Dacian capital, Sarmizegetusa, captured by Trajan in 106 must have paled in significance. Osroes knew very well that the Romans were masters at siege warfare and therefore he had a greater chance of defeating them in the open field. However, Trajan's incredible pace had perhaps left no opportunity for Osroes to muster a large enough army in time and he had been forced to abandon his capital and presumably retreat east into the Zagros Mountains (Iran) in the eastern section of the Parthian Empire, a tactic used before by the Parthians in times of defeat. With little or no time for an orderly retreat, Osroes also left behind his daughter and a famous golden throne.[85] Both were captured by the Romans and were highly symbolic trophies for Trajan eventually to ship back to Rome to feature in his triumphal procession. One can easily imagine Trajan sitting on Osroes' golden throne inside a stunning Parthian royal hall, a remarkable accomplishment and an astonishing representation of Rome's power under Trajan's principate.

> When [Trajan] had taken possession of this place [Ctesiphon] he was saluted *imperator* and established his right to the title of *Parthicus*. In addition to other honours voted to him by the Senate, he was granted the privilege of celebrating as many triumphs as he should desire.
>
> Dio Cassius[86]

Despite being modest throughout his whole reign and always keen to display an image of restraint in the way he lived and acted, Trajan may have been temporarily blinded or bewildered by the overwhelming sense of power he must have felt in the summer of 116. In two and half years, he had annexed massive swathes of territory with no significant military losses and at the expense of Rome's traditional Parthian adversary. On an emotional wave of euphoria and invincibility, Trajan's better judgement was possibly blurred for a second time, and instead of personally orchestrating a thorough consolidation of the Adiabene and Babylonian territories he had gained, Trajan instead lapsed into what appears an indulgent mood and arranged a tour down the Tigris to the Erythraean Sea (Persian Gulf). Rather like Alexander the Great, who was supposedly corrupted by the decadent nature of the Persian court and its customs, Trajan 'desired to sail'[87] down the Tigris aboard his imperial barge. Alternatively, one could argue that Trajan remained focused and the goal of his tour was to determine if there was a superior frontier to guard his gains further down the Tigris. There was little or no information to guide any Roman general in this far-flung region, so personal investigation was required for such a decision.[88]

Whatever the reason, the journey down the Tigris from Ctesiphon to the Persian Gulf was over 500 km and would have taken a couple of weeks at a leisurely pace. Prior to arriving at the Gulf, Trajan reached the inspiring location where the Tigris and the Euphrates converged creating an immense area of marshland and a flooded delta region. The region fell within the small kingdom of Mesene which was ruled by a Parthian vassal, King Athambelus. At this time, a river tidal bore almost claimed Trajan's life presumably while he was on his imperial vessel.[89] Presumably an unusually high incoming tide from the Persian Gulf created a wave in the river that was funnelled by the banks as it travelled, forming into a substantial wave front that may have almost capsized or wrecked Trajan's boat.

Recovering from the near miss, Trajan received a congenial welcome from the kingdom of Mesene. Its king obviously sensed that it was futile to resist the mighty Roman emperor, whose reputation would have preceded his arrival. Although expressing his loyalty to Trajan, King Athambelus was still ordered to pay tribute to Rome, probably a significant sum of money given the extremely wealthy port in the kingdom called Spasinou Charax (near Basra, Iraq). This port was the focal point of trade with India and a starting point for lucrative trade routes through the deserts to Petra and Palmyra. Perhaps that had been another incentive for Trajan's excursion to the shores of the Persian Gulf.

Spasinou Charax represented Trajan's most easterly acquisition and would prove the farthest-flung of all his conquests and ultimately the high water mark of the Roman Empire.[90] From its harbour side, Trajan saw many ships depart for India and it stirred his sentiments as he gazed out to the hazing turquoise horizon of the Gulf and fantasised about the awe-inspiring conquests of Alexandria the Great in the distant mystical lands of the Indian subcontinent. Such was his despondency at being unable to emulate Alexander's deeds that on seeing a ship set sail for India one day, Trajan is known to have said,

> I should certainly have crossed over to the Indi, too, if I were still young.
> Dio Cassius[91]

This reflection may have been prompted by Trajan's approaching sixtieth birthday in September of that year. It is also likely that Trajan was now finding it hard to ignore signs of his declining health, which will be addressed in the next chapter. But not one to dwell on self-pity, Trajan countered his sense of regret at not being able to press on to India and declared, erroneously, in a letter to the Senate that he had in fact advanced farther than Alexander the Great. Conceivably he claimed Babylonia and Mesene as a new Roman province, alongside Armenia, Mesopotamia and Assyria. Travelling by the fastest imperial dispatch, the letter would have arrived at the Senate around December.[92]

Amazed by Trajan's accomplishments and equally unable to interpret the geographical locations of all his conquests, the Senate granted Trajan a triumph over as many peoples as he desired.[93] The common people of the imperial capital were also forthcoming in their recognition of Trajan's victorious:

> So the people in Rome were preparing for him a triumphal arch besides many other tributes in his own forum and were getting ready to go forth an unusual distance to meet him on his return.
> Dio Cassius[94]

To mark the most easterly point of his advance, Trajan deviated from his usual reluctance to erect statues of himself and allowed a statue to be positioned on the shores of the Persian Gulf,[95] perhaps symbolically gazing out to India.

Trajan continued his tour, returning north along the Euphrates for his first visit to Babylon. He left behind the fleet he had taken down to Spasinou Charax, repaired after the tidal bore, with perhaps the vain hope that he could return in the near future and venture military campaigns in India in spite of his age.[96] Arriving at the once majestic city of Babylon for what can only be described in modern terms as a sight-seeing visit, since the city by Trajan's time was nothing more than ruins in the desert, he viewed the tomb mound of the legendary Assyrian queen, Semiramis, and was led to the remains of the palace of Nebuchadrezzar II and into the very room where Alexander the Great had died on 11 June 323 BC. Attentive to his hero's honour, Trajan made a sacrifice to Alexander, who had passed away just short of turning thirty-three.

Rebellion in the New Roman Provinces

While in Babylon, Trajan received the first urgent dispatches carrying the grim news that there were organised revolts in all his new provinces resulting in the loss of a significant number of his garrisons. The news marked the end of the Trajan success story. The initial control of the vast area that he had captured had hinged on the continued distraction of the Parthians due to internal feuding. It was Trajan's third major error of judgement to have assumed that the Parthians were not close to uniting against the common enemy. The astonishing loss of Seleucia, Ctesiphon and the Babylonian lands had probably galvanised the resolve of the Parthians and allowed them to put their squabbles to one side to oust the Roman host.

In addition to the Parthians uniting, it is plausible that the Jews in Mesopotamia were instrumental in supporting the revolt against the occupying Romans. Since the annexation of Mesopotamia, Trajan would have begun to set up a new taxation system to benefit from the lucrative caravan trades, an act that would have greatly curtailed Jewish freedoms previously enjoyed in the Parthian Empire. Moreover, the inclusion of Mesopotamia within the Roman Empire meant the imposition of a specific tax on all Jews, the *Fiscus Judaicus*, applied universally as a consequence of Jewish revolts in the first century against Rome. In short, Trajan was not only dealing with a galvanised Parthian resistance, but also with a contemporaneous Jewish uprising in the newly acquired territories.[97]

In a coordinated manner, Parthian forces levied in the eastern section of their empire, dropped out of the north-eastern Iranian mountains into Adiabene under the command of Osroes' nephew, Sanatrukes, who was the next in line for the Armenian throne after the death of Parthamasiris. Unprepared and unconsolidated, Adiabene was easily overrun by Sanatrukes. At the same time, Sanatrukes' son Vologaeses led a Parthian army into Armenia which Severus was unable to repel with only two legions spread too thinly to defend the whole region. In a strong position, Vologaeses offered a truce to Severus in exchange for territory in Armenia. With no hope of sending sufficient relief forces to Armenia in time, Trajan was forced to dispatch a note to Severus instructing him to agree the truce with Vologaeses rather than risk losing the entire province and suffering further Roman casualties.

In the intervening time, Trajan reacted quickly, and he divided his available mobile forces into three sections, the first under Julius Maximus Manlianus, the governor of Mesopotamia, the second under Quietus and the last under the joint command of the legion legates Erucius Clarus and Julius Alexander. There was mixed success in the Roman counter-offensives. Given his consular rank, Maximus was charged with the direct confrontation of Sanatrukes,[98] probably taking two legions from Mesopotamia across into Adiabene.[99] But, overwhelmed in a mêlée, he was defeated and killed in battle. In all probability, his legions suffered major casualties and the survivors scrambled back into Mesopotamia. Typical for Parthian tactics, supply lines had probably also been attacked, even at night, undermining the Romans' strength prior to engagements.[100] The disgraceful loss of a consular command would have horrified contemporaries; it would be seen as a serious fault of Trajan as *imperator* to allow such a defeat.

Dashing at maximum pace up the eastern bank of the Euphrates and then along the bank of the Chaboras River, Lusius Quietus brought his division of two legions from the region of Babylonia to within sight of Nisibis in Mesopotamia after a long journey of about 650 km.[101] The reliable general recaptured the important city of Nisibis and, in revenge for King Abgarus' treachery, he captured Edessa, which he proceeded to sack and burn to the ground.[102] His successes were a critical factor in stabilising the Mesopotamian zone which would have otherwise been lost quickly after the defeat of Maximus.

The third division of two legions under the joint command of the legates Erucius Clarus and Julius Alexander advanced on Seleucia, which had risen up in revolt.[103] The city was captured without incident and it was also sacked and burned, a common Roman punishment for rebellious cities. Aware from his scouts of the whereabouts of Sanatrukes, Trajan may have united his personal division with that of Erucius Clarus and Julius Alexander to create an army of around five legions,[104] with an equivalent number of auxiliaries, and marched to meet Sanatrukes.[105] The moment had finally arrived for Trajan to face a major Parthian army in open-field battle, although paradoxically the elusive Osroes still did not appear to assist his nephew.

In the absence of any details about the battle or its location, we must rely entirely on the typical features of Parthian and Roman early second century warfare and battle tactics to understand the possible reasons for the outcome of the confrontation. Sanatrukes would have favoured open flat terrain, best suited for his cavalry, as the site for the battle, while Trajan would have preferred uneven and rising ground ill-suited for the Parthian cavalry but manageable for his legions. The actual location remains unknown, but one can assume that the victors may have had the ideal topography that they desired.

With both sides formed up into their battle lines, the Parthians most likely commenced the battle with initial skirmishes using light archer cavalry who could canter or gallop into missile range of the Roman lines, release volleys of arrows and then retreat while still maintaining fire over the rear of their horses using the 'Parthian shot' technique. This action was intended to rattle the resolve of the Romans, inflict casualties and disrupt their disciplined formations. If the latter was achieved, *azat* commanders or Sanatrukes himself would have promptly ordered the cataphracts to advance on the disarrayed Roman lines to open a wedge in their position and compel the Romans to draw into close order, which was effective against such heavy cavalry. Alternatively, a mock charge by the cataphracts could cause the Romans to group up tightly in anticipation. This in turn made the Romans an easier massed target for the horse archers who could then gallop swiftly in and out to release showers of arrows. The 'hit-and-run' methods of the horse archers combined with the cataphracts' shock attacks could force Roman legionaries into cycles of open and closed formation and were the mainstay of Parthian battle tactics. Sustained application could wear down their foes' morale and destroy an ill-prepared or weakened army, as had been done at the slaughter of Roman forces at Carrhae in 53 BC. The common 'end game' for the Parthians, once they had successfully routed an army, was to surround their distraught enemy and annihilate them with waves of missile fire and cataphract charges.

But Trajan was evidently prepared to cope with these Parthian tactics, resist their strengths and capitalise on their weaknesses. He was also able to recall his youthful experiences as a young tribune when the legion to which he was posted was engaged in action against the Parthians. There is little doubt that he had adapted his forces to field a substantial number of light cavalry and infantry who could at least temporarily disperse Parthian light horse archers. He also likely had specialised auxiliary and *symmachiarii* to match the Parthians' missile capabilities, such as archers and slingers, and he may even have had his own contingent of cataphracts. The Roman imperial army was far more diverse and versatile than the Republican army of the past that had been resoundingly defeated by the Parthians. In addition, in the Trajanic period, legionary plate body armour was less susceptible to piercing by the Parthian arrows than it had been at the time of the battle of Carrhae and the extended neck guard of the helmet afforded better protection from arrows hailing down from above. Serious injuries could still be inflicted to exposed arms, legs and feet, incapacitating legionaries, but overall there would be fewer fatalities. Trajan may have also implemented specific training for his men to hack low at the cataphract horses' legs, the one part of their bodies not protected by armour. Finally, Trajan's forces were well rested, apparently supported by sufficient supply lines and had even been accompanied by a fleet of ships for their journey down into Babylonia. As a result, Trajan was able to defeat Sanatrukes' force that was probably around 1,000 cataphracts and 10,000 horse archers; any Parthian survivors almost certainly retreated all the way into the mountains of Media.

With Sanatrukes defeated, Armenia and Mesopotamia provisionally stabilised, but Adiabene lost, Trajan needed urgently to augment his control in Babylonia and Mesene to prevent mass uprisings. He also needed to prepare for the eventuality of Osroes appearing with a large army to recover his capital, Ctesiphon. Unable to garrison the entire region strongly and at the same time retain a balance of sufficient mobile forces to hand, especially with Roman forces dangerously over-stretched in all the annexed areas, Trajan promptly appointed a puppet client king to the Parthian throne to rule from Ctesiphon. A viable candidate was found called Parthamaspates, a son of Osroes who had been exiled and raised in Rome. A member of the Arsacid dynasty and obviously a Roman collaborator in the war, Parthamaspates was crowned by Trajan on a vast plain near Ctesiphon in front of a large crowd of Roman soldiers and local Parthians.[106] The act was shameless Roman propaganda, intended to display Trajan's authority to appoint a Parthian ruler, distracting from the reality of his precarious position, which was on the brink of crumbling.

This silver *drachm*, struck in Ekbatana *ca.* 116, depicts King Parthamaspates with his diadem.

Sufficiently content with the arrangement at Ctesiphon and at least partly confident he could continue to manipulate Parthamaspates as needed, Trajan hastened north with his force to support the stabilisation of Mesopotamia and consequently maintain the new eastern frontier that had been one of his ultimate goals in the war. Adiabene could remain abandoned and Babylonia an obedient client state to buffer against Parthian incursions from the east. Hopefully, Parthamaspates could muster forces if civil strife arose or if Osroes appeared out of hiding. Although he retained the prized acquisitions in Babylonia like Ctesiphon, Trajan must have been despondent and seriously concerned. Did he regret his lapse in attention during his Persian Gulf excursion? Or did his keen military sense believe that the situation was recoverable in the following year with the appropriate campaigns? After so many years engrossed in military life, there can be no doubt that Trajan was determined to regain the stronger foothold he had held. During the many days of their advance north he would have contemplated the efforts now required in 117 to reaffirm absolute authority. But in the present, Trajan sought the recapture of Hatra and with it the kingdom of Arabae Scenitae; Hatra's advanced position was essential in establishing a zone of influence beyond the Mesopotamian frontier and along a critical access route into Babylonia.

Today a UNESCO World Heritage site, Hatra is situated in a remarkably harsh desert environment in a region known as Al-Jazīrah. Any army operating in this area had to contend with the utterly barren and exposed desert terrain, devoid of shelter, adequate water and any ready sources of food or forage.[107] In the month of October, when Trajan and his forces arrived at Hatra, the daytime extreme temperatures could reach over 45 °C and then plummet to lows around 7 °C at night. As they were dressed in their plate armour and with a helmet and weaponry to carry, the relentless heat of the day could be unbearable even for the hardiest legionaries. Adding to the extreme conditions, endless swarms of sand flies troubled the Roman soldiers, settling in their food and water,[108] and through bites spreading diseases such as the severe parasitic infection Leishmaniasis which is still endemic in Iraq today.[109]

Hatra itself was a pivotal trading centre despite its desolate location. It had established great wealth from the caravan routes passing from the east, especially the affluent oriental Silk Road. As a result, a highly sophisticated and refined city that blended many western and eastern cultures emerged out of the desert sands and rocks. By Trajan's time, Hatra was at its peak of prosperity, allowing it to maintain formidable city defences, bold public buildings and a spectacular temple complex still visible today and remarkably well preserved until the Islamic State insurgent group in 2017 attempted to destroy the remains. It was the defences that preoccupied Trajan and his senior commanders as they surveyed the challenges ahead. The entire city was contained within two circular walls around 2 km in diameter. The first was a solid wall of clay baked as hard as stone in the searing sun. Next came a wide, deep trench and then an inner wall. In effect, the area between the walls was a killing ground. Roman soldiers caught in that space, trying to struggle through the trench and trapped between the two walls were easy prey for missile fire from the Hatrian defenders mounted on the walls or in the multitude of defensive towers all along the perimeters.

Trajan had dealt with seemingly impenetrable fortresses and citadels before in Dacia, but it was the inhospitable environmental conditions described above that posed the greatest challenge to him and his forces now. Nevertheless, the emperor defaulted to the traditional Roman approach that if the fortresses could not be stormed immediately, siege works would be thrown around the defences. But despite the vast army at his disposal, Trajan's siege was limited, given that the majority of his force had to be sent to the vicinity of the Tigris around 50 km due east to have sufficient water and fodder or sent on to Mesopotamia to support operations there. The siege constructions were minimal because of the absence of timber in the area and time was against the Romans as the elements took their toll on their resolve and health. By now, Trajan also had the additional burden of his own declining health, which limited his personal endurance for a lengthy siege.

Mounting assaults from nominal siege positions, the Romans were eventually able to find a chink in Hatra's perimeter defences and in order rapidly to secure a momentary breach Trajan threw in his cavalry. In an act intended to rally the courage of his men under the evidently demoralising conditions, Trajan led his own mounted guard in support of the assault. Though he left aside his imperial attire in which he would have stuck out like a sore thumb among his guard, Trajan was nevertheless distinguishable from his grey hair or finer horse and he drew fire from Hatrene defenders trained to seek out Roman officers as targets. A horse guard within Trajan's immediate vicinity was killed by archers, suggesting Trajan was extremely close to the action and at great personal risk. Yet despite his valour and the efforts of his cavalry, the assault was fruitless and the Hatrenes were able to repel the attack and protect the breach in their defences.[110] Perhaps the killing zone between the walls was the undoing of the cavalry, unable to cope with the exposure.

Further Roman assaults failed and the approaching winter season brought new climatic conditions to endure, not untypical for the region:

> There were peals of thunder, rainbow tints showed, and lightning, rainstorms, hail and thunderbolts descended upon the Romans as often as they made assaults.
>
> Dio Cassius[111]

Ultimately, Trajan was forced to lift the siege.[112] His experience and the advice of his *comites* recognised that another carefully planned approach in the following year was required, perhaps bringing in ample timber for larger offensive siege platforms and engines. It was also time to pull out his forces to Syria and Cappadocia for the winter, except where Quietus had recaptured areas of Mesopotamia and where Severus had control over parts of Armenia that had not been given to Vologaeses. All was not yet lost as Trajan headed back to Antioch, even though Babylonia was a precarious client state and Adiabene was not in Roman hands. Roman authority in Mesopotamia had been partially restored and the whole of Armenia could possibly be won back. Moreover, despite the loss of garrisons and the major defeat of Maximus, no other legions had been lost, so the overall Roman force, while depleted, remained reasonably intact and restorable.

Aborted Campaign of 117 and Empire-wide Unrest

Agonising over plans for the new campaign to start in the spring, which was required to regain the losses in the previous year, Trajan received dispatches in the summer of 116 through into early 117 with news of escalating Jewish revolts in the diaspora of Libya, Egypt and Cyprus.[113] Long troubled in the eastern half of the empire, Jewish communities had incited or were the victims of riots. Greeks and Jews were intolerant of each other's communities and religious practices, the likely cause for the widespread Jewish revolts detailed in Trajan's dispatches. Perhaps extremists had recognised Rome's focus on the Parthian War and seen that it provided the perfect opportunity to incite riots and satisfy long-harboured vendettas against the Greeks. One can also speculate that, while the Jewish rebellions to the east in Mesopotamia and to the west in the diaspora of Libya, Egypt and Cyprus started independently, the Parthians may have attempted to fuel the uprisings to the west to undermine Trajan's position.[114] Regardless of the Parthians' potential involvement, Trajan had to respond to the very serious Jewish incitements in the diaspora or he risked the dissemination of disorder that could destabilise entire provinces. He therefore had to send significant sections of his Parthian invasion army or reserves out to suppress the Jewish revolts and restore order. Firstly, Marcius Turbo, the ex-commander of Rome's largest naval base at Misenum (Miseno) near Naples in Italy[115] and who had been on campaign with Trajan in the Parthian War, was appointed to deal with the riots in Egypt and Cyrene. Cyprus was dealt with by sending the sub-unit of the VII *Claudia* legion involved in the Parthian War: its commander remains unknown.[116]

It is possible that the Jewish rebellions in the diaspora spread to Judaea, or there was a significant risk that such a dissemination of chaos could occur.[117] As a consequence, in the spring of 117, Trajan had to select his most trusted and arguably his most capable general at the time, Lusius Quietus, to tackle or prevent unrest in Judaea.[118] Legion II *Traiana* may have been dispatched with Quietus.[119] The absence of Quietus from his *comites* was a major loss for Trajan, but he could almost certainly recall stories from his father (who was involved in the suppression of the Jewish Wars during the reign of Nero) about the delicate balance in Judaea that could easily explode into a provincial uprising. Therefore, Trajan knew that a ruthless and adept general like Quietus would be required there.

The prospect of pursuing the Parthian War looked increasingly unlikely when further news arrived in Antioch informing Trajan that there was a possible war imminent on the Danube, with the Roxolani and Iazyges threatening attacks on Dacia, and there were also insurgencies reported in Britain. The drain of legions or *auxilia* from these locations to support the Parthian War had initially passed unnoticed, but after three years of absence, the consequentially reduced provincial and regional security had left the gradual emergence of unrest in those areas unchecked.[120] As a result, Trajan was forced to send another of his valuable generals, Quadratus Bassus, who was probably Governor of Syria at the time,[121] to take over as Governor of Dacia to deal with the looming crisis in the Danube region.

To make already dire matters even worse, rebellion had arisen in Babylonia and Parthamaspates had struggled to retain the throne that Trajan had personally bestowed on him a few months before; he left as a fugitive. A serious blow to Trajan's reputation, this effectively left only the precarious gains in Mesopotamia and what was left of control in Armenia as the results of three years of military campaigning in the East. Surely it was not entirely unexpected that a Roman-appointed Parthian king would not reign long in Babylonia before rebellion broke out: there was no substantial Roman military and financial support; Osroes was still at large and the powerful eastern section of the Parthian Empire intact.

Taking all the disturbances together, the overall effect meant that Trajan had to postpone the spring offensives in 117 with which he had planned to regain control in Mesopotamia and Armenia.[122] It was a sensible decision to abort the campaign in order to stand his forces down in the east in case they were urgently needed elsewhere and to evaluate carefully how to deal with the emerging turmoil elsewhere in the empire. Trajan would have certainly regained control along his new eastern frontier and quelled disturbances across the empire through a careful combination of military action and diplomacy given that his universal and internal authority remained strong and he still had the military capacity to mobilise offensive campaigns.[123] But for now, his Parthian War was on hold.

CHAPTER 11

CONSPIRACY, DEATH AND DEIFICATION

Trajan's Declining Health and Death

The Romans viewed death as an inevitable work of nature. Given the plethora of pagan beliefs within the Roman Empire, as well as the diversity of cultural and socio-economic influences, it is hardly surprising that diverse views existed on the afterlife and they are impossible to generalise. These notions ranged from a belief in the existence of the soul after death, a deep-rooted Roman tradition, and conversely, a belief that death marked the final end of existence.[1] Greek philosophy is thought to have influenced the latter, teaching the dispersal of the soul after death into the wider universe with the loss of individual identity. This is attested by examples of Roman epitaphs that expressed the idea that death was the end to one's existence.[2] Perhaps one of the best of these comes from an epitaph of the Imperial period:

> I wasn't; I was; I'm not; I don't care.
>
> Roman epitaph

Interestingly, the philosopher and Roman emperor Marcus Aurelius (121–180), thought of death as something not to dread and wrote:

> Death is a cessation from the impression of the senses, the tyranny of the passions, the errors of the mind, and the servitude of the body.
>
> Marcus Aurelius[3]

Beyond these different views on the afterlife, it is striking that the majority of Roman epitaphs have one thing in common: they celebrate the achievements of life. Although one cannot generalise about Roman attitudes towards the afterlife,[4] it is thought that most Romans held some notion of existence beyond mortal death.[5] Trajan's views on death are not recorded, so we can only guess that his declining health towards the end of the Parthian

War may have prompted him to reflect on the destiny of his soul and on his major accomplishments in life.

No doubt, Trajan would have hoped that after his death the Senate would vote him into the company of the *divi*, the divine. This was the befitting end for a worthy emperor. However, it should be noted that a boundary was still retained between divine emperors and the traditional gods, the *dei*.[6] Julius Caesar was the first Roman to be voted this honour and other emperors like Augustus were likewise deified after their death. As a result, the imperial cult was established and the structure was developed during the principate of Augustus. Participation in or support of the cult did not indicate any personal belief on the part of the emperor himself about his own afterlife. Famously, the Emperor Vespasian (ruled 69–79) mocked deification on his deathbed, saying, 'Oh dear, I think I'm becoming a god.'[7]

Certainly, contemplations of death increasingly occupied Trajan's thoughts in the summer of 117 when his health drastically worsened. The decline was enough for Trajan to be unable to continue personally overseeing his plans for new campaigns in the Parthian War. He had started the Parthian War in reasonable shape. His years may have slowed him down somewhat, but he was still able to climb to the top of Mount Casius with Hadrian in early 114. During the three years that followed, the physical and mental stresses of campaigning, often under harsh conditions, took their toll on his constitution. Towards the end of the third year, extreme environments such as the desert terrain around Hatra and the deepening anxieties caused by the insurgencies, finally accentuated the underlying pathology behind his principal suspected affliction: high blood pressure.

Hypertension, or high blood pressure, is known today as a 'silent killer' as most people have no symptoms during the early stages of disease. In many cases, the causes of the condition remain unknown, and in Trajan's case we will never know the root causes. Maintaining a healthy balanced diet and taking sufficient exercise decrease the risk of developing high blood pressure. On both these counts, Trajan's modest lifestyle, vigorous hunting pursuits and years of campaigning, often on foot, may have helped delay the onset or worsening of the disease, perhaps even adding years to a life that might otherwise have been cut short after the Dacian Wars. However, these factors were somewhat countered by the effects of Trajan's heavy alcohol consumption, which may have significantly aggravated the condition.

The first acute signs probably materialised while Trajan was in Babylonia in 116 during the third campaign of the Parthian War. Symptoms could have included a general feeling of malaise, headache, increased fatigue, periodic dizziness or difficulty sleeping. Trajan may have become emaciated by this time; this and other emerging symptoms were doubtless recognised by those close to him.[8] In particular, the common complication of peripheral oedema, fluid accumulation in the extremities, eventually became visible.[9] His condition had weakened his heart, reducing its pumping efficiency and allowing a build-up of this fluid, especially in the ankles and feet. Trajan's personal physician could do little at this stage to help his patient except alleviate his symptoms, for example by asking him to raise his feet when possible or by administering ancient remedies.

Back in Antioch, probably in the summer of 117, Trajan had a stroke, another typical complication of high blood pressure.[10] Lucky to survive, he was crippled, with a portion of his body paralysed. Increasingly distraught by his afflictions in this period, Trajan was also becoming paranoid that he was being poisoned, an archetypal method used to dispose of one's enemies that many of Trajan's predecessors had feared.[11] Plotina, Hadrian and Trajan's closest friends and aides would have been horrified to see the emperor in his debilitated state. Speculation would surely have been rife: who would replace him?

It was certainly time for Trajan to return to Rome and he authorised the appointment of Hadrian as governor of Syria, replacing Quadratus Bassus who had left for Dacia to tackle the disturbances in the region. Trajan's rationale for returning to Italy, probably pressed upon him by Plotina, was additionally motivated by factors other than his desperately deteriorating health. Firstly, he could claim the triumphs for his achievements in the Parthian War, which would help maintain his prestigious reputation despite the subsequent losses and currently unstable situation in Mesopotamia, Armenia and Babylonia. It would also have allowed him to adopt a centralised 'command and control' position in Rome to manage the many disturbances throughout the empire, and he could direct the Parthian War through his generals. Finally, it would allow Trajan to appoint his heir in an appropriate manner, just as Nerva had done when he publicly announced Trajan's adoption from the *Rostra* in the forum. Trajan knew the importance of this approach to ensure a smooth and stable transition of power. The mere fact that Trajan did not officially appoint an heir before he left Antioch suggests he was in denial of his life-threatening condition and therefore assumed he would complete the journey back to Rome. He was probably adamant that a nomination was not needed and that any nominee required respectful presentation to the Senate, a principle that adhered to his policy of maintaining a fictitious façade of respectful consultation with the senators.

The once mighty Roman emperor had marched with his legions through the mountains of Dacia and Armenia, but now he almost certainly required help to walk after his stroke as he set sail for Rome from Seleucia Pieria towards the end of July. Trajan was accompanied by Plotina, Matidia, his Praetorian Guard Prefect Attianus, his personal secretary Marcus Ulpius Phaedimus, his personal physician and his usual close aides and imperial secretaries. As his vessel hugged the coast of the Roman province of Cilicia (Çukurova, Turkey), Trajan's condition declined enough to warrant halting the voyage. His physician doubtless predicted that the end was very near and the imperial party moored in the harbour of Selinus (Gazipaşa, Turkey) to find accommodation. The region is a picturesque strip of lower-lying land between the turquoise waters of the Mediterranean and the soaring western Taurus Mountains, but, unable to appreciate the beauty of the area, Trajan was carried to his bed in a villa at an unknown location nearby;[12] at this stage his physician could do little more than provide palliative care.

Shortly after arriving in Selinus, Trajan died. He was sixty and had ruled for nineteen and half years. He was the first emperor to die outside Italy. Perhaps that was fitting given that he was the first to be born outside Italy. We do not know today whether he muttered any dying words. After years of high blood pressure, his frail heart may have finally failed, or perhaps a dangerous amount of fluid had built up in his lungs causing progressive shortening of his breath and ultimately respiratory collapse. Trajan is said to have also had diarrhoea near the end, perhaps due to a secondary infection easily contracted if he had become immune-suppressed, but it is far more likely the fatal complications of high blood pressure ultimately caused the emperor's death.[13] So expired Rome's thirteenth emperor, its 'Father of the Country', its 'Best Prince' and its all-conquering hero who had expanded the empire to the greatest extent.

Accession Conspiracy

It is very possible that Trajan died without designating a *Caesar*, his heir to the Principate.[14] This posed a critical risk to the stability of the Roman Empire. To appreciate the imprtance of the absence of an heir apparent and the probable conspiracy that followed to secure Hadrian as the successor, one needs first to address the relationship between Trajan and Hadrian.

Over the years, Trajan had bestowed certain privileges and honours on Hadrian appropriate for a second cousin of the emperor. Indeed, the emperor had given his closest available female relation of an appropriate age, Vibia Sabina (his sister's granddaughter), to Hadrian as a wife. Hadrian's senatorial career had advanced and his appointments were made at the first opportunity.[15] He had held positions of importance during the Dacian Wars in keeping with the stage of his senatorial career and he was the first governor of the new province created by Trajan, Pannonia Inferior. Hadrian's successes commanding a legion in the Second Dacian War reportedly prompted Trajan to give Hadrian a diamond he had once received from Nerva.[16] During the Parthian War, Hadrian held a special legate position as military adviser to the emperor and, after the pause in the war in 117, Trajan gave Hadrian his first really important position, the governorship of Syria and command of the substantial forces associated with this province.[17]

However, with the possible exception of his marriage to Vibia Sabina, there was no sign of truly special distinction. Rather, it appears that Trajan had provided polite recognition for a distant cousin, once his ward, and his only male relation. The later historian Dio Cassius notes clearly this observation:

> Yet [Hadrian] had received no distinguishing mark of favour from Trajan, such as being one of the first to be appointed consul [at the start of the year.[18]

One can argue that Trajan even deliberately limited the advance of Hadrian beyond the familial regard he held for him. It is possible that Hadrian's inappropriate excesses and indebtedness, that once drew anger from Trajan, had revealed and tarnished Hadrian's character in the eyes of the emperor.[19] Even Hadrian's marriage to Vibia Sabina may have been pressed upon a reluctant Trajan due to the influence of Plotina.[20] The marriage was thought to be an unhappy one and the emperor may have been more in sympathy with his great niece than with Hadrian.

Trajan had not made Hadrian a patrician and had only allowed Hadrian to attain the 'replacement' consulship in 108.[21] Even Hadrian's second consulship, earmarked for 118, was apparently only attained because of Plotina's 'favour'.[22] These were immensely important socio-politico statements given that Trajan could have easily elevated the status of his male relative if he truly had a good opinion of him and trusted him.

One can compare the lack of Hadrian's distinctions to the early honours given to Tiberius by the Emperor Augustus. Tiberius was thrust into the Senate and made eligible for the consulship five years ahead of the normal age. When he was thirty-one (12 BC) he held critically important military command positions in Pannonia and Germania and subsequently went on to great victories as a general in the region. In his mid-thirties he had attained a second consulship (7 BC) and been granted tribunician power (*tribunicia potestas*) and offered control of the East (6 BC) which would have made him the second most powerful person after Augustus.

In the early stages of the important Parthian War, the situation had not changed: Hadrian was not given direct command of a legion or division. There had been enough time to arrange for Hadrian to hold a formal position in a province and to act as a general during the war, so this was surely a slight on his abilities. There is also no known contribution from Hadrian during the war. Even Hadrian's later appointment as governor of Syria suggests issues in his relationship with the emperor. One cannot deny the importance of this province, but the appointment was unplanned; the best man for the job, Quadratus Bassus, was required more urgently in Dacia to deal with the emergency there.

Above all else, Trajan had allowed Hadrian, even possibly compelled him, to waste precious years in Athens (roughly 111–113)[23] from the perspective of advancing his senatorial career, years in which Hadrian could have been groomed for the Principate under Trajan's guidance. Certainly, Hadrian would have hoped, as a minimum, for a consular command from Trajan in this period. Instead, Hadrian was at leisure in Greece, hardly a suitable position for a Roman senator on a path to take over the entire Roman Empire.

In summary, Trajan's failure to grant Hadrian patrician status, to award him only a suffect consulship and, most significantly, to allow him to be at leisure in Athens during crucial years of his career, all strongly suggest that Trajan could not bring himself to take the decisive action either to repudiate Hadrian, which would be needed if he were not to be the leading candidate, or to fully reconcile himself to the prospect. It is also a possibility that some of the privileges given to Hadrian were thanks in part to persuasion by Plotina, who is known to have frequently supported Hadrian. Perhaps Trajan was more in sympathy with Sabina. It could be that Trajan suspected that Hadrian was going to reject his policies but it could also be something else that eludes our understanding today.[24] As Trajan's health declined seriously in 117, with death an imminent possibility, he did not formally adopt nor designate Hadrian as his heir. He was clearly unable to accept the selection of Hadrian as the person to succeed him.

Therefore, with the emperor's condition visibly declining and no successor appointed, it is arguable that Hadrian conspired with Plotina and Attianus to secure his accession. Plotina is thought to have harboured real affection for Hadrian and she had promoted his advancement over many years. Of a similar age, they connected well, and it is said she may have even fallen in love with him;[25] perhaps this was a cause of Hadrian's unhappy marriage to Sabina. Hadrian later deified Plotina and erected a temple in her honour in Nemausus (Nîmes) where she had been born. Attianus, once a co-guardian of Hadrian along with Trajan, would naturally assume that he would benefit from his exward ascending to the Principate.[26] Ultimately, the three conspirators likely viewed their actions as entirely justified. After all, they were not going to kill Trajan or accelerate his death, but merely ensure that the best candidate in their view could claim the Principate through a falsified, but believable adoption and thereby secure a smooth accession that averted the ravages of civil war and allowed the continuation of action against the various revolts ongoing across the empire in this period. In part, these were noble intentions.

The success of such a conspiracy hinged on two major components: credibility and backing. Together, Plotina and Attianus provided both. For credibility, Plotina was Trajan's wife and a venerable *Augusta*. Attianus was the current Praetorian Guard Prefect and a lifelong friend of Trajan. In addition, Hadrian appeared to be a viable candidate for adoption as Trajan's heir. Although he had fallen out of favour with Trajan at times in his life and his *cursus* had no especially remarkable advances above and beyond his peers, he had gradually attained positions of increasing influence that culminated in his appointment as governor of Syria.[27] Hadrian could additionally claim family connections to Trajan, as well as his marital connection through Sabina, Trajan's great niece. His backers and, perhaps most important of all, his command of three legions in Syria meant that Hadrian could realistically rely on the majority of the eastern legions to rally to his cause. Such a massive force was rather like a modern-day nuclear deterrent in its political weight. Only someone able to command the majority of the western armies could stand a chance of opposing Hadrian.

Before Trajan's departure to return to Rome, Plotina, Hadrian and Attianus may have agreed upon the method of falsifying Hadrian's adoption that should ensure a smooth and uninterrupted transition of power. Matidia accompanied the party heading for Rome but it is thought that she was not involved at all in the conspiracy.[28] Thus, at Trajan's death bed in Selinus, the conspiracy was launched. Plotina and Attianus may have tightly controlled access to the emperor so that, as he drew his last breaths, only they were present. After his death, Trajan's body was presumably stowed away in a sufficiently cool and secure place whilst someone of a similar build, who could be silenced later if need be, was likely paid a handsome sum to lie in bed and pretend to be the emperor.[29] A vital account survives from Dio Cassius whose own father, later governor of Cilicia under Marcus Aurelius, was able to provide details of the conspiracy:

> My father, Apronianus, who was Governor of Cilicia, had ascertained accurately the whole story about [Hadrian], and he used to relate the various incidents, in particular stating that the death of Trajan was concealed for several days in order that Hadrian's adoption might be announced first.[30]

For the opening of his biography of Hadrian, Dio Cassius provides a frank and clear description of what he probably learned from his father:

> Hadrian had not been adopted by Trajan; he was merely a compatriot and former ward of his, was of near kin to him and had married his niece – in short, he was a companion of his, sharing his daily life, and had been assigned to Syria for the Parthian War. Yet he had received no distinguishing mark of favour from Trajan.[31]

If this conspiracy was true, one of the hardest persons to have fooled with the disguising of Trajan's death was his personal secretary Phaedimus. As a result, Plotina and Attianus would have prevented him from approaching and talking with the impersonator. Plotina could have easily insisted on being the only person to attend to the emperor personally at this stage to ward off would-be interferers like Phaedimus. Alternatively, they could have simply bought him off or threatened him.

In the meantime, Plotina and Attianus had to send an urgent dispatch to Hadrian in Antioch to inform him of Trajan's death. Trajan probably died on 7 August 117 with the private message reaching Hadrian on 9 August by the fastest courier.[32] Plotina is known to have started signing documents on behalf of Trajan, presumably after his stroke. Hadrian was therefore able to reveal adoption papers on the same day he received word from Plotina and Attianus, supposedly signed by Plotina on behalf of the emperor on his deathbed. This stunt could never have been achieved while Trajan was in Antioch; the conspiracy had relied on the high probability of Trajan's death during the long journey home, away from the multitudes of people in the imperial quarters, whose prying nature or meddling might have uncovered the invalidity of Hadrian's adoption announcement.

Concealing Trajan's death for as long as they dared, to allow time for Hadrian's adoption announcement to spread at the very least through Syria and to the many legions present in the province at that time, Plotina and Attianus then officially announced Trajan's death to the Roman world on 9 August. Again, an urgent dispatch was sent to Hadrian in Antioch, and when he received the news on 11 August he immediately claimed his accession to the purple and this became his future *dies imperii*, imperial day. In the intervening period one can reasonably assume that Phaedimus either proved difficult to convince that Trajan had designated Hadrian as his adoptee or plans to bribe or threaten him failed. He may have had access to papers or known Trajan's actual plans for the selection of his heir. Plotina and Attianus had to prevent Phaedimus from leaking accusations, so Attianus probably recruited a corruptible guard or two to have him discreetly disposed of. Phaedimus' mysterious death at only twenty-eight years of age is recorded on 12 August on his funerary epitaph discovered in Rome,[33] five days after Trajan's death and one day after Hadrian's accession. Adding to the suspicions, his remains were returned to Rome only thirteen years later.

The rest was up to Hadrian. As governor of Syria, he quickly solicited the allegiance of the Syrian legions, which were the first to hail him as emperor. To promote the notion of divine intervention in his accession, Hadrian announced a prophetic dream that he claimed to have had the day before Trajan's death, in which he was anointed by fire from the heavens.[34] Moreover, to solidify his accession further, Hadrian knew he needed the Senate to endorse his claim, even though they were effectively powerless to reject him at this point. Thus, he wrote a letter to the Senate asking for their constitutional confirmation and the bestowal of his official imperial power. With legions behind Hadrian, the Senate's endorsement was merely ceremonial. Finally, it was imperative that Hadrian ordered the issue of new coins that would circulate across the empire bearing the key initial messages he wanted to convey: his adoption by Trajan and his subsequent accession as emperor.[35]

With the Roman world gradually learning of Trajan's death, Plotina, Matidia and Attianus conveyed his body back to Seleucia Pieria.[36] Notwithstanding the putative accession conspiracy she may have helped engineer, Plotina appears to have remained otherwise faithful to her husband and she seems to have genuinely mourned his death, along with many others. The funeral party arrived with an escort to a reception befitting the death of Rome's great emperor; Hadrian had travelled down from Antioch to greet them and to see

Trajan's body before it was cremated. A wax mask, now lost, was probably cast of Trajan's face in the traditional manner to preserve his image for the Ulpii. Trajan's ashes were then placed in a golden urn for Plotina and Matidia to return to Rome. There is little doubt that a contingent of senators, friends and crowds would have greeted Plotina's return in late September bearing the ashes of their conquering emperor in a golden urn. His remains were placed in a purpose-built vestibule chamber within the pedestal base of his mighty column depicting the Dacian wars.[37] Sadly, we know that the chamber was later robbed because excavations in 1906 revealed a hole through the pedestal into the chamber.[38] The thieves were probably unaware of the urn's contents. Trajan's ashes are certainly lost, but to the speculative mind the urn may survive somewhere today. It was certainly a magnificent honour to place Trajan's ashes in his column, not so much because of the column itself but rather because it lay within the *pomerium*, the sacred boundary of Rome. Ancient laws forbade burying anyone within the *pomerium*. The great Julius Caesar, who had a temple erected to him in the middle of the Republican forum after his death, had received the same privilege of having his ashes interred within the *pomerium*.[39] Trajan was therefore granted an extremely rare honour.

In this same period, a letter from Hadrian to the Senate requested Trajan's deification and it was unanimously approved by the Senate, along with many other honours.[40] In Roman belief, his soul was therefore not destined for Hades, but instead transformed into a divine entity, *Divus Trajan*, who rose to the heavens to join the Pantheon of Roman gods and unite with Nerva, Traianus and Marciana.

Lastly, Hadrian respected the Parthian triumph that had been offered to Trajan by the Senate before his death and allowed the posthumous celebration to proceed, probably later when he eventually returned to Rome. With similar pomp and glory as was seen at Trajan's Dacian triumph, his effigy was carried on a four-horse triumphal chariot through the streets of Rome and presumably Hadrian made the dedications to Jupiter in the Capitoline temple on behalf of the deceased emperor. A series of public triumphal games also celebrated Trajan's Parthian War and were held annually for a number of years.[41] Few of those attending would have cared about the actual outcome of the war. It was a chance to celebrate the memory of Rome's divine conquering emperor.

As events settled after Trajan's death, rumours soon spread at dinner parties and in taverns regarding the circumstances of Hadrian's accession. When Nerva had announced Trajan as his adopted heir, there had been no doubt that Trajan was *Caesar*, the emperor in waiting, given that Nerva had ascended the *Rostra* in the forum and publicly proclaimed his adoptee. In the absence of Trajan making a similar public declaration, it is not at all surprising that stories of cheated legitimate candidates or foul play proliferated. Indeed, Trajan is thought to have once suggested that Lucius Neratius Priscus, a famous jurist and member of his *consilium*, would be his heir if anything should happen to him.[42] One can hypothesise that this suggestion was triggered after the failed attempt on Trajan's life in the winter of 105/106, reminding Trajan of his mortality and susceptibility, and while Priscus was close to hand as governor of the crucial province of Pannonia.[43] Priscus was clearly a very clever man who had been held in high regard by Trajan, and perhaps he would have regretted that he had no military power or leverage to back up his previously favoured position and could only languish in his thoughts of what might have happened if Trajan had made it back to Rome from the East.

In short, it was not a foregone conclusion that Hadrian was Trajan's only possible heir. Moreover, an anecdote records Trajan as asking diners at a banquet to name him ten men capable of being emperor, which he then amended to a request for only nine names since he had already considered Servianus, a trusted loyalist and able statesman, as one such successor.[44] Other rumours astutely cited Trajan's fascination with Alexander that Great and idle gossip fuelled speculation that Trajan imitated his hero by following his example of dying without an heir.[45] It was thought by some that Trajan had then intended to leave the Senate to appoint his heir from a list of his top candidates that he would bequeath to them.[46] In any event, Trajan had failed to make any formal announcements. Regrettably, we may never know the full truth of the circumstances surrounding Trajan's death and Hadrian's accession.

A gold aureus, struck in Rome in 117 depicts Hadrian's reputed adoption.
Trajan and Hadrian are shown facing each other and shaking hands.

Concluding the Parthian War and Removing Trajan's Supporters

Following Trajan's cremation, Hadrian returned to Antioch to lay out his plans. He intended to discontinue the Parthian War. After withdrawing Catilius Severus and the Roman forces from what remained of the Roman province of Armenia, Hadrian appointed Severus in his place as governor of Syria now that he was emperor. Severus was evidently a trusted man, needed in Syria to help Hadrian implement his new strategy for the region. It appears that Hadrian needed to release the concentration of legions readied for the continuation of the war, firstly, to be prepared to tackle any challenges to his new authority and, secondly, to address the pockets of unrest throughout the empire that had emerged before Trajan's death. Hadrian was therefore ready to abandon Trajan's vision for a new northerly section of the eastern frontier. His ethos for the frontiers of the empire would be very different from that of Trajan. This is no better demonstrated than the great 118-km-long wall that Hadrian later built in northern Britain, beckoning in a new era of static defence and shunning the expansionism of Trajan's principate.

Hadrian's new policy effectively reverted to Augustus' guiding principle that the empire should be kept within its main natural river boundaries; the Rhine, Danube and Euphrates. As a result, in what would later prove to be an unpopular move, all the lands under Roman control east of the Euphrates were relinquished by Hadrian to the Parthians and what remained of Armenia handed over to Vologaesus. To deal with the awkward situation of Parthamasiris, crowned by Trajan but essentially an outcast battling a rebellion in Babylonia, Hadrian found a compromise by appointing him king of neighbouring tribes.[47] Consequently, Trajan's great Parthian War was discarded in 117 and all the campaigns once praised by the Senate had been in vain. The frontier in the east returned to its old boundaries before the war, along the Euphrates.

With the war concluded, Trajan's generals and avid supporters nevertheless still lived on, and many would have keenly felt his absence. Whenever a new emperor established his power base, it was always a delicate time for acutely loyal supporters of the deceased emperor or for those who had attained great eminence and power under the previous regime. In this case, four such senators were perceived by Hadrian as a threat to his authority, though in reality they may well have not posed any real hazard. Their mistake may have been to complain openly about Hadrian's abandonment of the Parthian War and territories in the east, as well as criticise some of his emerging policies.

They may have privately thought that Hadrian's accession was not what Trajan had desired. The four senators were Cornelius Palma Frontonianus, Caius Avidius Nigrinus, Lusius Quietus and Lucius Publilius Celsus.[48]

Palma, consul in 99 and 109, had successfully annexed the province of Arabia while governor of Syria. Celsus was also twice a consul during Trajan's reign (102 and 113), and Trajan had even erected statues honouring the pair.[49] While Palma and Celsus appear to have fallen out of favour with Trajan during the Parthian War,[50] or were perhaps simply too old or frail to travel east, they almost certainly remained faithful to some of Trajan's ideologies and policies. Besides, they were long considered adversaries of Hadrian while Trajan was alive, conceivably resentful of his potential as a successor to the principate, which they may also have coveted. Avidius Nigrinus was consul in 110, after which he was appointed as an imperial legate with a special mission in Greece for Trajan.[51] Lusius Quietus, the highly successful general in Trajan's Parthian War, appointed to the Senate by Trajan for his remarkable deeds and then consul in 117, arguably one of the best generals of his day and an instrumental commander during the Dacian Wars, was governor of Judaea in 117 with a legion under his authority. Thus, all these men had been staunch partisans of Trajan and had 'great influence and enjoyed wealth and fame'.[52] Hadrian may simply have not wanted to risk them plotting his demise or calling for rebellion against him.

Hadrian clearly thought that Quietus had to be tackled first. Probably within weeks or even days after his accession, Hadrian first relieved him of his command of the Mauretanian *auxilia* cavalry, which he had famously led for over twenty-five years in service of Rome, and then relieved him of his governorship of Judaea.[53] The Mauretanian cavalry were so loyal to Quietus that when they returned to their homeland after their dismissal the whole affair incited a rebellion there that Hadrian then had to deal with.[54]

As regards Avidius Nigrinus, it appears that Hadrian had appointed him governor of Dacia following the unexpected death of Quadratus Bassus on campaign. Perhaps at that time, soon after his accession, they were on good terms and Nigrinus was therefore a suitable immediate replacement for Bassus at a time of crisis. Not long after the accession, though, the feared news of incursions by the Iazyges and Roxolani triggered Hadrian to send forces from the East to Moesia to shore up offensive and defensive capabilities and he probably also departed for the Danube region himself in October 117.[55] The facts are not clear as to what happened next, but one can assume that, early in 118 with Hadrian in the region, an unknown event seriously soured his relationship with Nigrinus. The circumstances were sufficiently grave for Nigrinus to be considered a threat to the new principate. Therefore, Hadrian appointed his friend Marcius Turbo, who had just quelled the rebellion in Mauretania, as governor of Pannonia Inferior and Dacia. This was a slight against Nigrinus who had been in office for only a few months. How dare Hadrian replace an ex-consul of Rome, former legate in Greece for the divine Trajan, with Turbo who had once been a lowly centurion?[56]

Probably very soon after dismissing Nigrinus, Hadrian was presented with an incident that either provided the perfect excuse for accusations of treason against Nigrinus or constituted a genuine attempt on his life devised by the disgraced Nigrinus and his accomplices. Whatever the reasons, while Hadrian and Nigrinus were part of the same hunting party, presumably in Dacia, an episode occurred that obviously threatened Hadrian's life and was later construed as an assassination attempt. Quietus, Palma and Celsus were all conveniently implicated in the conspiracy and Hadrian's henchmen in the Senate orchestrated charges that were essentially despicable. The Senate ordered their execution.[57] One can only assume that the majority of the senators were under duress to act ruthlessly and intimidated by the uncertainty of the new regime. Nigrinus in Faventia (Faenza), having been allowed to leave Dacia in the intervening period, Palma in Baiae (Baia), Celsus in Tarracina and Quietus while travelling somewhere were all executed, under orders from Attianus acting for the Senate.[58]

In conclusion, before the year 118 had closed, Hadrian had managed to purge four prominent senators likely because he wanted to eliminate his most immediate and powerful enemies in the Senate. Although the order had supposedly come from the Senate, Rome's elite would have noted that these callous acts contradicted a direct promise that Hadrian had made to the Senate after his accession. He had sworn in a letter to the Senate that he would never condemn a senator to death, even invoking 'destruction upon himself if he should violate these promises in any wise'.[59] Many senators, who had not felt threatened for over nineteen years during Trajan's reign, would now have been afraid. As a result, Hadrian drew severe criticism and he was forced to make an oath that he had not ordered their deaths and shamelessly blamed the affair on Attianus – who would of course never have acted in such a way without Hadrian's consent.[60] Few would have believed such an oath and the whole affair haunted Hadrian throughout his principate and incurred the simmering wrath of the Senate. But Hadrian could live with this; he was the new unopposed master of the Roman world.

Trajan's Legacy

In measurable terms, Trajan's single greatest legacy was to expand the size of the empire, through conquest, to the largest size it would ever attain. With the annexation of Dacia, Arabia, Armenia, Mesopotamia, Assyria and Babylonia, the empire controlled nearly six million square kilometres. Although the gains from the Parthian Empire were extremely short-lived, both Dacia and Arabia were major acquisitions that endured, though in Dacia's case, the province was trimmed back.[61]

From the perspective of the average Roman citizen, Trajan was perceived to have brought tangible benefits to society and individuals, paid for with booty and tribute from the conquered regions. In Rome, gracious new public buildings and renovations adorned the city. Across Italy and the empire, massive improvements in infrastructure transformed the daily lives of countless people. Although it had been promoted by Trajan prior to the Dacian wars, it is very likely that the same flush of money from these conquests also ensured continued funding for the *alimenta*.

In stark contrast, the indigenous peoples of Dacia and Arabia were arguably far more affected by Trajan's legacy of expansion. The futures of their homelands were irreparably changed and in the case of Dacia, Trajan's imposition of '*pax Romana*' amounted to widespread enslavement for the vanquished Dacians, the destruction of parts of their society, the eventual loss of the kingdom's language and dialects, the erosion of its cultural identity and exploitation of its natural resources. The effects of the conquest of Arabia were less dramatic but still substantial. It appears that there, too, there was a gradual loss of native dialects, along with culture and identity. Trajan had firmly put the regions of Dacia and Arabia on a different course in history by bringing them into the realm of Rome's authority. The Parthian Empire did not escape unscathed following its conflict with Rome. Trajan's Parthian War undermined the position of the king of kings, exposed the Parthians' acute vulnerability to invasion in the western half of their empire and significantly drained their resources in its defence. It surely marked a turning point in Parthia's history and arguably the start of the decline towards the collapse of their empire in 224.

Less quantifiable, one of Trajan's legacies to the Roman Senate and elite classes was the continuation of comparative liberty started by his predecessor Nerva after Domitian's more oppressive principate. Although Trajan had operated with firm autocratic authority, his administration had respected the diminished role of the Senate and even empowered it to some extent, resulting in what appears to have been a restoration of the amiable balance lost since Augustus. This included clamping down on informers and treason cases, factors that had previously destroyed the relationship of the emperor with the Senate. In addition, one of Trajan's core values that underpinned his principate was modesty and respectability, which he displayed and practised in his everyday life and acts. These characteristics allowed his subjects to connect with him in an open manner, and indeed the next three emperors would adhere to that persona in varying degrees. Furthermore, as the first emperor to be born outside Italy, Trajan had demonstrated clearly that the barriers that had once restricted provincial Roman citizens were now well and truly gone. This paved the way for Lucius Septimius Severus (193–211), of North African descent, who started the Severan imperial dynasty.

It therefore appears that Trajan was indeed regarded by subsequent generations of Roman citizens as an able and just ruler, 'conducting himself as an equal towards all' despite his position of incredible power.[62] Almost 250 years later, his reputation among Roman citizens was still so high that, in honour of his memory, people called out praise to later emperors, 'More fortunate than Augustus, better than Trajan!'[63]

Yet Trajan's apparently impeccable reputation goes beyond the fall of the Roman Empire, although he has not yet been made the subject of Hollywood movies or televised drama like many other Roman emperors. Spanning to the Dark Ages, Saint Gregory the Great, Pope from 590 to 604, according to an account written in the early eighth century, visited Trajan's Markets in Rome, which prompted his recollection of Trajan's many fine deeds and virtues.[64] He supposedly lamented Trajan's pagan faith and his suffering in hell as a consequence, and the account continues that God answered Saint Gregory's prayers for a reprieve, freeing Trajan's soul from hell.[65]

Dante's *Divine Comedy*, describing a medieval view of Christian afterlife in the early 14th century, recognises Trajan's just nature.[66] Dante refers to a story which had passed down over many generations to his time: when Trajan was riding out to battle in one of the Dacian Wars, a widow accosted him to ask him to avenge the unjust death of her son. After he promised to deal with the matter should he survive the battle, the widow challenged Trajan by asking who would deal with the case should he perish. Trajan responded that his successor would then be responsible, to which the widow replied was it not better for him to deal with the matter personally and gain credit for the noble deed. Thereupon, Trajan took pity on her and is said to have dismounted to hear the details of the case, then issued orders that resulted in her son's death being avenged. The story, which may well have been based on a real incident during Trajan's principate but possibly embellished over time, exemplifies his dutiful nature with which medieval scholars could identify. The famous episode was known as the Justice of Trajan and became the subject of numerous later works of art.[67]

But surely one of the most telling observations that exemplifies Trajan's legacy of integrity and efficient leadership is the accolade from the sixteenth-century philosopher Niccolò Machiavelli, who includes Trajan in a list of the 'good' emperors to have ruled Rome:

> All the emperors who succeeded to the throne by birth, except Titus, were bad, all were good who succeeded by adoption; as in the case of the five from Nerva to Marcus [Aurelius].[68]

In addition there is a view that Titus simply didn't live long enough to go bad.

Agreeing with Machiavelli, the renowned eighteenth-century historian Edward Gibbon went even further, stating that the period of rule by these five 'good' emperors, Nerva, Trajan, Hadrian, Antoninus and Marcus Aurelius, was the most prosperous in all Rome's imperial history and even that of the human race. Thus, there is no better way to sumarise Trajan's lasting reputation than to leave the final say in this book to Gibbon:

> If a man were called to fix the period in the history of the world during which the condition of the human race was most happy and prosperous, he would, without hesitation, name that which elapsed from the death of Domitian to the accession of Commodus. The vast extent of the Roman Empire was governed by absolute power, under the guidance of virtue and wisdom. The armies were restrained by the firm but gentle hand of four successive Emperors, whose characters and authority commanded involuntary respect. The forms of the civil administration were carefully preserved by Nerva, Trajan, Hadrian and the Antonines, who delighted in the image of liberty, and were pleased with considering themselves as the accountable ministers of the laws. Such princes deserved the honour of restoring the republic, had the Romans of their days been capable of enjoying a rational freedom.
>
> Edward Gibbon, *The History of the Decline and Fall of the Roman Empire*[69]

NOTES

Preface

1. Lepper, F. A., *Trajan's Parthian War*, 'The General Nature of the Problem'.
2. Duncan-Jones, R., *Money and Government in the Roman Empire*, 'The Imperial Budget'. Jones's lower limit estimate for *ca.* AD 150 is 643 m sestertii.

CHAPTER 1: Impressionable Years

1. Taagepera, R., *'Size and Duration of Empires: Growth–Decline Curves, 600 B.C. to A.D. 600'*, estimates the population in 25 BC as 56.8 million and in AD 117 as 88 million. Durand, J. D., *Historical Estimates of World Population: An Evaluation*, gives a population around Augustus' reign as 56.8 million and estimates the population at around 65 million in the middle of the second century.
2. I accept the analysis in Bennett, J, *Trajan Optimus Princeps*, 'The Rise of the Ulpii'. Bennett calculates Trajan's birth year as AD 56 based on Dio Cassius.
3. Harlow, M. & Laurence, R., *Growing Up and Growing Old in Ancient Rome: A life course approach*, 'The Beginning of life: Infancy and childhood'.
4. Pliny, *Panegyricus*, 14.
5. French., V., 'Rescuing Creusa: New Methodological Approaches to Women in Antiquity'. Wells, C., 'Ancient Obstetric Hazards and Female Mortality'.
6. Parkin, T. G., *Demography and Roman Society*, 'Demographic Impression of the Roman World'.
7. Grainger, J. D., *Nerva and the Roman Succession Crisis of AD 96–99*, 'The Aristocratic Network'.
8. For a full discussion and analysis of Trajan's ancestry and marriage, see Bennett, *Trajan Optimus Princeps*, 'The Rise of the Ulpii'.
9. Dupont, F., *Daily Life in Ancient Rome*, 'The Ages of Man'.
10. Dupont, *Daily Life in Ancient Rome*, 'Time and Action'.
11. Talbert, R., *The Senate of Imperial Rome*, 'The Senate'.
12. Bennett, *Trajan Optimus Princeps*, 'The Rise of the Ulpii'.
13. Personal Communication: Professor Barbara Levick. It is important to note that there were repeated rulings against governing one's own province during the imperial period, especially after the revolt of Avidius Cassius during the reign of Marcus Aurelius.
14. Rawson, B. & Weaver, P., *The Roman Family in Italy; Status, Sentiment, Space*, 'Rome and the Outside World: Senatorial Families and the World They Lived In'.

15. Caballos, A. & Leon, P., (eds), *Italica MMCC*, 'Early Roman Italica as the Romanisation of Western Baetica', by S. J. Keay.
16. Claridge, A., *Rome: An Oxford Archaeological Guide*, 'Some Other Sites'.
17. Caballos, & Leon, *Italica MMCC*, 'Early Roman Italica as the Romanisation of Western Baetica' by S. J. Keay.
18. Given the possibility that Traianus Pollio was in his late twenties to early thirties, when he was appointed as a priest in the cult of the deified Augustus (formed after AD 14), it means he was about the right age to have been Traianus' father. Moreover, the wealth available to Traianus to qualify for entry into the Senate could only have come from a father like Traianus Pollio who had the means privately to fund the construction or re-construction of Italica's theatre.
19. Caballos & Leon, *Italica MMCC*. Rodriquez-Hidalgo, J. M. & Keay, S., 'Recent Work at Italica', 395–420.
20. Strabo, *Geography*, 3.2.
21. Strabo, *Geography*, 3.2.
22. For a complete review of early Roman childhood life and initial education, see Harlow, & Laurence, *Growing Up and Growing Old in Ancient Rome*, 'The Beginning of Life: Infancy and childhood'.
23. Pliny, *Panegyricus*, 24.
24. Definitive evidence does not yet exist but the totality of findings supports the notion that Trajan's family had a home on the Aventine Hill that was progressively developed over time and presumably taken over by Trajan prior to his becoming emperor and subsequently kept within the family. Vermaseren, M. J., & van Essen, C. C., *The Excavations in the Mithraeum of the Church of Santa Prisca in Rome*, describe remains of a large Roman house dated to AD 95 that was possibly the private house of Trajan or his close friend L. Licinius Sura. The 4th-century inventory *Notitia regionum Urbis (Romae)* XIII-10, lists Trajan's house on the Aventine close to the baths built by his friend Sura. Wojciechowski, P., 'Cult Appellations and Hercules Worship in Imperial Rome', 'Hercules domus Augusti', references an inscription found in the vicinity of Saint Prisca church dedicated to *Herculi Conservatori domus Ulpiorum* as evidence that Trajan's house stood in the area. Carandini, A., *Atlas of Ancient Rome*, Tableau 162b, maps his private house in this area.
25. Excavations performed under the authority of Sovraintendenza Capitolina, Roma (www.sovraintendenzaroma.it/i_luoghi/roma_antica/monumenti/privata_traiani_domus).
26. Video footage of excavations (www.corriere.it/video-articoli/2017/11/28/a-casa-traiano-sotto-tombino-meraviglia-nascosta/75df108a-d475-11e7-b070-a687676d1181.shtml).
27. Capitoline Museum, Rome, Exposition on suburban villas, 2006.
28. Dupont, *Daily Life in Ancient Rome*, 'Living in Rome'.
29. Morris, I., *Social Development*, 'Organization'.
30. Claridge, *Rome: An Oxford Archaeological Guide*, 'The Roman Forum'.
31. For a complete description of Nero's Golden House, see Segala, E. & Sciortino, I., *Domvs Avrea*.
32. Millar, F., *The Roman Near East 31 BC–AD 337*, 'Bridgehead and Dependent Kingdom'.
33. Suetonius, *Vespasian* 4.
34. Total of 28 legions by the end of Nero's reign.
35. Levick, B., *Vespasian*, 'From Nero's court to the walls of Jerusalem'.
36. Shelton, J., *As the Romans Did – A Sourcebook in Roman Social History*, 'Education'.

37. For an extensive description of the civil wars, see Wellesley, K., *The Year of the Four Emperors*, 'Caecina and Valens', 'The Five Days Caesar', 'Otho's Reaction' and 'The First Battle of Cremona'.
38. There is no evidence that the family owned estates or houses outside Rome, but given their wealth, I consider this highly likely.
39. Bennett, *Trajan Optimus Princeps*, 'The Rise of the Ulpii'.
40. Levick, *Vespasian*, 'Stabilization: The Winning of Peace'. Wellesley, *The Year of the Four Emperors*. Grant, M., *The Roman Emperors. A Biographical guide to the rulers of Imperial Rome 31 BC– AD 476*, 'Year of the Four Emperors'.
41. Suetonius, *Vitellius*, 17.
42. Shelton, *As the Romans Did*, 'Education'.
43. For evidence of Trajan's inadequacies in rhetoric, see Bennett, *Trajan Optimus Princeps*, 'The Rise of the Ulpii'.
44. Military skills would remain undetected at this age.
45. His first consulship is dated in 70 by Morris, 'The Consulate of the Elder Trajan'. Syme states that Traianus' consulship was 'surely' in 70, Syme, R., 'Review'.
46. Bowersock, G. W., 'Syria under Vespasian'.
47. Suetonius, *Vespasian*, 8.
48. Harlow & Laurence, *Growing Up and Growing Old in Ancient Rome*. 'Transition to Adulthood 2: Male'.
49. Birley, A., *Hadrian: The Restless Emperor*, 'Military Tribune'.

CHAPTER 2: Young Adulthood in a New Era

1. Dupont, *Daily Life in Ancient Rome*, 'The Ages of Man'.
2. Keijwegt, M., 'Iuvenes and Roman Imperial Society'.
3. Personal communication: Professor B. Levick – *iuventus* is a technical term for youth while *adulescens* can be viewed as an 'emotive' reference to youth.
4. Keijwegt, 'Iuvenes and Roman Imperial Society'.
5. Harlow, & Laurence, *Growing Up and Growing Old in Ancient Rome*. 'Transition to Adulthood 2: Male'.
6. Juvenal, *Satires*, VIII 166.
7. Keijwegt, 'Iuvenes and Roman Imperial Society'.
8. Dio Cassius, 68.10.2., describes Trajan's passion for a male dancer. The *Historia Augusta*, 2.7, records that Trajan 'loved [boys] ardently' . In 362, the Emperor Julian wrote *The Caesars*, alluding to Trajan's sexuality, 'Now is the time for Zeus our master to look out, if he wants to keep Ganymedes for himself' (311). For further assessments, see Birley, A. R., *Hadrian: The Restless Emperor*, 'Principatus et liberates', and Bennett, *Trajan Optimus Princeps*, 'The New Ruler'.
9. For a contextual study, see Clarke, J. R., *Roman Sex 100 BC–AD 250*.
10. Dio Cassius, *Roman History*, 68.7.4.
11. Suetonius, *Vespasian*, 8 and *Titus*, 6.
12. I use the years 73/74 estimated by Bennett, *Trajan Optimus Princeps*, 'The Rise of the Ulpii'.
13. Bowersock, 'Syria under Vespasian'.
14. Birley, E., 'Senators in the Emperor's Service'.

15. McAlindon, D., 'Entry to the Senate in the early Empire'. Pink, K., 'The triumviri monetales and the structure of the coinage of the Roman Republic'.
16. Duncan-Jones, R., *Power and Privilege in Roman Society*. 'Introduction – Senate'.
17. Levick, B., 'Propaganda and the Imperial Coinage'. Levick provides a detailed argument against the idea that coinage types were intended as propaganda tools.
18. I have assumed this based on the typical activities of modern mints that are relevant to the ancient arrangements.
19. Claridge, *Rome: An Oxford Archaeological Guide*, The Roman Forum.
20. Josephus, *The Jewish Wars*, 7.5.5.
21. Millar, F., *The Roman Near East*, 'The Jewish War and its Aftermath'.
22. Claridge, *Rome: An Oxford Archaeological Guide*, 'Colosseum Valley and Esquiline Hill'.
23. Grant, *The Roman Emperors*, 'The year of the four emperors; & the Flavian dynasty'.
24. Suetonius, *Titus*, 6.
25. Levick, B., 'Worries about Vespasian: The Achievements of an Emperor'.

CHAPTER 3: The Making of a Military Officer

1. Roth, J., 'The Size and Organization of the Roman Imperial Legion'. There is much confusion about the size of an imperial legion in this period because of contradictory evidence and complex archaeological findings. Roth's systematic review is adopted here with the inclusion of officers at the cohort level and the addition of the dedicated squadron of cavalry for a legion cited by Josephus (*Jewish Wars*, 3.115): 1st cohort contained 6 (not the 5 widely accepted) double-sized centuries (6 × 160 legionaries, plus 1 centurion, 1 optio, 1 signifer, 1 tesserarius, and 1 cornicen or tubicen for each century = 990) and 2nd to 10th cohorts contained 6 centuries (6 × 80 legionaries, plus 1 centurion, 1 optio, 1 signifer, 1 tesserarius, 1 cornicen or tubicen per century= 510), as well as 120 cavalry. A grand total of 5,700 men, at full theoretical strength, not counting senior officers.
2. For a definitive review of the Roman army in our period, see Goldsworthy, A. K., *The Roman Army at War 100 BC–AD 200*.
3. Goodman, M., *The Roman World 44 BC–AD 180*. 'The Army in Society'.
4. Connolly, P., *The Roman Army*, 'The Officers'.
5. Luttwak, E., *The Grand Strategy of the Roman Empire*, 'From the Flavians to the Severi'.
6. Hamblin, W., 'The Roman Army in the First Century'. Using estimates for total army of 25 legions, based on 5,700 men per legion (see above note).
7. Bowman, A. K., Garnsey, P., Rathbone, D., (eds), *The Cambridge Ancient History – The High Empire, AD 70–192*, 'Nerva to Hadrian', by M. Griffin.
8. Using size examples of permanent legion fortresses in the UK: Caerleon *ca.* 200,000 m^2, Chester *ca.* 243,000 m^2, York *ca.* 189,700 m^2, Colchester *ca.* 229,000 m^2. A typical soccer pitch is 6,900 m^2.
9. Towards the end of the 1st century and through the 2nd century forts were gradually converted to complete stone construction.
10. Campbell, B., *Greek and Roman Military Writers*, Reading 277: 'Pseudo-Hyginus, On Camp Fortifications 12–14'.
11. Connolly, *The Roman Army*, 'The Army of the Empire'.
12. Crow, J. G., *Housesteads Roman Fort*.

13. Goldsworthy, *The Complete Roman Army.* 'Joining the Roman Army'. Connolly, P., *The Roman Army.* 'The Army of the Empire'.
14. For an example of a duty roster for a unit in the 3rd Legion *Cyrenaica* in the late 1st century, see Goldsworthy, *The Complete Roman Army*, 'The life of a Roman soldier'. For a description of a military *consilium* see, Goldsworthy, *The Roman Army at War*, 'The General's Battle'. Punishments, see Campbell, *Greek and Roman Military Writers*, Reading 8: 'Polybius, Histories 6.38'. An example of a commander ordering tribunes to accompany him in negotiations, see Goldsworthy, *The Roman Army at War*, 'The General's Battle'. For Arrian's *Ectaxis* as an example of the command structure in fighting divisions, see Goldsworthy, *The Roman Army at War*, 'The General's Battle'. Hand-to-hand combat, see Appian, *Roman History*, 12.50.
15. Tacitus, *Agricola*, 5.16.
16. Birley, E., *The Roman Army Papers, 1929–1986*, 'Promotion and Transfer in the Roman Army'.
17. Bowman, A. K. & Thomas, J. D., *Vindolanda: The Latin Writing-Tablets*, number 4.
18. Brown, A., Meadows, I., Turner, S., & Mattingly, D., 'Roman vineyards in Britain'. This large Roman vineyard discovered in the UK may have played a significant role on the local market and potentially supplied Roman forces in the North.
19. Sealey, P. R. & Davies, G. M. R., 'Falernian Wine at Roman Colchester'.
20. Shelton, *As the Romans Did*, 'Leisure and Entertainment'.
21. Dalby, A. and Grainger, S., *The Classical Cookbook*. Pliny the Elder, *The Natural History*, 14.
22. Bennett, *Trajan Optimus Princeps*, 'The New Ruler'.
23. Dio Cassius, 68.7.4.
24. Goldsworthy, *The Complete Roman Army.* 'The life of a Roman soldier'.
25. Full a complete assessment of the strategy and deployment of forces throughout the Empire during the early Principate, as well as the role of client-states, see Luttwak, *The Grand Strategy of the Roman Empire*, 'The Julio-Claudian System'.
26. 'Major expansionism': examples include Caesar in France and Belgium, Augustus in northern Spain, the Alpine regions, Illyricum, Pannonia, Egypt & areas of north-eastern Africa (plus failed attempts in Germany) and Claudius in Britain. Vespasian's advances in Britain, Germany and the East, and Domitian's annexation of the Wetterau and Agri decumates regions in Germany were smaller gains.
27. Luttwak, *The Grand Strategy of the Roman Empire*, 'From the Flavians to the Severi'.
28. Personal communications, Michael Slansky.
29. Fitzpatrick, M. P., 'Provincializing Rome'.
30. Lloyd B. J., 'Royal Purple of Tyre'.
31. Burns. R., *Monuments of Syria*, 'Syria – Historical Sketch'.
32. Millar, *The Roman Near East*, 'From Actium to the Death of Herod'.
33. Millar, *The Roman Near East*, 'The Bridgehead and Dependent Kingdoms'.
34. Bowman, Garnsey, Rathbone, *Cambridge Ancient History XI*, 'The Flavians – Vespasian'. The four legions would be reduced under Vespasian to three with a legion moved to Judaea.
35. In AD 20, the Emperor Augustus sent the young Tiberius with an army to place their candidate Tigranes on the Armenian throne as a Roman vassal. Terms were agreed without conflict with Parthia.
36. Ben-Sasson, H. H., *A History of the Jewish People*, 'The Political and Social History of Judaea under Roman Rule'.
37. Luttwak, *The Grand Strategy of the Roman Empire*.

38. Bennett, *Trajan Optimus Princeps*, 'The Rise of the Ulpii'. Bennett hypothesises that Traianus was appointed as proconsular *legatus* of Cappadocia before his attested Syrian posting. Griffin, in Bowman, Garnsey, Rathbone, *The Cambridge Ancient History XI*, 'The Flavians – Vespasian', revises the opinion that two legions were stationed in Cappadocia, with XVI *Flavia Firma* coming later in 75/76 given that it was occupied in Syria in March and July 75 in the construction of a canal at Antioch on the Orontes. Thus, as of 70 until around 75/76, only XII *Fulminata* was at Melitene in Cappadocia.
39. It had previously been stationed in Raphanaea under Nero.
40. Talbert, R., *Barrington Atlas of the Greek and Roman World*.
41. Millar, *The Roman Near East*, 'Imperialism and Expansion'.
42. McElderry, R. K, 'The Legions of the Euphrates Frontier'.
43. Bowman, Garnsey, Rathbone, *The Cambridge Ancient History XI*, 'The Flavians – Vespasian'.
44. For evidence of constructions in Syria under Traianus' governorship and references to improvements by Roman legionaries around Antioch and Seleucia during the mid-seventies, see Millar, *The Roman Near East*, 'Imperialism and Expansion'.
45. Bowman, Garnsey, Rathbone, *The Cambridge Ancient History XI*, 'The Flavians – Vespasian'.
46. *Dio Cassius*, 65.15.3.
47. Assumed based on sensitivities formed after historical encounters between Rome and Parthia.
48. Not attested, but arguable given the reference by Pliny to Trajan's involvement with his father in military action in this period.
49. Talbert, *Barrington Atlas of the Greek and Roman World*.
50. Strabo, *Geography*, Book XVI, 2.3.
51. Vegetius, *De Re Militari*, Book I: 'The Selection and Training of New Levies'. Writing in the late 4th century, Vegetius describes the need for recruits to march with the 'common military step' to achieve 'twenty miles [29.6 km] in five summer-hours', and with the 'full step' to achieve 'twenty-four miles [35.5 km] in the same number of hours'.
52. Pliny, *Panegyricus*, 14.
53. Bowman, Garnsey, Rathbone, *The Cambridge Ancient History*, 'Nerva to Hadrian: Trajan', by M. Griffin.
54. Bennett, *Trajan Optimus Princeps*, 'The Rise of the Ulpii'. Bennett provides evidence and arguments to support the hypothesis for Trajan's second tribunate placement in Germania Inferior, which I have accepted here.
55. Talbert, *Barrington Atlas of the Greek and Roman World*.
56. Hornblower, S. & Spawforth, A., (eds), *The Oxford Classical Dictionary*.
57. Tribunes who were transferred between legions would likely have relied on a reference from their previous *legatus legionis*.
58. Pliny, *Panegyricus*, 15.2–4.
59. Pliny, *Panegyricus*, 14.1–2.
60. Dupont. *Daily Life in Ancient Rome*, 'The Family'.
61. Grainger, *Nerva and the Roman Succession Crisis*, 'The Aristocratic Networks'.
62. Shelton, *As the Romans Did*, 'Marriage'.
63. For wedding rituals in the context of a female life course, see Harlow & Laurence, *Growing Up and Growing Old in Ancient Rome*, 'Transition to adulthood I: Female'.
64. In the absence of documented ancient rumours about a poor marriage between Plotina and Trajan, I argue that they adapted well to each other and settled into married life accordingly.

65. *Historia Augusta*, 1.1.
66. Harlow & Laurence, *Growing Up and Growing Old in Ancient Rome*, 'The Place of Marriage in the life course', provides an example of a wealthy widow able to remain independent.
67. Personal communication: Professor Barbara Levick argues that the normal and mechanical system of allocating Asia and Africa could be left alone, thus saving senatorial self-esteem unless there was an overriding reason to interfere: a favourite to be pleased (e.g. Vespasian and Eprius Marcellus), a dangerous candidate (e.g. Agricola), or a potentially greedy one (e.g. Galba), or a serious military situation (e.g. Tiberius managing the choice for Africa).
68. Goodman, M., *The Roman World 44 BC–AD 180*, 'Greece and the Aegean Coast'.
69. Bennett, *Trajan Optimus Princeps*, 'The Rise of the Ulpii'.
70. Suetonius, *Vespasian*, 24.
71. Suetonius, *Vespasian*, 24.
72. Bennett, *Trajan Optimus Princeps*, 'The Rise of the Ulpii'.
73. The date for the eruption is now considered to be 24 October 79, based on a new inscription found in October 2018.
74. Derived from data compiled by the Center of Educational Technologies, US (www.cotf.edu/ete/modules/volcanoes/vsizeserupt1.html).
75. Estimate based on the following assumed populations: 20,000 Pompeii, 5,000 Herculaneum, 5,000 Stabiae, 5,000 Oplontis and 10,000 in small towns and the surrounding countryside.
76. Suetonius, *Titus*, 8.
77. Jones, B. W., *The Emperor Titus*, 'Reign of Titus'.
78. Suetonius, *Titus*, 8.
79. Claridge, *Rome: An Oxford Archaeological Guide*, 'The Capitoline Hill'.
80. Suetonius, *Titus*, 8. There is no direct evidence that the plague came after the fires in Rome in 80, but it can be hypothesised that poor living conditions in Rome resulting from the fire increased the spread of the disease.
81. Full account of the opening ceremony and seating arrangements, see Connolly, P., *Colosseum – Rome's Arena of Death*, 'Vespasian's Vision' & 'In the Arena'.
82. In 81, the mandatory period after the vigintivirate was over and Trajan fulfilled the necessary age for entry, i.e. in his 25th year.
83. Bennett, *Trajan Optimus Princeps*, 'The Rise of the Ulpii'.
84. Jones, *The Emperor Titus*, 'Reign of Titus'.
85. Talbert, *Barrington Atlas of the Greek and Roman World*.
86. Tacitus, *Germania*, 30.
87. For an evaluation of Domitian's actions against the Chatti, see Jones, *The Emperor Domitian*, 'War I'.

CHAPTER 4: **The Making of a General**

1. Bennett, *Trajan Optimus Princeps*, 'The New Ruler'. Bennett deduces the date based on age and by working from Dio Cassius' statement that Trajan was forty-one years old in January 98.
2. Jones, *The Emperor Domitian*, 'Administration I'.
3. Talbert, *The Senate of Imperial Rome*. 'The Senate'.
4. Acts 25:10, 'I am standing at Caesar's judgment seat now, where I should be judged', St Paul.
5. Pliny, *Letters*, 92 & 93.

6. If no written law existed, jurists acknowledged that local custom could apply and if not specific, the nearest custom could be applied. Failing that, the law in Rome applied. For details, see Shelton, *As the Romans Did*, 'Legislation'.
7. Great Britain is a partial exception.
8. Speculation based on the fact that Trajan later amended inheritance laws suggesting he had particular reasons to make such changes based on his experiences in the *centumviri*.
9. Quintilian, *Institutio Oratoria*, 12.5.
10. For details of a praetor's role, see Talbert, *The Senate of Imperial Rome*, 'Meeting places', 'Senators' & 'Routine'.
11. Tacitus, *The History*, 2.86. Jordanes, *De Origine Actibusque Getarum*, 13.78.
12. Domitian was frequently in the field to oversee significant military operations but it is not known if he was involved in battles. This was in line with his seemingly autocratic nature.
13. Account of Domitian's actions in 86 after the death of Fuscus, see Jones, *The Emperor Domitian*, 'War I'.
14. It is assumed that both were still alive in the mid-80s as there is no evidence to the contrary.
15. Harlow & Laurence, *Growing Up and Growing Old in Ancient Rome*, 'Getting Old'.
16. It is assumed that Plotina was born in 64.
17. Bennett, *Trajan Optimus Princeps*, 'The New Ruler'. Bennett references good relations between Plotina and Marciana after Trajan's accession. I assume that their relationship also flourished prior to Trajan's accession.
18. Assumed born around 67.
19. Given his close relationship with his sister and the title of *Augusta* later granted to Salonina Matidia, it is assumed that Trajan felt affection towards her.
20. Bennett, *Trajan Optimus Princeps*, 'The New Ruler'. Birley, A., *Hadrian: The Restless Emperor*, 'A Childhood in Flavian Rome'.
21. Assumes that Hadrian's father died in 85.
22. Birley, *Hadrian: The Restless Emperor*, 'A Childhood in Flavian Rome'.
23. Talbert, *The Senate of Imperial Rome*, 'The Senate'. Talbert states that 'no more than perhaps half of those who embarked upon a senatorial career' became consuls.
24. Jones, R. F. J., 'The Roman Military Occupation of North-West Spain'.
25. Mierse, W. E., *Temples and Towns in Roman Iberia*, 'Architectural Experiments'.
26. Goldsworthy, *The Complete Roman Army*, 'The Army of the Principate'.
27. Connolly, P., *Greece and Rome at War*, 'The Empire 140 BC–AD 200 – Army Organisation'.
28. Dio Cassius, 67.10.2.
29. Jones, *The Emperor Domitian*, 'War I'. Jones postulates that this edict was similar to the rewards issued after Domitian's success against the Chatti in 83 to strengthen military loyalty.
30. Dio Cassius, 67.10.2.
31. Syme, R., 'Antonius Saturninus'.
32. Dio Cassius, 67.11.4. Dio tells the story of Saturninus' close relations with a military tribune called Julius Calvaster.
33. Evidence of Saturninus' behaviour, Bennett, *Trajan Optimus Princeps*, 'Imperial Expansion and Crisis', and Jones, *The Emperor Domitian*, 'War II'.
34. Personal communication: Professor B. Levick argues that Saturninus was 'cornered' by Domitian. He was not like Vitellius against Galba as the Flavians were well installed. The revolt had more similarities with Vindex against a hostile Nero.

35. Jones, *The Emperor Domitian*, 'War II'.
36. Mogontiacum to Rome approximately 1,250 km. Assuming a rider can cover an average distance of 95 km a day, with a well-organised system of stations for relief horses, the message of Saturninus' revolt would have taken around 13 days to reach Rome.
37. Pliny, *Panegyricus*, 14.
38. Pliny, *Panegyricus*, 14.
39. Here it is assumed that the Guard covered an average 30 km a day.
40. Luttwak, *The Grand Strategy of the Roman Empire*, 'From the Flavians to the Severi'.
41. Tarraco to Legio along good Roman roads was approximately 770 km. The message of Saturninus' revolt would have taken around eight days to reach Rome at the rate described above.
42. *Dio Cassius*, 67.11.1.
43. Suetonius, *Domitian*, 6.
44. Jones, *The Emperor Domitian*, 'War II'.
45. Pliny, *Panegyricus*, 14.
46. Leaving Legio on 28 January.
47. Suetonius, *Domitian* 10.
48. Jones, *The Emperor Domitian*, 'War II'.
49. Jones, *The Emperor Domitian*, 'Amici'.
50. Pliny, *Panegyricus*, 14.3–15. Pliny states that 'After that journey he [Domitian] judged you [Trajan] worthy to conduct a series of campaigns.' This suggests that Trajan may have served Domitian in military operations after arriving in Germania.
51. Aftermath of Saturninus' revolt and the subsequent Chattan War in 89, Bennett, *Trajan Optimus Princeps*, 'Imperial Expansion and Crisis', and Jones, *The Emperor Domitian*, 'War II'.
52. During Tiberius' reign: Germania Superior – II *Augusta*, XIII *Gemina*, XIV *Gemina*, and XVI *Gallica*; Germania Inferior – I *Germanica*, V *Alaudae*, XX *Valeria Victrix*, and XXI *Rapax*.
53. Comprehensive review of legion distribution in this period: Syme, R., 'Rhine and Danube Legions under Domitian'.
54. *Dio Cassius*, 67.7.1.
55. Tacitus, *Germania*, 38.
56. Peck, H. T., *Harpers Dictionary of Classical Antiquities*.
57. Tacitus, *Germania*, 42.
58. Talbert, *Barrington Atlas of the Greek and Roman World*.
59. *Dio Cassius*. 67.7.1.
60. Bennett, *Trajan Optimus Princeps*, 'Imperial Expansion and Crisis'.
61. I postulate that Trajan, as early as 89/90, was increasingly involved in Domitian's *consilium*. This would allow the emperor to observe Trajan at close hand to vet him for greater posts such as *consul ordinarius* in 91.
62. Talbert, *The Senate of Imperial Rome*, 'Senatorial Legislation'.
63. Gallivan, P., 'The Fasti for A. D. 70–96'.
64. Dupont, *Daily Life in Ancient Rome*. 'Time and Action'.
65. Jones, *The Emperor Domitian*, 'Court II'.
66. Jones, *The Emperor Domitian*, 'War II'. Evidence for diplomacy in the region around 90–91.

67. Millar, F., 'The Emperor, the Senate and the Provinces'. Millar breaks from the traditional view that imperial and public provinces were managed separately by the emperor and Senate, suggesting a more diffuse arrangement.
68. Bennett, *Trajan Optimus Princeps*, 'Domitian's General, Nerva's Heir'. I have adopted Bennett's hypothesis that the appropriate gap in the governorships of either Germania Inferior or Superior could have been filled by Trajan and that these provinces were suitable for the ex-consul. I have assumed that Germania Superior was the likelier option given Trajan's possible previous experience in the region and the need for Domitian to place a trusted man there soon after Saturninus' rebellion. Moreover, it would have been a slight on Trajan, *consul ordinarius* in 91, to have to wait several years for such a posting and at odds with the very apparent favour that Domitian held for Trajan.
69. Based on notes after visiting sites and museums in and around Mainz. Trajan's residency is conjecture.
70. Saddington, D. B., 'Roman Soldiers, Local Gods and "Interpretatio Romana" in Roman Germany'.
71. Talbert, *Barrington Atlas of the Greek and Roman World*.
72. Syme, 'Rhine and Danube Legions under Domitian'.
73. Based on notes after visiting *limites* in the Taunus mountains and personal communications with Michael Slansky.
74. Matthew 27: 26 (*New Living Translation*).
75. *Dio Cassius*, 67.5.2.
76. Jones, *The Emperor Domitian*, 'War II'.
77. Evidence for the 2nd Pannonian War, as well as details surrounding Domitian's ovation, see Jones, *The Emperor Domitian*, 'War II' and Bennett, *Trajan Optimus Princeps*, 'Imperial Expansion and Crisis.'
78. Duncan-Jones, R., *Money and Government in the Roman Empire*, 'Surplus and Deficit'. Syme, R. 'The Imperial Finances under Domitian, Nerva and Trajan'.
79. Watson, G. R. 'The Pay of the Roman Army, The Auxiliary Forces'.
80. Roman historians have unfairly treated Domitian because of a hostile contingent of senators that despised him.
81. For a detailed assessment of Domitian's attitude to patricians, the Senate and senators, see Jones, *The Emperor Domitian*, 'Aristocracy I'.
82. Jones, *The Emperor Domitian*, Court I.
83. Bowman, Garnsey, Rathbone, *The Cambridge Ancient History XI*, 'The Flavians'.
84. *Suetonius*, Domitian, 8.
85. Roman pantomimes were hugely popular events in which solo dancers performed an array of mythical stories. It is thought that they sometimes danced erotically, but did not sing or speak. Riots had broken out at pantomimes likely due to the attendance of factions at odds with each other, perhaps aroused by the political content of the story being performed. See Slater, W. J. "Pantomime Riots." *Classical Antiquity*, vol. 13, no. 1, University of California Press, 1994, pp. 120–44, https://doi.org/10.2307/25011007.

    For the dismissed senator: *Dio Cassius*, 67.13. *Suetonius*, Domitian, 8.
86. Bowman, Garnsey, Rathbone, *The Cambridge Ancient History XI*, 'The Flavians – Domitian'.
87. Syme, R., 'The Imperial Finances under Domitian, Nerva and Trajan'.

88. Jones, *The Emperor Domitian*, 'Aristocracy I'. Jones cites the execution of at least eleven senators, but still fewer than Claudius who executed at least thirty-five.
89. Bennett, *Trajan Optimus Princeps*, 'Domitian's General, Nerva's Heir'. Bennett postulates that Trajan was appointed governor of Pannonia in 95–97 and this notion is adopted. No governor is attested in the province in this period until Pompeius Longinus in February 98. It is otherwise problematic to reconcile Trajan's later acceptance as emperor by the armies and senators without such a prominent posting. In personal communication with Dr. Bennett, referring to the 11th-century Byzantine historian Cedrenus who wrote about Trajan and states that 'a message of victory came from Trajan in Paeonia…', one can hypothesise that Cedrenus meant Pannonia. Grainger, *Nerva and the Roman Succession Crisis*, 'Nerva & Choice'. In contrast to Bennett, Grainger places Trajan in Germania Superior as governor starting in October 96 and therefore present in Rome for Domitian's assassination and Nerva's accession. Dusanic, S. & Vasic, M., 'An Upper Moesian Diploma of AD 96', argue for the appointment of Pompeius Longinus as governor of Pannonia at the end of the summer of 96; but the evidence shows he was governor of Moesia Superior in 94 and was still there in July 96. The only attested evidence for Pompeius Longinus in Pannonia is for 20 February 98 and he likely arrived in Pannonia the autumn before.
90. Dusanic & Vasic, 'An Upper Moesian Diploma'.
91. Millar, 'The Emperor, The Senate and the Provinces'.
92. Jones, *The Emperor Domitian*, 'War II'. It remains unknown why there was a switch over to the Suebi and Jones postulates that another Suebi–Sarmatian alliance was the reason. I have assumed that it was in fact pre-mediated to subdue the Sarmatians and then the Suebi rather than risk having to take on both.
93. Brzezinski, R. & Mielczarek, M., *The Sarmatians 600 BC–AD 450*, 'Who Were the Sarmatians?', 'Appearance and Customs' & 'Organization and Tactics'.
94. Conjecture based on the geography of the Hungarian Plain.
95. Dusanic and Vasic, 'An Upper Moesian Diploma', dates the switch between Sarmatian and Suebi opponents to late 96 or early 97. It is assumed here that it was late in 96.
96. *Historia Augusta*, 10.1
97. Pliny, *Panegyricus*, 24 & 55.

CHAPTER 5: **Adoption and Accession**

1. Suetonius, *Domitian*, 10.
2. Dio Cassius. 67.14.
3. Dio Cassius. 67.14. Suetonius, *Domitian*, 15.
4. Bowman, Garnsey, Rathbone, *Cambridge Ancient History XI*, 'The Flavians – Domitian'.
5. Dio Cassius. 67.15.
6. Detailed evaluation of conspirators, see Grainger, *Nerva and the Roman Succession Crisis*, 'Conspiracy'.
7. Bennett, *Trajan Optimus Princeps*, 'Imperial Expansion and Crisis'.
8. Grainger, *Nerva and the Roman Succession Crisis*, 'Conspiracy'. Grainger discusses the evidence and theories for the involvement of the Praetorian Guard prefects, concluding that Secundus removed Norbanus.

9. Grainger, *Nerva and the Roman Succession Crisis*, 'Conspiracy'. Grainger suggests this critical military component for the success of the conspiracy, but he cites Pompeius as the general and places Trajan in Rome at the time of the assassination.
10. *Dio Cassius*. 67.15.
11. *Dio Cassius*. 67.15.5–6.
12. Detailed evaluation of features that secured Nerva's selection, see Grainger, *Nerva and the Roman Succession Crisis*, 'Conspiracy'.
13. Tomei, M. A., *The Palatine*, 'The palace of the Flavians'. Tomei provides details for the palace layout. I have suggested the route that Domitian likely took just before his assassination.
14. Suetonius, *Domitian*, 16–17. *Dio Cassius*. 67.15–17. Events are pieced together from both of their accounts, although Suetonius' narrative is considered more reliable given the fact he claims to have spoken with the page boy who survived as a witness.
15. Suetonius, *Domitian*, 18.
16. Suetonius, *Domitian*, 16–17.
17. Talbert, *The Senate of Imperial Rome*, 'Routine – Summons'.
18. Suetonius, *Domitian*, 18. Eutropius, 7.23.
19. Talbert, *The Senate of Imperial Rome*, 'Routine – Time and duration of sessions'. Although the Senate could meet at night, I believe that Fronto wanted to delay the session until the following dawn to ensure more senators could attend.
20. Conjecture based on likely pre-arranged discourse delivered to the Senate to distance the conspirators from suspicion of involvement.
21. Suetonius, *Domitian*, 23. Although Suetonius states that the senators were 'delighted', this view reflects the somewhat unjust damnation of Domitian and it is more likely that many loyal to Domitian who had prospered under his rule were deeply disappointed.
22. Speculation based on his absence from source references and his loyalty to Domitian.
23. Suetonius, *Domitian*, 23.
24. Grainger, *Nerva and the Roman Succession Crisis*, 'Reactions'. Grainger discusses evidence of damnation being carried out, concluding that it was never fully executed because of apathy in the provinces.
25. *Dio Cassius*. 68.2.
26. *Epitome de Caesaribus*, 12.
27. Grainger, *Nerva and the Roman Succession Crisis*, 'Reactions'. Grainger provides evidence for the plebeian reaction to Domitian's death and Nerva's accession.
28. Suetonius, *Domitian*, 23.
29. Suetonius, *Domitian*, 23.
30. Suetonius, *Domitian*, 23.
31. Bennett, *Trajan Optimus Princeps*, 'The New Emperor'. Bennett refers to Pliny's remark (*Panegyricus*, 47) that Nerva opened Domitian's palace to the public and concludes that Nerva took residence in the Domus Tiberiana.
32. Personal communication: Professor Barbara Levick cites Brunt, P. A., 'Did Emperors ever suspend the law of *Maiestas*?' regarding treason charges. Brunt argues that Roman emperors never renounced the Julian Law of treason, *maiestas*, which would have meant leaving Rome without legal protection against rebellion or armed assault. Rather some emperors renounced only defamation as a charge for treason.
33. *Dio Cassius*. 68.1.

34. *Dio Cassius*. 68.1.3
35. Duncan-Jones, *Money and Government in the Roman Empire*, 'The Economics of Empire'. Provides details for previous *congiaria* and *donativa*. It is assumed that Nerva would have given an amount in the high range to the Praetorian Guard given their unhappiness with his accession.
36. 150,000 on the corn dole receiving 300 *sestertii* plus 30 × 5,000 troops receiving 400 *sestertii* each.
37. Sutherland, C., 'The State of the Imperial Treasury at the Death of Domitian'.
38. For details of Domitian's financial policies, see Jones, *The Emperor Domitian*, 'Administration I' and Syme, 'The imperial finances under Domitian, Nerva and Trajan'.
39. *Dio Cassius*. 68.2.
40. Grainger, *Nerva and the Roman Succession Crisis*, 'The Emperor's Work'. Grainger argues that Nerva initiated the *alimenta* scheme and early successes were applied extensively across Italy by Trajan who claimed credit. Grainger provides details of the land allotments and their scale in relation to the imperial revenue. Bennett, *Trajan Optimus Princeps*, 'Imperial Expansion and Crisis', provides an assessment of the rationale for the *alimenta*. O'Brien, G. C., *Trajan's Imperial Alimenta*, provides an extensive evaluation of the societal value of children and the *alimenta*.
41. Syme, 'The imperial finances under Domitian, Nerva and Trajan'.
42. Sutherland, 'The State of the Imperial Treasury at the Death of Domitian'.
43. Personal communication: Professor Levick describes the possible purpose of the commission as essentially to give more cash to the *aerarium* and thereby more power to the Senate. The case is further evaluated in Levick's *Vespasian*, 'Financial Survival'.
44. Pliny, *Letters*, 10.58 (d)
45. Pliny, *Letters*, 10.58 (c)
46. Grainger, *Nerva and the Roman Succession Crisis*, 'The Succession Problem'.
47. *Epitome de Caesaribus*, 12.
48. No details of the Third Pannonian War are known, but it is assumed that campaigns in 95–96 had weakened the Suebic–Sarmatian forces and opened access routes for easier incursions into their territory in 97.
49. Eck, W., *Philosophy and Power in the Graeco-Roman World*, 'An Emperor is Made'.
50. *Dio Cassius*, 68.3.
51. *Epitome de Caesaribus*, 12
52. Personal communication: Professor Barbara Levick. Nobility in Roman parlance meant having a consular ancestor in the male line. Traianus was a *novus homo*, the first in his family to become a senator.
53. *Historia Augusta*, 10.1
54. Germania Inferior – Licinius Sura; Moesia Inferior – Octavius Fronto; Moesia Superior – Pompeius Longinus.
55. Grainger, *Nerva and the Roman Succession Crisis*, 'The Aristocratic Networks'.
56. Jones, *The Emperor Domitian*, 'Court II'. He served either as an imperial *comes* or as governor of Lower Germany.
57. Jones, *The Emperor Domitian*, 'Court II'. Ursus was from Gallia Narbonensis.
58. Syme, R., 'Guard Prefects of Trajan and Hadrian'.

59. Jones, C. P., 'Sura and Senecio'. Jones suggests 93 as a possible year for his consulship in the absence of an attested date. Sura may have been appointed governor by Domitian and held the post through Nerva's reign.
60. *Martial*, VII, 47.
61. Syme, R., 'People in Pliny'.
62. There is no direct evidence for Verus as an ally except that his involvement in Nerva's *consilium* made it likely that he agreed to or advocated Trajan's candidacy as Nerva's heir. Verus originated from Uccibi and was enrolled as a patrician when Vespasian and Titus were censors, like Traianus. Verus was loyal to Domitian, sufficient enough to be awarded a consulship during Domitian's reign.
63. Personal communication: Professor A. Birley argues that Servianus probably took Ursus' names when the latter died and left him a legacy and there is no reason to believe he was Ursus' son.
64. Personal communication: Professor Levick. One could assume that Quadratus was a friend given his career during Trajan's reign including the award of a second consulship. However, Professor Levick suggests that Quadratus could equally have been someone pacified by Trajan, in a similar manner as Licinius Mucianus was tolerated and pacified by Vespasian (see Levick, *Vespasian*).
65. Birley, *Hadrian: The Restless Emperor*, 'A Childhood in Flavian Rome'.
66. Walton, C. S., 'Oriental Senators in the Service of Rome: A Study of Imperial Policy down to the Death of Marcus Aurelius'.
67. Pompeius Longinus is attested as governor on 12 July 96.
68. Gallivan, 'The Fasti for A. D. 70–96'.
69. Stout, S. E., 'The Governors of Moesia'.
70. Personal communication: Professor A. Birley: Two diplomas for 9 September 97 show (a) the outgoing governor of Moesia Inferior as [Octavius] Fronto; the new incoming governor is named in a missing part, and his name is supplied in (b) as L. [mistake for Q. – or he may have had more than one *praenomen*] Pom[ponius Rufus]. Diploma references in Holder, P., *Roman Military Diplomas V* (London, 2006) nos. 337 (originally published *ZPE* 138: 225–8, 2002) and 338 (originally published ibid. 117: 233–8, 1997). This evidence shows that Fronto was still governor until shortly before 9 September 97. Pomponius Rufus was still in office in 99. Thus, Julius Marinus, once thought to be in place as governor of Moesia Inferior at the time of Trajan's adoption, was probably an erroneous interpretation of the diploma *CIL* XVI 41 for January 97.
71. Jones, 'Sura and Senecio'. Jones states that this meant Sosius was under Sura.
72. Eck, W., *Philosophy and Power in the Graeco-Roman World*, 'An Emperor is Made'.
73. Jones, 'Sura and Senecio'.
74. Bennett, *Trajan Optimus Princeps*, 'Domitian's General, Nerva's heir'.
75. Tully, G. D., 'A Fragment of a Military Diploma for Pannonia Found in Northern England?'
76. Syme, R., 'The Friend of Tacitus'. Syme, R., 'Consulates in Absence'. Syme suggests that Agricola may have been absent from Rome for his consulship in Sept.–Oct. 97.
77. Syme, 'Guard Prefects of Trajan and Hadrian'.
78. Syme., R., review of: '*I Fasti Consolari dell' Impero Romano dal 30 Av anti Christo al 613 Dopo Christo*'. Syme suggests that Sabinus may have still been alive in 97, although 'he cannot have survived for many months'.

79. Considering overlapping networks between senators, it is assumed that each faction member could rally six or seven other senators as supporters.
80. Pliny, *Panegyricus*, 9.2–10. Pliny suggests that Trajan only reluctantly accepted adoption. However, it was conventional to feign a refusal initially and therefore Pliny's claim must be regarded with some suspicion. Rather, it was advantageous for Trajan carefully to consider his support and overall position.
81. Pliny, *Panegyricus*, 5.
82. *Epitome de Caesaribus*, 13.6
83. *Dio Cassius*, 68.5.1.
84. Eck, W., *Philosophy and Power in the Graeco-Roman World*, 'An Emperor is Made'. The other two were Cn. Domitius Tullus and T. Vestricius Spurinna.
85. Pliny. *Panegyricus*, 8.2. 'Laurels had been brought from Pannonia, at the god's behest, for the symbol of victory to mark the rise of a ruler who would never know defeat.' Although Trajan is not explicitly referred to as the general behind this victory, it is assumed they were sent by Trajan. Why would Pliny otherwise refer to an important victory won by someone else thereby placing emphasis on another's merits as a military genius?
86. Pliny, *Panegyricus*, 8.2.
87. *Dio Cassius*, 68.3.
88. *Dio Cassius*, 68.3: 'Afterwards in the Senate he [Nerva] appointed him [Trajan] *Caesar* and sent a message to him written with his own hand (Trajan was governor of Germany).' This could mean two things: firstly, that the message appointing him *Caesar* was prepared very soon after Nerva's announcement and therefore against the idea that Trajan was governor of Pannonia and rather a governor of one of the German provinces; or, secondly, there was some time between the announcement and the message about being named *Caesar*, during which time Trajan was appointed proconsul of both Germanies.
89. Pliny, *Panegyricus*, 9.
90. *Historia Augusta* 3.7.
91. Personal communication: Professor Levick refers to the fact that the title of Augustus was exclusive to the emperor except in the case when Lucius Verus and Marcus Aurelius shared the title uniquely as co-emperors.
92. Pliny, *Panegyricus*, 8.
93. Pliny, *Panegyricus*, 8.
94. Personal communication: Professor A. Birley – it is known that Pompeius Longinus was governor in February 98 and therefore it is likely that he was not sent there during that winter, but instead arrived in the previous autumn. Jones, *The Emperor Domitian*, 'War II'. Jones concludes that the Third Pannonian War was over by October 97.
95. *Historia Augusta*, 2.3.
96. *Historia Augusta*, 2.5.
97. Bennett, *Trajan Optimus Princeps*, 'Domitian's General, Nerva's Heir'. Grainger, *Nerva and the Roman Succession Crisis*, 'Heir'. Both argue that Trajan's role was to review the organisation of the Rhine frontier.
98. *Historia Augusta*, 2.6.
99. Pliny, *Panegyricus*, 8.
100. Pliny, *Panegyricus*, 8.

101. Smallwood, M., *Documents illustrating the Principates of Nerva, Trajan and Hadrian*, 'Consular Fasti'.
102. Claridge, *Rome: An Oxford Archeological Guide*, 'Historical Overview'.
103. *Epitome de Caesaribus*, 12.
104. *Dio Cassius*, 68.4.
105. *Epitome de Caesaribus*, 12.
106. Bennett, *Trajan Optimus Princeps*, 'Domitian's General, Nerva's Heir'.
107. Taagepera, 'Size and Duration of Empires: Growth–Decline Curves, 600 B.C. to 600 A.D.'
108. *Dio Cassius*, 68.5.
109. Pliny, *Panegyricus*, 11. *Epitome de Caesaribus*, 13.6.
110. Bowman, Garnsey, Rathbone, *The Cambridge Ancient History XI*, 'Nerva to Hadrian; Trajan'. Griffin cites coins RIC II 313 nos. 835–6.
111. Assumed immediate correspondence from Trajan across his network of command.
112. Bickerman, E., 'Diva Augusta Marciana'. They did not receive the title until 100–5.
113. *Dio Cassius*, 68.5.
114. Levick, B., *Claudius*, 'Accession'.
115. *Dio Cassius*. 68.5. It is not mentioned specifically that they were executed nor does it suggest who would have actually killed Aelianus, but one can reasonably argue that Trajan's guards were involved in any dispatch. An alternative theory is that Trajan was directly involved in Nerva's ordeal with Aelianus and therefore needed to silence him on his accession.
116. Jones, B., 'Casperius Aelianus. An Enigma?'
117. For a definitive description of the Imperial Horse Guard, see Speidel, M., *Riding for Caesar: The Roman Emperor's Horse Guard*.
118. Syme, 'Guard Prefects of Trajan and Hadrian'.
119. *Dio Cassius*. 68.16.
120. Pliny, *Panegyricus*, 22.
121. Bowman, Garnsey, Rathbone, *Cambridge Ancient History XI*, 'Nerva to Hadrian: Trajan'. Grainger, *Nerva and the Roman Succession Crisis*, 'The New Emperor'.
122. Pliny, *Panegyricus*, 18.
123. Bowman, Garnsey, Rathbone, *Cambridge Ancient History XI*, 'Nerva to Hadrian: Trajan'.
124. Townend, G. B., 'The Post of Ab Epistulis in the Second Century'. It is generally accepted that Capito was secretary for both languages, Latin and Greek.
125. Pliny, *Panegyricus*, 18.
126. Connolly, P., *The Cavalryman*, 'The soldier's Emperor'.
127. Bennett, *Trajan Optimus Princeps*, 'Domitian's General, Nerva's Heir'. Lepper, F., & Frere, S., *Trajan's Column*, Notes E3.
128. Smallwood, *Documents illustrating the Principates of Nerva, Trajan and Hadrian*, 'Consular Fasti'.
129. Bennett, *Trajan Optimus Princeps*, 'Domitian's General, Nerva's Heir'.
130. Pliny, *Panegyricus*, 22.

CHAPTER 6: The Dawning Trajanic Age

1. Bennett, *Trajan Optimus Princeps*, 'The New Emperor'. Bennett proposes this northerly entrance which is adopted here in the account of Trajan's entry into Rome.
2. Pliny, *Panegyricus*, 22.
3. Pliny, *Panegyricus*, 22.

NOTES TO PAGES 104–114

4. Pliny, *Panegyricus*, 23.
5. Pliny, *Panegyricus*, 23. Pliny states 'soldiers' but it is assumed he meant the newly appointed Horse Guard.
6. Speidel, *Riding for Caesar*, 'Riding High in the Second Century'.
7. Pliny, *Panegyricus*, 23.
8. Pliny, *Panegyricus*, 23.
9. For details of the temple, see Claridge, *Rome: An Oxford Archaeological Guide*. Platner, S. B., *A Topographical Dictionary of Ancient Rome*, 'Aedes Iovis Optimi Maximi Capitolini'.
10. Pliny, *Panegyricus*, 23.
11. It is assumed that Trajan continued in the footsteps of Nerva, allowing public access to Domitian's palace and taking residence in the Domus Tiberiana.
12. For details of the Domus, see Tomei, *The Palatine*, 'Domus Tiberiana'.
13. Dio Cassius, 68.5.
14. It remains unknown when Trajan's parents died. However, assuming that Pliny's *Panegyricus* refers to Trajan's father looking down on Trajan like Nerva, and the average life expectancy, the father and mother had likely died before 100.
15. Examples include, RIC II 764; Strack 154; Calicó 1136; BMCRE 506 note; Cohen 3.
16. Pliny, *Panegyricus*, 84.
17. Birley, *Hadrian: The Restless Emperor*, 'Prinipatus et Libertas'.
18. *Historia Augusta*, 2.7
19. *Historia Augusta*, 4.1. Hadrian benefited from the 'favour' of Plotina. *Historia Augusta*, 9 & 19.5. After Matidia's death Hadrian honoured her in several ways, suggesting a special relationship between them.
20. First reprimand for excessive hunting and second for excessive debts and pleasure seeking.
21. Duncan-Jones, *Money and Government in the Roman Empire*. 'The Economics of Empire' and 'The Coin Evidence'.
22. Pliny, *Panegyricus*, 25. The exact amount if not stated and described as a 'half-donation'.
23. No evidence available and therefore an estimate.
24. Pliny, *Panegyricus*, 25.
25. Duncan-Jones, *Money and Government in the Roman Empire*. 804 m *sestertii* from tax and revenues.
26. Levick, *Propaganda and the Imperial Coinage*.
27. Van Meter, D., *The Handbook of Roman Imperial Coins*, 'Trajan'.
28. Dio Cassius, 68.10.
29. Pliny, *Panegyricus*, 33.
30. Bennett, *Trajan Optimus Princeps*, 'The Inauguration of a New Era'.
31. Pliny, *Panegyricus*, 66.2.
32. Pliny, *Panegyricus*, 66.4.
33. Pliny, *Panegyricus*, 93.1–2.
34. Assumed circuit distance of 1,300 m and average speed around 35 km/hr.
35. Pliny, *Panegyricus*, 51. Roman Coin, BMC853, RIC 571.
36. Pliny, *Panegyricus*, 51.4–5.
37. For reviews of Trajan's public works in this period, see Bennett, *Trajan Optimus Princeps*, 'Pater Patriae', and Syme, 'The Imperial Finances under Domitian, Nerva and Trajan'. On the Portus Centumcellae and Trajan's villa see Pliny, *Letters*, 6.31; Thermae Traiani see Anderson, J. C.,

'The Date of the Thermae Traiani and the Topography of the Oppius Mons' & Carandini, *Atlas of Ancient Rome*, Bk 2 Tab. 118–19; Circus Maximus see Carandini Bk 1 Region XI & Bk 2 Tab. 117, 175–7; Vestae see Carandini Bk 1 Region VIII & Bk 2 Tab 40–1.
38. Pliny, *Panegyricus*, 30.
39. Africa was likely able to help given that it produced two-thirds of the overall supply for Rome. For regional corn supply, see Bowman, Garnsey, Rathbone, *Cambridge Ancient History XI*, 'Vespasian'.
40. Pliny, *Panegyricus*, 31.
41. Bowman, Garnsey, Rathbone, *Cambridge Ancient History XI*, 'Nerva to Hadrian: Trajan'.
42. Pliny, *Panegyricus*, 28.
43. Syme, R., 'The Imperial Finances under Domitian, Nerva and Trajan', 55–70.
44. Spalding Jenkins, A., 'The "Trajan-Reliefs" in the Roman Forum'.
45. Pliny, *Panegyricus*, 34.
46. Pliny, *Panegyricus*, 34.
47. Rutledge, S., *Imperial Inquisitions: Prosecutors and Informants from Tiberius to Domitian*. Personal Communication: Professor Barbara Levick confirms that Titus performed a similar parading of informers in his reign.
48. Arguments for and against suspension, see Brunt, 'Did Emperors Ever Suspend the Law of Maiestas?' Investigators, see Bennett, *Trajan Optimus Princeps*, 'Law, Finance and Literature'. Trajan's impact, see Bowman, Garnsey, Rathbone, *Cambridge Ancient History XI*, 'Nerva to Hadrian: Conclusions', by Miriam Griffin.
49. Pliny, *Panegyricus*, 42.
50. Pliny, *Panegyricus*, 42.
51. Pliny, *Natural History*, 36.122, gives 180 m *sestertii* for the cost of an aqueduct as a benchmark for a large public construction. It is assumed that Trajan's works in this period cost around 350 m *sestertii*. For Trajan's aid to Egypt, one can suggest 10 m *sestertii* based on aid given to Sardis in AD 17, Tacitus *Annals* 2.47. Dole expansion estimated as 5 m *sestertii*. *Alimenta* expenses of 60 m *sestertii* using Nerva's figure spent on land grants for the poor, *Dio Cassius*, 68.2. Polybius, *Histories*, 31.28, describes 0.75 m *sestertii* for a costly gladiatorial show in 160 BC. The *Senatus Consultum de Pretiis Gladiatorum Minuendis* decree of AD 177 to standardise the cost of gladiators references games costing in the hundreds of thousands of *sestertii* range. Cost of Trajan's games estimated at 10 m *sestertii*. Total estimate of 435 m *sestertii*, plus 45 m *sestertii congiarium* and 26 m *sestertii donativum*.
52. Duncan-Jones, *Money and Government in the Roman Empire*, Chapter 4.
53. Duncan-Jones, *Money and Government in the Roman Empire*, Chapter 15.
54. Pliny, *Panegyricus*, 41.

CHAPTER 7: Trajan's First Dacian War

1. Personal communication. David Thomas – Quintus Fabius Maximus Verrucosus, or Fabius 'Cunctator' (the 'delayer') is a prominent exception, choosing stalling tactics during the Second Carthaginian War.
2. *Dio Cassius*, 68.6.1.
3. Lepper & Frere, *Trajan's Column*, Notes E2.
4. Lepper & Frere, *Trajan's Column*, Notes E2.
5. There is no evidence of any opposition to the war.

NOTES TO PAGES 122–127

6. Talbert, *Barrington Atlas of the Greek and Roman World*.
7. Eliade, M., & Trask, W., 'Zalmoxis'.
8. Teodorescu, D. M., *Cercetari arheologice in Muntii Hunedoarei*. Teodorescu was the first archaeologist to identify the hilltop fortress remains in Gradistea Muncelului as Sarmizegetusa Regia.
9. For meaning, see Strabo, *Geography*, VII 3.12 and Ramsay, W., 'Pisidian Wolf-Priests, Phrygian Goat-Priests, and the Old-Ionian Tribes'. Draco, see Tudor, D., *Corpus Monumentorum Religionis Equitum Danuvinorum: The Analysis and Interpretation of the Monuments*.
10. Ligt de, L., Hemelrijk, E., & Singor, H. W., (eds), *Roman Rule and Civic Life: Local and Regional Perspectives*, 'The Legend of Decebalus' by Bruun, C.
11. Trajan's Column, Rome.
12. Eliade, M., & Trask, W., 'Zalmoxis'.
13. Herodotus, *The Histories*, IV 93–6.
14. Dumitru, C., Cristina, A. I., Viorel., A., *From the History of the Romanian Apiculture*.
15. Matyszak, P., *The Enemies of Rome*, 'Decebalus of Dacia: The Braveheart of the Carpathians'.
16. Goldsworthy, *The Roman Army at War*, 'The Generals' Battle'.
17. Bennett, *Trajan, Optimus Princeps*, 'Dacicus'. Bennett lists Servianus as governor of Pannonia, replaced by Agricola at the start of the war. Syme, 'People in Pliny' notes that Neratius Priscus is cited as governor of Pannonia *ca*. 102–5 AD, and one could assume he was a general in the second campaign of the First Dacian War until the start of Trajan's Second Dacian War. Syme states that Atilius Agricola was Priscus' predecessor and therefore held the post for at least a year (through 101) and was a general in the first campaign of the First Dacian War. He had replaced Servianus, who had prepared the province in advance of conflict and was presumably seconded for the start of the war before claiming his *consul ordinarius* in Rome in January 102. Birley, *Hadrian: the restless Emperor*. Birley cites Neratius Priscus as governor of Pannonia *ca*. 102–5.
18. Lepper & Frere, *Trajan's Column*, Notes E4. Bennett, *Trajan, Optimus Princeps*, 'Dacicus'. Both authors review senior commanders involved in the First Dacian War.
19. Bassus was previously *legatus* of XI *Claudia* and later legate of Judaea from 102/3 to 104/5.
20. Jones, 'Sura and Senecio'.
21. Bennett, *Trajan, Optimus Princeps*, 'Dacicus'.
22. Lepper & Frere, *Trajan's Column*, Notes E4.
23. Lepper & Frere, *Trajan's Column*, Notes E4.
24. Lepper & Frere, *Trajan's Column*, Notes E4.
25. Lepper & Frere, *Trajan's Column*, Notes E4.
26. Lepper & Frere, *Trajan's Column*, Notes E4.
27. Rossi, L., *Trajan's Column and the Dacian Wars*, Chapter 4.
28. Assumed around 1,000 men.
29. Bennett, *Trajan, Optimus Princeps*, 'Dacicus'. Bennett describes reference to Palmyrenes, Getae, Daci, Britons and Cantabri.
30. Rossi, *Trajan's Column and the Dacian Wars*, Chapter 4.
31. Assumed around 1,000 mounted.
32. Assumed around 500 slingmen.
33. Assumes Lepper & Frere (*Trajan's Column*, Notes E4) citation of legions that participated in the campaign force (IV *Flavia Felix*, XIII *Gemina*, I *Adiutrix*, II *Adiutrix*, I *Minervia*, VII *Claudia*

= 34,200 theoretical strengths reduced by 20% attrition = 27,360) and vexillations (1,000 each from XV *Apollinaris*, XIV *Gemina Martia Victrix*, V *Macedonica*, I *Italica*, IV *Scythica* [Syria], XII *Fulminata* [Syria] and an unknown legion [Syria] = 7,000). Total 34,360 legionaries and an equivalent number of auxiliaries. Plus, all the available Guards and *symmachiarii*.

34. Postulated given the nature of sovereignty.
35. Trajan's Column, Rome.
36. Based on a gross population estimate of around 800,000, one could broadly equate that only a fraction were suitably aged, fit for combat, in possession of arms and successfully mustered for war.
37. Brzezinski & Mielczarek, *The Sarmatians*, 'Who Were the Sarmatians?'.
38. Brzezinski & Mielczarek, *The Sarmatians*, Plate E.
39. Around 9,000 men were involved in the raid of 69 into Moesia. It is assumed that subsequent raids in 85–88 had fielded an equivalent number, which if depleted had recovered in numbers by 101.
40. Talbert, *Barrington Atlas of the Greek and Roman World*.
41. Lepper & Frere, *Trajan's Column*. Extensive evidence is examined for the onset of campaigning and I have assumed that operations were launched from Viminacium and moved east to cross at Lederata.
42. Trajan's Column, casts 12–15.
43. For the imperial army on the march, see Connolly, *The Roman Army*, 'The Army of the Empire'. Goldsworthy, *The Complete Roman Army*, 'The Army at War'.
44. Goldsworthy, *The Complete Roman Army*, 'The Army at War'.
45. *Dio Cassius*, 68.8.1. Trajan's Column, casts 25–26.
46. Talbert, *Barrington Atlas of the Greek and Roman World*.
47. Trajan's Column, cast 55.
48. Trajan's Column, casts 59–60.
49. Trajan's Column, cast 62.
50. Trajan's Column, casts 59–61.
51. Trajan's Column, cast 60.
52. Trajan's Column, cast 61.
53. Trajan's Column, cast 63. Trajan inspects a bow captured from the Dacians. The fact that this is depicted on the column speaks to their surprise that the enemy had this technology.
54. Trajan's Column, cast 60.
55. Goldsworthy, A., *In the Name of Rome*, 'Caesar in Gaul'. Goldsworthy gives the example of Julius Caesar close behind fighting lines.
56. Lepper & Frere, *Trajan's Column*, 'Thunderstorm Battle'. Trajan's Column, casts 63–4.
57. Trajan's Column, cast 71.
58. Trajan's Column, cast 71.
59. Trajan's Column, cast 66.
60. Trajan's Column, casts 68–70.
61. Trajan's Column, cast 72.
62. Trajan's Column, cast 73. Lepper & Frere, *Trajan's Column*, 'Thunderstorm Battle'. I have assumed a chronology for the capture during the period of consolidation after the second battle of Tapae.
63. Trajan's Column, cast 74–5.

64. Trajan's Column, casts 77–9.
65. Trajan's Column, casts 79.
66. Lepper & Frere, *Trajan's Column*. The authors alternatively propose Oescus/Novae further east, based on the rationale that the Roxolani depicted on the Column were located further east. However, it is problematic to reconcile why Trajan would seek a counter-offensive so far east that then required a lengthy journey north to enter the Hateg Plain where his forces were presumably not yet stationed. It is assumed that his offensive needed to focus on the Bistra Valley area or immediately to the east of the Iron Gates Pass. He could have then returned via Tibiscum, or alternatively through the region of modern-day Teregova from Dierna. The latter seems more probable if he wanted to seize an initiative.
67. Mounts Tarcu 2,190 m, Godeanu 2,229 m and Gugu 2,291 m.
68. Trajan's Column, cast 91.
69. Trajan's Column, casts 92–4.
70. Trajan's Column, casts 95–8.
71. Lepper & Frere, *Trajan's Column*, Section VI. The authors argue the location of the battle depicted (casts 102–9). Dio Cassius (68.8.2) recalls an incident involving a field bandage station and considering his previous account (68.8.1) could place the station at Tapae. Given the symbolic and strategic advantages of the area, I have assumed here that this major battle was again in the Tapae region.
72. Cruse, A., *Roman Medicine*, 'Physicians and Healers in the Roman World'.
73. Trajan's Column, casts 102–3.
74. Dio Cassius, 68.8.2.
75. Trajan's Column, cast 106.
76. Goldsworthy, *The Roman Army at War*, 'The Unit's Battle'.
77. Trajan's Column, casts 106–7.
78. Trajan's Column, casts 104–5.
79. Feugere, M., *Weapons of the Romans*, 'Torsion powered war machines'.
80. Trajan's Column, casts 108–9.
81. Historia Augusta, *Hadrian*, 3.2
82. Bennett, *Trajan, Optimus Princeps*, 'Dacicus'.
83. Trajan's Column, casts 121–2.
84. Lepper & Frere, *Trajan's Column*, 'Commentary Part I'. Multiple theories are described for the route and manner of the second campaign season. Given the victory at the third battle of Tapae that removed Dacian control of the Iron Gates Pass, it is assumed here that this pass was the path of choice. Additionally, a network of forts had been established in the Banat region.
85. Trajan's Column, casts 143–4.
86. Trajan's Column, cast 145. *Dio Cassius*, 68.9.1–3.
87. *Dio Cassius*, 68.9.2.
88. Trajan's Column, casts 160–1.
89. Lepper & Frere, *Trajan's Column*, Section VII. The authors cross reference Lino Rossi's identification of the fort shown in casts 163–72 as Costeşti. That Decebalus capitulated shortly after the strike suggests this is Costeşti because of its importance and close proximity to the capital.
90. Trajan's Column, casts 162–72.
91. Trajan's Column, cast 171.

92. Postulated given their nearby locations.
93. *Dio Cassius*, 68.9. 5–6.
94. Lepper & Frere, *Trajan's Column*, Section VII.
95. Personal communication: David Thomas – civic and societal activities were crucial to ensure long-term military success.

CHAPTER 8: Trajan's Second Dacian War

1. *Dio Cassius*, 68.10.1.
2. Personal communication: David Thomas – events depicted on Trajan's Column suggest that Decebalus had started disquieting activities that Trajan needed to observe himself and violence against Romans did not occur until the emperor was on his way.
3. *Dio Cassius*, 68.10.4.
4. For these close advisers, see Jones, '*Sura and Senecio*' and Bennett, *Trajan, Optimus Princeps*, 'Dacicus'.
5. Bennett, *Trajan, Optimus Princeps*, 'Dacicus'. Bennett suggests that these forts created a system for advanced warning of incursions.
6. Lepper & Frere, *Trajan's Column*, Notes E4.
7. Bennett, *Trajan, Optimus Princeps*, 'Dacicus'.
8. It is assumed that these vexillations were recalled given their involvement in the first war.
9. The campaign force included the legions selected for the first war (depleted because of casualties – total attrition around 30% = 24,000) with additional support from the new II *Traiana* legion (full strength) and new vexillations from XXX *Ulpia* and X *Gemina* (2,000 each) and prior vexillations (7,000).
10. Birley, *Hadrian: The Restless Emperor*, 'The Young General'. Probably 11 June 106.
11. *Dio Cassius* 68.10.3.
12. There are no major set-piece battles shown on Trajan's Column relating to this second war.
13. 84–85: first war with Dacia with Domitian expelling the Dacians from Moesia; 86–88: Domitian's second war with Dacia; and 101–2: Trajan's First Dacian War.
14. For justification of the route, see Lepper & Frere, *Trajan's Column*, 'Trajan's Journey Section IX', and Bennett, *Trajan, Optimus Princeps*, 'Dacicus'.
15. *Dio Cassius*, 68.11.1–2.
16. *Dio Cassius*, 68.11.1–2.
17. Trajan's Column, casts 249–54.
18. Trajan's Column, casts 255–6.
19. Trajan's Column, casts 259–61.
20. *Dio Cassius*, 68.13.6.
21. *Dio Cassius*, 68.13.1–6.
22. Drobeta-Turnu Severin Historical & National History Museum, Romania.
23. Trajan's Column, casts 259–261.
24. Lepper & Frere, *Trajan's Column*, Interlude Section XI. The authors discuss the various possible embassies (plates LXXII–LXXIII) and favour the Roxolani over the presence of the Iazyges.
25. *Dio Cassius*, 68.11.3.
26. *Dio Cassius*, 68.12.1.
27. *Dio Cassius*, 68.12.1.

28. *Dio Cassius*, 68.12.2.
29. *Dio Cassius*, 68.12.1. Dio is unclear on the source of the poison. Bennett, *Trajan, Optimus Princeps*, 'Dacicus', suggests it was a freedman of Decebalus.
30. *Dio Cassius*, 68.12.4.
31. *Dio Cassius*, 68.12.4.
32. Trajan's Column, casts 265–6
33. Trajan's Column, casts 274–7.
34. Lepper & Frere, *Trajan's Column*, Interlude Section XI.
35. Personal communication: Peter Connolly – The practical nature of the Roman army would have adopted many techniques to defile in an orderly manner through such passes.
36. Hent, Alin., 'The Fortifications in Orastie Mountains as Enclosures'.
37. Lepper & Frere, *Trajan's Column*, Sarmizegetusa Section XIII.
38. Taylor, T., 'Aspects of Settlement Diversity and Its Classification in Southeast Europe before the Roman Period'.
39. Opreanu, C. H., 'The Enigmatic Dacia Architecture at Sarmizegetusa Regia, Profane versus Sacred Purpose', *EphNap*, 29: 177–92, 2019.
40. For archaeological studies and descriptions of the Dacian citadel, see Apostol, V., 'A Few Indications on the Architecture of Sarmizegetusa Regia, about the Andesite Columns and the Measurement Unit'. Apostol, V., and Matesscu, R., 'The Great Limestone Temple at Sarmizegetusa Regia, Reanalysis of Archaeological and Architectural Data'. Bodo, C., 'Muntii Orastiei, Centrul Regatului Dac'. Daicoviciu, H., 'Le Sanctuaire A de Sarmizegetusa Regia'. Daicoviciu, C, 'Studiul Traiului Dacilor in Muntii Orastiei'. Daicoviciu, C., and Ferenczi, A., *Asezariledacice din Muntii Orastiei*. Petan, A., 'The Dacian Fortress of Gradistea Muncelului: from the Legend of the White King to its Identification with Sarmizegetusa Regia'. Teodorescu, D. M., *Cercetari arheologice in Muntii Hunedoarei*.
41. There is no direct archaeological evidence to date that the Romans completely surrounded the capital with typical siege walls, barriers and fortifications. Any siege works were likely temporary structures that have avoided modern-day detection. Possible evidence of siege construction can be seen on Trajan's Column, casts 306–8, showing Trajan surveying the Dacian defences from a raised rampart. Advanced satellite-generated high- and mid-resolution topographic data suggest that Roman forces at Sesului and Muncelu could have worked in tandem to besiege and subdue Sarmizegetusa Regia.
42. An assumption, given that no women or children are shown in any of the scenes on the column depicting the final fall of Sarmizegetusa Regia.
43. Trajan's Column, casts 291–2.
44. Trajan's Column, casts 301–4.
45. Trajan's Column, casts 301–4.
46. Trajan's Column, casts 306–8.
47. Trajan's Column, casts 309–12
48. Trajan's Column, casts 309–12
49. Trajan's Column, casts 313–14. The small doorway is significant as depictions of the fortress only show walls without entrances. Combined with the fact that Dacians are shown standing directly over the scene, but not engaged in fighting, suggests they were traitors letting Romans in through the normally concealed doorway. Roman forces had not managed to scale the walls

and their sudden appearance inside the fortress further supports the notion that these Dacians betrayed Decebalus.
50. Trajan's Column, casts 316–18.
51. Julius Caesar prevented the vulnerable from leaving Alesia in 52 BC for this same reason.
52. Josephus, *The Jewish Wars*, 3.7.23
53. Trajan's Column, casts 326–8. This is a hotly debated interpretation. One could conclude differently this was the dispensing of final water rations before escape attempts but the immediately following scene (cast 329) of Dacians carrying their dead is hard to reconcile. It would also not be the first time suicide was taken as an option by the besieged – Zealots trapped in Masada are suspected of mass suicide just prior to its captured in 73 by Roman forces – Kolitz, Z., 'Masada – Suicide or Murder?'
54. Trajan's Column, casts 331–2.
55. Florea, G., 'Archaeological Observations Concerning the Roman Conquest of the Area of the Dacian Kingdom's Capital'.
56. Makkay, J., 'The Treasures of Decebalus'.
57. Bennett, *Trajan, Optimus Princeps*, 'Dacicus'. Provides corrected figures for the numbers cited by the ancient sources. For examples of treasures, see Deppert-Lippitz, B., 'Dacian Gold Treasures from Transylvania'.
58. Using 804 m *sestertii* as the annual revenue, see Hopkins, K., 'Taxes and Trade in the Roman Empire'.
59. Trajan's Column, casts 384–7. Speidel, M., 'The Suicide of Decebalus on the Tropaeum of Adamklissi'. Speidel, M., 'The Captor of Decebalus a New Inscription from Philippi'.
60. Lepper & Frere, *Trajan's Column*, XIV 'Mopping Up'.
61. Bennett, *Trajan, Optimus Princeps*, 'Dacicus'.
62. Bradley, K., 'On Captives under the Principate'.
63. Bennett, *Trajan, Optimus Princeps*, 'Redacta in formam provinciae'.
64. Wade, D., 'More Ado about Dacia'.
65. Lepper & Frere, *Trajan's Column*, Note F2.
66. Ellis, L., '"Terra Deserta": Population, Politics, and the [de]Colonization of Dacia'.
67. Syme, R., 'Some Friends of the Caesars'.
68. Bennett, *Trajan, Optimus Princeps*, 'Redacta in formam provinciae'.
69. For a comprehensive description of town planning, occupancy and excavations, see Alicu, D. & Paki, A., *Town-planning and Population in Ulpia Traiana Sarmizegetusa*.
70. Bennett, *Trajan, Optimus Princeps*, 'Redacta in formam provinciae', cites 15,000 auxiliaries. Using my figure for the size of two legions considering attrition (9,120 men) this totals around 24,000.

CHAPTER 9: **Biding Time between Great Wars**

1. In-depth review of imperial virtues, see Norena, C. F., 'The Communication of the Emperor's Virtues'.
2. The date, Bennett, *Trajan, Optimus Princeps*, 'Dacicus'. Details of Roman triumphs, Makin, E., 'The Triumphal Route, with Particular Reference to the Flavian Triumph', and Beard, M., *The Roman Triumph*. The night before for Vespasian and Titus, Josephus, 7.123. I have adopted the hypothesis that the Villa Publica was destroyed by this time but part of its park space was not developed and therefore a suitable location to muster troops.

3. Smith, W., *A Dictionary of Greek and Roman Antiquities*, 'Triumphus'.
4. Ibid.
5. Beard, *The Roman Triumph*. The author reviews the diversities of triumphs and warns against assuming that the slave and his words were permanent fixtures.
6. Smith, *A Dictionary of Greek and Roman Antiquities*, 'Triumphus'.
7. Josephus, *The Jewish Wars*, 7.122. A reference to Vespasian and Titus' triumph.
8. Makin, 'The Triumphal Route, with Particular Reference to the Flavian Triumph'.
9. Dio Cassius. 68.15.1.
10. Smith, *A Dictionary of Greek and Roman Antiquities*, 'Triumphus'.
11. *Dio Cassius*, 68.14.6.
12. *Dio Cassius*, 68.16.2.
13. Historia Augusta, *Hadrian*, 3.6.
14. Personal communication: Professor Barbara Levick.
15. Around 150,000 recipients.
16. 2.5 *sestertii* per *modius* of wheat, Duncan-Jones, R., 'An Epigraphic Survey of Costs in Roman Italy'. 1 *modius* weighed 6.5 kg, Rickman, G., 'The Grain Trade under the Roman Empire'. Thus, 500 *sestertii* could buy 200 *modii* weighing 1,300 kg.
17. Weaver, P., 'Freedmen Procurators in the Imperial Administration'. Saller, R., 'Promotion and Patronage in Equestrian Careers'.
18. Bennett, *Trajan, Optimus Princeps*, 'Optimus Princeps'.
19. Bennett, *Trajan, Optimus Princeps*, 'Optimus Princeps'. Bennett proposes an argument for the constitutional changes.
20. Personal communication: David Thomas suggests that this constitutional change reflects Trajan's objective to represent his power transparently, as opposed to the masquerade of Augustus.
21. Bennett, *Trajan, Optimus Princeps*, 'Optimus Princeps'. Bennett's hypothesis is based on the title of *Optimo Principi* and other factors.
22. Bennett, *Trajan, Optimus Princeps*, 'Optimus Princeps'.
23. Example of numerous letters between Trajan and Pliny while governor of Bithynia-Pontus.
24. Norena, C., 'The Social Economy of Pliny's Correspondence with Trajan'.
25. Eutropius, 8.2.
26. Sherwin-White, A. N., 'Trajan's replies to Pliny: authorship and necessity'.
27. Pliny, *Letters*, 5.9.
28. Personal communication: David Thomas.
29. Pliny, *Letters*, 5.13.
30. Ibid.
31. Bennett, *Trajan, Optimus Princeps*, 'Optimus Princeps'. Bennett refers to senators in this episode.
32. Pliny, *Letters*, 6.19.
33. Ibid.
34. Pliny, *Letters*, 6.31.
35. Merrill, E., 'On the Date of Pliny's Prefecture of the Treasury of Saturn'. Harte, R., 'The Praetorship of the Younger Pliny'.
36. Bowman, Garnsey, Rathbone, *Cambridge Ancient History. The High Empire, A.D. 70–192*, 'Nerva to Hadrian'.

37. Pliny, *Letters*, 10.17a.
38. Pliny, *Letters*, 10.32.
39. Detailed evaluation of Trajan and Pliny's letters, see Sherwin-White, 'Trajan's replies to Pliny: authorship and necessity'. Woolf, G., 'Pliny/Trajan and the Poetics of Empire'. Radice, B., 'A Fresh Approach to Pliny's Letters'.
40. For the day and month, see Pliny, *Letters*, 10.17b. For the year, see Sherwin-White, 'Trajan's replies to Pliny: authorship and necessity'.
41. Pliny, *Letters*, 10.60.
42. Precedent, Pliny, *Letters*, 10.7 & 10.57. Compromise, 10.115.
43. Pliny, *Letters*, 10.9, 10.18, 10.20, 10.22, 10.40.
44. Pliny, *Letters*, 10.9.
45. Pliny, *Letters*, 10.40. Henrichs, A., 'Graecia Capta: Roman Views of Greek Culture'.
46. Pliny, Letters, 10.32, 10.38.
47. Pliny, Letters, 10.38.
48. Pliny, Letters, 10.22.
49. Pliny, Letters, 10.34.
50. *Dio Cassius*, 68.3.2, 68.16.2.
51. Bennett, *Trajan, Optimus Princeps*, 'Optimus Princeps'. Bennett questions the involvement of Laberius Maximus. However, Historia Augusta, *Hadrian* 5.5, although an unreliable source, clearly states that Laberius Maximus was already in exile at the start of Hadrian's reign presumably as punishment for his involvement.
52. Anderson, J. & Haverfield, F., 'Trajan on the Quinquennium Neronis'.
53. There were buildings before and after this period, but 109–12 appears to have been a period of intensive construction.
54. *Dio Cassius*, 69.4.
55. Trajan's forum, see Packer, J. E., *The Forum of Trajan in Rome*. Claridge, *Rome: An Oxford Archaeological Guide*, 'Imperial Forums'. Packer, J., 'Trajan's Glorious Forum'.
56. *Ammianus Marcellinus*, 16.10.15.
57. Syme, 'The Imperial Finances under Domitian, Nerva and Trajan'.
58. Duncan-Jones, *Money and Government in the Roman Empire*, 'Change and Deterioration'.
59. I estimate a total income for 106–13 of 11,030 m *sestertii* and total expenses in the same period of 8,725 m *sestertii*.
60. Lo Cascio, E., 'State and Coinage in the Late Republic and Early Empire'.
61. Eutropius, 8.2.
62. Bennett, *Trajan, Optimus Princeps*, 'Redacta in formam provinciae', gives 105 and 106 as probable years.
63. Pliny the Elder, *The Natural History*, 12.41.
64. Bowersock, G. W., 'A Report on Arabia Provincia'.
65. *Dio Cassius*, 68.7.4, refers to the 'subdued' kingdom of Petra. Bowersock, 'A Report on Arabia Provincia', arguments for and against open conflict.
66. Bowersock, 'A Report on Arabia Provincia'.
67. Consulship, Harrer, G., & Griffin, M., 'Fasti Consulares'. Statue, Chenault, R., 'Statues of Senators in the Forum of Trajan and the Roman Forum in Late Antiquity'. Insignia, Kropp, A., *Images and Monuments of Near Eastern Dynasts, 100 BC–AD 100*, 'Methods, Dynasts and Kingdoms'.

NOTES TO PAGES 186–200

68. Bowersock, 'A Report on Arabia Provincia'.
69. Bowersock, G., 'The Annexation and Initial Garrison of Arabia'.
70. Graf, D., 'The Via Nova Traiana between Petra and 'Aqaba'.
71. Graf, D., 'The "Via Militaris" in Arabia'.
72. Bowersock, 'A Report on Arabia Provincia'.
73. Boatwright, M. T., 'The Imperial Women of the Early Second Century A.C.'
74. Oliver, J., 'The Empress Plotina and the Sacred Thymelic Synod'.
75. Danziger, D. & Purcell, N., *Hadrian's Empire: When Rome Ruled the World*, 'Belonging'.
76. *Epitome De Caesaribus*, 14.8.
77. Birley, *Hadrian: The Restless Emperor*, 'The Young General'.
78. *Historia Augusta, Hadrian*, 3.
79. *Dio Cassius*, 68.15.5.
80. First 93 (Domitian), second 102 (Trajan).
81. *Dio Cassius*, 68.15.6.
82. Vermaseren & van Essen, *The Excavations in the Mithraeum of the Church of Santa Prisca in Rome*.
83. Bust of Trajan (1805,0703.93), British Museum, London.
84. Pliny, *Panegyricus*, 81.1
85. *Dio Cassius*, 68.15.1.
86. *Dio Cassius*, 68.15.3.
87. Pliny, *Letters*, 6.31.
88. Eutropius, 8.2.
89. *Dio Cassius*, 68.7.4.
90. Bennett, *Trajan, Optimus Princeps*, 'The New Ruler'.

CHAPTER 10: The Parthian War

1. Examples of blame for conflict between Rome and Parthia, see Crook, J., Lintott, A., & Rawson, E., *Cambridge Ancient History, The Last Age of the Roman Republic, 146–43 BC*, 'Lucullus, Pompey and the East', by A. Sherwin-White; Bowman, A. K., Champlin, E., Lintott, A., *Cambridge Ancient History, The Augustan Empire, 43 BC–AD 69*, 'The expansion of the Empire under Augustus – Armenia & Parthia', by E. S. Gruen; Levick, B., *Tiberius, the Politician*, 'Provincial and Foreign Policy'.
2. Bowman, Champlin & Lintott, *Cambridge Ancient History*, 'The expansion of the empire under Augustus – Armenia & Parthia'. Tigranes, made King of Armenia by Tiberius in the very year of the 20 BC peace treaty, was Rome's nominee, not Parthia's. In AD 2, Augustus ultimate acceptance of the Parthian candidate in return for recognition of Roman authority appears more like a recognition of current realities in the region than proof that this was what had been agreed in 20 BC.
3. Lepper, *Trajan's Parthian War*, 'Conclusion'. I have adopted Lepper's views on frontier motivations.
4. *Dio Cassius*, 68.17.1.
5. Assumed that Dio was writing and researching his histories around 200.
6. Birley, *Hadrian: The Restless Emperor*, 'The Parthian War'.
7. Duncan-Jones, *Money and Government in the Roman Empire*, 'Reign-studies: Chronology and Structure'. Duncan-Jones suggests that this increased production was specifically to support

the Parthian War. Bennett, *Trajan, Optimus Princeps*, 'Parthicus'. Bennett cites large outputs in the mints of Flaviopolis, Anazarbos and Alexandreia kat'Isson.
8. Invernizzi, A., 'Parthian Nisa: New Lines of Research'.
9. Lendering, J., *History of Iran – Parthian Empire*.
10. Arsacid dynastic history, see Daryaee, T., *Oxford Handbook of Iranian History*, 'The Arsacid Empire', by E. Dabrowa. Bennett, *Trajan, Optimus Princeps*, 'Parthicus'.
11. Longden, R. P., 'Notes on the Parthian Campaigns of Trajan'.
12. Shahbazi, A. Sh., *Parthian Army*.
13. *Justinus*, 41.3.
14. Plutarch, *Life of Crassus*, 24.1–2.
15. Bennett, *Trajan, Optimus Princeps*, 'Parthicus'.
16. Kawami, T. S., 'Archaeological Evidence for Textiles in Pre-Islamic Iran'.
17. Gruber, J. W., 'Irrigation and Land Use in Ancient Mesopotamia'.
18. Bennett, *Trajan, Optimus Princeps*, 'Parthicus'.
19. Bickerman, E. J., 'Diva Augusta Marciana'.
20. Lepper, *Trajan's Parthian War*, 'The General Nature of the Problem'.
21. 42 days in total assuming Rome to Brundisium along the Via Appia and Via Traiana (22 km per day; total 21 days), Brundisium to Corinthus (coastal sailing; total 14 days), Corinthus to Athens (22 km per day; total 7 days).
22. Birley, *Hadrian: The Restless Emperor*, 'The Young General'.
23. Birley, *Hadrian: The Restless Emperor*, 'Archon at Athens'.
24. *Dio Cassius*, 68.17.2–3.
25. *Dio Cassius*, 68.17.3.
26. Calculation assumes Athens to Ephesus (sailing, 6 days), Ephesus to Attaleia (22 km per day; total 14 days), Attaleia to Seleucia (coastal sailing, 4 days).
27. Bennett, J., *Trajan, Optimus Princeps*, 'Parthicus'.
28. Lepper, *Trajan's Parthian War*, 'The General Nature of the Problem'.
29. *Dio Cassius*, 68.18.
30. Bennett, J., *Trajan, Optimus Princeps*, 'Parthicus'. Bennett cites *Dio Cassius* (68.21.1) as referring to this period Jan.–April 114.
31. *Dio Cassius*, 68.19.2.
32. McDermott, W., 'Homullus and Trajan'. I have assumed that following his governorship of Cappadocia, Trajan may have retained him as an adviser.
33. Birley, *Hadrian: The Restless Emperor*, 'The Parthian War'.
34. It is assumed that Quietus had been elevated by now to a more senior position.
35. Assumed, based on the similar number for the Dacian wars.
36. Wilcox, P., *Rome's Enemies 3: Parthians and Sassanid Persians*, 'The Parthians'.
37. Shahbazi, A. Sh., *Parthian Army*. Shahbazi provides an overview of Parthian command structures and military tactics.
38. For a comprehensive overview of Parthian weapons and armours, see Wilcox, *Rome's Enemies*, 'The Parthians'.
39. Burris-Davis, B., *Parthian Horses – Parthian Archers*, parthia.com
40. Conflict in Nero's reign ended in 63.
41. Assumes 19–20 km a day through difficult mountainous terrain.
42. *Dio Cassius*, 68.19.3.

43. *Dio Cassius*, 68.19.
44. Syme, R., 'The Enigmatic Sospes'.
45. *Dio Cassius*, 68.20.4. Dio states that Parthamasiris was allowed to go 'to any place he pleased', but he surely meant banishment from Armenia and subsequent events suggest it was anyway a hollow offer.
46. For ancient reference to the Mardi, see Strabo, *Geography*, 11.13.6. Location east of Lake Van, see Longden, 'Notes on the Parthian Campaigns of Trajan'.
47. Personal communication: Professor Barbara Levick suggests that Quietus' Moorish origins would have made him familiar with the Atlas regions.
48. Syme, R., 'The Career of Arrian'.
49. Bennett, *Trajan, Optimus Princeps*, 'Parthicus'.
50. Ibid.
51. Lepper, *Trajan's Parthian War*, 'The Chronological Problem'.
52. Coinage struck 112–14.
53. *Dio Cassius*, 68.18.3.
54. *Dio Cassius*, 68.23.
55. Assumes that Trajan left Elegeia around April 115, with a distance of around 500 km to the Nisibis area.
56. *Dio Cassius*, 68.23.2.
57. Ibid.
58. *Dio Cassius*, 68.22.2.
59. *Dio Cassius*, 68.26.1.
60. Plutarch, *Life of Crassus*, 3.17.
61. Bennett, *Trajan, Optimus Princeps*, 'Parthicus'.
62. *Dio Cassius*, 68.21.
63. Ibid. Described as a 'barbaric' dance.
64. Bennett, *Trajan, Optimus Princeps*, 'Parthicus'.
65. It is assumed that they met in south-eastern Mesopotamia where Quietus had not been able to advance.
66. Lepper, *Trajan's Parthian War*, 'The General Nature of the Problem'. Lepper suggests Hatra which I have adopted here given its tactical position, after having seized Singara. For Singara, see *Dio Cassius*, 68.22.
67. For theories of their capture, see Lepper, *Trajan's Parthian War*, 'The General Nature of the Problem'.
68. For examples of coins with PARTHICO or PARTHIA CAPTA, see Sear, D., *Roman Coins and Their Values*, 3099 & 3140. Date and letter, see Bennett, *Trajan, Optimus Princeps*, 'Parthicus'.
69. *Dio Cassius*, 68.24. The details provided by Dio suggest that he drew evidence from eyewitness accounts.
70. Estimate based on historical events.
71. *Dio Cassius*, 68.25.
72. *Dio Cassius*, 68.25.6.
73. 331 BC.
74. The actual crossing point is unknown, but assumed to be somewhere in the vicinity of modern-day Mosul, Iraq. For Mount Masius as a location for timber, see Millar, *The Roman*

Near East, 'The Roman Presence, AD 114–161'. I agree with Bennett, *Trajan, Optimus Princeps*, 'Parthicus', that pontoons were constructed rather than the ships cited by Dio Cassius.
75. Dio Cassius, 68.26.2.
76. Dio Cassius, 68.26.3–4.
77. Dio Cassius, 68.22.3.
78. Bennett, *Trajan, Optimus Princeps*, 'Parthicus'. Bennett provides arguments for and against the name of the new province.
79. Dio Cassius, 68.26.4
80. Lepper, *Trajan's Parthian War*, 'Strategy and Topography'.
81. Lepper, *Trajan's Parthian War*, 'Arrian's Parthika' (trans. J. G. DeVoto) – *Arrianus 67*.
82. Assumes leaving Antioch for the Tigris in early April 116.
83. Dio Cassius, 68.28.2. Describes the use of 'hauling-engines'.
84. Dio Cassius, 68.28.2.
85. Bennett, Trajan, Optimus Princeps, 'Parthicus'.
86. Dio Cassius, 68.28.2–3.
87. Dio Cassius, 68.28.3.
88. This is supported by Roman senators being unable to recognise the names of many places included in Trajan's dispatches.
89. Dio Cassius, 68.28.4.
90. 30°53'52.0"N, 47°32'51.0"E
91. Dio Cassius, 68.29.1.
92. Assuming 10–12 weeks and sent second half of September.
93. Dio Cassius, 68.29.2.
94. Dio Cassius, 68.29.3.
95. Longden, 'Notes on the Parthian Campaigns of Trajan'.
96. Lepper, *Trajan's Parthian War*, 'Arrian's Parthika'. Eutropius 8.3.3.
97. For a review of the uprising causes, see Ben Zeev, M. P., *Diaspora Judaism in Turmoil, 116/117 CE: Ancient Sources and Modern Insights*, 'Mesopotamia'.
98. Longden, 'Notes on the Parthian Campaigns of Trajan'.
99. Lepper, *Trajan's Parthian War*, 'The Causes of the War'.
100. Goldsworthy, *In the Name of Rome: The Men Who Won the Roman Empire*, 'Imperial Legate: Corbulo and Armenia'.
101. It is assumed that Quietus was still in Babylonia having captured Adiabene earlier in the year and then proceeded down to Babylon along the Tigris.
102. Dio Cassius, 68.30.2.
103. Ibid.
104. Lepper, *Trajan's Parthian War*, 'The Causes of the War'. Based on Lepper's arguments for the division of legions between commanders, I have assumed that Trajan had a personal force with him at all times of around three legions.
105. Bennett, *Trajan, Optimus Princeps*, 'Parthicus'. Bennett suggests that Trajan met and defeated Sanatrukes. Dio Cassius (86.30) mentions no field battle. Malalas is vague (11.6), stating that Parthamaspetes was 'bribed' into becoming a Roman ally. Trajan then 'set out against Sanatrukes, emperor of the Persians… many Persians fell and [Trajan] captured Sanatrukes' and had him killed. I assume that Malalas is describing a field battle against Sanatrukes in which sizeable forces were engaged, many Parthians were slain and the Parthian leader

captured alive. Malalas does not mention any specific battle or location for these events. I also assume that the sack of Seleucia likely attracted Sanatrukes from wherever he was located. There is no evidence that Trajan joined his two legates, but it is reasonable to postulate that they united to have five legions in total to ensure victory against Sanatrukes. David Thomas, in a personal communication, notes that one could postulate alternative events in which Sanatrukes was heading for Armenia, intending to join Vologaeses, and Trajan pursued him northwards seeking battle.

106. *Dio Cassius*, 68.30.3.
107. *Dio Cassius*, 68.31.1.
108. *Dio Cassius*, 68.31.4.
109. Salam, N., et al., 'Leishmaniasis in the Middle East: incidence and epidemiology'.
110. *Dio Cassius*, 68.31.3.
111. *Dio Cassius*, 68.31.4.
112. *Dio Cassius*, 68.32.1.
113. Ben Zeev, *Diaspora Judaism in Turmoil*, 'The Order, Possible Interrelations, and Achievements of the Uprisings'.
114. Birley, *Hadrian: The Restless Emperor*, 'The Parthian War'.
115. Syme, R., 'The Wrong Marcius Turbo'.
116. Collins, J. J. and Harlow, D. C., (eds), *Early Judaism*, 'Jewish History from Alexander to Hadrian', by C. Seeman and A. Marshak.
117. Ben Zeev, *Diaspora Judaism in Turmoil*, 'Judaea'.
118. *Dio Cassius*, 68.32.3.
119. Ben Zeev, *Diaspora Judaism in Turmoil*, 'Judaea'.
120. Examples include, XV *Apollinaris* from Pannonia, I *Italica* from Novae (modern Svishtov), V *Macedonica* from Moesia, XI *Claudia* from Moesia Inferior and X *Fretensis* from Judaea. It is probable that auxiliary units were taken from Britain.
121. Campbell, B. *The Roman Army 31 BC–AD 337. A Source Book*, 'The Officers' (112).
122. *Dio Cassius*, 68.33.1. Dio only references Mesopotamia but surely Armenia was considered as well.
123. Lepper, *Trajan's Parthian War*, 'Conclusion'. I agree with Lepper that the situation could have been remedied in Mesopotamia, and I assume was recoverable in Armenia and Babylonia. The unrest in the Danube region may have been manageable through diplomacy or force. Quietus would probably have dealt with Judaea and then returned to the Parthian war.

CHAPTER 11: **Conspiracy, Death and Deification**

1. For a review of beliefs, see Toynbee, J. M. C., *Death and Burial in the Roman World*, 'Roman beliefs of the afterlife'.
2. Beard, M., North, J., Price, S., *Religions of Rome: Volume 2, A Sourcebook*, 'Individuals and Gods: Life and Death'.
3. Marcus Aurelius, *Meditations*, 6.26.
4. Toynbee, *Death and Burial in the Roman World*, 'Roman beliefs of the afterlife'.
5. Beard, North & Price, *Religions of Rome*, 'Individuals and Gods: Life and Death'.
6. Personal communication: David Thomas
7. Suetonius, *Vespasian*, 23:48

8. Mitchell, S., 'The Trajanic Tondo from Roman Ankara: In Search of the Identity of a Roman Masterpiece'. Mitchell rejects the traditional identification of the bronze bust in the Museum of Anatolian Civilizations (Ankara) as Trajan. Regardless, I assume that Trajan would have had an emaciated appearance similar to the bust's depiction.
9. *Dio Cassius* 68.33.2–3.
10. *Dio Cassius* 68.33.3. Whisnant, J. P., 'Effectiveness versus efficacy of treatment of hypertension for stroke prevention'. 35–50% of strokes are caused by high blood pressure.
11. *Dio Cassius*, 68.33.3.
12. Personal communication: Dr Claudia Winterstein, an archaeologist working in Selinus states that there is no evidence to date that the Şekerhane Köşkü (the so-called cenotaph to Trajan) marks the site of the villa in which Trajan died.
13. Eutropius, 8.5.
14. *Dio Cassius* 69.1.1. Eutropius, 8.6.
15. Bennett, *Trajan, Optimus Princeps*. 'Parthicus'.
16. Historia Augusta, *Hadrian*, 3.7
17. Historia Augusta, *Hadrian* 4.1
18. *Dio Cassius*, 69.1.2.
19. Historia Augusta, *Hadrian*, 2.6
20. Historia Augusta, *Hadrian*, 2.10
21. Birley, *Hadrian: The Restless Emperor*, 'The Young General'.
22. Historia Augusta, *Hadrian*, 4.4
23. Birley, *Hadrian: The Restless Emperor*, 'Archon at Athens'.
24. Personal communication: David Thomas cites several possible reasons for Trajan's failure to appoint Hadrian as his heir.
25. *Dio Cassius*, 69.1.2.
26. Attianus ended up losing his job as prefect of the Praetorian Guard not long after when he became the scapegoat for the execution of four senators; Syme, R., 'Guard Prefects of Trajan and Hadrian.'
27. Lepper, *Trajan's Parthian War*, 'The Causes of the War'. Lepper states that Hadrian had no record of 'continuous or accelerated promotion'.
28. Historia Augusta, *Hadrian*, 5.9.
29. Historia Augusta, *Hadrian*, 4.10
30. *Dio Cassius*, 69.3.
31. *Dio Cassius*, 69.1.1–2
32. Historia Augusta, *Hadrian*, 4.6–7. Hadrian announced his adoption in Antioch on the fifth day before the Ides of August (9th) and received official news of Trajan's death on the third day before the Ides (11th) that marked his accession. The sailing distance between Selinus and Antioch is first around 30 nautical miles along the coast and then around 150 nautical miles across open waters to Seleucia Pieria. Casson, L., 'Speed under Sail of Ancient Ships', estimates that ancient vessels, with favourable winds, averaged between 4 and 6 knots over open water, and 3 to 4 knots along coasts. Thus, I estimate a dispatch from Selinus to Seleucia took around 40 hours and then around 4 hours by horse to Antioch. Thus, if sent during the early hours of 7 August, a message could have reached Hadrian on the morning of the 9th.
33. Vatican Museum, Epitaph of a Lictor (cat. 6961), dated 130 from Rome, CIL VI 1884.
34. *Dio Cassius*, 69.2.1.

35. Mattingly, H., 'Some Historical Coins of Hadrian'.
36. Historia Augusta, *Hadrian*, 5.9
37. *Dio Cassius*, 69.3. Eutropius, 8.5.
38. Platner, *Topographical Dictionary of Ancient Rome*, entry: Forum Traiani.
39. *Dio Cassius*, 44.7.
40. Historia Augusta, *Hadrian*, 6.1
41. *Dio Cassius*, 69.2.3.
42. Historia Augusta, *Hadrian*, 4.8
43. Syme, 'People in Pliny'. Syme dates Priscus' governorship of Pannonia to *ca.* 102–5.
44. Birley, *Hadrian: The Restless Emperor*, 'The Young General'. Birley reviews the arguments that Priscus and Servianus were potential heirs.
45. Historia Augusta, *Hadrian*, 4.9
46. Ibid.
47. Historia Augusta, *Hadrian*, 5.4
48. Syme, R., '*Die Reichsbeamten von Dazien* by Arthur Stein'.
49. Syme, 'The Friend of Tacitus'. Career details for Palma and Celsus.
50. Birley, *Hadrian: The Restless Emperor*, 'The Young General'.
51. Birley, A., 'Hadrian and Greek Senators'.
52. *Dio Cassius*, 69.2.5.
53. Historia Augusta, *Hadrian*, 5.8.
54. Ibid.
55. Birley, *Hadrian: The Restless Emperor*, 'The Young General'. Birley reviews events in Dacia and the Danube region in this period.
56. *Dio Cassius*, 69.19.1.
57. Historia Augusta, *Hadrian*, 7.2
58. Ibid.
59. *Dio Cassius*, 69.2.4.
60. Oath, see *Dio Cassius*, 69.2.6. Blame on Attianus, see Birley, *Hadrian: The Restless Emperor*, 'The Young General'.
61. Lepper and Frere, *Trajan's Column*, Note F1.
62. Eutropius, 8.4.
63. Eutropius, 8.5.
64. Trumbower, J. A., *Rescue for the Dead: The posthumous salvation of Non-Christians in early Christianity*, 'Gregory the Great's Prayer for Trajan'.
65. Vickers, N. J., 'Seeing Is Believing: Gregory, Trajan, and Dante's Art'.
66. Dante, *The Divine Comedy, Paradiso* Canto 20.1–72.
67. Seznec, J., 'Diderot and "The Justice of Trajan"'. Sharnova, E., 'A Newly Discovered "Justice of Trajan" from the Second School of Fontainebleau'.
68. Machiavelli, Niccolò, *Discourses on the First Decade of Titus Livius*, Chapter 10.
69. Gibbon, E., *The History of the Decline and Fall of the Roman Empire*, Vol. 1, 'The Constitution in the Age of the Antonines'.

BIBLIOGRAPHY

Ancient Authors

Ammianus Marcellinus, trans. J. C. Rolfe, Harvard University Press, 1935–1940.
Appian, *Roman History, Volume II,* ed. & trans. B. McGing, Loeb Classical Library, Harvard University Press, 1912.
Dio Cassius, *Roman History, Books 61–70,* trans. E. Cary, Loeb Classical Library, Harvard University Press, 2000.
Epitome De Caesaribus, trans. T. M. Banchich, Canisius College, 2018.
Eutropius, *Abridgement of Roman History,* trans. J. S. Watson & H. G. Bohn, 1853.
Herodotus, *The Histories,* trans. A. D. Godley, Harvard University Press, 1920.
Historia Augusta, Volume I, trans. David Magie, Loeb Classical Library, Harvard University Press, 1921.
Julian, *The Caesars,* trans. W. C Wright, 1913.
Justinus, *Epitome of Pompeius Trogus 'Philippic histories', Books 40–44,* trans. J. S. Watson, 1853.
Jordanes, *De Origine Actibusque Getarum,* trans. C. C. Mierow, Princeton University Press, 1915.
Josephus, *The Jewish Wars,* trans. M. Hammond, Oxford University Press, 2017.
Juvenal, *The Satires,* trans. A. S. Kline, Poetry in Translation, 2001.
Marcus Aurelius, *Meditations,* trans. M. Casaubon, Project Gutenberg, 2021.
Malalas, *The Chronicle of John Malalas,* trans. E. Jeffreys, M. Jeffreys, R. Scott, Australian Association for Byzantine Studies, 1986.
Martial, *Epigrams,* Bohn's Classical Library, 1897.
Pliny the Elder, *The Natural History,* J. Bostock & H. T. Riley, (eds), Taylor & Francis, 1855.
Pliny, *Letters, Books 1–7,* trans. B. Radice, Loeb Classical Library, Harvard University Press, 1997.
Pliny, *Letters, Books VIII–X, Panegyricus,* trans. B. Radice, Loeb Classical Library, Harvard University Press, 1997.
Plutarch, *Lives Volume III,* trans. B. Perrin, Loeb Classical Library, 1916.
Polybius, *The Histories, Volume VI: Books 28–39,* trans. W. R. Paton, Loeb Classical Library, Harvard University Press, 2012.
Publius Cornelius Tacitus, *The Agricola and Germania,* trans. A. S. Kline, Poetry in Translation, 2015.
Publius Cornelius Tacitus, *The History,* trans. A. J. Church & W. J. Brodribb, Perseus, 1942.
Quintilian, *Institutio Oratoria,* trans. H. E. Butler, Loeb Classical Library, 1920.

Strabo, *Geography*, trans. H. L. Jones, Loeb Classical Library, Harvard University Press, 1923.
Suetonius, *The Twelve Caesars*, trans. Robert Graves, Penguin Books, 1980.
Tacitus, *Histories Books 4–5, Annals: Books 1–3*, trans. C. H. Moore & J. Jackson, Loeb Classical Library, Harvard University Press, 1931.
Vegetius, *De Re Militari*, trans. J. Harper & L. Adet, Harper-McLaughlin-Adet Publications, 2019.

Modern Works

Alicu, D., & Paki, A., *Town-planning and Population in Ulpia Traiana Sarmizegetusa*, Tempus Reparatum, 1995.
Anderson, J., & Haverfield, F., 'Trajan on the Quinquennium Neronis', *Journal of Roman Studies (JRS)*, 1: 173–9, 1911.
Anderson, J. C., 'The Date of the Thermae Traiani and the Topography of the Oppius Mons', *American Journal of Archaeology*, 89(3): 499–509, 1985.
Apostol, V., 'A Few Indications on the Architecture of Sarmizegetusa Regia, about the Andesite Columns and the Measurement Unit', *Caiete ARA*, 10: 55–87, 2019.
Apostol, V., and Matesscu, R., 'The Great Limestone Temple at Sarmizegetusa Regia, Reanalysis of Archaeological and Architectural Data', *Caiete ARA*, 11: 67–124, 2020.

Beard, M., *The Roman Triumph*, Harvard University Press, 2009.
Beard, M., North, J., & Price, S. R. F., *Religions of Rome: Volume 2, A Sourcebook*, Cambridge University Press, 1998.
Bennett, J., *Trajan Optimus Princeps*, 2nd edn, Indiana University Press, 2001.
Ben-Sasson, H. H., *A History of the Jewish People*, Harvard University Press, 1985.
Ben Zeev, M. P., *Diaspora Judaism in Turmoil, 116/117 CE: Ancient Sources and Modern Insights*, Peeters, 2005.
Bickerman, E., 'Diva Augusta Marciana', *American Journal of Philology*, 95(4): 362–76, 1974.
Birley, A., 'Hadrian and Greek Senators', *Zeitschrift für Papyrologie Und Epigraphik*, 116: 209–45, 1997.
———, *Hadrian: The Restless Emperor*, Routledge, 2001.
Birley, E., 'Senators in the Emperor's Service', *Proceedings of the British Academy*, 1953, 39: 197–214.
———, *The Roman Army Papers, 1929–1986*, Gieben, 1988.
Boatwright, M. T., 'The Imperial Women of the Early Second Century A.C.', *American Journal of Philology*, 112 (4): 513–40, 1991.
Bodo, C., 'Muntii Orastiei, Centrul Regatului Dac', *Judetul Hunedoara Monografie*, 1: 90–166. 2012.
Bowersock, G. W., 'Syria under Vespasian', *JRS*, 1973, 63: 133–40.
———, 'The Annexation and Initial Garrison of Arabia', *Zeitschrift für Papyrologie Und Epigraphik*, 5: 37–47, 1970.
———, 'A Report on Arabia Provincia', *JRS*, 61: 219–42, 1971.
Bowman, A. K., Champlin, E., Lintott, A., (eds), *The Cambridge Ancient History, The Augustan Empire, 43 BC–AD 69*, Cambridge University Press, 1996.
Bowman, A. K., Garnsey, P., Rathbone, D., (eds), *The Cambridge Ancient History, Volume XI, The High Empire, AD 70–192*, Cambridge University Press, 2nd edn, 2000.
Bowman, A. K., & Thomas J. D., *Vindolanda: The Latin Writing-Tablets*, Society for the Promotion of Roman Studies, 1983.
Bradley, K., 'On Captives under the Principate', *Phoenix*, 58(3/4): 298–318, 2004.

Brown, A., Meadows, I., Turner, S., & Mattingly, D. 'Roman vineyards in Britain: Stratigraphic and palynological data from Wollaston in the Nene Valley, England', *Antiquity*, 2001, 75(290): 745–57.

Brunt, P. A., 'Did Emperors Ever Suspend the Law of *Maiestas*?', *Sodalitas, Scritti in Onore de Antonio Guarino*, 984: 469–80, 1984.

Brzezinski, R., & Mielczarek, M., *The Sarmatians 600 BC–AD 450*, Osprey Publishing, 2002.

Burgers., P., 'Coinage and State Expenditure: The Reign of Claudius AD 41–54', *Historia: Zeitschrift für Alte Geschichte*, 50(1): 96–114, 2001.

Burns. R., *Monuments of Syria, An Historical Guide*, Tauris Publishers, 1999.

Caballos, A & Leon, P., (eds), *Italica MMCC*, Consejeria de Cultura Seville, 1997.

Campbell, B., *The Roman Army 31 BC–AD 337: A Source Book*, Routledge, 2003.

———, *Greek and Roman Military Writers – Selected Readings*, Routledge Classical Translations, 2004.

Carandini., A., (ed.), *The Atlas of Ancient Rome*, Princeton University Press, 2017.

Casson, L., 'Speed under Sail of Ancient Ships', *Transactions and Proceedings of the American Philological Association*, 82: 136–48, 1951.

Chenault, R., 'Statues of Senators in the Forum of Trajan and the Roman Forum in Late Antiquity', *Journal of Roman Studies*, 102: 103–32, 2012.

Claridge, A., *Rome: An Oxford Archaeological Guide*, Oxford University Press, 1998.

Clarke, J. R., *Roman Sex 100 BC–AD 250*. Abrams Publishers, 2003.

Collins, J. J., & Harlow, D. C., (eds), *Early Judaism*, Eerdmans Publishing, 2012.

Connolly, P., *The Roman Army*. Purnell & Sons, 1984.

———, *Greece and Rome at War*, Greenhill Books, 1998.

———, *Colosseum – Rome's Arena of Death*, BBC Books, 2003.

———, *The Cavalryman*, Oxford University Press, 2003.

Crook, J., Lintott, A., & Rawson, E., (eds.), *The Cambridge Ancient History, The Last Age of the Roman Republic, 146–43 BC*, Cambridge University Press, 1994.

Crow, J. G., *Housesteads Roman Fort*, English Heritage, 2005.

Cruse, A., *Roman Medicine*, Tempus, 2004.

Daicoviciu, C, 'Studiul Traiului Dacilor in Muntii Orastiei', *SCIV*, 2(1): 95–126, 1951.

Daicoviciu, C., & Ferenczi, A., *Asezariledacice din Muntii Orastiei*, Bucuresti, 1951.

Daicoviciu, H., 'Le Sanctuarie A de Sarmizegetusa Regia', *AMN* 17: 65–79, 1980.

Dalby, A., & Grainger, S., *The Classical Cookbook*, British Museum Press, 1996.

Dante, *The Divine Comedy*, trans. A. S. Kline, Poetry in Translation, 2000.

Danziger, D., & Purcell, N., *Hadrian's Empire: When Rome Ruled the World*, Hodder, 2005.

Daryaee, T., (ed.), *The Oxford Handbook of Iranian History*, Oxford University Press, 2012.

Deppert-Lippitz, B., 'Dacian gold treasures from Transylvania', *Jewellery Studies*, 12: 55–66, 2012.

Dumitru, C., Cristina, A. I., Viorel., A., *From the History of the Romanian Apiculture*, Free Library, 2011.

Duncan-Jones, R., 'An Epigraphic Survey of Costs in Roman Italy', *Papers of the British School at Rome*, 33: 189–306, 1965.

———, *Money and Government in the Roman Empire*, Cambridge University Press, 1998.

———, *Power and Privilege in Roman Society*, Cambridge University Press, 2016.

Dupont, F., *Daily life in Ancient Rome*, Blackwell, 1992.

Durand, J., 'Historical Estimates of World Population: an Evaluation', *Population and Development Review*, 3: 253, 1977.
Dusanic, S., & Vasic, M., 'An Upper Moesian Diploma of AD 96', *Chiron*, 1977, 7: 291–304.

Eck, W., *Philosophy and Power in the Graeco-Roman World: Essays in honour of Miriam Griffin*, Oxford University Press, 2002.
Eliade, M., & Trask, W., 'Zalmoxis', *History of Religions*, 11(3), 257–302, 1972.
Ellis, L., '"Terra Deserta": Population, Politics, and the [de]Colonization of Dacia', *World Archaeology*, 30(2): 220–37, 1998.

Feugere, M., *Weapons of the Romans*, Tempus, 2002.
Fitzpatrick, M. P., 'Provincializing Rome: The Indian Ocean Trade Network and Roman Imperialism', *Journal of World History*, 22(1): 27–54, 2011.
Florea, G., 'Archaeological Observations Concerning the Roman Conquest of the Area of the Dacian Kingdom's Capital', *Lucrarile Coloviului National AMN* 1(1): 33–7, 1994.
French., V. 'Rescuing Creusa: New Methodological Approaches to Women in Antiquity', *Helios*, New Series, 13(2): 69–84, 1986.

Gallivan, P., 'The Fasti for A. D. 70–96', *Classical Quarterly*, 31(1): 186–220, 1981.
Gibbon, E., *The History of the Decline and Fall of the Roman Empire*, Fred de Fau & Co., 1906.
Goldsworthy, A. K., *The Roman Army at War 100 BC–200 AD*, Clarendon Paperbacks, 1998.
———, *The Complete Roman Army*, Thames & Hudson Ltd., 2003.
———, *In the Name of Rome: The Men Who Won the Roman Empire*, Phoenix, 2003.
Goodman, M., *The Roman World 44 BC–180 AD*, Routledge, 2003.
Graf, D., 'The Via Nova Traiana between Petra and 'Aqaba', *Syria*, 70(1/2): 262–3, 1993.
———, 'The "Via Militaris" in Arabia', *Dumbarton Oaks Papers*, 51: 271–81, 1997.
Grainger, J. D., *Nerva and the Roman Succession Crisis of AD 96–99*, Routledge, 2004.
Grant, M., *The Roman Emperors. A Biographical Guide to the Rulers of Imperial Rome 31 BC–AD 476*, Phoenix Giant, 1997.
———, 'Irrigation and Land Use in Ancient Mesopotamia', *Agricultural History*, 22 (2): 69–77, 1948.

Hamblin, W., 'The Roman Army in the First Century', *Brigham Young University Studies*, 36(3), 337–49, 1996.
Harlow, M., & Laurence, R., *Growing Up and Growing Old in Ancient Rome: A life course approach*, Routledge, 2002.
Harrer, G., & Griffin, M., 'Fasti Consulares', *American Journal of Archaeology*, 34(3): 360–4, 1930.
Harte, R., 'The Praetorship of the Younger Pliny', *Journal of Roman Studies*, 25: 51–4, 1935.
Henrichs, A., 'Graecia Capta: Roman Views of Greek Culture', *Harvard Studies in Classical Philology*, 97: 243–61, 1995.
Hent, A., 'The Fortifications in Orastie Mountains as Enclosures', *Analele Banatului: Arheologie Istorie* 24: 255–72, 2016.
Hopkins, K., 'Taxes and Trade in the Roman Empire', *JRS*, 70: 101–25, 1980.
Hornblower, S., & Spawforth, A., (eds), *The Oxford Classical Dictionary*, 3rd rev. edn, Oxford University Press, 2005.

Invernizzi, A., 'Parthian Nisa: New Lines of Research', *Iran & the Caucasus*, 1: 107–19, 1997.

Jones, B., 'Casperius Aelianus. An Enigma?', *Classical Journal*, 68(3): 277–9, 1973.
Jones, B. W., *The Emperor Titus*, Croom Helm/St Martin's Press, 1984.
———, *The Emperor Domitian*, Routledge, 1993.
Jones, C. P., 'Sura and Senecio', *JRS*, 60: 98–104, 1970.
Jones, R. F. J., 'The Roman Military Occupation of North-West Spain', *JRS*, 66: 45–66, 1976.

Kawami, T. S., 'Archaeological Evidence for Textiles in Pre-Islamic Iran', *Iranian Studies*, 25 (1/2): 7–18, 1992.
Keijwegt, M., 'Iuvenes and Roman Imperial Society', *Acta Classica*, XXXVII, 79–102, 1994.
Kolitz, Z., 'Masada – Suicide or Murder?', *Journal of Orthodox Jewish Thought*, 12(1): 5–26, 1971.
Kropp, A., *Images and Monuments of Near Eastern Dynasts, 100 BC–AD 100*, Oxford University Press, 2013.

Lendering, J., *History of Iran – Parthian Empire*, Iran Chamber Society, 2001–21.
Lepper, F. A., *Trajan's Parthian War*, Ares Publishers, 1948.
Lepper, F., & Frere, S., *Trajan's Column*, Alan Sutton, 1988.
Levick, B., 'Propaganda and the Imperial Coinage', *Antichthon*, 16: 104–16, 1982.
———, *Claudius*, Yale University Press, 1990.
———, 'Worries about Vespasian: The Achievements of an Emperor', *Acta Classica*, 42: 121–37, 1999.
———, *Tiberius, the Politician*, Routledge, 1999.
———, *Vespasian*, Routledge, 1999.
Ligt de, L., Hemelrijk, E., & Singor, H. W., (eds), *Roman Rule and Civic Life: Local and Regional Perspectives*, Proceedings of the Fourth Workshop of the International Network Impact of Empire, Brill, 2003.
Lloyd, B. J., 'Royal Purple of Tyre', *Journal of Near Eastern Studies*, 22(2): 104–18, 1963.
Lo Cascio, E., 'State and Coinage in the Late Republic and Early Empire', *JRS*, 71: 76–86, 1981.
Longden, R. P., 'Notes on the Parthian Campaigns of Trajan', *JRS*, 21: 1–35, 1931.
Luttwak, E., *The Grand Strategy of the Roman Empire; from the First Century AD to the Third*, Johns Hopkins University Press, 1979.

Machiavelli, N., *Discourses on the First Decade of Titus Livius*, trans. N. H. Thomson, Pennsylvania State University, 2007.
Makin, Ena, 'The Triumphal Route, with Particular Reference to the Flavian Triumph', *Journal of Roman Studies*, vol. 11, [Society for the Promotion of Roman Studies, Cambridge University Press], 1921, pp. 25–36.
Makkay, J., 'The Treasures of Decebalus', *Oxford Journal of Archaeology*, 14(3): 333–45, 1995.
Mattingly, H., 'Some Historical Coins of Hadrian', *JRS*, 15: 209–22, 1925.
Matyszak, P., *The Enemies of Rome. From Hannibal to Attila the Hun*, Thames & Hudson, 2004.
McAlindon, D., 'Entry to the senate in the early Empire', *JRS*, 47: 191–5, 1957.
McDermott, W., 'Homullus and Trajan', *Historia: Zeitschrift für Alte Geschichte*, 29 (1): 114–19, 1980.
McElderry, R. K., 'The Legions of the Euphrates Frontier', *Classical Quarterly*, 3(1): 44–53, 1909.

Merrill, E., 'On the Date of Pliny's Prefecture of the Treasury of Saturn', *American Journal of Philology*, 23(4): 400–12, 1902.
Mierse, W. E., *Temples and Towns in Roman Iberia*, University of California Press, 1999.
Millar, F., *The Roman Near East 31 BC–AD 337*, Harvard University Press, 1993.
———, 'The Emperor, the Senate and the Provinces', 1966, 56: 156–66, 1966.
Mitchell, S., 'The Trajanic Tondo from Roman Ankara: In Search of the Identity of a Roman Masterpiece', *Journal of Ankara Studies*, 2(1), 1–10, 2014.
Morris, I., *Social Development*, Stanford University, 2010.
———, 'The Consulate of the Elder Trajan', *JRS*, 43: 79–80, 1953.

Norena, C., 'The Communication of the Emperor's Virtues', *JRS*, 91: 146–68, 2001.
———, 'The Social Economy of Pliny's Correspondence with Trajan', *American Journal of Philology*, 128(2): 239–77, 2007.

O' Brien, G. C., *Trajan's Imperial Alimenta: An analysis of the values attached to children in Roman society in the alimenta of Trajan*, University of Leiden, 2019–2020.
Oliver, J., 'The Empress Plotina and the Sacred Thymelic Synod', *Historia: Zeitschrift für Alte Geschichte*, 24(1), 125–128, 1975.
Oltean, I. A., & Fonte, J., 'GIS Analysis and Spatial Networking Patterns in Upland Ancient Warfare: The Roman Conquest of Dacia', *Geosciences*, 11: 17, 2021.
Opreanu, C. H., 'The Enigmatic Dacia Architecture at Sarmizegetusa Regia, Profane versus Sacred Purpose', *EphNap*, 29: 177–92, 2019.

Packer, J. E., 'Trajan's Glorious Forum', *Archaeology*, 51(1): 32–41, 1998.
———, *The Forum of Trajan in Rome*, University of California Press, 2001.
Parkin, T. G., *Demography and Roman Society*, Johns Hopkins University Press, 1992.
Parvan, V., *An Outline of the Early Civilizations of the Carpatho-Danubian Countries*, Cambridge University Press, 2015.
Peck, H. T., (ed.), *Harpers Dictionary of Classical Antiquities*, Harper and Brothers, 1898.
Petan, A., 'The Dacian Fortress of Gradistea Muncelului: from the Legend of the White King to its Identification with Sarmizegetusa Regia', *ReDIVA*, 5: 65–98, 2016.
Pink, K., 'The triumviri monetales and the structure of the coinage of the Roman Republic', Numismatic Studies no. 7., American Numismatic Society, 1952.
Platner, S. B., *A Topographical Dictionary of Ancient Rome*, Oxford University Press, 1929.

Radice, B., 'A Fresh Approach to Pliny's Letters', *Greece & Rome*, 9(2): 160–8, 1962.
Ramsay, W., 'Pisidian Wolf-Priests, Phrygian Goat-Priests, and the Old-Ionian Tribes', *Journal of Hellenic Studies*, 40, 197–202, 1920.
Rawson, B., & Weaver, P., *The Roman Family in Italy; Status, Sentiment, Space*, Oxford University Press, 1999.
Rickman, G., 'The Grain Trade under the Roman Empire', *Memoirs of the American Academy in Rome*, 36: 261–75, 1980.
Rodriquez-Hidalgo, J. M., & Keay, S., 'Recent Work at Italica', *Proceedings of the British Academy*, 1985.
Rossi, L., *Trajan's Column and the Dacian Wars*, Cornell University Press, 1971.

Roth, J., 'The Size and Organization of the Roman Imperial Legion', *Historia: Zeitschrift für Alte Geschichte*, 43(3), 346–62, 1994.
Rutledge, S., *Imperial Inquisitions: Prosecutors and Informants from Tiberius to Domitian*, Routledge, 2001.

Saddington, D. B., 'Roman Soldiers, Local Gods and "Interpretatio Romana" in Roman Germany', *Acta Classica*, 42: 155–69, 1999.
Salam, N., et al., 'Leishmaniasis in the Middle East: incidence and epidemiology', *PLoS neglected tropical diseases*, 8(10): e3208, 2014.
Saller, R., 'Promotion and Patronage in Equestrian Careers', *JRS*, 70: 44–63, 1980.
Sealey, P. R., & Davies, G. M. R., 'Falernian Wine at Roman Colchester', *Britannia*, 15: 250–4, 1984.
Sear, D., *Roman Coins and Their Values*, Volume II, Spink, 2002.
Segala, E., & Sciortino, I., *Domvs Avrea*, Electa, 1999.
Seznec, J., 'Diderot and "The Justice of Trajan"', *Journal of the Warburg and Courtauld Institutes*, 20(1/2): 106–11, 1957.
Shahbazi, A. Sh., *Parthian Army*, Iran Chamber Society, 2001–2021.
Sharnova, E., 'A Newly Discovered "Justice of Trajan" from the Second School of Fontainebleau', *Burlington Magazine*, 142 (1166): 288–91, 2000.
Shelton, J., *As the Romans Did – A Sourcebook in Roman Social History*, 2nd Edn, Oxford University Press, 1998.
Sherwin-White, A. N., 'Trajan's replies to Pliny: authorship and necessity', *JRS*, 52: 114–25, 1962.
Smallwood, M., *Documents illustrating the Principates of Nerva, Trajan and Hadrian*, Cambridge University Press, 1966.
Smith, W., *A Dictionary of Greek and Roman Antiquities*, John Murray, 1875.
Spalding Jenkins, A., 'The "Trajan-Reliefs" in the Roman Forum', *American Journal of Archaeology*, 5(1): 58–82, 1901.
Speidel, M., 'The Captor of Decebalus: a New Inscription from Philippi', *JRS*, 60: 142–153, 1970.
———, 'The Suicide of Decebalus on the Tropaeum of Adamklissi', *Revue Archéologique*, 1: 75–78, 1971.
———, *Riding for Caesar. The Roman Emperor's Horse Guard*, Batsford, 1994.
Stout, S. E., *The Governors of Moesia*, Princeton University, 1911.
Sutherland, C., 'The State of the Imperial Treasury at the Death of Domitian', *JRS*, 25: 150–62, 1935.
Swan, P., *The Augustan Succession: An Historical Commentary on Cassius Dio's Roman History, Books 55–56 (9 B.C. – A.D. 14)*, Oxford University Press, 2004.
Syme, R., 'Rhine and Danube Legions under Domitian', *JRS*, 18: 41–55, 1928.
———, 'The Imperial Finances under Domitian, Nerva and Trajan', *JRS*, 20: 55–70, 1930.
———, '*Die Reichsbeamten von Dazien* by Arthur Stein', *JRS*, 36: 159–68, 1946.
———, '*I Fasti Consolari dell' Impero Romano dal 30 Av anti Christo al 613 Dopo Christo* by Attilio Degrassi', *JRS*, 43: 148–61, 1953.
———, 'The Friend of Tacitus', *JRS*, 47: 131–5, 1957.
———, 'Consulates in Absence', *JRS*, 48: 1–9, 1958.
———, 'The Wrong Marcius Turbo', *JRS*, 52: 87–96, 1962.
———, 'Some Friends of the Caesars', *American Journal of Philology*, 77(3), 264–73, 1965.
———, 'People in Pliny', *JRS*, 58: 135–51, 1968.
———, 'The Enigmatic Sospes', *JRS*, 67: 38–49, 1977.

———, 'Antonius Saturninus', *JRS*, 68: 12–21, 1978.
———, 'Guard Prefects of Trajan and Hadrian', *JRS*, 70: 64–80, 1980.
———, 'The Career of Arrian', *Harvard Studies in Classical Philology*, 86: 181–211, 1982.

Taagepera, Rein, 'Size and Duration of Empires: Growth–Decline Curves, 600 B.C. to 600 A.D.', *Social Science History*, 3: 125, 1979.
Talbert, R., *The Senate of Imperial Rome*, Princeton University Press, 1984.
———, *Barrington Atlas of the Greek and Roman World*, Princeton, 2000.
Taylor, T., 'Aspects of Settlement Diversity and Its Classification in Southeast Europe before the Roman Period', *World Archaeology*, 19(1), 1–22, 1987.
Teodorescu, D. M., *Cercetari arheologice in Muntii Hunedoarei*, Cluj, 1923.
Tomei, M. A., *The Palatine*, Soprintendenza Archeologica di Roma Electa, 1998.
Townend, G. B., 'The Post of Ab Epistulis in the Second Century', *Historia: Zeitschrift für Alte Geschichte*, 10: 375–81, 1961.
Toynbee, J. M. C., *Death and Burial in the Roman World*, Johns Hopkins University Press, 1971
Trumbower, J. A., *Rescue for the Dead: The posthumous salvation of Non-Christians in early Christianity*, Oxford University Press, 2001.
Tudor, D., *Corpus Monumentorum Religionis Equitum Danuvinorum: The Analysis and Interpretation of the Monuments*, Brill Academic, 1976.
Tully, G. D., 'A Fragment of a Military Diploma for Pannonia Found in Northern England?', *Britannia*, 36: 375–382, 2005.

Van Meter, D., *The Handbook of Roman Imperial Coins*, Canterbury Press, 2000.
Vermaseren, M. J., & van Essen, C. C., *The Excavations in the Mithraeum of the Church of Santa Prisca in Rome*, Brill, 1965.
Vickers, N. J., 'Seeing Is Believing: Gregory, Trajan, and Dante's Art', *Annual Report of the Dante Society*, 101: 67–85, 1983.
Vindolanda Tablets, Online, vindolanda.csad.ox.ac.uk.

Wade, D., 'More Ado about Dacia', *Classical World*, 64(4): 114–16, 1970.
Walton, C. S., 'Oriental Senators in the Service of Rome: A Study of Imperial Policy down to the Death of Marcus Aurelius', *JRS*, 19: 38–66, 1929.
Watson, G. R., 'The Pay of the Roman Army, The Auxiliary Forces', *Historia: Zeitschrift für Alte Geschichte*, 1959, 8(3): 372–8.
Weaver, P., 'Freedmen Procurators in the Imperial Administration', *Historia: Zeitschrift für Alte Geschichte*, 14(4): 460–9, 1965.
Wellesley, K., *The Year of the Four Emperors*, 3rd edn, Routledge, 2000.
Wells, C. 'Ancient Obstetric Hazards and Female Mortality', *Bulletin of the New York Academy of Medicine*, 51: 1235–49, 1975.
Whisnant, J. P., 'Effectiveness versus efficacy of treatment of hypertension for stroke prevention', *Neurology*, 46(2): 301–7, 1996.
Wilcox, P., *Rome's Enemies 3: Parthians and Sassanid Persians*, Osprey Publishing, 2003.
Wojciechowski, P., 'Cult Appellations and Hercules Worship in Imperial Rome', *The Roman Empire in the Light of Epigraphical and Normative Sources*, vol. 4, 2013.
Woolf, G., 'Pliny/Trajan and the Poetics of Empire', *Classical Philology*, 110(2): 132–51, 2015.

INDEX

❦

Roman personalities generally have their full names given in this index but are normally placed alphabetically according to their *nomen*, usually the second of their names. Cross-references in the form 'Attianus, *see* P. Acilius Attianus' are included where an individual is also referred to by another of their names, with the main entry in this case found under 'P. <u>Acilius</u> Attianus'.

Abgarus, king, 202, 206, 217, 226
P. Acilius Attianus, 49, 237, 239–42, 247
M. Acilius Glabrio, 60, 71, 72
adulescentia, 18–21
Ad Flexum, 80
Adenystrae, *see* Parthia
Aelana (Aqaba), 185, 186
P. Aelius Hadrianus Afer, 39
Aerarium, 83
afterlife, Roman beliefs, 234–5
Agri Decumates, 43
Alexander the Great, 199, 219, 220, 223–4, 225
Alexandria, 11, 14, 32
Alimenta, 82, 115–16, 118, 248
Apollodorus of Damascus, 155, 182
Aquincum, 80
Alani, 35
Ammianus Marcellinus, 184
Anatolian Mountains, 211
M. Annius Verus, 89
Anthemusia, *see* Parthia

Antioch, 22, 32, 34–5, 94, 205–6, 217–19, 231–2, 241–2, 245
C. Antius Aulus Julius Quadratus, 89
Antoninus (emperor), 250
Antonius Primus, 14, 15
L. Antonius Saturninus, 54–8, 62–3, 67, 73
Apulum (Alba Iulia), 168
Arabia Provincia, 185–7
Arbandes, 217
Argentorate, 63
Armenia:
    Alani invasion, 35;
    capital, *see* Artaxata;
    coronation crisis, 196–7, 198, 199;
    kings, 33, 196, 206, 212, 225, 245;
    Parthian War, 196–8, 206–9, 211–15, 218–19, 224–5, 228, 231–3, 236;
    Roman province, 213–15, 224, 245, 248;
    strategic value, 16, 33–4, 196, 198–9, 207
Arrian (L. Flavius Arrianus), 221
Cn. Arrius Antoninus, 78, 88
Arsamosata (Aršamšat), 207, 212, 213
Artaxata (Artashat), 211, 214
Athambelus King, 223
Athens, 105, 205–6
Attianus, *see* P. Acilius Attianus
S. Attius Suburanus Aemilianus, 90, 99
Augusta, 98, 187–8, 204, 240
Augustus (emperor), 7, 11, 23, 31, 33, 45, 67, 93, 97–8, 107, 149, 175, 181, 188, 190, 191, 203, 235, 238–9, 245, 249

INDEX

C. Avidius Nigrinus, 246–7
Axidares King, 205, 211

Baiae (Baia), 247
Banat region, 69, 121, 130, 132–3, 137, 139, 143, 150
Bastarnae, 129–30, 155
battles, *see individual battle names*
Bedriacum, Battle of, 13–15
Belgica, 90
Berzobis (Busra ash-Sham), 151, 168
Bithynia-Pontus, 89, 177, 178, 180, 199
L. Blattius Traianus Pollio, 7
Bostra, 185–7, 206
Brigetio, 80
Bructeri, 36–7, 44
Bruttius Praesens, 213–14
A. Bucius Lappius, 56–7
bulla, 3, 17
Buri, 129, 132, 154

Caesarea Mazaca (Kayseri), 16
Caesennius Paetus, 34
Caligula (emperor), 99, 104, 106–7
C. Calpurinus Crassus Frugi, 84, 180
Capitoline Games, 47
Carnuntum (Bad Deutsch-Altenburg), 68
Carpathian Mountains, 53, 58, 101, 120–2, 129, 132–4, 138, 149, 159, 167, 170
Carrhae, Battle of, 211, 217, 227–8
Casperius Aelianus, 81, 85, 99, 213
Caspian Gates, 214
Caspian Sea, 214
L. Cassius Dio Cocceianus, *see* Dio Cassius
L. Catilius Severus, 212, 215, 225–6, 231, 245, 249
T. Catius Caesius Fronto, 73–4, 76–8, 81
Caucasus Mountains, 35, 198, 214, 219
censorship, 21, 23
centumviri, 46, 176
Cestius Gallus, 10
Chaboras River, *see* Parthia
Chatti, 42–3, 55, 57, 59–60, 62, 65, 67, 70, 87
Cilicia, 237, 241
C. Cilnius Proculus, 124, 131, 142
Claudius (emperor), 4
M. Claudius Livianus, 124, 131, 144, 150, 170

C. Claudius Severus, 187, 199
Colonia Claudia Ara Agrippinensium, 94, 96
Commagene, 34
Commodus (emperor), 250
congiarium, 82, 109, 111, 174
Constantius II (emperor), 183–4
consuls, 4, 39, 45–7, 59–60, 62, 113
Cordvba (Cordoba), 6
Cornelius Fuscus, 43, 47–8
Cornelius Nigrinus, 43, 85, 90–2
P. Cornelius Scipio, 5
Cornutus Tertullus, 199
cursus honorum, 4, 16, 21, 25, 28, 31, 37, 39–44, 45, 48, 50, 74, 84, 86, 150, 180, 189, 240

Dacia/Dacians:
   annexation, 167–8;
   allies First Dacian War, 128–9, 130;
   Banița, 160;
   Bistra River, 133–4, 136–9;
   Blidaru, 145, 160;
   Căpâlna, 160;
   comati, 122, 127–8, 135, 137, 142–3, 146, 153, 160, 172;
   command of forces, 127–8;
   Costești Cetățuie, 146, 160;
   council of war, 128;
   Dacia Capta, 169 (coin);
   Dacian Dragon, 122, 137, 171;
   ethnicity, 122;
   falx sword, 128, 130, 135, 140, 164–5, 167;
   Hațeg plain, 136–7, 144, 146, 151, 159, 166, 168;
   Iron Gates Pass, 53, 131, 133–4, 136–7, 143, 151, 154, 158–9, 168;
   justification, First Dacian War, 119–21;
   Keys of Teregova, 138, 159;
   lands, 121–2;
   military strengths and weaknesses, 130;
   murus Dacicus, 161;
   natural resources, 123;
   Orăștie River, 161;
   Piatra Roșie, 145, 160;
   pileati, 122, 127–8, 139, 143, 145–6, 153, 160, 172;
   religion, 122–3, 127–8, 161–2, 166–7;
   Sarmizegetusa Regia, *see separate entry*;

Sarmizegetusa Ulpia, 168;
society, 122;
Vulcan Pass, 158–9;
wildlife, 121–2, 171
Dante, 249
Darial Gorge, 214
Darius III, 219
Decebalus:
  allies, 120, 128–30, 153;
  assassination attempt on Trajan, 156;
  capture of Longinus, 157–8;
  capture of sister, 137, 172;
  conflict with Domitian, 47, 53–4, 59, 119;
  council of war, 128, 143, 145;
  death, 167;
  defeat of Fuscus, 47, 144;
  engagements in battle, 134–6, 138–9, 140, 142, 154, 164;
  envoy, 144;
  poison event, 166;
  provocation second war with Trajan, 148–9;
  royal treasure, 166–7;
  ruling authority, 122, 127, 152, 153;
  siege of Sarmizegetusa Regia, 160–6;
  sons, 127, 167, 172
  surrender, 146–7;
  use of Roman engineers, 120
Dierna, 132, 138, 158
dies lustricus, 3
Dio Cassius, writings about:
  earthquake, 219;
  field bandages, 141;
  Hadrian, 238, 241;
  Nerva's adoption of Trajan, 74;
  Nerva's reign, 81;
  Parthian War, 198, 199, 205, 215, 221–2, 224, 231;
  Plotina, 107;
  Praetorians, 99;
  statues, 173;
  Sura 190–1;
  Trajan's behaviour, 192;
  Trajan's dream, 91;
  Trajan's drinking, 30;
  Trajan's games, 173;
  Trajan's sexuality, 21
Djerdap Gorge, 101, 138
Domitian (emperor):
  accession, 42;
  assassination, 74–6, 84, 85, 97, 99;
  Capitoline Games, 47;
  Capitoline Hill, 15;
  Chattan conflicts, 42;
  constructions, 45, 114, 181, 182;
  Dacian conflicts, 43, 47, 53–4, 119, 120–1, 133;
  damnation, 78;
  First Pannonian War, 58–9;
  fiscal balance, 82, 184;
  fear and conspiracy, 71–4;
  Germanicus, 43;
  Gibbon, 250
  laws, 83;
  Minerva, 71;
  military popularity, 79, 82;
  nurse (Phyllis), 78;
  Parthenius, 72–6, 85;
  Praetorian Guard, 47, 72, 85;
  Saturninus' revolt, 54–8;
  Second Pannonian War, 65–7;
  sexual morality, 71;
  start of *cursus*, 25;
  Third Pannonian War, 67–70
Domus Traiana, 9
donativum, 82, 109, 111
Drobeta bridge, 155 (coin), 158
Dura-Europos (Salhiyé), *see* Parthia

Elegeia (Erzurum), 211, 213–15
Emesa (Homs), 32, 34
Ephesus, 39
equestrian, 2, 11, 22, 27, 41, 62, 100, 174–5
Erucius Clarus, 226
Euphrates, *see* Parthia/Parthians
Eutropius, 176, 185, 193

L. Fabius Justus, 150
fascis, 46
Faventia (Faenza), 247
First Dacian War:
  Battles of Tapae, 133–6 (2nd), 139–42 (3rd);

INDEX

Blidaru, 145;
Buri mushroom message, 132;
booty, 139;
Costeşti Cetăţuie, 145;
Dacian counter-offensive, 136–9;
Dacian people, 121–3;
Dacian forces and allies, 128–9;
Dacian senior command, 127–8;
Dacian strongholds, 144, 145;
Dacian surrender, 146–7;
diplomacy, 139, 144;
legion standard recovered, 144;
justification of war, 119–21;
Piatra Roşie, 145;
prisoners, 141, 143;
Roman forces, 125–7;
Roman consolidation, 136–9;
Roman offensive campaign I, 131–6, 142–3;
Roman offensive campaign II, 143–6;
Roman Senior Command, 123–5
Fiscus Judaicus, 225
Flavia Domitilla, 71, 75, 188
L. Flavius Arrianus, *see* Arrian
T. Flavius Clemens, 71–2, 75
Fossa Traiana, 114;
Fronto, *see* T. Catius Caesius Fronto
frumentationes, 115
Funisulanus Vettonianus, 43

Galba (emperor), 11–13, 50
Gaugamela, Battle of, 219–20
Gaul, 37, 47, 67, 149
Germania Inferior:
  Batavians, 99;
  Bructeri, 36;
  governors, 12, 36, 56, 87–8, 90, 94, 125, 190;
  revolt, 12, 57;
  Roman forces, 54, 57, 126
Germania Superior:
  campaigns against Chatti, 42, 59;
  governors, 54, 62, 67, 87, 94, 96;
  limites, 64–5;
  roads, 43;
  Roman forces, 63, 126;
  revolt, 54, 56

Gibbon, Edward, 250
Glabrio, *see* M. Acilius Glabrio
Q. Glitius Atilius Agricola, 90, 124, 131, 142
gold mines, 51, 120, 123
grammaticus, 12
Gregory the Great, Pope, 249

Hadrian:
  accession, 242;
  adoption, 240–1, 244;
  Archon Eponymos, 205;
  Athens, 205, 239;
  childless, 188;
  conspiracy, 237–41;
  consul suffectus, 189, 238;
  deification of Trajan, 243;
  diamond ring gift from Trajan, 174, 238;
  executing senators, 246–7;
  extravagances, 95;
  First Dacian War, 125, 142;
  Gibbon, 250;
  guardians, 49;
  governor of Pannonia, 189;
  governor of Syria, 236, 240, 242;
  marriage, 108–9, 188–9;
  news of Nerva death, 96
  Parthian War, 205, 208, 219, 235, 239, 245;
  Plotina, 240;
  reprimanded by Trajan, 50, 95, 108–9, 190;
  Second Dacian War, 150, 174;
  sexuality, 108;
  tribunus laticlavius, 94;
L. Herennius Saturninus, 150
Hispania Tarraconensis, 11, 50, 51, 52 (map), 53, 55, 59, 90
Horti Sallustiani, 95

Iazyges, 58, 61, 65, 68–70, 80, 87, 92, 111, 130, 132, 149, 189, 232, 246
Imperial Horse Guard, 99, 104, 124, 126, 132, 137–8, 146, 152, 154, 156, 158, 209, 230
Imperium, 1, 69, 77, 93, 94, 97
infans, 3
Italica, 2–9, 39, 49, 52, 204

Jerusalem, 10–11, 24, 35, 206
Jewish Revolts, 10–11, 14, 24, 225, 231–2
Judaea:
    governors, 24, 64, 246;
    Lusius Quietus, 232, 246;
    peace, 24;
    Roman forces, 10–11, 14, 33, 35, 206, 208;
    Titus, 11, 14, 16, 24;
    Traianus, 10, 11, 14, 16, 24;
    Vespasian, 11, 14, 16, 24, 33, 35
Julius Alexander 226
Julius Caesar, 67, 101, 110, 149, 172, 181, 235, 243
Julius Civilis, 24, 36, 42
S. Julius Frontinus, 88, 90
L. Julius Ursus, 90–2, 94, 101, 111
L. Julius Ursus Servianus:
    First Dacian War, 124–5, 142;
    governor of Germania Superior, 94;
    governor of Pannonia, 142;
    Hadrian, 95, 96;
    possible successor to Trajan, 244;
    Trajan's adoption, 89;
    Trajan's *consilium*, 100
M. Junius Homullus, 199, 208
Juno, 105–6
Jupiter, 47, 71, 104, 106, 136, 175
juvenis, 17

King's Highway (Arabia), 185–7

Manius Laberius Maximus, 124, 131, 137, 180
latus clavus, 22
Lederata, 131, 133
legati Augusti pro praetore, 62
legatus legionis, 10, 28, 29, 34, 36, 50–1, 55, 57
Legio, 51–3
Legions:
    I *Adiutrix*, 48, 68, 80, 125, 151, 207, 208;
    I *Italica*, 125, 151, 208;
    I *Minervia*, 126, 150, 151, 174, 189;
    II *Adiutrix*, 48, 68, 80, 125, 151, 189;
    II *Traiana*, 151, 208, 232;
    III *Cyrenaica*, 14, 186, 206, 208;
    III *Gallica*, 35, 206, 208;
    IV *Flavia*, 48, 125, 151, 168;
    IV *Scythica*, 34–5, 126, 151, 207–8;
    V *Alaudae*, 47;
    V *Macedonica*, 11, 94, 125, 151, 208;
    VI *Ferrata*, 34–5, 90, 207–8, 213–14;
    VI *Victrix*, 36;
    VII *Claudia*, 125, 151, 208, 232;
    VII *Gemina felix*, 14, 50–2, 55–7, 59, 87, 90;
    VIII *Augusta*, 63;
    X *Fretensis*, 11, 24, 35, 206, 208;
    X *Gemina*, 36, 151;
    XI *Claudia*, 63, 126, 151, 208;
    XII *Fulminata*, 11, 34, 126, 151, 207, 208;
    XIII *Gemina*, 68, 125, 151, 168, 208;
    XIV *Gemina*, 54, 57, 63, 68, 80, 125, 151;
    XV *Apollinaris*, 11, 68, 125, 151, 203, 207–8;
    XVI *Flavia Firma*, 35, 207–8;
    XXI *Rapax*, 36, 55, 57, 65;
    XXII *Deiotariana*, 14;
    XXII *Primigenia*, 36, 63, 94;
    XXX *Ulpia Victrix*, 151, 208
Lex imperii, 175
M. Licinius Crassus, 199
Licinius Mucianus, 11, 14
L. Licinius Sura:
    baths, 110 (map);
    death, 190, 194;
    dinner with Trajan, 190–1;
    First Dacian War, 125, 131, 142, 144;
    Hadrian, 108;
    governor of Germania Inferior, 94, 194;
    Second Dacian War, 150;
    third consulship, 174;
    Trajan's adoption, 88, 91;
    Trajan's *consilium*, 100;
    Trajan's triumph, 170, 172;
    trusted friend of Trajan, 88, 190–1, 204
lictors, 46, 104, 172
limites, 32, 42–3, 64, 68–9, 95, 100, 168, 197–8, 214
Longinus, *see* Pompeius Longinus
ludi, 46–7
Lusius Quietus:
    death, 246–7;
    First Dacian War, 125, 144;
    Jewish revolts, 232;

Parthian War, 208, 213, 215–17, 220, 226, 231

Machiavelli, 250
Manisarus, King, 202, 217, 220
C. Manlius Felix, 125
Mannus, King, 201, 206, 216, 217
Marcia (Trajan's mother), 3, 8, 39, 48
Marcia Furnilla, 3
Marciana (Trajan's sister):
 Augusta, 98, 188;
 birth, 3;
 daughter, 12;
 death, 204;
 deification, 204, 243;
 Domus Tiberiana, 107;
 marriage, 12;
 patriarchal, 108;
 Plotina, 48, 80, 91, 95, 108;
 teaching Trajan, 8;
 widow, 39
Marcomanni, 58, 59, 61, 67, 79, 92, 120, 129
Marcus Aurelius (emperor), 234, 241, 250
Marcus Trahius, 7
Marcius Turbo, 208, 232, 247
Q. Marius Barea Soranus, 3
Mark Antony, 199
Mars, 131, 158, 171
Masada, 24, 165
Matidia (Salonia):
 Augusta, 204;
 daughters, 49, 188;
 father's death, 39;
 Hadrian, 109;
 marriage, 48–9;
 mother, 12;
 patriarchal, 108;
 relationship with Trajan, 190;
 remarriage, 49;
 Trajan's death, 237, 240, 242–3;
 Vibius Sabinus, 90
Matidia the younger, 49, 108, 188
Maximus, General, *see* Manius Laberius Maximus,
J. Maximus Manlianus, 226
Meharaspes, King, 202, 217, 220

Melitene (Malatya), 34, 207
P. Metilius Nepos, 150
Minerva, 71, 105–6
Mithridates II, 200
Moesia:
 capital, 131;
 civil war, 14;
 Dacian incursion, 43, 119;
 division, 47;
 First Dacian War, 120–1, 124–5, 127, 142;
 frontier, 43;
 governors, 53, 87, 89, 90, 124–5, 142;
 posted legions, 68, 94, 150–1, 246;
 Pannonian War, 68–9, 73, 87;
 Second Dacian War, 150–4, 156
Mogontiacum (Mainz), 54–8, 62–3
Mount Casius, *see* Parthian War
Mount Kogaionon, 122
Murex trunculus, 32
Mursella (Petrijevci), 68

Nabataean kingdom, *see* Arabia
Nebuchadrezzar III, 225
L. Neratius Priscus, 88, 142, 244
Nero (emperor), 2, 5, 10, 11, 33, 50, 73, 89, 99, 106, 107, 181, 197, 232
Nerva:
 accession, 76–80;
 adopting Trajan, 80, 83–93, 101, 111, 204, 234;
 alimenta, 82, 115;
 chief secretary, 100;
 coins, 93, 108;
 congiarium and *donativum*, 82, 109;
 consilium, 68, 84–5, 88–9;
 conspiracy, 84;
 consuls, 81, 92;
 cursus, 74, 84;
 death, 95–6;
 deification, 97, 114;
 diamond ring, 174, 189, 238;
 Domitian's assassination, 74;
 Domitian's palace, 80;
 edicts, 83;
 forum, 110 (map);
 fourth consulship, 95;

laurelled letter, 92;
noble birth, 74;
policies, 80, 81, 83, 112, 118, 184, 248;
Praetorian Guard, 78, 81–2, 85;
Third Pannonian War, 92–4
Norbanus, 56–7, 73, 77
novi homines, 5
Noviomagus (Nijmegen), 151

Obobas, 186
Octavius Fronto, 89–90, 94
Cn. Octavius Titinius Capito, 100
olive oil, 6–7
Oltenia region, 121–3, 151, 159, 189
Orăștie Mountains, 122, 136, 140, 143–4, 158–62
Orăștie River, 161
Orontes River, 22, 32, 34, 205
Osrhoëne, 35, 202, 206, 216–17
Osroes I:
  Armenian throne, 196–7;
  daughter, 222;
  coin, 197;
  command of forces, 209–10;
  embassy, 205–6;
  evading engagement, 229, 233;
  golden throne, 222;
  losses (Parthian War), 218, 220, 222;
  Parthamasiris, 211–13;
  Parthamaspates, 228;
  Sanatrukes, 210, 225–6;
  Vologaeses III, *see separate entry*
Ostia, 55, 114, 181
Otho (emperor), 12–14

paedagogue, 3
C. Palma Frontonianus, 89, 101, 111, 173, 186, 208, 246–7
Palmyra, 32
Panegyricus, 37
Pannonia:
  Augustus in, 149;
  civil war, 12–14;
  division, 189, 238;
  First Dacian War, 119–20, 124–5, 127, 142;
  First Pannonian War, 58–9, 119;

frontier, 43, 80;
governors, 67–8, 87, 91, 100, 107, 124–5, 142, 150, 157, 189, 238, 244, 247;
posted legions, 50–1, 63, 68, 80, 127, 151–2, 189, 207–8;
Second Dacian War, 149–52, 167;
Second Pannonian War, 65, 67, 90;
Third Pannonian War, 67–70, 73, 79–80, 81, 92–4, 98, 106, 157;
Tiberius, 238–9
Parthamasiris, King, 196–7, 200, 205–6, 211–12, 225, 245
Parthamaspates, King, 228 (coin), 229, 232
Parthenius, 72–6, 85
Parthia/Parthians:
  Abgarus, *see separate entry*;
  Adenystrae, 220;
  Adiabene, 202, 215–16, 220, 223, 225–6, 228–9, 231;
  Anthemusia, 202, 206, 216;
  Arbela (Erbil), 202, 220;
  Arsacid dynasty, 196, 200–2, 228;
  Assyria, 202, 219, 220, 224, 225, 248;
  Athambelus, *see separate entry*;
  Axidares, *see separate entry*;
  Babylonia/Babylon, 201, 217, 219–21, 223–6, 228–9, 231–2, 235–6, 245, 248;
  Batnae, 202, 216;
  Chaboras River, 226;
  conflict with Vespasian, 35;
  Ctesiphon, 201–2, 219, 221–3, 225, 228–9;
  Dura-Europos, 217, 221;
  Edessa (Şanlıurfa), 198, 202, 217, 226;
  Empire, lands, 200–2;
  equestrian skills, 203, 210;
  Erythraean Sea (Persian Gulf), 223, 224, 229;
  Euphrates, 34–5, 37, 44, 186, 196–8, 201–2, 204, 207, 211, 217, 221, 223–4, 226, 245;
  Gaugamela, 219–20;
  golden throne, 222;
  Gordyene, 202, 217, 220;
  Hatra (al-Hadr), 202, 217, 229, 230, 235;
  Lake Van, 202, 213;
  Manisarus of Gordyene, *see* Manisarus;

Mannus of the Arabes Scenitae, *see* Mannus;
Masius Mountains, 216, 220;
Meharaspes of Adiabene, *see* Meharaspes;
Mesene, 223–4, 228;
Mesopotamia, 201–2, 213, 215–19, 224–6, 228–33, 236, 248;
Mithridates II, *see separate entry*;
Nisibis (Nusaybin), 198, 201, 202, 216, 220, 226;
Nineveh (near Mosul), 220;
Osrhoëne, 35, 202, 206, 216–17;
Osroes I, *see separate entry*;
Parthamasiris, *see separate entry*;
Parthamaspates, *see separate entry*;
religion, 203;
ruling structure, 200–1;
Sanatrukes, *see separate entry*;
Satala (Sadak), 35, 207–8, 211;
Seleucia, 202, 222, 225, 226;
Singara (Sinjar), 201, 217, 221;
Sippar (Tell Abu Habbah), 221;
social class and culture, 203–4;
Spasinou Charax (near Basra), 223–4;
Taq-i Kisra, 202;
Taurus Mountains, 34, 198, 206, 213, 237;
Tigris, 198, 201–2, 204, 213, 216, 220, 221, 222, 223, 230;
Vologaeses III, *see separate entry*
Parthian War:
  Abgarus, *see separate entry*;
  Adiabene, *see* Parthia;
  Arbela, *see* Parthia;
  Armenian annexation, 212–14;
  Armenian throne, 196, 206, 212–13, 225;
  Arsamosata, *see separate entry*;
  Bitlis Pass, 213, 215–16;
  cataphracts, 210, 217, 227–8;
  Ctesiphon, *see* Parthia;
  conclusion, 245;
  diplomacy, 205–6, 214, 217, 220;
  earthquake, 218–19;
  Edessa, *see* Parthia;
  embassies and ambassadors, 205–6;
  Gordyene, *see* Parthia;
  Hadrian, 205, 208, 219, 235, 239, 245;

Hatra, *see* Parthia;
imperial headquarters, 206, 218;
invasion of Armenia, 211;
invasion of Mesopotamia, 215–16;
frontier improvement, 197–9;
justification of war, 196–9;
major battle, 226–7;
Manisarus of Gordyene, *see* Manisarus;
Mannus of the Arabes Scenitae, *see* Mannus;
Meharaspes of Adiabene, *see* Meharaspes;
Mount Casius, 205–6, 219, 219, 235;
Nisibis, *see* Parthia
Osroes I, *see separate entry*;
Parthamasiris, *see separate entry*;
Parthamaspates, *see separate entry*;
Parthian command, 209–10;
Parthian forces and allies, 210–11;
Parthicus, 218;
premeditation, 199–200;
river crossing, 216, 220;
rebellion, 225–31;
Roman command, 207–8;
Roman forces, 208–9;
Roman campaign AD 114, 211–15;
Roman campaign AD 115, 215–19;
Roman campaign AD 116, 219–25;
Roman campaign (aborted) AD 117, 231–3;
Sanatrukes, *see separate entry*;
Seleucia, *see* Parthia;
siege, Hatra, 230–1;
Singara, *see* Parthia;
Sporaces, *see separate entry*;
tidal bore, 223;
Tigris, *see* Parthia;
Trajan's departure East, 204–5;
Trajan's return to Rome, 236–7;
triumph (posthumous), 243;
truce with Vologaeses, 226;
Vologaeses III, *see separate entry*
Pax Romana, 26, 169, 248
M. Pedo Vergilianus, 218
Q. Petillius Cerialis, 25
Petra, 185, 223
T. Petronius Secundus, 73, 77–8, 81, 85
Phyllis, 78

Pia Fidelis Domitiana, 56
Pliny the Younger (C. Plinius Caecilius Secundus):
  consul suffectus, 178;
  death, 180, 199;
  governor of Bithynia-Pontus, 178–80, 199;
  letters, 83, 176–7, 178, 180, 193;
  Panegyricus (speech), 9, 37, 55–6, 93, 108, 112–13, 115, 117, 192;
  uncle (Pliny the Elder, C. Plinius Secundus), 186
Pompeia Plotina:
  Augusta, 98, 187–8;
  childless, 45, 188;
  conspiracy, 238–42;
  Epicurean philosophy, 188;
  family relations, 48–9, 108, 109, 188, 204;
  marriage, 38–9, 49, 87;
  origins, 38;
  support of Trajan, 80, 95, 236, 237;
  Trajan's ashes, 243;
  virtues, 39, 48, 107, 208
Pompeius Longinus, 89, 94, 100, 125, 131, 150, 156–8
Pontius Pilate, 64
population, Roman Empire, 174
Porta Flaminia, 103–4
Portus Centumcellae, 114, 192–3;
Portus Traiani, 114
praefectus castrorum, 27, 52
praetorships, 4, 43, 45–7, 50, 60
Praetorian Guard:
  camp, 110 (map);
  diminished role, 98–9;
  financial reward, 12, 82;
  imperial betrayal, 11–12, 73, 75, 77–8, 85, 91–2, 239–42;
  imperial protection, 72;
  military activities, 13, 43, 55, 57, 126, 132, 134, 146, 152, 208–9;
  prefects, 25, 40, 47, 73, 81, 88, 99, 124, 144, 150, 237;
primus pilus, 27, 52
Proconsules, 62
Publilius Celsus, 173, 208, 246–7

Pylades, 194

J. Quadratus Bassus, 125, 131, 150, 199, 232, 236, 239, 246
quaestorships, 4, 37, 41, 42, 44

Rabbel II Soter, 186
Raetia, 56, 64
Raphanaea, 35, 206
Regulus, 96
River Nile, 114
Roman army:
  auxilia/auxiliaries, 27, 64, 68, 79, 85, 131–2, 134–5, 137, 139–40, 142, 145–6, 154, 159, 162–4, 167, 226;
  bridges, 51, 131, 143, 216, 220;
  camp layout, 28, 29;
  cavalry, 134, 227;
  centurions, 27–9, 51–2, 125, 135, 140, 157, 220, 247;
  command, 26, 27, 28, 123–5;
  equipment, 162;
  engineers, 59, 120, 128, 131, 133, 146, 162–3, 216, 219–20;
  field medicine/*medici*, 141;
  forces in First Dacian War, 125–7;
  helmets, 15, 128, 130, 159, 162, 163, 228;
  javelins, 135, 164, 172;
  legionaries, 26–30, 34, 36, 79, 130, 135, 140–2, 144, 146, 154, 159, 162–4, 167–8, 227, 229;
  lorica segmentata, 27, 228;
  marching column, 131–2, 159;
  missile weapons, 135, 142, 145, 163, 227;
  navy, 126, 152, 221–2, 232;
  shields, 15, 27, 135, 137, 163;
  snow shoes, 214;
  strengths and weaknesses, 129–30;
  structure and size, 26;
  suovetaurilia, 131, 143, 158;
  sword, 27, 135, 140;
  symmachiarii, 126–7, 132, 134–5, 139, 152, 159, 209, 227;
  total size, 27;
  wages, 82
Roman law, 45–6, 66, 83, 115–16, 175, 176–8, 243

INDEX

Rome:
  Aqua Traiani, 110 (map), 114;
  Aventine Hill, 9, 113, 191;
  Basilica Aemilia, 10;
  Basilica Julia, 115, 172;
  Basilica Ulpia, 183;
  Baths of Sura, 110 (map), 191;
  Campus Martius, 110 (map), 171;
  Capitoline Hill, 9, 10, 15, 41, 92, 104, 106, 110 (map), 167, 172–3;
  Circus Flaminius, 172;
  Circus Maximus, 10, 110 (map), 113, 114, 172, 191;
  Clivus Capitolinus, 104–5;
  Clivus Victoriae, 106;
  Colosseum, 24, 25, 41, 110 (map), 111, 114, 116, 172;
  Curia, 47, 76, 78, 93;
  Domitian's palace, 74–5;
  Domus Tiberiana, 80, 106–8, 110 (map), 188;
  Domus Traiana, 9;
  Forum Boarium, 172;
  Forum Romanum, 110 (map), 172;
  Mamertine Prison, 173;
  Palatine Hill, 9, 72, 74, 80, 106–7, 110, 113, 172, 181, 18;
  pomerium, 243;
  Porticus Octavia, 171;
  Quirinal Hill, 96, 182;
  Rostra, 93, 191, 236, 244;
  Saint Peter's Basilica (Vatican), 105;
  Scalae Gemoniae steps, 167;
  Subura district, 18, 22;
  Temple of the Flavians, 78, 104;
  Temple of Isis, 171;
  Temple of Julius Caesar, 172;
  Temple of Jupiter, 10, 15, 41, 45, 92, 105, 110 (map), 173, 181, 243;
  Temple of Saturn, 104, 172;
  Temple to Pax, 24;
  Thermae Traiani, 114;
  Tiber, 2, 6, 9, 15, 77, 103, 110 (map), 114, 172;
  Trajan's Column, 183–4 (coin), 243;
  Trajan's Forum, 182–4;
  Trajan's Markets, 249;
  Velabrum, 172;
  Vestal Virgins *atrium*, 113
Roxolani, 69, 120–1, 128–30, 138–9, 153–5, 232, 246
Rutilius Gallicus, 36
Rutilius Lupus, 199

C. Salonius Matidius Patruinus, 12
Samosata (Samsat), 34–5, 207
Sanatrukes, 210, 225–8
Sarmizegetusa Regia, 53, 122, 143–6, 158–66, 168
Satala, *see* Parthia
Saturninus, *see* L. Antonius Saturninus
T. Statilius Crito, 204
Second Dacian War:
  assassination attempt on Trajan, 156;
  Banița, 160;
  Blidaru, 160;
  Căpâlna, 160;
  capture of Decebalus and annexation of Dacia, 166–9;
  capture of Longinus, 156–8;
  Costești Cetățuie, 160;
  Dacian capital, *see* Sarmizegetusa Regia;
  Dacian forces and allies, 153, 154;
  Dacian senior command, 152–3;
  Dacian strongholds, 160;
  Dacian treasure, 166–7;
  diplomacy, 153, 155;
  Drobeta bridge, 155 (coin), 158;
  escalations and the partial campaign of AD 105, 153–4;
  fall of Sarmizegetusa Regia and the Dacian kingdom, 160–6;
  justification of war, 148–50;
  mounted relief, 154;
  murus Dacicus, 161;
  Piatra Roșie, 160;
  peace terms violated, 148;
  poison scene, 166;
  Roman forces, 150–2;
  Roman offensive campaign of AD 106, 158–9;
  Roman senior command, 150;
  siege, 160, 162–6;

winter AD 105/106, 155–8
Secundus, *see* T. Petronius Secundus
Seleucia Pieria, 34, 205, 237, 242
Selinus (Gazipasa), 237, 240
Semiramis, 225
Senate meetings, 17, 176
Senecio, *see* Q. Sosius Senecio
Sentius, 220
Septimius Severus (emperor), 249
Servianus, *see* L. Julius Ursus Servianus
Singara, *see* Parthia
Sirmium (Sremska Mitrovica), 68
Q. Sosius Senecio, 90, 101, 111, 125, 131, 142, 150, 170
Spasinou Charax, *see* Parthia
Sporaces, king, 202, 206, 216
Stephanus, 75–6
Suebic Quadi, 58, 61, 67, 69, 79, 92, 111, 120, 129
Suetonius (C. Suetonius Tranquillus), 57, 175
Sura, *see* L. Licinius Sura
Syria:
    capital, *see* Antioch;
    governors, 10, 18, 22, 34–6, 85, 92, 186, 199, 232, 236, 238–2, 245–6;
    Parthian War, 197–9, 205–6, 208, 221, 231–2;
    Roman forces, 11, 14, 28, 30, 33–5, 90, 126, 145, 151, 197, 206, 208, 231;
    strategic value, 31, 33, 197–8;
    trade, 185;
    Traianus in, 22, 34, 35, 36

Tacitus (Publius Cornelius Tacitus), 42, 58
Tapae, 53, 59, 127, 133–4, 136–7, 139–40, 142–3
Tarracina, 246
Tarraco (Tarragona), 51, 52 (map), 190
Taunus Mountains, 42–3, 63–4
D. Terentius Scaurianus, 167
Tettius Julianus, 53–4, 55, 133
Thermae Traiani, 114
Tiberius (emperor), 94, 106, 107, 238
Tiberius Claudius Maximus, 167
Tiberius Julius Alexander, 14
Tigris, *see* Parthia/Parthians
Titus (emperor):
    accession, 39–40;
    Caesar, 25;
    catastrophic events, 40–1, 219;
    censorship, 21, 24;
    Colosseum, 41;
    death, 42;
    Judaea, 14, 16, 24;
    Legion XV *Apollinaris*, 11;
    marriage, 3, 60;
    Praetorian Guard prefect, 25
tribunus laticlavius, 4, 26, 28, 29, 30
toga praetexta, 3, 17
toga virilis, 17, 18
Traianus (Trajan's father), *see* M. Ulpius Traianus
Traii or Trahii, 3
C. Traius Pollio, 7
Trajan:
    accession, 96–7;
    adoption by Nerva, 83–93;
    adoption of Hadrian, 240–1, 244 (coin);
    adulescentia, 18–21;
    alimenta, 115–16, 118 (coin), 248
    alcohol consumption, 30, 61, 142, 193;
    ancestors, 7;
    Arabia annexation, 185–7 (coin)
    assassination attempt, 156
    Augustus, 98;
    birth, 1, 2, 5;
    Caesar, 93, 95, 98, 214;
    childless, 49;
    Christianity, 180;
    coinage, 111;
    congiarium and *donativum*, 109, 111, 174;
    consilium, 100, 109, 149, 175–6, 178, 190, 192, 198, 244;
    conspiracy, 180–1, 237–44;
    constitution, 175–6;
    consulships, 60–1 (1st), 95, 98 (2nd), 111 (3rd), 121 (4th), 181 (5th), 214 (6th);
    Dacian triumph (2nd), 170–3;
    Dacicus, 153, 214;
    dealing with corruption, 176–80, 194;
    death, 237, 240–3;
    deification, 243;
    Domitian's *consilium*, 59–61, 67;

INDEX

Domitian's Third Pannonian War, 69–70, 79–80, 85, 92, 94;
education, 8, 12, 15, 16, 17;
Egypt drought, 114–15;
enjoyment of hunting, 19;
family estates, 19;
festival of Liber, 16;
finances, 116–17, 184–5;
first governorship, 62–5;
first legion command, 50–3;
first military action, 35–6;
Fossa Traiana, 114;
frumentationes, 115;
Germania Inferior, 36;
Germanicus, 93, 98, 214;
governor of Pannonia, 67–70;
guardianship of Hadrian, 49;
Imperium, 93, 98, 214;
Italica, 7, 8, 9;
justice of Trajan, 249–50;
latus clavus, 22;
law and order, 115–16, 175–6, 177–8, 192;
legacy, 248–50;
Legion, IV *Scythica*, 35;
Legion VI *Ferrata*, 35;
Legion VII *Gemina*, 50–2, 55–7, 59, 87, 90;
marching on foot, 215, 235;
marriage, 38–9;
modest living, 107, 193;
mounted military action, 154, 230;
naming, 2;
Optimus Princeps, 176, 214–15;
Parthian triumph (posthumous), 243;
Parthicus, 218, 222;
Pater Patriae, 101–2, 214;
patrician class, 21–2;
personal protection, 156;
personal secretary, 204, 237, 241, 242;
physical, health and appearance, 8, 12, 19, 50, 70, 191–3, 205, 234–7;
Pontifex Maximus, 97, 98, 214;
Portus Traiani, 114;
praetorship, 45–7;
private house, 9;
proconsul of Germania, 94;

prophetic dream, 91;
public games, 111, 116;
public works, 113–14, 181–4;
plutei Traiani, 115;
quaestorship, 41–2;
returning to Rome, 103–6;
roads, 114;
Saturninus revolt, 54–8;
sexuality, 20, 21, 30, 193–4, 217;
studiis, 175;
style of ruling, 109, 112–13, 175, 193;
Tribunicia potestas, 93;
tribunus laticlavius, 28, 29, 30, 35–6;
typical day in Rome, 176;
vigintivirate, 22, 23
Tibiscum (Jopta), 133, 137–9, 159
Tribunicia potestas, 77, 93, 98, 239
Tuder (Todi), 2
Tullius Justus, 83
Turdetanians, 5
Tzon Pass, 214

Ulpii, 3
M. Ulpius Phaedimus, 204, 237, 241, 242
M. Ulpius Traianus (Trajan's father):
ancestors, 3, 7;
allegiance to Vespasian, 14, 15, 16, 21;
bringing up children, 3, 8;
Caesarea Mazaca, 16;
consul suffectus, 16, 21;
death, 107–8;
deification, 107–8 (coin);
early career, 4, 5;
eastern postings, 13, 14, 32;
governor of Cappadocia, 16, 18, 19, 21, 34, 35;
governor of Syria, 22, 28, 34, 35;
legatus legionis, 10, 11, 24;
ornamenta triumphalia, 36, 197;
patrician class, 21, 22;
patronage of Claudius, 4;
proconsul of Asia, 39;
retirement, 48;
sodalis Flavialis, 40
wife, 3;
wealth, 7, 18

Vespasian (emperor):
   accession, 15;
   censorship, 21, 23;
   death, 39–40;
   declarations of allegiance, 14;
   eastern policies, 16, 22, 31, 32, 33, 34, 35;
   fiscal policies, 25;
   imperial ambitions, 13, 14;
   Judaea, 11, 24;
   Julius Civilis, 24;
   new Flavian dynasty, 23;
   temple to Pax, 24;
   triumph, 24
Vestal Virgins, 66, 71, 113
Vesuvius, 40, 219
S. Vettulenus Civica Cerialis, 11
Via:
   Aemilia, 114;
   Amerina, 2, 3;
   Appia, 114;
   Augusta, 7, 52 (map);
   Domitia, 56;
   Flaminia, 103, 110 (map);
   Labicana, 114;
   Puteoli, 114;
   Sacra, 172–3;
   Sublacensis, 114;
   Traiana, 194 (coin);
   Traiana Nova, 187, 194 (coin)
Vibia Sabina, 49, 108, 188–9, 194, 238–40
L. Vibius Sabinus, 49, 90
vigintivirate, 4, 22, 23
Viminacium, 53, 131–3, 137–8, 155
Vindobona, 68
Vindonissa (Windisch), 63
Vitellius (emperor), 12, 13, 14, 15
Vologaeses I, 33, 35
Vologaeses III, 196, 201, 210, 231

Wallachia region, 121–3, 150

Zagros Mountains, 222
Zalmoxis, 122–3, 127–8, 166–7
Zeugma, 34, 35, 198, 207